FASHIONS IN SCIENCE

FASHIONS IN SCIENCE

OPINION LEADERS AND COLLECTIVE BEHAVIOR IN THE SOCIAL SCIENCES

IRWIN SPERBER

University of Minnesota Press • Minneapolis

Illustrations on pages 51, 181, and 189 by Erica Sher.

Published by the University of Minnesota Press
2037 University Avenue Southeast,
Minneapolis MN 55414.
Printed in the United States of America.

Library of Congress Cataloging-in-Publication Data

Sperber, Irwin.
    Fashions in science: opinion leaders and collective behavior in the social
sciences/Irwin Sperber.
       p.   cm.
    Bibliography: p.
    Includes index.
    ISBN 0-8166-1758-9   ISBN 0-8166-1759-7 (pbk.)
    1. Sociology—Philosophy. 2. Sociologists—Psychology. 3. Social sciences—
Research—Moral and ethical aspects.   I. Title.
HM24.S696   1990   89-5098
301'.01—dc20   CIP

The University of Minnesota
is an equal-opportunity
educator and employer.

CONTENTS

PREFACE

In our earliest impressions of the social environment, while still innocent of any abstractions about justice and truth, we already feel what we cannot explain: we are sometimes blamed for misbehavior we did not commit and praised for good deeds we have not done. We are made uneasy, sometimes hurt or frightened, by parents punishing the innocent and praising the guilty. We are sometimes mortified when our parents and teachers lie to us, to each other, to themselves. We eventually reconcile ourselves to the fact that blame and praise are often not fairly allocated, that the road to "maturity" consists in quietly adjusting to the eccentricities of parental authority. We gradually find ourselves telling other people what they want to hear, what is in good taste, not what we know to be the truth.

As we are socialized into the larger society, we continue to observe punishments and rewards given out for blatantly cruel, unfair, or inappropriate reasons. We become less and less surprised to hear that a man is lynched because he is black, that a second is promoted because he is well connected and white, or that a third is fired because he is gay. We are hardly startled to hear that a woman is beaten because her husband does not want her working outside the home, that a second is hired for soap commercials because she "passed the couch test," or that a third is fired because she is a lesbian. And we are accustomed to a candidate's victory in an election because he has a nice smile, while his opponent is defeated because he says what he means and means what he says; we commonly see voters all but ignoring the substantive issues that might divide the candidates. Although such injustices and irrationalities are sometimes recognized and even condemned, little is done to examine why they take place or how to prevent them. Yet we always feel uneasy about them. We believe that they should not prevail in our educational system, that they must be held to a minimum in those domains in which the pursuit of reason is the declared objective. But why is praise so often given to those who do not deserve it? Why is ridicule heaped on those who deserve praise? Why are these practices so widespread, so taken for granted, in our political system? *Why do these things happen even in the realm where they are least expected, in the very embodiment of human reason and the search for truth, in the temple of science itself?* These questions, however crudely formulated, have troubled me ever since I was old enough to understand such vernacular wisdom as "Nice guys finish last"; "It's not what you know but who you know"; and, "Only the good die young." In the embryonic stages of this research, I wanted to find out why anyone would want to accept or follow such unjust and corrupt beliefs. I eventually realized that these questions were unduly simplistic, one-dimensional, and unanswerable so long as they were cast in such a moralistic form; that an explanation of these absurdities in the realm of science, in which they are most openly disavowed in principle, would be necessary before attempting to explain their presence in those political, entrepreneurial, and cultural realms in which they are more readily accepted.

A number of important forces have profoundly shaped and conditioned the growth of science in the twentieth century: the rise of fascist and totalitarian states as well as the less direct but equally effective trend toward the commercialization of knowledge, commonly called "sociology for sale" in my own discipline, have been particularly influential. I do not wish to minimize their importance per se or the extensive research done by social scientists and historians on their continuing effects. Indeed, I am indebted to this research literature in the pages to follow. But far less recognized and far more influential than these well-recognized forces in the shaping of irrationality in science is the play of fashion or the fashion process in the scientific community.

The purpose behind the present study of irrationality in the scientific community is not to offer just another account of the social forces shaping the rise of modern science. Rather, it consists in an article of faith: I hope that an explanation of irrationality where it is least expected and least acknowledged can help to serve as a basis for understanding the forces responsible for injustice as well as irrationality in the more familiar domains of everyday life. This article of faith guides the task at hand:

to investigate the processes at work when the undeserving are praised, when the truth is dismissed, when the scientific community compromises itself and deceives the public in rituals of self-celebration.

Organized religion and monarchies in centuries past indeed suppressed and played havoc with scientific inquiry: it was for good reason that Robert Boyle and Isaac Newton felt compelled to go underground in their "invisible college" even as late as the seventeenth century. But other forces, perhaps more subtle, have emerged to produce new distortions, new orthodoxies, new forms of irrationality in the modern scientific community. I will show that even those scientists who try to study the scope of irrationality in general and its presence in the scientific community in particular are themselves caught up in the same social forces that shape their object of study.

Although congressional committees do at times investigate some of the more glaring manifestations of outright fraud in the scientific community (e.g., the Subcommittee on Fraud and Plagiarism in Science ably chaired by Congressman Ted Weiss), public officials, historians, and sociologists alike have neglected the larger issues raised by these episodes. My original concerns needed revision, expansion, and historical specification: (1) Why is the scientific community so lenient, even indifferent, toward these intellectual misdemeanors? (2) To what extent are these recurring manifestations of blatant fraud only the tip of an iceberg, suggestive of a vast array of dubious scientific activities commonly passed off as valid or even certified as major breakthroughs and achievements by all concerned? (3) What are the long-term consequences of such activities and their celebration by the scientific community and the larger society? (4) How are these activities and the scientists who become role models or exemplars of these activities selected for adoption or approval in the first place? (5) What are the underlying causes of and possible means of preventing such styles of research, such modes of discourse, such paradigms in the face of their certification as orthodox or in good taste?

To begin to come to terms with these questions—and I only *begin* to answer them—I advance a series of working hypotheses to the effect that the scientific community, like the domains of costume adornment and automobile design, is profoundly influenced by a particular form of collective behavior, that is, the play of fashion. I suggest that styles or models of scientific thought rise to and fall from prominence just as shifting hemlines and chrome fenders are brought onto and cast off center stage, that their fate is governed by the operation of collective tastes or sentiments that are shifting, amorphous, pervasive, and usually unacknowledged by the audience. I further suggest that opinion leaders in the scientific community are comparable to those in commercial design; that the emergence of a Kroeber, a Simmel, a Merton, a Kuhn, an Alexander in the social sciences, for example, is a manifestation of the same process that elevates a Christian Dior, an Yves St. Laurent, a Gloria Vanderbilt, a Max Factor, a Lucien Picard to prominence in the world of costume adornment and cosmetics. I propose that this same process is equally responsible for relegating some opinion leaders, designers, and models to obscurity, for designating some candidates as modern and in good taste and others as old-fashioned and in bad taste; that the fashion process is uncritically and routinely passed off as equivalent to the application of objective criteria for the evaluation of competing models in the scientific community as well as the world of commercial design.

The praise given to bad ideas and undeserving people along with the scorn given to the good and the deserving seemed to be a tantalizing mystery, even a morality play. But the puzzle called for further redefinition so that it could be described, explained, and solved in researchable terms. For example, could it be that these practices are only the manifestations of underlying social forces found in some historical contexts rather than others? Could it be that these seemingly eccentric, erratic, unjust, irrational tendencies are crucial mechanisms of institutionalized social control, that they represent a structure of domination largely unrecognized by its own participants? Could it be that these practices are neither random nor bizarre? I could not help but marvel at their ubiquitous and persistent nature in modern society. Most remarkable, I thought, was the great extent to which they seemed to operate without regard to any objective criteria of validity, truth, or precedent. I eventually suspected that I was dealing with special patterns of collective behavior rather than immoral conduct and idiosyncrasies. I accordingly drew upon concepts in the sociology of collective behavior to sketch a map of the territory I wished to explore.

The dimensions of this map can be outlined by reference to "the fashion process" and "the play of fashion in science" as well as the observations made by applying them to the task of understanding the acclaim given to some opinion leaders rather than others in the scientific community.

The fashion process is a form of collective behavior marked by a series of normative preoccupations: keeping in step with the times, with the latest developments; following the example of prestigious opinion leaders who "keep their ears to the ground" and articulate the shared and implicit sentiments of the public; admiring proposals for adoption when they are in good taste and new, discarding them when they are in bad taste and old; dismissing the weight of tradition while rediscovering and repackaging old proposals as though they were unprecedented, exciting, and modern; ignoring or downgrading explicit criteria by which competing proposals can be evaluated. The identity and well-being of opinion leaders, participants, and groups in modern society are often profoundly affected by the degree to which they are deemed to be in step with the latest developments, in tune with modernity itself.

The operation of the fashion process or the play of fashion in science is indicated by the pattern of collective behavior of participants in the scientific community: the design, packaging, and articulation of the "latest developments" presented by opinion leaders and the praise given to those opinion leaders by the audience in accordance with its collective tastes; the adoption of some paradigms and rejection of others on the basis of those same collective tastes that ordinarily remain unrecognized by opinion leaders and followers alike in this community. Opinion leaders as well as rank-and-file participants in the scientific community are under relentless pressure to adhere to the latest styles or trends considered to be in "good taste"; to think and work only within the boundaries of the perceived social consensus, the mainstream, the orthodoxy of the "intellectual vanguard" of the moment; to refrain from going so far out in experimentation with unrecognized models as to incur the disapproval of peers in that community; and to avoid at all costs any interest in any trends considered to be old or "dated" on pain of ostracism or any association with opinion leaders and followers still clinging to obsolete models.

The first case study of a scientific opinion leader caught up in the fashion process examines the theoretical research of Georg Simmel and calls attention especially to his essay "Fashion." The many serious fallacies identified in Simmel's research are traced to the unacknowledged yet pervasive operation of this same process in his own sociological thought. The equally serious fallacies in Alfred Kroeber's empirical research on the play of fashion are also traced to the unacknowledged operation of this process in his own investigations. Nearly all contemporary studies of the fashion process are inadequate and misleading because of their uncritical acceptance or "rediscovery" of the precedents established by such prestigious opinion leaders as Simmel and Kroeber in the history of social science.

With the stage set for the submission of new models and for the competition among various designers and performers to gain recognition as the new savior of the discipline, the stature of Thomas S. Kuhn in modern sociology in general and the sociology of science in particular is critically examined. The many fallacies and ambiguities in Kuhn's claims about the scientific community are traced to the operation of the fashion process in his own thought. These fallacies and ambiguities receive enthusiastic applause from his audience and help to explain his rise to prominence. His stature is the result more of his unwitting accommodation to collective tastes in the discipline than of the alleged validity of his research. Kuhn's most important contributions to the sociology of science, especially his efforts at critical self-awareness and his recognition of the need to study anomalies on a systematic basis, are consistently ignored by the sociologists who most acclaim his work.

The next case study examines the ascendance of Robert Friedrichs's model of dialectical pluralism in American sociology. The ahistorical assumptions and caricature of the sociology of knowledge taken for granted in his model lead to grave misrepresentations, both theoretically and empirically, of developments in sociological inquiry. Friedrichs's model is a skillful modification of Kuhn's paradigm in the service of legitimating the present and proximate future of the discipline. His work is yet another instance of the unacknowledged but pervasive fashion process at work in the thinking of an opinion leader in the scientific community.

The next case studies call attention to the far-reaching influence of Pitirim Sorokin and Robert K. Merton in the development of American sociology. These eminent opinion leaders are unwittingly caught up in the fashion process even as they attempt to investigate fads, foibles, rivalries, and irrationality in the scientific community. Merton's professional stature is attributed in part to his ingenuity in representing trivial research and ideological polarization in the discipline as proof of a bountiful future for "world sociology" rather than a threat to its very existence.

The final case study examines the rise of Jeffrey Alexander to prominence as an opinion leader in sociological theory. It traces the boundaries of collective taste within which the doctrines of "neofunctionalism" and "postpositivism" have been celebrated as new and exciting paradigms in the scientific community. This analysis emphasizes the conservative mood in sociology as the impetus to the adoption of a new paradigm and the emergence of a new opinion leader onto center stage. The ideological requirements of capitalist society in general and the shifting collective tastes of the sociological profession in particular have combined to shape a selection process favorable to the adoption of seemingly revolutionary concepts and themes: politically sanitized and up-to-date meanings for "structural analysis," "dialectics," "transcendence," and "feeling the pain of others" have emerged as the ostensibly daring language, as the scientific orthodoxies, of the day.

These case studies indicate that the fashion process can have immense influence on all social participants—even on those scientists who critically study it. The play of fashion can render the self into an object readily caught up in the appeal of "keeping in step with the times." It can be a major determinant of what Fromm calls "the marketplace personality," the implied declaration that "I am as you desire me." It has great influence under conditions of organized insecurity and alienated intellectual labor, especially in the context of the modern scientific community.

I also show that an understanding of the fashion process helps to illuminate the rise to prominence of the functional theory of stratification; that the functional account of differential rewards based on social need and personal merit obscures the systematic rewards given to the incompetent and mediocre; and that the adoption of this model is specifically a manifestation of collective tastes formed in a crisis-ridden scientific community.

Beyond an analysis of opinion leaders in social science, the present study examines the origins and scope of collective taste in the scientific community in general and sociology in particular. Such an examination helps to explain why some proposals and opinion leaders are deemed orthodox one moment only to be discarded as obsolete the next. One set of forces shaping these collective tastes derives from the requirement of an advanced capitalist society for the appearance, indeed the illusion, of "new solutions to new problems," "better living through science," and an endless proliferation of scientific projects and models leading to "progress just over the horizon."

A closely related requirement for the maintenance of legitimacy in an advanced capitalist society is a disdain, even a sense of revulsion, for historical self-awareness; there must be an especially pronounced disdain for any interest in the accumulated wisdom and wealth in society made possible by the past struggles, sacrifices, and contributions of the working class. There must also be a correspondingly great faith in the doctrine that all progress is due to the contributions of the Rockefellers, the Du Ponts, the Carnegies, the Mellons, the Fords, and the boundless energies of the scientists whose work they sponsor and direct.

An effect of these requirements is an ongoing preoccupation with the present and the proximate future, not with the long-term origins and consequences of a given problem or trend. Its manifestation is typically in the formation of *ahistorical thought*: it becomes an institutionalized and pervasive orientation taken for granted as good social adjustment, as the normal way for scientists and laypersons alike to perceive themselves and their society, as the celebration of the here-and-now above all else. This mode of thought is given expression through such beliefs as "Keep in step with the times"; "Stay abreast of latest developments";

"What is new is true and good, what is old is false and bad"; and through the reverence for modern science as an end in itself. This ahistorical outlook is strongly reinforced by the satisfaction of yet another requirement of capitalist society: the task of creating and playing upon the perception of artificially heightened needs for new and sensational products, services, and ideas to ensure a demand for all manner of commodities sold to consumers. That most of these commodities are, upon closer inspection, neither new nor sensational (and for that matter, are often unnecessary, useless, even downright unhealthy or dangerous) must be systematically ignored, trivialized, or suppressed; those who try to bring this fact to the attention of the scientific community or the larger society are ostracised, ridiculed, and worst of all, labeled as "old-fashioned," "out of step with the times," "out of touch with reality," and perhaps just a little senile.

Another set of forces behind these collective tastes in the scientific community is the alienation of intellectual labor, the exclusion of scientists as part of the working class from positions of corporate and state power, the artificially contrived and culturally reinforced distinction between mental and manual labor. A result of this alienation is the decline of any sense of intellectual craftsmanship, the decline of pride in one's participation in the scientific community, with a corresponding rise of vanity, other-directedness, and unabashed pursuit of self-aggrandizement by any means necessary and regardless of its consequences for one's colleagues, students, or fellow citizens.

Without self-esteem, without pride in their role as ineffectual or token participants in the larger decision-making process, scientists engage in all manner of secondary adjustments to their environment: they become academic entrepreneurs, devise strategies to market and package their ideas and services as though they were commodities, learn that career mobility depends on selecting the appropriate means of transportation—not rocking the boat while riding on the gravy train. They launch an attendant search for compensations to ameliorate the anguish of their powerlessness to control the applications, the fruits, the profits generated by their intellectual labor and scientific discoveries. The most important of these compensations, and the most plausible means by which to deny the realities of political impotence in the scientific community, is the ongoing proliferation of new awards, prizes, and grants administered by miscellaneous groups of scientists, by quasi-public agencies, by corporate think tanks, by universities. These groups and agencies administer a flood tide of rewards to scientists who engage in "vanguard" research, who are at "the cutting edge of the future," who are certified as advancing this or that "revolutionary paradigm," who must embody the very latest developments in the field. *The ritual process of giving out rewards, especially when they are capriciously given to mediocre candidates heralded for the moment as geniuses and prophets in the professional priesthood, maintains the illusion that the scientific community is in control of its own destiny.* This same ritual process also drives scientists to compete fiercely with one another and to compromise themselves for a few crumbs, for a ride on the gravy train. Scientists quickly abandon any critical perspective on their own discipline and on the making of social policy precisely because they get the message loud and clear that any irreverent or distasteful conduct leads to banishment from the promised land.

Even though scientists may well be *legally* and *technically* protected from political repression through academic tenure and civil service codes, the fact remains that their intellectual and political activity is profoundly shaped and mutilated by the mechanism of arbitrary, capricious, and even sleazy issuance of professional awards. The grim and incessant competition for individual rewards helps to ensure that scientists view each other as *rivals*; that they dismiss cooperative efforts as a sign of weakness or maladjustment; that their debilitating search for recognition leaves little time or energy for pursuing science in the service of social justice or progress, much less criticizing any of the antics, foibles, and orthodoxies in their own discipline.

The most ominous and pervasive sign of alienated intellectual labor in the scientific workplace is *cynicism*: cynicism about the validity of one paradigm versus another, cynicism about the role of scientists in the larger society, and cynicism about the legitimacy and worth of science itself. Even when a scientist is proved to have committed acts of fraud or plagiarism, the standard response is, "He was stupid to have gotten caught" or "So what else is new?" No effort is made to reexamine, much less to tighten, the standards of peer review by which the culprit was awarded a grant, prize, promotion, or other recognition for work that was bogus or not his own. In the context of such cynicism, objective truth-content is not a decisive factor in the selection of competing models. Standards of good taste (based on whatever is felt to be the latest development, the most pleasant, in the mainstream) become the governing criteria for the rise of some models to prominence and the decline of others to obscurity. Cynicism in the scientific community, in turn, promotes *relativism*; this ideology assumes that all ideas are more or less valid from one standpoint or another, that there is no objective criterion by which a given idea can be proved superior to others, that it does not make much difference which idea is adopted today because it will not be around for long in any case, that whatever looks good, feels good, or seems advantageous at the moment is superior to competing models. This ideology is an essential part of the soil in which endless varieties of new models sprout and proliferate, a precondition for the play of fashion in science.

Despite the corrosive effects of the fashion process in the scientific community, they are not inevitable or irreversible. Indeed, the play of fashion can help to facilitate the introduction and serious consideration of new models that would otherwise be suppressed at the outset. Just as the fashion process establishes an orthodoxy of what is in good taste at a given moment, it also allows for the entertainment and proliferation of new ideas, even those that some opinion leaders might dismiss as unduly "visionary" or "too far out." But the fashion process can have this constructive effect only if its presence is explicitly and candidly acknowledged (as it is in the domain of costume adornment), if its range of operation is itself subjected to critical *public* scrutiny and its potential mischief kept at the forefront of attention. An obstacle to the recognition of the fashion process within the scientific community is that its participants are loathe to admit to any irrational collective behavior in the evaluation and adoption of competing paradigms. Yet the constructive role of the fashion process cannot take effect unless its presence is candidly acknowledged by its adherents and critics alike. (Indeed, some of the opinion leaders in the scientific community who expose and condemn manifestations of the fashion process in sociology, for example, are themselves unwittingly caught up in that same process; even Sorokin and C. Wright Mills are very much under its influence despite their assaults against other sociologists for a miscellany of irrational collective behaviors.)

One rule within the scientific community is suggestive of what Sumner meant by a *folkway*, and is not unlike the Mafia's principle of *omertà*: those who break the code of silence within the community and wash dirty linen in public by "ratting" on their brethren are severely taken to task. There is a tacit but compelling rule that scientists must not expose or criticize other scientists caught in acts of fraud and plagiarism. How can the presence and strength of such a rule be ascertained? One reliable way to estimate the salience, sanctity, and level of consensus behind this (or any other) rule as viewed by social participants is to note their collective response to those who violate it. What happens when a scientist identifies colleagues engaged in the production of bogus research findings and plagiarism in their quest for grant money and proceeds to notify the appropriate federal agencies (HEW, NIH) of the irregularities? The scientist filing the well-documented charges is subjected to retribution (discontinuation of funding, ostracism) for his trouble while the culprits fudging and plagiarizing their "hard data" are neither investigated nor penalized for their antics by the same agencies. The testimony given to the congressional Subcommittee on Fraud and Plagiarism in Science has aired instructive testimony about the normative pattern according to which fraud in science is condoned and efforts to expose it are suppressed.

Most of the irrationality in science is far more subtle, unwitting, and pervasive than suggested by a given scandal or even a series of scandals uncovered by conscionable scientists and well-intended muckrakers: most of this irrationality is the unfolding or playing out of the collective behavior inherent in the fashion process and the collective tastes that give it scope and direction. A defining characteristic of this collective behavior is the emergence of opinion leaders who serve for the most part unwittingly to reflect and reinforce the collective tastes within their community. We will see that even those scientists who specifically investigate the fashion process in modern society, the play of fashion within the scientific community, and the manifestations of irrationality in science and society can themselves be intimately caught up in this very same process. It is now time to direct our attention to such opinion leaders as Simmel, Kroeber, Friedrichs, Sorokin, Kuhn, Merton, and Alexander in order to ascertain what they say about the play of fashion, how much they are themselves subject to its influence, and what we can learn from their insights, their myopia, and their role in the scientific community. We will then examine the origins and consequences of alienated intellectual labor as well as the structural and ideological conditions that shape the pattern of rewards and recognition conferred by the scientific community on its opinion leaders. We will also examine the degree to which rewards are systematically allocated to the undeserving, the marginally competent, or the mediocre as an important mechanism of social control in the scientific community. Last but not least, we will explore the possibility that *the fashion process rather than the Protestant ethic may well have been the major impetus to the rise of modern science; that the widely held view of the Protestant ethic as the driving force behind scientific ferment and discoveries from the seventeenth century to the present era, the Weberian thesis popularized by Merton, is itself a manifestation of the fashion process in the scientific community.* The excursion is a long one, I hope you enjoy it.

ACKNOWLEDGEMENTS

Much of the credit for whatever value this work may have belongs to a number of scholars and teachers.

During my formative days as a graduate student at the City College of New York in the early 1960s, I was encouraged to pursue studies in the sociology of knowledge and allowed to write a master's thesis on Karl Mannheim's contributions to this domain. I was allowed to utilize the remarkable faculty resources on all five CUNY campuses and even to take courses at other nearby universities toward my degree. I had the benefit of instruction from Alfred McClung Lee at Brooklyn College, Joseph B. Gittler at City College, and Robert K. Merton at Columbia University. From these three I learned much about collective behavior, symbolic interactionism, and classical social theory, respectively. To CUNY in general and these faculty in particular, I remain deeply grateful for my initiation into the discipline.

This work is a substantially revised and expanded version of a doctoral dissertation on the sociology of science I completed at the University of California at Berkeley. During my studies at Berkeley in the more turbulent period of the 1960s, I was fortunate to have had the opportunity to learn more deeply about collective behavior and symbolic interactionism from Herbert Blumer and Erving Goffman; I learned much about the history of social thought, especially the bearing of evolutionism and the Enlightenment on sociology itself, from Kenneth Bock and Ernest Becker. I am indebted to Richard Lichtman for enabling me to appreciate the relevance of historical materialism for the tasks of social theory and practice, and to go beyond the caricatures of Marxism all too often on display in graduate sociology programs. I am also indebted to Hanan Selvin and Robert Somers for their tireless efforts at convincing an impatient antiwar activist that methodological self-awareness is an essential goal in the analysis of public policy.

During that stormy decade, these faculty constituted a "critical mass" of original scholarship, dedicated teaching, and, in the case of Ernest Becker, charismatic leadership as well; these faculty educated and inspired a generation of graduate students in a progressive, critical, and interdisciplinary tradition. I was fortunate to have been part of that generation.

I would like to thank Stanley Aronowitz for his suggestions and pleadings that I take leave of more mundane tasks in order to revise and complete this work at long last. I am glad I did so, for it has taken me back to my roots and reminded me just how much I owe to the teaching and research of others.

Terry Cochran, my editor at the University of Minnesota Press, deserves special thanks for his excellent suggestions as to matters of substance and style as well as his understanding and patience with an author prone to work in fits and starts. Mary Byers has been a most capable, caring, and meticulous copy editor whose suggestions and corrections have been invaluable. For all the shortcomings of substance and style in the pages to follow, I am alone responsible.

Last but not least, I want to thank Erica Sher for her artistic talent and keen sense of irony in drawing the sketches of three figures whose works are examined in this study. I trust that the irreverence in these portraits of Mills, Sorokin, and Merton is understood in the context of respect for the scholarship these theorists have exemplified. A sense of humor is necessary for life and growth; I think it has a place in the scientific community.

The next generation is entitled to a world more just, honest, and nurturing than the one it will inherit. To my own wonderful daughters, Janette and Claudia, already striving to make the world a more fit place in which to live, and to all those contributing to the struggle for justice and reason however they can and wherever they are, this book is dedicated.

FASHIONS IN SCIENCE

CHAPTER 1
INTRODUCTION
SCOPE AND PRECEDENTS FOR THE STUDY OF FASHIONS IN SCIENCE

The central purpose of the present study is to clarify the scope and magnitude of the play of fashion or the "fashion process" in modern society by demonstrating that it increasingly pervades even an academic or scientific institution in which its presence might be least expected. It will be shown that this process exerts a far-reaching influence on (i) the substantive research carried out by prominent sociologists who have studied the fashion process, as well as (ii) the major investigations of those sociologists of science and knowledge who have themselves studied the growth of modern science in general and the discipline of sociology in particular. Some of the intensive case studies to follow deal with the research of such prominent scholars as Thomas Kuhn, Robert Friedrichs, Pitirim Sorokin, and Robert K. Merton; they serve to indicate that even the sociology of science and the sociology of knowledge, academic domains usually regarded as devoted to the values of rationalism and critical self-awareness and immune to the pressures of the day, are themselves fertile soil in which this process has taken root and blossomed in many guises that are consistently ignored by those same scholars.

A second aim of the present work is to examine critically the contributions to the study of the fashion process in modern society to be gleaned especially from the writings of such social scientists as Georg Simmel, Alfred Kroeber, and Herbert Blumer. Such a focus enables one to evaluate the theoretical assumptions, hypotheses, and ranges of applicability of the perspectives or schools of thought with which these scholars are

associated in the history and current development of sociological inquiry. One can then take advantage of the illumination each perspective
adds to an understanding of this complex, pervasive, and unduly ignored aspect of modern society; the contributions of the aforementioned investigators will be compared and synthesized at several junctures here. The value of the symbolic interactionist perspective in
highlighting some of the weaknesses in conventional approaches to the
study of the fashion process and calling attention to certain crucial
aspects of this process that are otherwise overlooked altogether will become evident from the substantial utilization of this perspective in
general, and my indebtedness to Blumer's analysis of the fashion process in particular.

A third aim of this volume is to demonstrate (a) that ahistorical and
mechanistic assumptions about human nature are taken for granted by
prominent sociologists in their studies of the fashion process and of the
scientific community in modern society; (b) that these assumptions consistently lead to the neglect or denial of the capacity of the social self to
redefine the meaning of forces or "variables" in everyday life and in the
scientific community; and (c) that these assumptions lead to an uncritical acquiescence or endorsement of both the fashion process as well as
the operation of that process in the scientific community. It will be
shown that these assumptions lead to a preoccupation with the study of
the present as given, with the result that the serious investigation of the
historical origins and long-term consequences of the fashion process
are ignored, and that these assumptions similarly lead to a myopic
preoccupation with the present structure and trends in the scientific
community as though they were necessary, natural, universal, timeless,
and desirable for the growth of scientific knowledge. In my examination
of these assumptions, I hope to show that they are rarely if ever acknowledged or critically examined by the many scholars who incorporate them into the models or perspectives submitted for adoption in
the discipline of sociology. It will also be shown that these assumptions
serve to accelerate the play of fashion in the scientific community and
to bring about substantial distortions of the actual characteristics of the
fashion process, the scientific community, and the operation of the fashion process in the scientific community.

A fourth aim of this study is to demonstrate that the sociology of
knowledge is an essential part of any comprehensive effort to investigate the trends and social crises in which social scientists are themselves participants; that the failure to apply the perspective and the lessons of this scholarly domain to such an investigation, a deficiency that
has become virtually institutionalized in the contemporary intellectual

culture of American society, renders difficult the task of recognizing the fashion process in one's own research. This same failure renders still more difficult the urgent task of critically examining those ideological presuppositions and vested interests in the academic community that lead to self-celebration and insensitivity to negative evidence and is therefore conducive to an intellectual climate in which the fashion process is accelerated in modern science. The sociology of knowledge is all too often dismissed as a product of Karl Mannheim's relativism and idealism, as incompatible with the advancement of an objective science of society. The sociology of knowledge, however, is not meant to repudiate the goals of an objective and reliable social science; it *does* emphasize the misleading assumptions and implications of the doctrines of value-neutrality, self-celebration, and neglect of negative evidence by many scholars. It also emphasizes the ideological and structural sources of such myopia. Despite contemporary notions concerning its allegedly "esoteric" character, the "inconsequential" status it deserves as an offshoot of classical epistemology, and its "dated" or obsolescent condition, the trivialization, neglect, and, at times, caricature of this field by prominent social scientists are responsible for much of the faulty logic, dubious evidence, and unwarranted conclusions found in the substantive research on the fashion process, the scientific community and the nature of modern society itself.

Few scholars have seriously investigated the fashion process in modern society, but a substantial number have investigated the development of scientific institutions in modern society. Those who have studied the fashion process usually *assumed* that it does not operate in the contemporary scientific community and that it can only (or primarily) affect such ordinary domains as costume adornment, popular art, and architecture. Those who have studied the scientific community from a sociological standpoint have also *assumed* that the fashion process is by definition incompatible with and inoperative in the scientific community, that it could not possibly be a characteristic of the modern scientific world in particular, and that its existence or presence at any time in the scientific world is such a remote issue as to be unworthy of systematic investigation. These assumptions, though often taken for granted and sometimes openly declared as self-evident, have never been systematically investigated or demonstrated. It is my intention to show here, however, that the most prestigious and influential social scientists who accept these unproven assumptions are themselves (1) unwittingly yet profoundly caught up in the fashion process even as they attempt to investigate the play of fashion and the nature of the scientific community; (2) led thereby to rely on spurious or nonexistent evidence, to employ fallacious logic, and to reach untenable conclusions about the fashion process and the scientific community in modern society; (3) uncritically reflecting and reinforcing the collective behavior and sentiments of the audience that acclaims their research and expects scientific opinion leaders to act "in good taste" and "in step with the times"; (4) establishing unsound and unexamined precedents for the study of the fashion process, the scientific community, and the human condition in general—thereby hindering the advancement of reliable sociological knowledge about major trends and forces in modern society.

The fashion process in the scientific community is difficult to investigate not only because the operation of this process is subtle, widely misunderstood, and often ignored by sociologists but also because the very meaning of the scientific community is open to differing interpretations. The "scientific community" all too often connotes a high degree of interpersonal collegiality among its participants and an abstract consensus around certain allegedly universal assumptions concerning value-neutrality, egalitarianism among scientists, rationalism and devotion to truth as an end in itself. These and similar connotations, it will be shown, are misleading portraits of modern science and are themselves conducive to a climate in which the fashion process is accelerated in the scientific community. For purposes of the present study, then, the term "scientific community" refers to any discipline, profession, institution, or network of organizations regarded as both responsible for producing and conveying ideas about a given order of social or physical phenomena and the source of those particular ideas defined as *authentic, certified*, and *valid* descriptions or explanations of such phenomena. There is no necessary relationship between what is socially defined to be authentic knowledge and what is actually proven to be a valid claim about a given phenomenon. I will show that social perceptions of scientific truth, including those of the scientists I will examine below are readily caught up in the fashion process. An *opinion leader* in the scientific community is any scholar whose work is regarded as highly influential and prestigious by his or her peers, reasonably representative of the most important and best research in a given area of study, and generally successful in "staying on top" (at least in the short run) despite the entry of rival designers into the selection process. For purposes of the present study, the operation of the fashion process in the scientific community refers primarily, first, to the manifestations of this process in the assumptions, uses of evidence, conclusions, and modes of exposition in the research done by opinion leaders in that community; second, to the fact that the presence of this process is unacknowledged and often denied categorically by those opinion leaders; and finally, to the tendency of this process to cause serious distortion or neglect of important aspects of the phenomena investigated by them.

In investigating the degree to which the fashion process operates in the scientific community, one must explicitly state the criteria by which the hypotheses about its scope and magnitude can be verified, the logical assumptions on which those criteria are based, the methodological grounds on which the hypotheses about its scope and magnitude can be verified, the potential sources of ideological distortion or oversight, and the substantive grounds on which the hypotheses are initially formulated. These considerations are necessary, not only because they call attention to the substantive issues at hand, but also because they guard against the possibility that the present study itself might become caught up in the fashion process under investigation. If the fashion process is as subtle and pervasive as I hope to show, then one would be naive to ignore the risk that the present study might be susceptible to its operation. To avoid or minimize its impact on one's assumptions and research, this process must be critically taken into account rather than righteously denied or casually dismissed.

Some Cautionary Methodological Considerations: Criteria of Validity and Tentative Assumptions

The criteria or indicators for the verification of hypotheses about the scope and magnitude of the fashion process in science are complex; they must be understood at several levels of theoretical and empirical investigation. Where the fashion process exerts a major and fairly constant influence on scientific inquiry, one should be able to demonstrate the following points.

(1) The most widely acclaimed research carried out by the most eminent scholars in a given discipline may be marked by serious defects in the logic, evidence, and conclusions of that research.

(2) These defects are primarily the result of the unwitting, uncritical, and ongoing endorsement of such themes as "what is new or modern is necessarily best"; "the emerging social consensus is the ultimate arbiter of scientific truth"; "the scholar who works alone is irresponsible and his findings are suspect"; "good taste, congeniality, and moderation are preferable to heated debate, political conflict and disruption of the professional status quo in the scientific community." These defects are found so frequently in a representative group of the most prominent and articulate scholars that they are attributable to the social context in

which they occur and not to any eccentricity, aberration, or intellectual mediocrity on the part of the scholars whose work is examined.

(3) There are considerable numbers and varieties of models competing for adoption in the scientific community, and the dominant models (e.g., those intensively examined in terms of the two immediately preceding criteria) are in fact the ones that triumph in the selection process of that community.

(4) The selection process in which various models compete for acceptance is governed more by the implicit values of good taste, social consensus, and modernity than by the considerations of logical adequacy or empirical validity of claims being presented to an audience (i.e., a professional constituency).

(5) The most prestigious and influential scholars in the discipline enjoy their coveted status primarily because they accommodate, legitimize, and crystallize the collective tastes and amorphous sentiments of their audience. They are not elevated to positions of high stature primarily because of any superiority in their scholarly vision, rigor, or originality; their work is not systematically evaluated by comparison with the work of actual or potential rivals in the discipline.

(6) The prevailing views and the ascendant scholars in the discipline constitute such an orthodoxy in the scientific community as to produce severe reprisals, including personal denunciation and institutionalized ostracism, against those who openly attack their legitimacy and who are defined as "out of step with the latest developments."

(7) This orthodoxy, however much it may appear all-powerful and permanent, nevertheless represents a model or configuration of closely related models that once managed to displace the previous orthodoxy and might in turn be displaced by still newer models as the audience considers them in the competition for center stage. Thus, the apparent orthodoxy at one time is discarded as an obsolete model at a later time and may be yet again rediscovered as though it were a daring new innovation in still a subsequent period in the development of the scientific community.

(8) The ordinary members of the scientific community are under relentless pressure to keep abreast of new styles and shifting emphases displayed by those opinion leaders who are considered "in the vanguard," to adjust to those particular styles or models around which a consensus forms, and to refrain from going so far out in experimenting with generally unrecognized models as to incur the disapproval of peers in that community.

These criteria or indicators are designated in this order because they indicate a methodologically coherent sequence of steps by which the investigation of the fashion process in modern science can be brought to an unambiguous conclusion regarding the presence or absence of this process in the scientific community and the scope and magnitude of this process in the event that its presence is in fact ascertained. These eight criteria of the fashion process in science are essential to any definitive and irreproachable demonstration of the hypothesis that the play of fashion pervades a given scientific discipline. But one should note that the evidence obtained for each of them is of considerable value and, indeed, necessary to the analysis of evidence for the succeeding step in such an effort to verify the hypothesis. As already noted, there is a paucity of research to which one may turn in the study of fashions in science; since the need for exhaustive evidence on which to test such a hypothesis is still unmet, the present study must be guided by the following cautionary considerations.

First, the evidence assembled at each step of investigation must be searchingly analyzed to ensure that it is in fact (a) representative of the trends and forces in the scientific community in a given historical period, (b) an accurate indication of the essential arguments and studies carried out by the particular opinion leaders whose scholarly work is chosen for intensive examination, and (c) specifically relevant to the task of ascertaining the validity of the hypotheses advanced. In my analysis I call attention to the representativeness, accuracy, and relevance of the material presented as evidence for the hypothesis that the fashion process does operate in social science.

Second, alternative interpretations of the evidence, including the possibility that defects in a given piece of research might be attributable to idiosyncracies or aberrations on the part of the individual scholar, must be examined. One of the most effective means by which such alternative explanations can be ruled out is to demonstrate both that the defects in a given piece of research are similar to defects in the research of other prominent scholars in the given area and that these defects are consistently associated with certain assumptions and modes of thought traceable to the larger context of collective behavior, vested interests, and ideologies in which scientific institutions develop. At various junctures in this study I point out the continuities in the substantive defects, assumptions, and ideologies of such a seemingly disparate group of promiment social scientists as Georg Simmel, Alfred Kroeber, Thomas Kuhn, Robert Friedrichs, Pitirim Sorokin, and Robert K. Merton, and Jeffrey Alexander.

Third, the limitations on the applicability of the evidence presented must be realistically acknowledged in order to distinguish warranted inferences from plausible but tentative assertions on the one hand and idle or untenable speculation on the other hand. One limitation on the evidence presented here is that virtually all of the case studies refer to the play of fashion in the social sciences rather than the physical sciences. Hence, no attempt can be made to conclude that all of the disciplines in the physical and social sciences are equally affected by the fashion process. Moreover, the intensive case studies used here are focused chiefly on the discipline of sociology per se; one must be extremely cautious even in drawing tentative conclusions about the fashion process in such allied disciplines as anthropology, psychology, political science, and history on the basis of such evidence. One can note that Kroeber is not only an anthropologist but one of the most prestigious anthropologists in that discipline as well as a highly influential figure in the social sciences more generally; this fact is highly suggestive of the possibility that his assumptions and claims about the nature of fashions in modern society, which are shown here to be themselves caught up in the fashion process, may be characteristic of the research done by other opinion leaders in the discipline of anthropology. But such a suggestion, however reasonable and plausible it might be, should be considered as a problematic rather than conclusively demonstrated hypothesis; it requires independent investigation and cannot be proved or disproved on the basis of intuitive beliefs or highly suggestive data. One can note that Simmel is as much a social psychologist as a sociologist, moreover, and that the same suggestive but not conclusive implication would seem to be in order as a basis for investigating the domain of social psychology. One can also note that Sorokin enjoys considerable stature in certain circles of historical inquiry, social philosophy, and international social science; again, it is essential to distinguish between a tentatively, cautiously advanced suggestion that requires independent investigation from a verified hypothesis holding that the fashion process is operative in the disciplines of history and philosophy. Finally, one can note that Kuhn was originally trained in the physical sciences and that his *Structure of Scientific Revolutions* has been favorably received by many physical scientists. But this in no way proves that any of the physical sciences correspond in their internal structure or development to the features Kuhn has proposed for his model of the scientific community. Indeed, I hope to show that Kuhn's model is laden with so many ambiguities as to cast the most serious doubt on the claims he wishes to advance. One can note in passing, as explained in my discussion of Kuhn's admiration for modern physics textbooks, that the decline of interest in classical physics and in the need for methodological rigor in experimental research may well open the door to the fashion process in modern physics. But the fact that a given scientific discipline has some of the characteristics (e.g., an ahistorical orientation, vagueness in the use of basic concepts and units of observation) that are conducive to the play of fashion can only be suggestive of the possibility that the discipline may be caught up in this process; such a possibility must be independently investigated as a working hypothesis and not uncritically translated into a self-evident conclusion.

Fourth, in view of the many lacunae in the literature on the fashion process and the even more serious paucity of research on the play of fashion in science, it is essential that any evidence presented here be meticulously assembled in the first place. I have therefore made a strategic decision to concentrate on the criteria 1 and 2 discussed earlier in order that subsequent research on the fashion process be established on a firm footing. Although the following intensive examinations of work done by major opinion leaders also have some fruitful implications here and there for the remaining criteria to be investigated, the fact remains that the present study undertakes to accomplish only the first two criteria and should therefore not be considered a conclusive and exhaustive demonstration of all aspects of the fashion process in modern science. Still another reason to concentrate on only a limited number of criteria is that those undertaken herein already entail a formidable range of problems that require much attention in their own right and that, when clarified and solved, should greatly facilitate the advancement of future research on the fashion process; these many-sided problems of interpretation, both methodological and theoretical, are defined and solved at a number of appropriate points (especially in the discussion of Kroeber's and Kuhn's research) in the pages to follow. An argument could be made that the case studies below do substantially address and document criteria 4 and 5 in the task of identifying fashion in science. But this has not been my primary objective at the present stage of research.

These cautionary considerations lead to a question still facing this study of an inadequately explored conceptual terrain: just what is being *assumed* and what is being *demonstrated* in this study?

This investigation assumes that if each of the eight criteria enumerated earlier were satisfied, then the evidence so obtained would generally corroborate the findings thus far reached through ascertainment of the first two criteria in the following discussions. This assumption implies neither that the necessary evidence for its validation has already been obtained nor that such evidence must perfectly corroborate it in every detail. This assumption also does not imply that the task of carrying out the remaining steps of this investigation is rendered superfluous because of the evidence obtained from an ascertainment of the first two criteria; on the contrary, the analysis of fashions in science based on the evidence presented here can only be sharpened and, where called for, extended or corrected in light of additional knowledge. In a somewhat more positive but still provisional sense, this assumption can be restated as follows. The considerable evidence presented in this study indicates that the works of prominent opinion leaders examined herein are marked by grave substantive defects; that these defects are largely attributable to the operation of the fashion process in the scientific community rather than to idiosyncratic aberrations; and that the possibility of demonstrating the operation of the fashion process in terms of all eight criteria for ascertaining it in the scientific community can be reasonably, fairly, and tentatively *assumed* for our purposes.

This assumption is no less reasonable and, indeed, is more plausible than the possibility that the widely acclaimed works of the prominent scholars under examination are unrepresentative of the research carried out by peers in the discipline or that an altogether different interpretation of the evidence would be as adequate as the one presented herein to account for the many defects found in those works. Various arguments and documentations to rule out such a possibility are emphasized at appropriate junctures. Nevertheless, there might be a limited degree to which one or another aspect of this possibility (however remote) would be thereby brought to light. Although the material presented here renders this possibility most unlikely, the need for sensitivity to negative evidence must be kept in mind rather than honored in the breach. I intend to show that an insensitivity to negative evidence, especially as found in tendencies toward self-celebration among prominent social scientists, is yet another form of myopia that reflects and reinforces the play of fashion in modern science.[1] For this reason, I would prefer to err on the side of extreme caution and sensitivity to negative evidence rather than on the side of premature conclusions and dogmatic denials that alternative interpretations of the fashion process in science might arise in the course of future research. As the following case studies make clear, the need for intellectual humility is rarely given even a passing nod in the social sciences today; the only opinion leader in the sociology of science who occasionally attempts to engage in critical self-examination, Thomas Kuhn, was by his own admission never really socialized into the academic culture of modern American sociology.

Definition of the "Fashion Process"

The *fashion process* refers to the preoccupation with keeping in step with the times; second, to following the example of prestigious opinion leaders who crystallize and reinforce the vaguely expressed collective tastes of the public; admiring proposals for adoption when they are in "good taste" and new, and discarding them when they are in "bad taste" and old; opposing the weight of tradition in general while rediscovering and modifying old proposals as though they were unprecedented, daring, and modern; ignoring or downgrading the importance of explicit criteria by which competing proposals for adoption can be rationally evaluated. The fashion process facilitates major forms of change, continuity, and control in modern society: those who resist new and popular proposals are condemned as being old-fashioned or "too straight." Once a proposal is in fact widely adopted, it is defended as though it were sacrosanct because "it's the latest thing," only to be subsequently repudiated in favor of a newer one that is "more in step with the times."[2]

The fashion process can open the door to innovative solutions and challenges against those traditions that render difficult or impossible any new response to problems in the social order. However, the preoccupation with the here-and-now together with an indifference (or even a hostility) to tradition leads to a markedly ahistorical view of the problems to be solved and a myopic neglect of the wisdom and mistakes of the past. For example, the fashion process is especially pronounced in modern American society: old ideas and elderly persons, regardless of their possible value in solving the problems of the day, tend to be downgraded or "put away" in favor of new ideas and young persons regardless of their lack of value in solving those same problems.

One manifestation of the scornful treatment of old ideas and elderly persons is that social scientists themselves often assume that innovation is the essence of modern civilization and proceed to analyze obstacles to this allegedly natural or self-evident tendency. According to a study by Rogers and Shoemaker, for example, "although it is true that we live more than ever before in an era of change, prevailing social structures often serve to hamper the diffusion of innovations."[3] The possibility that old ideas and practices might be superior to new ones and that their defenders might be more enlightened than their assailants is generally discounted by social scientists who adopt this perspective.

Still another manifestation of the same perspective is found in the literature on aging. Sociological research on the aged is narrowly concerned with describing the patterns of rejection to which the aged are subjected and the related priorities in favor of youth and novelty in American culture rather than explaining either the causes of such discrimination or the operation of the fashion process as an impetus to it. Raab and Selznick, for example, make only an incidental effort to take note of these causes or to recognize the play of fashion that reinforces their impact on the aged:

> Because of the swiftly changing nature of our society, the cultural differences between the older and younger generations are often marked. . . . The older people in our society tend to feel useless, unimportant, out of place, in the way, discarded, isolated, lonely and idle. It has been said that these feelings are deepened by the accent on youth in our society. The pleasures, romance and energies of youth have been enshrined in our mass advertising, our mass media, and our general attitudes.[4]

The authors imply that discrimination against the aged is a necessary consequence of any swiftly changing society, but give neither logical reasons nor empirical evidence to support this view. Because they neglect to examine the causes of the strong emphasis on youth, which clearly has a grave impact on the aged, Raab and Selznick permit the impression that this value is an immutable feature of modern society and that the only appropriate recourse is the partial amelioration of its more acute symptoms. The cultural definition of old ideas and aged persons as obstacles to progress is also uncritically expressed in those areas of scholarly inquiry in which one might least expect to find it; the emergence of such an ahistorical bias in social science warrants careful examination.

The Conventional Wisdom Regarding the Nature of Fashion

There is a slowly growing recognition that the fashion process operates in areas far beyond the scope of costume adornment and styles of art and literature, and that it even extends to such seemingly unlikely fields as science and religion.[5] But there remains a tendency to explain this process ahistorically in terms of psychological needs inherent in human nature and to espouse a cynical view regarding the futility of its operation without recognizing the special conditions in modern society that produce and accelerate it in everyday life. Even in such a widely accepted source as the *Encyclopedia Americana*, for example, one reads that:

the dynamic element in fashion is traceable to the activity for fresh experience that seems to characterize the human psyche, and may be explained by its recurrent dissatisfaction with the conditions of existence and the desire to improve these conditions through change.[6]

Maurice Valency gives no evidence to support his claim that human beings are driven by an innate need for new experience; he offers no explanation for the fact that some people are more preoccupied with fashion than others and that the rates and patterns of acceleration in the fashion process vary greatly from time to time and place to place. Similarly, he provides no argument to justify his sweeping claim that human beings are inherently dissatisfied with their environment and devoted to its improvement through social change. Indeed, the rapid decline in major forms of social protest in the 1970s and the emergence of increasingly conservative electoral politics in American society while revolutionary movements in the Third World simultaneously became successful would suggest that any dissatisfaction felt toward the environment and any desire to improve it are neither constant nor universal in human nature.

This same authoritative source proceeds to hold that the late 1960s can be characterized by a "romanticism" that allegedly produced the "cult of the bizarre," and that any attempt to correct or replace this trend would be an exercise in futility. Illustrative of this genre of speculation about the fashion process is the assumption that human beings are permanently at the mercy of orthodoxies created by their own psychological needs, that they are everywhere doomed to a fate they once set into motion but are now powerless to control and that they are now creatures of fashion rather than seekers of freedom:

> It was not until the late 1960's that a new wave of romanticism brought about the development of the cult of the bizarre and the extreme in dress and manners, art, music, and literature. As usual, these manifestations seemed to have more to do with fashion than with freedom, since those who revolted were more strictly regimented than those who did not. In the swings of fashion, it seems hardly possible to revolt against the despotism of the past save in terms of one more despotic.[7]

To explain away the forms of protest and innovation of the 1960s as a "cult of the bizarre," to conclude that struggles for social change are necessarily self-defeating, and to ignore the constellation of problems and crises in modern society to which the fashion process is a response are all features of the conventional wisdom on this matter. These tendencies are themselves part of the ahistorical and cynical "conservative mood" in American culture;[8] their clearly negative connotations concerning the "romanticism" of social participants are themselves part of the fashionable practice in the academic world to label protest movements in the 1960s as frivolous, irresponsible, utopian, or immature. Although Valency presumes to clarify the essence of the fashion process by claiming that "the ultimate arbiter of fashion is public opinion,"[9] he discounts the vast degree to which public opinion and collective taste are shaped by the historical context in which they emerge and manipulated deliberately by vested interests in the social order. Despite his prominence as an opinion leader and world traveler in search of the latest designs in furniture for upscale clients, Maurice Valency's ahistorical assumptions about "fashion" serve only to reflect and reinforce the fashion process in modern society.

Approaches to the Study of Fashion: Major Precedents in the Work of Simmel and Kroeber

Although costume adornment is the most familiar arena for the play of fashion in modern society, science is another arena in which the fashion process operates with considerable impact on the direction of social change as well as on sociological explanations of social change. Symptomatic of the operation of the fashion process is an ahistorical bias—an insensitivity to learning from the mistakes or the wisdom of the past. This bias has been criticized especially by those who survey the history and current status of sociological theory,[10] while the forces responsible for its persistence have been accorded scant attention. Regardless of the vehemence with which some scholars have attacked the ahistorical bias in sociological inquiry, criticisms and moral exhortations to abandon it have been thus far unsuccessful. The present study is an effort to analyze origins and consequences of the underlying fashion process itself in the discipline of sociology.

Before the fashion process in sociological inquiry can be analyzed, a number of questions must be answered. Why do we so often associate the fashion process with costume adornment alone? Why are fields other than costume adornment so rarely examined in terms of the fashion process even by sociologists who might be expected to go beyond such a limited empirical terrain? Why do we so often consider the fashion process to be a frivolous, superficial, or harmless feature of modern social life? Why do we generally consider the manifestations of the fashion process in material and highly visible styles of modern living but not in subtle styles of scientific thought or politics? Why do we usually discount the economic and political structure of society, the prevailing cultural values, the subjective meaning of a new style or practice when the play of fashion is investigated? Why is the play of fashion itself so often studied in an ahistorical manner? To answer these questions, the legacy of the most important architects of the scientific study of the fashion process must be examined.

This examination will also indicate the fallacy of Whitehead's belief that "a science which hesitates to forget its founders is lost." It will show that the originators of an area of study can be at least partially responsible for a discipline becoming lost and that a most searching analysis of their work is necessary if a discipline is to find itself.

An analysis of the precedents for the ahistorical approach to the study of fashions and the tendency to associate the study of costume adornment (usually of women's clothing) with the study of fashions is now in order. Since the former orientation is most fully articulated by Georg Simmel and the latter orientation is most fully articulated by Alfred Kroeber, and since these are the most influential scholars who have devoted substantial attention to the study of fashion, the work of both writers becomes all the more significant for any current investigation of fashion for the purpose of this study.

More than a decade before Alfred Kroeber attempted to identify the principle of order in civilization by the statistical analysis of fashion, Georg Simmel had advanced what seemed to be a comprehensive theoretical and epistemological approach to the discovery of this same principle.[11] A review and critical evaluation of this approach to the study of fashion, advanced by Simmel as a key to an understanding of modern civilization itself, is now in order.

Simmel's Theory of Human Nature and the Play of Fashion

According to Simmel, the individual as well as the public mind are governed by the limiting principle of the social paradox:

> We recognize two antagonistic forces, tendencies, or characteristics, either of which, if left unaffected, would approach infinity; and it is by the mutual limitation of the two forces that the characteristics of the individual and the public mind result. (541)

Since there is no single, ultimate, or controlling force that always determines all of human behavior, it follows that

> we must establish the degree of limitation exercised by the counteraction of some other force, as well as the influence exerted by the latter upon the primitive force. (541)

Simmel claims that the dualism inherent in human nature, in the individual mind and the public mind, has its origin in the human organism itself:

> The physiological basis of our being gives the first hint, for we discover that human nature requires motion and repose, receptiveness and productivity—a masculine and feminine principle are united in every human being. This type of duality applied to our spiritual nature causes the latter to be guided by the desire to describe the single, special element. Thus generalization gives rest to the soul, whereas specialization permits it to move from example to example; and the same is true in the world of feeling. On the one hand we seek peaceful surrender to men and things, on the other an energetic activity with respect to both. (542)

Simmel offers no evidence to support the claim that there is a need for motion and repose in the physiological basis of our being. Although most persons engage in activities at some time and rest at other times, such an observation is hardly grounds for claiming that there is an *innate* need for both motion and repose in the human organism. Even if such a biological need exists, Simmel gives no justification for assuming that it is necessarily and directly translated into the attitudes and customs of all human groups and that it will be uniformly perceived and acted upon by each person in a given group. To claim that such a need operates as a fixed and determining principle is to ignore (a) the historical contexts in which human groups develop various modes of action or *inaction* in response to any given need; (b) the individual's life history through which he or she learns to discount or minimize some needs while concentrating on or exaggerating others; and (c) the ongoing interplay between the historical context and human group life. Redefinitions of and readjustments to collective as well as individual interests are communicated, built upon, and discarded; they can hardly be explained as the acting out of alleged needs for motion and repose.

Although Simmel ignores these considerations and fails to specify the concrete conditions under which his claim might hold, he proceeds to invoke these needs and allegedly derived "antagonistic forces" as the bases for an ahistorical theory of human nature, of social change, of fashions in society:

> The whole history of society is reflected in the striking conflicts, the compromises, slowly won and quickly lost, between socialistic adaptation to society and individual departure from its demands. We have here the provincial forms of those great antagonistic forces which represent the foundations of our individual destiny, and in which our outer and inner life, our intellectual as well as our spiritual being, find the poles of their oscillations. Whether these forces be . . . ground in practical conflict representing socialism on the one hand or individualism on the other, we have always the same form of duality which is manifested biologically in the contrast between heredity and variation. The essential forms of life in the history of our race invariably show the effectiveness of the two antagonistic principles. (542)

Quite apart from Simmel's conceptual confusion between the forces mentioned at the beginning of this statement and the principles that would presumably enable one to explain the operation of these forces, he is here advancing major substantive claims that further warrant critical review. First, is there any evidence to support the claim that conflicts and compromises throughout all of human history can be characterized in terms of the collectivity (or "socialistic adaptation") versus the individual (or individualistic departure from collective demands)? Many, if not most, of the major struggles and accommodations in history are the result of one organized sector of society striving to control another sector or several sectors of that society. Wars and revolutions, for example, are neither created nor settled by virtue of the personality of a given dissident; they cannot be characterized by the acting out of an individual's desire to be different as an end in itself. Second, if these allegedly universal and antagonistic forces do in fact determine every person's individual destiny, then why is it that different individuals display such different outcomes in their destiny from time to time and place to place? Third, how can one ascertain whether a given act is or is not the mere acting out of these antagonistic forces? If these forces are innate and universal, and if the individual is the mere creature through which they work themselves out, then how can anyone, including Simmel, claim to have any rational knowledge of forces that, by definition, are omnipresent and omnipotent even in the areas of spiritual and intellectual life? Fourth, what characteristics of these antagonistic forces and what reasoning offered by Simmel can justify the assumption that the "form" of social life can be separated from the "content" of it? To claim that "we always have the same form of duality" and that "we have here the provincial forms of those great antagonistic forces" without giving evidence to support this claim or even specifying the kind of evidence that might be used to test its validity is to beg the question about the arbitrary dichotomy between the form and content of social life.

The antagonism between repose and motion, generalization and specialization, peaceful surrender and energetic activity is the source of experimentation in human endeavors and, by implication, of the fashion process as well:

> There is no institution, no law, no estate of life which can uniformly satisfy the full demands of the two opposing principles. The only realization of this condition possible for humanity finds expression in constantly changing approximations and ever revived hopes. It is this that constitutes the whole wealth of our development, the whole incentive to advancement, the possibility of grasping a vast proportion of all the infinite combinations of the elements of human character, a proportion that is approaching the unlimited itself. (542)

Thus, according to Simmel, the only incentive for improvement and innovation in history has derived from the aforementioned innate, fixed, and universal antagonism. But why are some societies far more progressive and innovative than others at the same point in time? Why is the same society more innovative at some times than at others? None of these differences would exist if the forces for innovation were fixed and inherent in human nature. Simmel could perhaps have extricated himself from these various difficulties by arguing that "human nature" is itself plastic, historically conditioned, and capable of redefinition by the social self at least in certain circumstances. But his steadfast adherence to a biologically reductionist view of antagonistic forces renders such extrication impossible. The consequences of this reductionist view for Simmel's analysis of subjectivity in the fashion process are now examined.

Imitation and the Play of Fashion

Despite Simmel's insistence on the study of the form (the processes and laws) rather than the content (the motives and values) of social life, he made a number of claims about the subjectivity of actors and assumed that his views concerning individual psychology applied universally. These claims about the content of social life were intended to complement the foregoing epistemology regarding the antagonistic forces in civilization and specifically to lay the groundwork for his theory of fashion. He thus considered it necessary to postulate the existence of a

> . . . psychological tendency towards imitation. The charm of imitation in the first place is to be found in the fact that it makes possible an expedient test of power, which, however, requires no great personal and creative application, but is displayed easily and smoothly, because its content is a given quantity. . . . It affords the pregnant possibility of continually extending the greatest creations of the human spirit, without the aid of the forces which were originally the very condition of their birth. (542)

Another feature of this psychological tendency toward imitation is that

> whenever we imitate, we transfer not only the demand for creative activity, but also the responsibility for the action from ourselves to another. Thus the individual is freed from the worry of choosing and appears simply as a creature of the group, as a vessel of the social contents. (542–43)[12]

For whom does imitation serve as a possibility for "extending the greatest creations of the human spirit?" Why is this possibility so often neither brought to fruition nor recognized by those who engage in imitative acts? Simmel at one point argues that imitation is an uncritical act of very ordinary or common scope. He also argues, however, that one becomes so conscious of this act as to see its alleged "charm." Simmel ignores the possibility that one may consciously choose to imitate the practices of someone else because (1) he might be severely punished unless he did so, and he rationally comprehends the consequences of defiance; (2) the practices of someone else may have proved more effective in reaching a given goal than alternative practices would allow for; (3) those practices may produce the necessary material resources, political unity, and personal security to serve as a basis for otherwise impossible experiments or rebellions; (4) it is often only by first imitating or memorizing a poem, play, dance, or other ritual that a full appreciation and creative modification of it can be accomplished. Finally, a great deal of extraordinary courage is sometimes essential to the task of imitation: soldiers who follow the example of a heroic commander under combat, guerrilla fighters who follow the example of a revolutionary leader, frightened children who follow the example of older siblings by learning to swim in deep water are among the instances of great courage in the face of real risks associated with the act of imitation. Simmel nevertheless speaks of imitation as if it is always performed "easily and smoothly," as if it universally guarantees "freedom from worry," as if it renders the individual into a mere "vessel of the social contents," as if it were necessarily an escape from responsibility. He ignores the possibility that "experimentation" can itself often be an uncritical adherence to demands for innovation as an end in itself; that new and "sensational" experiments or discoveries may be far inferior to traditional practices; that imitation under certain conditions can lead to creative results and under other conditions to conventional results; that there is nothing inherent in imitation, as either a social form or a psychological striving, to indicate the uses to which it may be put or the meaning it may have for social participants.

The view Simmel is presenting, then, is that imitation is not only "one of the fundamental tendencies in our character" but also the guarantor of uniformity and continuity in social change. In defending this view, Simmel adds:

> Wherever prominence is given to change, wherever individual differentiation, independence and relief from generality are sought, there imitation is the negative and obstructive principle. . . . For this very reason social life represents a battleground and social institutions may be looked upon as the peace-treaties in which the constant antagonism of both principles has been reduced externally to a form of cooperation. *The vital conditions of fashion as a universal phenomenon in the history of our race are circumscribed by these conceptions.* (543; emphasis added)[13]

Although vast numbers of subjugated individuals find it necessary to act in solidarity (to "imitate" one another) to win their independence from tyranny, Simmel claims that their real enemy is neither the structure of domination nor the men at the top of it, but rather "the negative principle of imitation." But he does not propose that even this negative principle can or should be the target of any struggle for independence. On the contrary, the principle of imitation and the principle of experimentation, he maintains, are satisfactorily and permanently reconciled in the fashion process. Indeed, the indefinite ranges of conflicting tendencies in human nature are already permanently reconciled by this process:

> Fashion is the imitation of a given example and satisfies the demand for social adaptation; it leads to individual upon the road which all travel; it furnishes a general condition, which resolves the conduct of every individual into a mere example. At the same time, it satisfies in no less degree the need of differentiation, the tendency towards dissimilarity, the desire for change

and contrast, on the one hand by a constant change of contents, . . . on the other hand because fashions differ for different classes—the fashions of the upper stratum of society are
never identical with those of the lower. (543)

Toward what end does Simmel devote so much emphasis to the "demand" for social adaptation, the "need" for differentiation, the "desire"
for change? Despite his failure to demonstrate the universality and in-
herency of such demands, needs, and desires, one may still consider the
reason behind Simmel's burst of interest in the *content* of social life at
this juncture of his analysis.

Simmel straightforwardly reveals the far-reaching logic behind this
sudden focus on the content of social life:

If we should study the history of fashions in connection with
their importance for the form of the social process, we should
find that it reflects the history of the attempts to adjust the
satisfaction of the two counter-tendencies more and more perfectly to the conditioned individual and social culture. The various psychological elements in fashion all conform to this fundamental principle. (543–44)

Simmel further amplifies the importance of a general theory of the "content" as well as the "form" of the fashion process:

In fashion the different dimensions of life, so to speak, acquire
a peculiar convergence, that fashion is a complex structure in
which all the leading antithetical tendencies of the soul are represented in one way or another. . . . Thus fashion can to all appearances and *in abstracto* absorb any chosen content: any
given form of clothing, of art, of conduct, of opinion may become fashionable. And yet many forms in their deeper nature
show a special disposition to live themselves out in fashion, just
as others offer inward resistance. (544)[14]

For Simmel, then, a theory of fashion is necessary and sufficient for a
theory of history, a science of society, a veritable key to unlock the mys-
teries of "the antithetical tendencies of the soul" itself.

Simmel did not attempt to examine empirically those characteristics
of modern society specifically responsible for the drastic acceleration of
the fashion process; he gave little attention to the effects of an open
class structure, the sale of mass-produced commodities, and the social
crises to which they give rise. Much to his credit, however, he clearly
recognized not only the operation of the fashion process in a wide vari-

ety of domains but also the function it serves as a symbolic boundary between the "privileged stratum" of society and the "lower classes":

> Fashion is a product of class distinction and operates like a number of other forms, honor especially, the double function of which consists in revolving within a given circle and at the same time emphasizing it as separate from others. . . . Fashion on the one hand signifies union with those in the same class, the uniformity of a circle characterized by it, and, *uno actu*, the exclusion of all other groups. (544)

Simmel went on to observe that

> fashion occasionally will accept objectively determined subjects such as religious faith, scientific interests, even socialism and individualism; but it does not become operative as fashion until these subjects can be considered independent of the human motives from which they have arisen. For this reason the rule of fashion becomes in such fields unendurable. (544)

But who sets the pace for others to follow in these fields? How is the climate conducive to the rise of an opinion leader brought about?

Opinion Leaders in "Objectively Determined" Fields: Fashion Dudes and Sociological Inquiry

Simmel does not explain why he believes that religious faith, scientific interests, socialism, and individualism are necessarily and exclusively the fields that can be "objectively determined." Although these fields are clearly amenable to the systematic application of explicit criteria of virtue, elegance, truth, or validity, the same abstract opportunity or logical possibility for such application also exists in such fields as art, music, dance, and literary criticism. Religious faith and scientific interests are not always "objectively determined" merely because the possibility of such determination logically exists. Many astronomers denounced the data and the telescopic device used to prove that the earth revolves around the sun. Even the discoveries concerning relativity, for example, were initially greeted with shock and disbelief by some prominent physicists. Although such fields as physics and astronomy are logically amenable to "objective determination," they are not inherently the fountainhead of rational debate and judgment in the face of new discoveries. Hence, Simmel's conclusion that the play of fashion cannot endure in these disciplines is based on the premise that they approximate in reality what they profess in principle. Even if the premise were empirically tenable, however, there is no reason to believe that it would absolutely preclude the play of fashion in a given scientific discipline. For example, the fashion process might be operative in the selection of social statistics rather than historical sociology or political economy as the "latest thing" in which a scholar is encouraged to carry out research. But rigorous, well-informed, and enduring research based upon explicit criteria of validity might be produced in the fashionable specialization anyway. Finally, Simmel ignores the fact that leaders and practitioners in "objectively determined" disciplines may be more adept at rationalizing rather than eliminating the operation of the fashion process, more concerned with presenting the appearance of infallibility and objectivity than cultivating the substance of this lofty ideal.[15] Despite his vagueness concerning the role of opinion leaders and practitioners in giving direction to the play of fashion in "objectively determined" fields, Simmel offers an insight into this role useful to the study of fashions in sociological inquiry.

Simmel's analysis of the opinion leader in the play of fashion, although derived from observation regarding the clothing "dude," is applicable to many domains beyond that of costume adornment:

> He leads the way, but all travel the same road. Representing as he does the most recently conquered heights of public taste, he seems to be marching at the head of the general procession. In reality, however, what is so frequently true of the relation between individuals and groups applies also to him: as a matter of fact, the leader allows himself to be led. (549)

We shall later examine the extent to which prominent leaders in the sociological profession tend on the one hand to appear entirely original in their work as perceived by their many followers and on the other hand to accept the prevailing orthodoxies about the nature of sociological inquiry.

Still more to the point for the study of fashions in social science is Simmel's observation regarding competition within a privileged stratum:

> The same process is at work as between the different sets within the upper classes, although it is not always as visible here as it is, for example, between mistress and maid. Indeed, we may often observe that the more nearly one set has approached another, the more frantic becomes the desire for imitation from below and the seeking for the new from above. (545)

Simmel argues that there is *within* a privileged group, such as that of social scientists, an intense but subtle rivalry to display the latest styles not only to awe the "outsiders" from below (e.g., students, the lay public) but also to establish command within the group itself. We will have occasion to examine how prominent opinion leaders within the major schools of thought in sociological inquiry are concerned with the problem of "keeping a few steps ahead" of their rivals as well as the consequences of this problem for the discipline as a whole.

The Fashion Process as a Civilizing Tendency

Simmel holds that the appeal of fashion is increasingly widespread because it represents a sharp and total break with traditional values:

> In these latter days fashion exercises such a powerful influence on our consciousness in the circumstance that the great, permanent, unquestionable convictions are continually losing strength, as a consequence of which the transitory and vacillating elements of life acquire more room for the display of their activity. The break with the past, which for more than a century civilized mankind has been laboring unceasingly to bring about, makes the consciousness turn more and more to the present. This accentuation of the present evidently at the same time emphasizes the element of change, and a class will turn to fashion in all fields, by no means only in that of apparel, in proportion to the degree to which it supports the given civilizing tendency. (548)

Simmel does not explain why the decline of one set of "permanent" convictions leads to the rise of transitory elements of life rather than another set of "permanent" convictions. When one traditional mode of domination or thought is overthrown, there is no reason to believe a priori that another and perhaps more absolutist mode will not replace it. Simmel assumes that a vacuum necessarily results when traditional values decline and that only the new transitory values of modernity are available to fill the void. He is so convinced of the abstract inevitability of these new values that he does not consider the specific historical conditions under which seemingly permanent values have been undermined by the economic and ideological currents of twentieth-century Europe and the specific reasons for the replacement of those values by transient values rather than an alternative set of traditional values. He is clearly so optimistic about the advent of the new society as to characterize it as a "civilizing tendency," and does not consider this development as problematic in its own right or as subject to a less optimistic interpretation than the one he takes for granted. Simmel claims, for example, that any group will support new values in any field to the degree that it is committed to this "civilizing tendency." He ignores the possibility that a group may well adopt a new value out of desperation in trying to cope with changes that are increasingly unpredictable and uncontrollable and not because of an abstract devotion to an allegedly "civilizing tendency."

Simmel's conviction that fashion is a progressive force, indeed the most liberating development in all of human history, is illustrated by his unrestrained delight in the personal freedom it and it alone allegedly facilitates:

> Fashion is also a social form of marvelous expediency because, like the law, it affects only the externals of life, only those sides of life which are turned to society. It provides us with a formula by means of which we can unequivocally attest our dependence upon what is generally adopted, our obedience to the standards established by our time, our class, and our narrower circle, and enables us to withdraw the freedom given us in life from externals and to concentrate it more and more in our innermost natures. (554).

Simmel gives no evidence or logical argument in support of the claim that fashion and law affect only the external aspects of social life. The great extent to which many persons are preoccupied with staying in fashion and defending law and order, the anxiety they experience when they are criticized for being out of style or violating the law, would indicate that both fashion and law can be of salient concern to the identity of large numbers of persons in modern society. Indeed, Simmel himself fleetingly recognizes the profound cultural and psychological impact of fashion on the formation of identity:

> It may almost be considered a sign of the increased power of fashion, that it has overstepped the bounds of its original domain, which comprised only personal externals, and has acquired an increasing influence over taste, over theoretical convictions, and even the moral foundations of life. (548)

Exactly why the fashion process should have been operative only on "personal externals" in traditional society, granting that the process was not yet pronounced, is not made clear. The crucial point here is that the fashion process does have a substantial influence on the "innermost nature" of human identity and that Simmel's claim regarding its appeal only to the external aspects of personality is rendered untenable because of his own astute observations to the contrary.

Simmel is cynical about human nature ("man is a rather unfaithful being"; 551) and pessimistic about oppressed masses in general ("the lower classes are difficult to put in motion and they develop slowly" 555). His optimism is reserved for the new middle classes whose very existence ensures the progressive unfolding of the fashion process in modern society:

> The real variability of historical life is therefore vested in the middle classes, and for this reason the history of social and cultural movements has fallen into an entirely different pace since the *tiers état* assumed control. For this reason fashion, which represents variable and contrasting forms of life, has since become much broader and more animated, and also because of the transformation in the immediate political life, for man requires an ephemeral tyrant the moment he has rid himself of the absolute and permanent one. The frequent change of fashion represents a tremendous subjugation of the individual and in that respect forms one of the essential complements of the increased social and political freedom. (555–56)

Simmel's reference to the human need for tyranny of some kind, permanent or ephemeral, is again a symptom of his ahistorical perspective; he ignores the extent to which even the allegedly creative middle classes are socialized into the value of obedience to authority and therefore also overlooks the possibility that the "need" for domination is socially derived rather than inherent in human nature. Simmel imputes a high level of rational calculation to the middle classes in their leadership as animators of the fashion process, but he ignores their organized insecurity and desperation, which may be their real impetus to attempt innovations in many different spheres of life.

The Fashion Process and Modern Economics

Simmel barely touched upon the profound effects of the industrial revolution in the latter part of the nineteenth century on the acceleration of the fashion process. He had so little grasp of the relationship between emerging corporate power and the play of fashion in his own era that he juxtaposed them merely for the sake of contrasting a stable, well-modulated system with one that displays extreme oscillations:

> Especially in the older branches of modern productive industry, the speculative element gradually ceases to play an influential role. The movements of the market can be better overlooked, requirements can be better foreseen and production can be

more accurately regulated than before, so that the rationalization of production makes greater and greater inroads on chance
conjunctures, on the aimless vacillation of supply and demand.
Only pure articles of fashion prove to be an exception. The po-
lar oscillations, which modern economics in many instances
knows how to avoid and from which it is visibly striving to-
wards entirely new economic orders and forms, still hold sway
in the field immediately subject to fashion. The element of
feverish change is so essential here that fashion stands, as it
were, in logical contrast to the tendencies for development in
modern economics. (556)

However striking this contrast may appear, one must carefully examine
its validity and implications for the systematic study of fashions.

Simmel's devotion to the search for paradoxes led him to ignore the
intimate causal relationships and points of similarity between modern
economics and the play of fashion. First, modern economics in Simmel's
own era was already becoming a field in which new palliatives and
stereotyped explanations for business upheavals were already gaining
in popularity.[16] New labels for recurrent economic crises as well as
seemingly new solutions for chronic economic problems enjoyed credibility because of their apparent novelty. Modern economics was evolv-
ing into what has long since become an arena for the play of fashion in
the twentieth century. To characterize modern economics (either in
1904 or today) as immune to the fashion process is to ignore the ample
evidence to the contrary. Second, the play of fashion can to some degree
be stimulated, accommodated, channeled, and exploited by corporate
producers with an interest in selling their commodities as "the latest
thing"; the cultural emphasis on discarding obsolete products is an essential and carefully calculated means by which consumers are induced
to believe that "spending is better than mending" in the market economy. Hence, the play of fashion is a crucial feature of an expanding capitalist economy in which the defining characteristics are profit accumulation through mass production, mass consumption, mass exploitation,
and mass culture.

Third, a number of drastic, unpredicted and largely uncontrolled
booms and busts took place in Simmel's era. Despite his vision of modern economics as the guarantor of "entirely new economic orders and
forms," these extreme business cycles have continued to the present
day. The play of fashion, however, does not necessarily oscillate in the
extreme and senseless manner Simmel implies; its upper and lower
limits of style are often consciously held in check by the selective application of collective taste to a specific trend, and its individual par-

ticipants often devote much time and energy to the task of appearing exactly proper as adherents to the latest style. In short, modern economics is far from the purely rational and stable domain Simmel had supposed; the play of fashion is far from the irrational and unstable domain he had supposed. The ongoing relationship between modern economics and the fashion process is far more intimate and reciprocal than he had uncritically supposed. His obsessive search for logical paradoxes and contrasts regardless of their often dubious empirical basis blinded Simmel to the consideration of these matters.

Simmel's View of the Harmless Effects of Fashion on the Class Structure, the Identity of Women, and Social Freedom

Some of the most questionable elements in Simmel's view of fashion result from vague and contradictory claims he himself makes. Simmel briefly observes that the play of fashion is absent in tribal and classless societies. But he fails to spell out the dimensions of a "classless" society and ignores the continuing presence of such institutions as ethnocentrism and racism as well as other forms of prejudice in modern society that are equivalent to certain features of what he viewed as "tribal" civilization. A "classless" society might refer in one sense to a system based exclusively upon caste relationships; or it might refer in another sense to a system in which every person and social group had the same interests in and control over scarce resources. He further observes that the play of fashion is absent in a given social class where tangible harm might result from its operation—it is present only where superficial and external aspects of life are affected. But he himself points out (1) that fashion is a crucial means of crystallizing differences in wealth and power among the upper, middle, and lower classes; (2) that its operation helps to exclude lower classes from "getting too close" to the privileges of the upper classes; (3) that it is, in effect, a means of keeping the lower classes in their place and therefore perpetuating their deprivations. He even notes with a tone of muted scorn the harmful and stifling effects of the fashion process on women and the profound, enduring nature of these effects on their identity:

> It is one of the pleasures of the judge of human nature, although somewhat cruel withal, to feel the anxiousness with which woman clings to the commonplace contents and forms of social intercourse. The impossibility of enticing her beyond the most banal and trite forms of expression, which often drives

one to despair, in innumerable instances signifies nothing more than a barricade of the soul, an iron mask that conceals the real features and can furnish this service only by means of a wholly uncompromising separation of the feelings and the externals of Life. (552–53)

In light of the impact of the fashion process as an "iron mask" responsible for suppressing and even smothering the subjective feelings, needs, and aspirations of women, Simmel's characterization of the fashion process as "harmless" is in error. His remark that fashion is irrational but harmless is further to be questioned because he elsewhere admits that it has penetrated the domains of science and politics. The play of fashion in the choice of medical procedures or political leaders can certainly be harmful to those victimized by ineffective treatment for illness or capricious decisions emanating from high office. He observes that the play of fashion finds its most receptive practitioners among women and the middle classes, for they lose personal freedom as they gain social freedom and the play of fashion gives expression to this feature of the new society. But he gives no clear evidence for the notion that the lower classes culturally or psychologically are unreceptive to the play of fashion; they may simply lack the time and money to indulge in the latest lifestyles. He ignores the possibility that they have gained *more* social freedom and lost *less* personal freedom than the middle classes in the new society as a consequence of the breakdown of feudalism; the rise of unemployment and chronic job insecurity among those who are professionally trained and salaried is a sharp restriction on the social freedom of the middle classes. Similarly, the *appearance* of social freedom and the *substance* of such freedom must be distinguished. As Michels pointed out in the study of personnel employed by trade union organizations and Weber noted in his study of bureaucracy, the ostensibly successful person in a professional hierarchy of administration is not necessarily as free of regimentation and surveillance as might be supposed. Simmel nevertheless uncritically equated the appearance and the substance of increased social freedom; he therefore concluded that there has been much progress from feudal to modern society in the direction of social experimentation and that the growing presence of the fashion process was rendered inevitable because of it.

Simmel's inability to understand fully the special importance of the fashion process in modern society is illustrated by his single and brief remark about "differences in standards of life" in the twentieth century:

Fashion plays a more conspicuous role in modern times, because differences in our standards of life have become so accentuated, for the more numerous and sharply drawn these differences are, the greater the opportunities for emphasizing them at every turn. . . . This has become all the more pronounced since legal restrictions prescribing various forms of apparel and modes of life for different classes have been removed. (546)

One difficulty with Simmel's version of modern society is that there are extremely powerful leveling pressures that lead not to diversity but rather to conformity in the urbanized and regimented mass society; Simmel does not acknowledge that much of the diversity in modern society may be more apparent than real. A second difficulty with his version of modern society is that the diversity of life-styles is not a necessary impetus to the play of fashion in any case; Simmel ignores the possibility that the same forces that generate diversity in life-styles are also responsible for the play of fashion. Finally, the absence of legal restrictions on the play of fashion cannot be considered a major or sufficient *cause* of this phenomenon. The fashion process is not an inherent striving in human nature; the removal of legal restrictions on its operation cannot be seen as tantamount to the removal of unnatural obstacles to the natural expression of the social self.

Control of the Lower Classes: The Fashion Process and the Natural Tendency to Imitate the Upper Classes

When the "lower classes" vicariously identify with the interests of the privileged and are co-opted into support for the status quo by material or cultural rewards, a great deal of imitation by the lower classes of the upper classes is likely; one might then speak of the fashion process operating efficiently to maintain social order. But when a society becomes increasingly unable to deliver on even the most minimal promises of affluence and success and its resources for the co-optation of the lower classes are sharply diminished, the possibility of rebellion rather than adherence to an allegedly timeless principle of imitation is on the agenda; one might then speak of the fashion process operating inefficiently to maintain social order. Simmel's conception of the fashion process, however, assumes that it always operates efficiently and to the advantage of the upper class:

Just as soon as the lower classes begin to copy their style, thereby crossing the line of demarcation the upper classes have drawn and destroying the uniformity of their coherence, the upper classes turn away from this style and adopt a new one, which in its turn differentiates them from the masses; and thus the game goes merrily on. Naturally the lower classes look and strive toward the upper classes, and they encounter the least resistance in those fields which are subject to the whims of fashion; for it is here that mere external imitation is most readily applied. (545)

Simmel's claim that the lower classes are always and naturally driven to copy the latest styles of the upper classes rests on the assumption that human nature is governed largely by the principle of imitation. He does not examine or even acknowledge the conditions under which the lower classes seek to destroy the life-style and privileges of the upper classes. Had Simmel seriously investigated these conditions, he would have opened the door to questioning whether (1) the fashion process is really the permanent guarantor of orderly social change as alleged; (2) a theory of fashion is sufficient for a general theory of history and a key to "the human soul" itself; (3) a theory of fashion can be deduced from a series of arbitrarily declared logical possibilities about antagonistic forces in human nature; and (4) the apparent tendency of a lower class to copy the styles of the upper class in one historical context (e.g., in Germany in the 1890s) is proof of a general tendency to do so under all conditions at all times. Simmel consistently avoided facing these questions by avoiding the prior question of the conditions under which the oppressed identify with the privileged in contrast to the conditions under which the oppressed seek to overthrow the privileged and to redefine the prevailing standards of good taste.

What are the methodological consequences of Simmel's neglect of the aforementioned considerations? What is the general value of his conception of the antagonistic forces and imitative tendencies in human nature? What are the implications of his theoretical perspective for an understanding of social change and continuity in modern society? These questions can be most instructively answered by contrasting Simmel's perspective with Kroeber's empirical approach to the study of the fashion process and the principle of order. Kroeber's influential work in this connection is now critically examined and then compared with that of Simmel.

Kroeber's Statistical Approach to the Study of Fashion

Although Alfred L. Kroeber's work is most closely associated with the discipline of anthropology, his long and productive career exerted a lasting effect on many fields of social science. Pitirim Sorokin and Talcott

Parsons, for example, have repeatedly acknowledged Kroeber's importance in the development of sociological inquiry.[17] Kroeber's earliest study of fashions in women's skirts already included the major assumptions and arguments amplified in his subsequent and voluminous writings on civilization and cultural growth;[18] it therefore takes on added importance in evaluating the literature on the fashion process in society. Kroeber's exemplary candor in recognizing some of the limitations in his quantitative approach as well as his neglect of the other and more serious weaknesses in it can prove instructive in formulating the study of fashions in science so as to avoid the pitfalls of previous research on this process.

Kroeber begins his study by noting the features of social phenomena that can be traced statistically over time, including their origin, growth, and death.

> The rise and fall of national arts and of national fortunes certainly seem to bear out [the] conception that most social phenomena are expressible by nearly similar and presumably simple geometric curves. . . . The classic French drama, that of Spain, of Ancient Athens; the briefly great literatures of Rome, Portugal and Germany; the so-called romantic poetry of England, even the minor stirring known as American literature; Italian art of the Renaissance; the Dutch and Flemish schools of painting; Greek sculpture—and we might add, philosophy—each of these insolable movements has been traced through a similar course of origin, growth, climax, decline, and either death or petrification, analogous to the life stories of organisms.[19]

Kroeber observes that the study of these "isolable movements" is extremely difficult to approach scientifically because the "laws" governing their course and the determinants underlying them in the first place must be stated in quantitative form, while the course of these movements is intrinsically and clearly qualitative in nature.[20]

Kroeber overlooks the possibility that the assumptions behind these criteria for a scientific principle might themselves serve to reflect and reinforce a prevailing fashion in social science, namely, to equate the establishment of a "workable law" or "scientific principle" with the quantification of the data to be explained. He does not come to grips with the clear contradiction between (i) his own acknowledgment that the course of the movements under study is in fact *qualitative*, and (ii) his insistence that its features must be described in *quantitative* terms if the principle governing it is to attain scientific status. The criterion of validity he is imposing on the study of fashions is, by his own admission, unsuitable for and distortive of the subject matter itself. Instead of developing the tools of analysis and the theoretical concepts appropriate to the study of the phenomena in question, Kroeber is clearly arguing that qualitative phenomena must be translated into quantitative categories whether or not they can be so translated without grave distortion. Far from maintaining that the perspective of the researcher should respect the nature of the subject matter to be investigated, Kroeber is arguing that the subject matter should be forced into line with the prevailing perspective and tools of research at hand regardless of the misrepresentations that might ensue.

Kroeber's criteria of validity for a scientific law clearly override all other considerations regarding the problem or process selected for investigation. They would seem to lead one to conclude that those phenomena amenable to quantification should be investigated regardless of their substantive triviality and that those phenomena not amenable to quantification should be ignored regardless of their substantive importance. This is the conclusion Kroeber himself reaches. Early in this influential essay, he considers the potential value of studying fashions in politics but abandons this line of inquiry solely because the subject matter is too complex. He proceeds to devote the remainder of it to an analysis of variations in the length and width of women's skirts in the period 1844–1919. After ruling out the study of fashions in art because it would also be too "subjective" and "complex," he calls for research on jewelry, silverware, and furniture similar to his analysis of women's skirts:

> Political fortunes have this advantage over the fluctuations of the arts: they are readily expressible, and with substantial accuracy, in such quantitative terms as drachmas or pounds of tribute and revenue. On the other hand, they suffer, as a medium for analysis, through their complexity. . . . Then, too, where a concentrated political organization has been achieved, opportunities are put in the hands of an occasional genius or even the man of unusual talent, for much more spectacular accomplishment, perhaps, than in the fields of artistic and intellectual endeavor. . . . I may here express my conviction that any further quantitative investigation that may be undertaken as to the course of stylistic changes should be planned to cover if possible a period of from one to two centuries, whether they concern fashions of dress, or of jewelry, silverware, or furniture.[21]

In addition to discounting the proposal to study fashions in politics because the topic is too "subjective" and "complex," Kroeber has now gone so far as to reject the possibility of studying fashions in any field in which a "man of unusual talent" or "an occasional genius" might bring about marked changes or "spectacular accomplishments." This approach to the study of fashion explicitly rules out the study of prestigious leaders who might faithfully reflect or creatively reinforce or innovate in the expression of collective tastes in a given field. Since prestigious opinion leaders, "occasional geniuses," and "men of unusual talent" may sometimes be all the same individuals, Kroeber has in effect foreclosed the study of one of the defining characteristics of the fashion process itself. The ongoing role of opinion leaders in the selection process by which proposals are designed and introduced for possible adoption therefore becomes unworthy of serious investigation. Indeed, Kroeber was far more concerned with the quantitative representation of the time span involved in tracing the fashion process than with the identification of the forces that give rise to this process.

On the one hand, Kroeber expresses concern over the need for a longer time span in his study than the period he was able to encompass:

> In fact it would have been desirable if the range of investigation could have been extended from 75 years to 125. The net result of a larger series of cases would therefore have been a probable smoothing and increased regularity of the plotted curves expressive of the course of fashion. (242)

On the other hand, such a longer time span would add nothing substantively to one's understanding of the trends: "Presumably nothing more would have eventuated from the increase of data." (242).

As early as 1919, then, Kroeber was already echoing the sentiments for a "hard science" of the human condition as an end in itself. A major opinion leader in anthropology and the social sciences more generally, Kroeber was among those who helped to reinforce and consolidate the emerging trend toward raw empiricism in American culture, and especially in the academic world. An increasingly fashionable intellectual and ideological lens was used uncritically to study the play of fashion, with the result that some of the crucial features of the subject matter under investigation were treated as unworthy of scientific study.

Simmel and Kroeber on the Distinction between the "Form" and "Content" of Fashion

Simmel's epistemological arguments and sweeping claims regarding the antagonistic forces responsible for the play of fashion and his qualitative (indeed, his largely intuitive) observations about the main features of this phenomenon would seem at first glance to be altogether incompatible with such a strongly empiricist approach to this topic as Alfred Kroeber's methodology clearly calls for. The conflict is more apparent than real, however, for they disagree chiefly on the use of specific research methods rather than on the acceptance of ahistorical assumptions. Kroeber's ahistorical and mechanistic view is reminiscent of Simmel's claim that the lower classes are always and naturally driven to copy the latest style of the upper classes. They both accept the assumption that human nature is governed largely by the principle of imitation. Since Kroeber's effort is exemplary in terms of adherence to the requirements of technical precision, an intensive analysis of his own data and the problems he encountered in interpreting his own tabulations as well as the underlying assumptions responsible for those problems is in order.

Simmel's and Kroeber's logical agreement on the distinction between "form" and "content" in the study of fashion has major consequences for the way in which this phenomenon is described and explained. One serious consequence of this distinction for Kroeber's approach is that he chose to examine only those historical records about fashions which could be translated into statistical regularities regardless of their possible inaccuracy or unreliability for the purpose at hand. Similarly, he chose to ignore those historical records that would not be readily amenable to quantification regardless of their possible accuracy and reliability for the purpose at hand. Thus, he concentrated his attention on "hard" data gleaned exclusively from fashion *magazines* in ascertaining trends in the style of women's skirts although he admitted that such sources were unsatisfactory on a number of important technical and quantitative grounds. Upon completion of the research, Kroeber observed that

> fashion journals of the middle of the nineteenth century contain fewer illustrations than recent ones. It sometimes happened therefore that only seven or eight toilettes [rather than the intended "ten figures measured for each calendar year"] were represented in it. Insufficiency of material or oversight has resulted in a few years being represented by only nine sets of measurements.[22]

For each of the first ten fashion illustrations found in each magazine, Kroeber had intended to record eight sets of measurements. But he discovered that

unfortunately also, there is scarcely a year for which ten illustrations could be found in each of which all eight measurements
were recordable. . . . In [some periods] waist widths are hard
to get. The consequence of all these little circumstances is that
the majority of the eight features are represented, year by year,
by less than ten measurements, sometimes by only four or five.
(241)[23]

Kroeber found himself irritated by these obstacles to his intended
statistical research; he criticized the American draftsmen producing the
pictures in the magazines as well as the designers producing the skirt
styles for their culpability in this setback to a scientific investigation of
this field:

The Parisian journal contained beautiful lithographs only, the
American exponent of fashion woodcuts of a horribly crude
kind. The American waists seemed at least a quarter inch
thicker, and all of the proportions clumsier. Juxtaposition of the
percentages for adjacent years however proved at once that the
difference was only in artistic execution. The American drafts-
man fell as far short of his French colleague as the American
designer was obviously doing slavish imitations of French
models. (243)

In addition to his impatience with poor workmanship in American fashion magazines and fashion designs, Kroeber complained of the extreme
inaccessibility of those magazines that did exist; his reluctant decision
to designate 1844 as the beginning year for his now sharply curtailed
scope of quantitative analysis was governed by the availability of magazines as of that date and not by any substantive interest in that particular
period. He also expressed concern over the vast degree of visual distortion in the width of a skirt that is possible in photographic representations of its form, and implies at one point a tone of methodological
despair:

I began the measurements in the year 1844 for the reason that
that was the first volume of a fashion journal which I happened
to know to be accessible in New York City, where I then
was. . . . It is surprising how poorly equipped in fashion journals the greater institutional libraries in our larger cities
are. . . .
    A skirt may be of almost any width or narrowness in a fash-
ion plate or on a posed model. When slenderness is desired,
one leg is put behind the other, in a front view, and the dress is

made to cling to an exaggeratedly slim calf or ankle. In other words, there is no fixed limit of extremity. (243, 245, 252)

Such was the quality of the sources of data on which one of the most prominent social scientists in the annals of American scholarship undertook to pursue and defend the quantitative study of regularities or forms in the play of fashion. These sources were chosen because they were deemed by Kroeber himself to be the most accurate and comprehensive materials on trends in women's skirts that had been published; the topic of fashions in women's skirts was itself chosen for study because these specific sources of data, the most amenable to quantification known to Kroeber at the time, were available for the declared purpose at hand. Although he is to be credited for his exemplary candor in recognizing some of the serious deficiencies in the quality of these sources of data, other, even more serious deficiencies arise from their use which Kroeber's one-sided interest in the quantification of trends over time led him to overlook. The deficiencies indicated in the following discussion further illustrate the distortions in an understanding of trends likely to result from the arbitrary distinction between the "form" and "content" of social life.

Kroeber's Neglect of Fashion Dolls

If Kroeber had been concerned more with the historical context in which fashions in women's skirts developed and less with the statistical regularities in their appearance per se, he might have discovered that fashion magazines were not the only or the most important vehicle through which the latest styles for adoption were publicized. He might have discovered that one reason for the shoddy workmanship in the appearance of pictures in those magazines had nothing to do with the alleged crudeness of American craftsmen and designers in comparison with their French colleagues. *Indeed, the most talented American workmanship in the design, production, and conveyance of the latest styles of dress was concentrated in an entirely different medium, namely, the creation and distribution of fashion dolls during most of the time span covered by Kroeber's quantitative investigation.*[24] Fashion dolls made during the period 1850–90 were carefully, realistically, and beautifully made by the individuals and groups actually planning to use them as a basis for style innovations. They were made of the same materials as the design actually called for; they were deliberately designed to cater to the prevailing and shifting tastes of the time.

Kroeber was so severely restricted in what he could quantify because of the various inadequacies in the fashion magazines that he was able to establish usable statistical data only for silk skirts. Silk is a most arbitrary and possibly unrepresentative material that could at best indicate what a relatively prosperous woman might afford on rare occasions. In view of the prolonged periods of austerity and depression in the United States encompassed by Kroeber's time span of 1844–1919, this possibility should have received at least some consideration, even from a narrow statistical standpoint, in order to control for the risk of systematic error in the frequency distribution of wide and narrow silk skirts in the "boom and bust" eras.

Had Kroeber been at least minimally familiar with the "content" or the meaning of the fashions he undertook to study, he would have been able to take into consideration a far greater scope of evidence that would also have been more reliable and representative of the actual trends of the time. Had he done so, he would have been able to establish generally accurate dates as well as the original designers and regions of the country associated with these trends over a far longer period of time than the use of fashion magazines could possibly have allowed for: the designers took great pride in their work, and the relevant information about these dolls was included in the labels sewn into the finished product. These fashion dolls were often eventually given to children for play in the nursery, but only after their intended purpose as a salient object of style for emulation was accomplished.

Kroeber's Interpretation of Data on Fashions in Women's Skirts

Quite apart from the unreliability of the source materials he chose to employ, one can question Kroeber's decision to single out certain periods of fashion rather than others and certain aspects of the changing shape of women's skirts rather than others. What criteria governed his choice of the periods to be emphasized or interpreted one way rather than another?

The absence of a theoretical framework to illuminate the greater importance of certain trends over others led Kroeber to reach conclusions that do not go beyond the immediate descriptive boundaries of what he represented statistically and to ignore the meaning of the trends from the standpoint of the social participants. In his summary of the data on décolletage widths from 1844 to 1919, for example, social participants (the creatures, carriers, and creators of culture) have virtually ceased to exist:

This trait [width of decolletage] appears to have a very long periodicity. The first few years of the record are indecisive: they may represent the end of a period of broadening of shoulder exposure. At any rate by 1851–53 a maximum is reached above 21. . . . By 1876 the percentage has fallen to 13.5, and the plates evince a strong inclination to show the busts in profile; which is likely itself to be a symptom of aversion for expanse of shoulders. 1877 to 1883 are reactionary, with an increase to 17.[25]

It is instructive to note that Kroeber had first *rejected* the study of fashions in art and politics because these domains were too "subjective" and "complex" for scientific investigation. But he himself does not hesitate to indulge in a series of unfounded speculations about the "symptom of aversion for expanse of shoulders" and a "strong inclination to show the busts in profile," which, he believes, was followed by a "reactionary" period in 1877. For whom was it an "aversion"? Did those who designed these décolletages and the women who chose them perceive the alleged aversion? For whom was the "reactionary" period a reactionary one? The present trend toward long gowns and skirts, for example, does not necessarily imply a tightening up of sexual morality, and there is sometimes an *inverse* relationship between the appearance of modesty in costume adornment and the actual practice of social participants. Hence, Kroeber's ostensible repudiation of topics for study because they are too "subjective" and "complex" must be viewed in light of his own indulgence into far-fetched speculation about one of the most subjective and complex of topics—the relationship between costume adornment and the sexual attitudes and practices of women. He imputed his own moral judgments of "progressive" and "reactionary" trends to the era he investigated. Indeed, the well-known and scandalous sexual derring-do of such prominent figures as Grover Cleveland in the 1880s did not deter millions of citizens from supporting them, and the characterization of this period as "reactionary" in terms of the width of the décolletage (or any other aspect of sexual symbolism at the time) is by no means as self-evident as Kroeber supposed.

Kroeber's massive effort to assemble quantitative data gleaned from fashion magazines published over a period of seventy-five years yielded an impressive total of three graphs and eight tables of statistical information on trends in the size and shape of women's skirts. The inferences and generalizations he reached on the basis of this evidence deserve critical review.

Kroeber begins his discussion of "conclusions as to change in civilization" by holding that the fact of regularity in social change is the primary inference from our phenomena. The amplitude of the periodicities is of hardly less importance. Their very magnitude dwarfs the influence which any individual can possibly have exerted in an alteration of costume. . . . No matter how isolated one's point of view, how resistant to a social or super-individual interpretation, how much inclined to explain the general from the particular and to derive the fashions of a world from the one focus of Paris, the fact remains that a succession of human beings have contributed successively to the same end.[26]

Although Kroeber's data do unquestionably demonstrate a pattern of regularity in social change, the statistical research of Durkheim and the historical research and comparative investigations of Sumner and Weber had already demonstrated this point many times.[27]

There was no need specifically for a quantitative study of such a relatively unimportant topic as the width of women's skirts to prove the same point that had been thoroughly documented in the study of such a relatively important topic as the rate and pattern of suicide over time. That Kroeber's data indicate a minimal or even nonexistent role for individual innovators should also be questioned, for he deliberately selected only those aspects of the fashion process and those sources of evidence that would exclude any cases of "occasional genius" or men of "unusual talent" whose leadership might be substantial in a given field. The evidence he chose to use inevitably ruled out any findings to the contrary, and Kroeber failed to demonstrate that the play of fashion in women's skirts is in any way representative of the play of fashion in other aesthetic or political fields; indeed, he himself gave convincing reasons earlier in the same article to expect that contrary findings might well have been reached if he did study fashions in art or politics.

Moreover, regardless of the extent to which Kroeber and other commentators may have assumed that all style innovations emanate from Paris, an assumption likely to be reinforced by confining one's attention to the inadequate fashion magazines of the time, the producers, designers, and users of fashion dolls were fully aware of and gave continuing expression to the domestic tastes, models, and innovations in costume adornment that characterized the American cultural landscape itself.[28]

Although Kroeber makes clear that he recognizes the distinction between genius and mediocrity, he himself confesses bewilderment over the possible determinants of the trends he has meticulously graphed and tabulated:

What it is that causes fashions to drive so long and with ever increasing insistence toward the consummation of their ends, we
do not know; but it is clear that the forces are social, and not
the fortuitous appearance of personalities gifted with this taste
or that faculty. Again the principle of civilizational determinism
scores as against individual randomness.[29]

The major purpose of engaging in this research from its inception, according to Kroeber, was to discover in quantitative terms a "workable
law" or "deterministic principle" (236) governing the fashion process;
this purpose avowedly guided his selection of the specific topic of
fashions in women's skirts and the specific sources of evidence to be
consulted. He found that the data presented shed no light whatsoever
on the causes of the fashion process, that "we do not know" any more
now of what social forces are responsible for it than we knew before the
research was carried out.

Kroeber's Criticism of Psychological Reductionism

Kroeber regarded his statistical approach to the study of fashions in
women's skirts as an occasion for repudiating all forms of psychological
reductionism:

The existence of varying degrees of intellectual quality does not
touch, one way or the other, the finding that there operate
super-individual principles which determine the course of social
events. The content of history as a sum and in its parts, so far
as these have civilizational meaning, is the product of such principles.[30]

But Kroeber deliberately ruled out any interest in studying the varying
degrees of intellectual quality of leaders in such fields as art and politics;
therefore, by his own admission, he did not have access to the evidence
that could test the validity of his claim that variations in the quality of
individual leaders do not affect the "super-individual principles which
determine the course of social events." Since Kroeber actually concluded that the nature of these determining principles has not been illuminated by his statistical data, his claim that these principles are never
affected by opinion leaders or "men of unusual talent" seems premature
and dubious. That society is more than and not reducible to the attitudes
of particular individuals, moreover, was already a widely accepted and
documented view in the social sciences prior to Kroeber's research.
Cooley, for example, had published his major study on social organiza-

tion a full decade before Kroeber launched his research on fashions.[31] Albion Small, a theoretical and administrative architect of one of the earliest and most influential schools of thought in American social science, had stated as early as 1905 that

> not merely in sociology, but in every department of knowledge, the organic concept is the most distinctive modern note. . . . The most intimate and complex and constructive coherence of elements that we discover, previous to our study of society, is the coworking of part with part in vital phenomena. About a generation ago, men who wanted to understand the social reality more precisely began to make use of ascertained vital relationships as provisional symbols of societary relationships.[32]

The interest of any social scientist in cautioning against the possibility of psychological reductionism is always well taken. But Kroeber was unjustified to assume that this possibility actually prevailed in American social science and that his research on fashion was necessary for the correction of an intellectual culture that in any case had long since rejected this oversimplified paradigm.

Kroeber's Conclusions about Human Nature and the Superorganic Features of Civilization

One major generalization Kroeber derives in this research pertains to the nature of human nature:

> Being human, we cannot however divest ourselves of inquisitiveness about other human beings as human beings, nor of inquisitiveness into their morality and psychology and for the desire for an aesthetic representation of their actions. Only, the pursuit of such does not lead to knowledge that is scientifically applicable; nor to a comprehension of what lies beyond ourselves as individuals.[33]

Although Kroeber claims that one can never divest oneself of inquisitiveness about the subjective meaning of morality and aesthetics from the standpoint of social participants, his own research on fashions is clear evidence of remarkable success in performing this very feat. That he succeeded all too well in this task is, as previously suggested, a major reason for the methodological and theoretical shortcomings of his study. Moreover, Kroeber's own data do not prove that human inquisitiveness into the meaning of morality and aesthetics necessarily hinders the pursuit of "knowledge that is scientifically applicable." His data do indicate that statistical regularities can be studied in the absence of such curiosity and that such study, even when rigorously executed, can lead to bias and distortion in the interpretation of those regularities.

Kroeber's final generalization based upon his research is the most far-reaching assertion to be found in the entire essay:

> The super-organic or superpsychic or super-individual that we call civilization appears to have an existence, an order, and a causality as objective and determinable as those of the subpsychic or inorganic. At any rate, no insistence on the subjective aspects of personality can refute this subjectivity, nor hinder its ultimate recognition; just as no advance in objective understanding has ever cramped the activity of personality. (263)

Although other scholars have demonstrated the causes and effects of various trends in society and of transformations of society as a whole, there is nothing in Kroeber's own data or in his inferences about such data to indicate the nature of this causality or determining principle. There is nothing in Kroeber's data to warrant his conclusion that his inferences were necessarily objective; his expression of value judgments concerning "reactionary" trends and "aversion" to profiles of the female bust suggests that a good deal of bias was in fact operative in the inferences he did draw. His data have at best only a remotely illustrative bearing on his generalizations about "the principle of order in civilization" and the extent to which fashion may exemplify this principle. Indeed, Kroeber does not actually state the scope of the assumptions or the means of testing the principle he has been investigating; if the principle is as objective and "determinable" as he claims it is, then his previous statement that "we do not know" what brings about changes in fashion is mistaken. Clearly, the principle is so difficult to ascertain using the approach and sources of evidence he consulted that he never explicitly states what the principle really is. To say that the principle is "superindividual," "objective," "statistical," "determinable," or superorganic is to say nothing of its substantive content or actual verifiability.

Despite Kroeber's candor, statistical thoroughness, and ingenuity in extrapolating a wide range of tabulations from inadequate raw data, his approach to the study of fashion can serve as a lesson in the steps to be avoided rather than followed in the future studies of this phenomenon. The present study of fashion in sociological inquiry takes into account the pitfalls of Kroeber's research and therefore does not accept the assumptions he regarded as self-evident or the allegedly objective methodology he equated with the identification of statistical regularities over time.

Simmel and Kroeber on the Study of Fashion:
The Major Contributions and Shortcomings in Their Legacies

Far from being an incidental concern to Simmel and Kroeber, the study of fashion was central to their own work as well as to their commitment to the larger search for the basic principles on which civilization must ultimately rest. Simmel's approach to the study of this phenomenon concentrated on (1) the formulation of such basic tendencies in human nature as "imitation" and "experimentation," (2) an absolute distinction between the form and content of fashion as a social process, and (3) those logical deductions from this formulation that would be tantamount to a theory of fashion and therefore a general theory of order and change in history. Kroeber's approach to the study of this phenomenon concentrated in (1) the identification of statistical regularities in the play of fashion over time, (2) an absolute distinction between the forms of regularities in social life on the one hand, and the content or meaning they have on the other hand, and (3) those inferences about the superindividual nature of civilization that would reveal the principle of order in civilization and that could be strictly based on that data.

Simmel and Kroeber are among the first social scientists in the twentieth century who can be justly credited with identifying the study of fashion as vital to the advancement of social science. Despite the ambitious scope and originality of their efforts, however, they failed in a number of ways to recognize the importance of the fashion process. First, Simmel and Kroeber failed to identify the rapidly accelerating rate of change in all spheres of society in the twentieth century and the rapidly increasing pervasiveness of the fashion process in everyday life as well as in science itself. They did not systematically examine the already emerging effects of the new capitalist society—urbanization, depersonalization, mass production, boom-and-bust cycles in the economy—and their bearing on the play of fashion. Second, both men ignored the reasons for a sudden growth of scholarly interest in the study of new trends, the social forces to which such an interest was a response, and the value of the sociology of knowledge as applied to their own respective lines of inquiry. Third, they failed to investigate or even acknowledge the possibility that their own methodological and theoretical assumptions might reflect and reinforce the play of fashion in social-science itself. They ignored the possibility that the widespread commitment by many able scholars to the enhancement of the public image of the fledgling disciplines of sociology and anthropology might lead to excessive tendencies toward "packaging" and "overselling" the product and catering more to the tastes of the time than to the need for verifiable hypotheses and relevant data on the play of fashion in society.

Simmel, for example, ignored the degree to which his preoccupation with the study of paradoxes or "antagonistic forces" might be a fashionable alternative within the boundaries of Hegelian thought to the momentum of dialectical materialism as a political and intellectual development in Europe. His search for paradoxes in the play of fashion, although sometimes insightful and even ingenious, obscured the fact that abstract possibilities of an indefinite series of contradictions do not necessarily correspond to the empirical evidence for or against such possibilities. Hence Simmel uncritically imputed empirical tendencies to the phenomena he presumed to investigate on the basis of deductions about alleged paradoxes in human nature. These alleged paradoxes were themselves derived from an ahistorical, mechanistic, and simplistic psychological model that Simmel smuggled back into his sociological study of pure "forms" after he ruled out the "contents" of social life as the primary subject matter of sociology. Simmel was devoted far more to the appearance of his version of scientific sociology as the sweeping and universal means to understand the social order than to the verification and logical consistency of the grandiose claims about the fashion process he advanced in the service of this aim.[34]

Kroeber similarly ignored the degree to which his preoccupation with the quantification of social trends might reflect and reinforce an increasingly fashionable alternative to the traditionally individualistic and intuitionist doctrines in moral philosophy and in American culture more generally. He ignored the possibility that the equally doctrinaire equation between statistical regularities and "super-individual principles of order" might itself by symptomatic of the increasingly popular raw empiricism and vulgar utilitarianism, which, in their extreme form, assumed a sacrosanct equivalence between quantifiability and validity in science.[35] As an attempt to oppose "science by assertion" and the moralistic exhortations of scholars from assorted religious backgrounds, Kroeber's purpose was timely and admirable enough. But his categorical rejection of "subjectivity" as the proper concern of an objective social sicence opened the door to the uncritical introduction of his own ideological biases in the study of fashions and the systematic inattention to the meaning of social trends (such as those in styles of women's skirts) from the standpoint of the participants themselves.

Simmel and Kroeber admirably attempted to differentiate their own work from the tendency in traditional historical investigations to emphasize isolated or unique events in a chronological sequence. But they succeeded in repudiating the study of social content only to make unfounded assumptions in turn about human subjectivity in historical developments associated with the fashion process anyway. In their exemplary zeal to make social science as scientific as possible, they correctly recognized that the study of fashion is an urgent priority on the scholarly agenda. However, Simmel and Kroeber are together responsible for helping to establish a number of precedents in the study of fashion that enjoy a lively persistence in the study of all aspects of social life in the twentieth century. These precedents include the imputation of the researcher's own biases to the meanings developed by social participants; insensitivity to historical evidence coupled with characteristically grandiose generalizations about a "theory of history" or "laws of the social system"; the repudiation in principle and in practice of empathy as a significant tool of sociological investigation; the construction of oversimplified psychological and social-psychological paradigms that are mechanistic and distortive of the human condition; the presentation of elegantly deduced logical possibilities at one extreme and technically precise findings at the other having little relevance to the substantive conclusions reached by the investigator. These precedents further include failure to recognize the extent to which scholarly inquiry into social life is itself an important response to the trends and crises, both obvious and inobvious, in the society in which such inquiry emerges; failure to identify the specific connections, for example, between the sudden proliferation of fashions and the growth of scholarly interest in this topic in modern society; failure to appreciate the need for critical self-awareness and the value of applying the sociology of knowledge to one's own intellectual endeavors. With such prominent and influential scholars as Simmel and Kroeber to legitimize these precedents in the name of an objective social science, one need not be surprised to find that studies of the fashion process in particular and the social sciences in general are today still inundated with these same difficulties. These precedents are themselves in part manifestations of the fashion process, and in part ideological conditions conducive to the fullest operation of this process. The specific tendencies to engage in ahistorical speculation as though it were "general theory" and to indulge in professional self-celebration in the name of value-neutral science are to be highlighted through an examination of the work of such opinion leaders as Thomas Kuhn, Robert Friedrichs, Pitirim Sorokin, Robert K. Merton, and Jeffrey Alexander in modern sociology; they are both manifestations of and ongoing reinforcements for the play of fashion in scholarly inquiry, as the following case studies indicate.

CHAPTER 2
THE EMBARRASSMENT OF RICHES, THE NATURE OF SCHOLARLY DEBATE, AND THE CALL FOR A SOCIOLOGICAL NEWTON

The degree to which the explicit criteria for rational criticism are operative in a scientific discipline can be ascertained by examining actual evidence of debate regarding the status of the discipline itself. Insofar as these criteria are in fact operative, one would expect that a moderate exchange of views concerning a minor issue about the discipline will evoke a mutual understanding that the differences are negotiable and reconcilable. Insofar as these same criteria are operative, one would expect that an intense exchange of views concerning a major issue about the discipline will evoke explicit and principled differences that cannot be easily reconciled, clear recognition of the competing interpretations or sources of data for each position, and equally clear recognition of the grounds on which the differences might be continued or eventually resolved. Hence, the analysis of an *intense* exchange of views concerning a *major* issue about the discipline is the most instructive evidence for the purpose of ascertaining the degree to which explicit criteria for rational criticism are operative in a given discipline. Insofar as this analysis indicates that such criteria are not operative, one can infer that the discipline in question is fertile soil in which the fashion process can grow.

If such an analysis is to be meaningful, a methodological problem in choosing relevant evidence for this purpose must first be solved. The danger remains that intense debate over a major issue in the discipline might only seem to reflect a minimal presence or even the total absence of criteria for rational criticism; inferences drawn from such a debate

PITRIM A. SOROKIN: Attacking the Fads and Foibles of Modern Sociology

might be highly misleading. It is possible that such criteria might well be operative and pervasive in the discipline but nevertheless absent in the particular debate chosen for analysis under any of the following conditions. First, the adversaries themselves might be unusually inept in public debate within the academic community, and this weakness might in turn cause the level of debate to be unrepresentatively low. Second, the adversaries might be ignorant of developments concerning the subject matter and resort to polemical attacks as a means of concealing intellectual weaknesses of their own: this circumstance also might render the level of debate to be unrepresentatively low. Third, the format of the debate might be so casually organized or spontaneously transacted as to encourage a frivolous or poorly argued exchange at an intellectual level far below that which generally prevails in the discipline. The most effective means by which the danger of such distortion can be overcome is to choose for analysis only the kind of intense and important debate in which (1) the adversaries are highly articulate in expressing their views; (2) the adversaries are well informed about their subject matter; (3) the format in which the debate takes place is formally organized, public, and representative of the official vehicles of communication in the discipline.

These potential sources of distortion can be avoided and the methodological problem of making unwarranted inferences from them can be solved if they are kept clearly in mind in selecting a debate for analysis. The record is available for an intense debate between Donald Horton and Pitirim Sorokin concerning the scientific status of sociology in the United States.[1] The choice of this record in particular as a test case for analysis fully takes into account the aforementioned considerations. Since it specifically deals with the validity of observations and conclusions presented by Sorokin in *Fads and Foibles in Modern Sociology and Related Sciences*, the subject matter of this intellectual confrontation takes on added importance for present purposes: it concerns not only the major issue of whether irrationality is present in modern sociological inquiry but also the specific kinds of evidence and the appropriate theoretical perspective by which the question can be answered. The fact that the adversaries are from two of the most influential and prestigious universities (the University of Chicago and Harvard, respectively) in which doctoral programs in sociology are offered is a further basis on which to consider this debate in a context conductive to a high level of rational criticism in the discipline. Therefore, any major shortcomings in the level of rational criticism in this debate are attributable to the actual level of scholarly communication in the discipline rather than the individual defects of the adversaries, the idiosyncracies of an editorial board, or any possible doubts about the standing of the journal itself as a serious medium for debates and publications in American sociology.

Horton begins his review of *Fads and Foibles in Modern Sociology* by stating that "many of [Sorokin's] criticism are astute" and that Sorokin "has many interesting things to say."[2] He concludes this review by characterizing Sorokin's lifelong work as testimony to "a distinguished career" (339). Most striking in Horton's review, however, is the omission of any examples of those criticisms of modern sociology advanced by Sorokin and found to be "astute" and "interesting" in Horton's scholarly judgment. He also omits examples of other works by Sorokin that might amplify the reasons for referring to Sorokin's "distinguished career."

There is no indication in this review of what Horton might mean by such terms as "astute"or "interesting" or "distinguished." Horton's failure to clarify the meaning of his own terms is instructive: he later severely criticizes Sorokin's theory of cognition because it "cannot be expressed in any words" (338).

How can Horton's failure to clarify his own terms be explained in view of the fact that he specifically attacks Sorokin's *Fads and Foibles* for this very same deficiency? A similar query, and one equally puzzling at first glance, arises in view of yet another criticism Horton makes of Sorokin's work:

> One might recommend this book to students of propaganda as a case study in the tactics of prejudice. The devices employed are too numerous to catalogue fully; we mention as examples . . . the coining of burlesque, derogatory terms such as "quantiphrenia" and "metromania"; . . . strategies of caricature in which the position of the opponent is exaggerated or oversimplified; dramatic sarcasm, mock modesty; and plain invective. (338–39)

In regard to the use of burlesque and derogatory terms, one should note Horton's characterization of Sorokin's appraisal of the social sciences:

> The manner is demagogic rather than scholarly. . . . The derogations and ridicule in this book can be interpreted only as an appeal to third parties against sociology as a science and profession. . . . Only the enemies of rational social inquiry can possibly benefit. This self-destructive act is a pitiable climax to a distinguished career. (338–39)

Horton goes so far as to accuse Sorokin of psychopathological disturbances that are alone responsible, in Horton's judgment, for the aforementioned demagoguery of the book and the downfall of its author:

> If Sorokin is no longer regarded as a creative power in sociology, it is because of the increasingly irrational and idiosyncratic character of his work, not because of any conspiracy against him. Professional isolation is the fate invited by any man who builds private systems of thought outside the collaborative development of the science to which he is nominally attached. (339)

Since Horton regards Sorokin as an irrational person whose failure to collaborate with others has justly led to his ostracism from the profession, the reasons for the failure to clarify the "astute" and "interesting" aspects of *Fads and Foibles in Modern Sociology* or to illustrate any aspects of Sorokin's "distinguished career" can now be discerned. First, Horton's intensions and conclusions have nothing to do with praise for any aspect of this publication, for the major emphasis is on discrediting the book as demagogic and the author is irrational, intuitionist, and self-destructive. Second, Horton does not really claim that Sorokin was once rational and only later became an irrational "pitiable" figure. He makes clear that, in his judgment, Sorokin was always irrational, that this defect has become increasingly pronounced in the course of his career and culminated in this most irrational act of all: the writing of an altogether "deplorable" book (337). Horton fleetingly mentions the possible value of Sorokin's distinction between "systems" and "congeries," but emphasizes that Sorokin's general position is neither new nor of any substantial value in its past or present form:

> The "Integral Sociology" offered by Sorokin as a saving grace
> has been described by him in more than a dozen volumes in re-
> cent years. The author's theoretical position is somewhat con-
> cealed in the polemic of the first ten chapters. Unfortunately for
> subscribers to Sorokin's program, it . . . can be only symbo-
> lized or "intuitively communicated by merging the minds of the
> communicants" in the manner of Yoga. (338–39)

Horton does not appraise the integralist position as a constructive or critical alternative to present forms of inquiry but rather as a "saving grace," which clearly implies that it is a theological or metaphysical approach unworthy of serious attention. He does not characterize those scholars in agreement with Sorokin as part of a theoretical tradition, but rather as "subscribers to Sorokin's program" based on intuitionism. Thus, neither Sorokin and his writings nor those who agree with him or engage in similar research are part of sociology as a science or a profession. On the one hand, Horton accuses Sorkin of unfairly labeling as cults a number of major theoretical and empirical perspectives in sociology. On the other hand, he engages in precisely the same tactic by accusing Sorokin of culpability in the formation of a cult and concludes that the sanctions of isolation and neglect of the cultist's work by sociologists in the mainstream of the profession are justified. According to Horton, then, a scholar who fundamentally challenges the modes of inquiry in a given discipline and refuses to perform as a team player in collaborative research activities will be inevitably brought to ruin. Any scholar, regardless of his or her professional stature or academic rank or evidence to support his or her position, is being warned to think twice before assaulting the intellectual orthodoxies and professional circles in command of the discipline on pain of receiving the treatment to which Sorokin has been subjected.

Although Horton points out that, in his opinion, Sorokin's views are sarcastic and inbued with "mock modesty" (338), there is no substantive indication of the possible bearing these shortcomings might have upon the validity of the criticisms Sorokin advances. The history of science, sociology very much included, is marked by frequent instances of major discoveries and creative syntheses carried out by investigators who were egomaniacal, abrasive, occasionally mystical or secretive, and even obsessed with the search for immortality as an impetus for their original research. But Horton's position makes clear that any psychological defects of an investigator judged to be sufficiently acute in the eyes of other members of a given discipline are a prima facie basis on which to reject any claims or findings he might produce.

Horton is satisifed that the quality of Sorokin's work has been evaluated fairly in every respect:

> There is nothing that most of us can do except evaluate his work on its merits. (339)

Horton ignores the possibility that none of the merits in Sorokin's work were ever actually discussed and that the accusations leveled against *Fads and Foibles* are more the defensive expression of the collective tastes of a profession in which many fashionable practices and the public image of a hard science are themselves under attack. The prefatory remarks about the "astute" and "interesting" aspects of this work are really meant, first, to show a perfunctory adherence to the standards of good taste in the profession; second, to utter some gratuitous and fleeting words of faint praise as a sign of civility; and finally, to ostracize, discredit and humiliate anyone who launches a major assault against the prevailing fashions in the profession itself. Horton takes Sorokin to task, for example, as a dissident who works alone in building "private systems of thought" rather than performing as a collaborator in an age of teamwork. Since Sorokin is uncongenially out of step with his peers, the substantive content of his work must also be seen, in Horton's view, as gravely in error. Because Sorokin attacks rather than praises prominent colleagues, the substantive content of his work must also be seen as "self-destructive" rather than constructive. Since the attacks on his colleagues include such explosive charges as plagiarism, intellectual incompetence, and indulgence in the equivalent of dianetics and astrology, the attacks must again be seen as baseless. These are among the measures used to sanction Sorokin for his refusal to abide by the prevailing rules in the profession for mutual adulation and celebration of sociology as a science. What are the consequences of such a refusal, and what do they indicate about the play of fashion in the discipline?

The publication of Fads and Foibles in Modern Sociology and Related Sciences is a gross violation of the rules by which the appearnce of moderation, personal conciliation, professional collaboration, and ideological consensus is produced in the profession. It is a clear and present danger to the play of fashion in a scientific discipline: through the fashion process, these rules are given sufficient latitude for diversified or novel implementation by a variety of schools of thought. It is a threat to the play of fashion by which these schools of thought can adapt (or at least seem to adapt) to new crises in the discipline and in the structure of society as a whole. Each school of thought in sociology may well devote some occasional energy to the criticism of rival schools, but it abstains from any outright attack on the state of the profession itself or the rules of the game by which its own legitimacy is negotiated and secured. Whatever the nuances of difference from one school to the next, the collective tastes of all major schools of thought were sharply offended by Sorokin's charges and the intransigent tone in which he made them. The concrete meaning of these collective tastes is especially crystallized when the style and values through which they are expressed become the object of attack and the culprit is singled out for the appropriate sanctions.

Horton's interest in appearing to maintain his professional composure and to represent the highest possible academic standards for the evaluation of Sorokin's work may well have caused him to neglect its most immediate and crucial implication: if even a few of Sorokin's charges are entirely correct or if many of them are only partially correct, then a devastating blow has been struck against the image of the profession. Sorokin exposed the styles and values of intellectual work in the profession in unmercifully sarcastic prose, and ridiculed the sacrosanct "publish or perish" rule in terms of the symptoms of charlatanism. One should note the unprecedented scope and intensity of the attack under the headings Sorokin himself employed to describe these symptoms:

> Obtuse jargon and sham-scientific slang; sham operationalism; the cult of numerology; amnesia and the new Columbuses; quantophrenia; the grand cult of "social physics" and mental mechanics;" the wonderland of social atoms and small groups; atomic humpty dumpty; the blind alley of hearsay stuff and negativism; sham objectivism; testocracy; senescent empiricism.[3]

Moreover, Sorokin links these characterizations specifically with the names of the most important opinion leaders and spokesmen in the major schools of thought within American sociology and related disciplines. Solomon Asch, Robert Bales, F. S. Chapin, Kingsley Davis, Morton Deutsch, Stuart Dodd, George Homans, Clyde Kluckhohn, Paul Lazarsfeld, Kurt Lewin, George Lundberg, Robert MacIver, Robert Merton, Wilbert Moore, Jacob L. Moreno, William Ogburn, Talcott Parsons, Anatol Rapoport, Stanley Schachter, Edward Shils, Samuel Stouffer, Melvin Tumin, and W. L. Warner are among the hundreds of nationally and internationally prominent figures attacked (often in great detail) under one or more of the aforementioned headings. No fewer than eleven past presidents of the American Sociological Association are among those repeatedly singled out for fierce attack in this work. Rather than publicly acknowledging the seriousness of this threat to contemporary American sociology, Horton implies that no threat exists at all because of the character defects of the person who produced it.

The only point in Horton's review of Sorokin's work that can be construed as a substantive criticism rather than a denunciation of it refers to:

> . . . the strategy of selecting extreme views and representing them as typical (e.g., the work of Dodd or Zipf), or alluding to writers whose work is marginal to the social sciences as if they were in the center (e.g., J. Q. Stewart), or referring to such quackeries as "dianetics" and astrology as in the same universe of discourse as the social sciences. (338)

Horton ignores the fact that the overwhelming majority of scholars criticized by Sorokin are figures whose work is widely published and known in the discipline, and that some of Sorokin's severest criticisms are aimed at the most eminent and influential leaders of American sociology. What vexes Horton is that Sorokin characterizes the scholarship in such fields as microsociology and functional theory in terms of a "wonderland" or a "cult," and that the conventional expressions of deference, demeanor, and congeniality are absent from those characterizations. Moreover, George Lundberg published a convincing article just a few months before the appearance of Horton's review for the purpose of documenting the strong convergences in the approaches of Parsons and Dodd;[4] although Dodd's views are academically marginal and extremist in Horton's own judgment, Lundberg and Parsons as well as the editors of the *American Journal of Sociology* would seem to agree that Dodd's views do receive a good deal of attention from those considered in the vanguard of sociology as a science.

How Vagueness and Ambiguity in Sociological Debate Facilitate the Play of Fashion

It should be noted here that Horton's dismissal of Dodd's work as marginal and extremist also clearly implies that it is unsound and therefore unworthy of serious attention. But we have just seen that George Lundberg, another prominent sociologist whose work is part of the mainstream of the discipline, finds Dodd's position substantially similar to that of an even more prominent sociologist whose position is perceived as the very fountainhead from which the various larger and smaller streams derive their intellectual current. This vagueness among opinion leaders regarding what is central and what is marginal, what is in step and what is out of step at a given time, illustrates the absence of systematic criteria by which the significance and validity of research can be evaluated. By keeping center stage ambiguously open to new *dramatis personae* and new styles of thought, this vagueness is an important facilitating mechanism for the ongoing play of fashion in the discipline. We will later examine the importance of vagueness and ambiguity in Kuhn's model of the scientific community to help explain his rapid rise to prominence in the academic community generally and even more so in the discipline of sociology.

Sorokin's response to Horton's review of *Fads and Foibles in Modern Sociology* is even more instructive than Horton's own statements regarding the work. He states that he heartily welcomes it:

> The strongly disparaging character of the review is a good omen for the book because of a high correlation between the damning of my books by the reviewers of the *American Journal of Sociology* and their subsequent career. The more strongly they have been damned (and practically all my books were damned by your reviewers), the more significant and successful were my damned works.[5]

Sorokin is clearly saying that any criticism of his work in the *American Journal of Sociology* is actually evidence of its scholarly merit and favorable reception elsewhere, and that such criticism is self-evidently false and therefore need not be taken seriously. He proceeds to argue that the more negative the criticism of his work at the hands of such reviewers as Horton,

> . . . the more they were translated and the more voluminous the scientific literature in the form of substantial articles, Ph.D. theses, and books about them, the greater the space given them in various sociological and philosophical lexicons and en-

cyclopedias, and the more substantial the chapters in texts and monographs on sociological, historico-philosophical, religious, ethical, political and aesthetic theories devoted to my "emotional outbursts."

Sorokin ignores the possibility that such a dramatic concentration of attention to his work might at least partially be attributable to the presence of a "Sorokin cult" in a number of disciplines. He also overlooks in this reply the fact that the amount of attention accorded a given idea or scholarly work has no necessary bearing on its possible truth-content. This is all the more significant because he argues at great length in *Fads and Foibles in Modern Sociology* that the works of many widely acclaimed figures in the discipline have serious theoretical and empirical deficiencies, that fame is often granted to scholars in the academic community on arbitrary or even irrational grounds, and that some of the most renowned figures of all are guilty of plagiarism, incoherence, and ignorance of the subject matter they purport to investigate.

Sorokin then claims his ideas are further vindicated because his detractors eventually adopt them anyway, and that the translation of his work into so many languages is additional corroboration of his views:

> Even more frequently my "yarns" have been appropriated by some of the damning reviewers a few years after publication of their reviews. So far, thirty-four translations of my volumes have been published, and several additional translations are under way. The total world literature about my "yarns" probably exceeds that about the works of any living sociologist highly praised by the reviewers of the *American Journal of Sociology*.

In view of the fact that he bitterly attacks "quantophrenia" and "numerology," Sorokin's invocation of the *number* of languages into which his works have been translated as a validation of their scholarly merit is a symptom of the same trends he criticized in previous works—including *Fads and Foibles in Modern Sociology*. The possibility that his work is not so drastically different from or superior to those he attacks is implied by Sorokin himself. First, he has frequently and convincingly shown that many of the most prominent figures in sociological inquiry (including former students and colleagues of his) do espouse theoretical and empirical approaches he himself developed decades earlier. Second, even his detractors sometimes utilize or adopt *in toto* the approaches he developed that they had once criticized. Given his claims about the mediocrity of scholarship in the discipline of sociology, he might have considered the possibility that widespread recognition of his work, however begrudging, could indicate some of its significant weaknesses. Sorokin gives no reason to expect that an academic community so inundated with charlatans, plagiarists, numerologists, social physicists, and wonderland theorists as the one he depicts would also be capable of recognizing the merit of anything other than the caliber of work conventionally regarded as in good taste.

Some of the most thoroughly documented views advanced by Sorokin in *Fads and Foibles* are (1) that a scholar who is considered unpopular may nevertheless be more insightful and sound in his observations than another scholar who is considered in fashion; (2) that ideas should always be evaluated on their merits and not on the basis of their prestige; and (3) that many of Sorokin's own ideas on which the principle of integralism is based derive from an appreciation of creative thinkers who are obscure, dead, or unrelated to American Sociology in any sense whatsoever. Moreover, Sorokin repeatedly makes clear his own judgment that he is central to the advancement of sociology as a science and his outrage at often being defined as marginal or even external to the discipline. Hence, one might expect that a sociologist so concerned with his own centrality to the discipline would be especially careful to agree or disagree with a critic on the substantive merit of the criticism and not on the basis of the critic's personal virtues and vices. But the very opposite is the case, for Sorokin ignores the content of Horton's criticism and proceeds to discredit the critic:

> I would like to know who or what authority entitled Professor Horton to speak on behalf and in the name of all American sociologists? So far as I know, no such authority empowered Horton to be an official or unofficial mouthpiece of American sociology. Neither can Horton claim such a right by virtue of his great contributions to sociology; to my knowledge, his contributions have been very modest, if any at all.

Moreover, Sorokin implies that Horton belongs to and is trying to defend the very cults in the sociological profession that are the object of attack in his book:

> As to Horton's laments about the professional interests of sociologists being possibly hurt by my book, these laments are either insincere or naive. . . . If by "professional interests of sociologists" he means "the existential interests" of various "sociological" Tammany Halls and "Mutual Back-Scratching Cliques," the less the number of such Tammany Halls and cliques in sociology, the better for the science of sociology.

In view of the considerable justification for Sorokin's own allegations, he is clearly implying that neither Horton's criticisms of his work nor the criticisms from any prominent sociologist or any prominent school of thought in American sociology deserve serious attention.

Although I will show that there are major conceptual and empirical oversights in Sorokin's critique of American sociology, it can already be noted that Horton's review of Sorokin's work and Sorokin's rejoinder fail to touch upon the substantive weaknesses or merits of *Fads and Foibles*. Despite the fact that Horton's article purports to be a review of this book and Sorokin's response supposedly addresses Horton's article, there is no evidence in either that the criteria for rational debate are operative.

Although Sorokin argues systematically for the *sociological* rather than psychological interpretation of social crises, he nevertheless claims that the crisis arising from the decadence of the discipline is exacerbated by the failure of the sensate leaders of the various cults in the discipline to heed his integralist approach to sociological inquiry. He maintains that his approach alone and necessarily will ensure a permanent solution to the problem of sensate sociology with its fads, foibles, cults, mediocrities, charlatanism, plagiarism, and Tammany Halls. Throughout his stormy career, all of Sorokin's writings and teachings have been avowedly organized and presented in terms of his integralist perspective. He has consistently expressed his alarm over the scope and gravity of this problem. But if so many sociologists have studied under him, if so many colleagues have been inspired by him, if so many scholars in so many disciplines have adopted his ideas, if this vast influence has actively persisted and even gained momentum over a period of several decades, then one might consider the possibility that *Sorokin's widely disseminated approach to the problem of social science is part of the problem itself*. Despite his voluminous writings on the sociology of culture and knowledge, despite his attack on American sociologists for their insensitivity to the need for self-knowledge, Sorokin consistently avoids any concrete analysis of this aforementioned possibility or even any abstract acknowledgment of its existence.

Diversity, Uncertainty, and Crisis: The Search for a Sociological Newton

Despite the shortcomings in Sorokin's analysis of fashions in sociology, his survey of the discipline can be credited for highlighting a rarely acknowledged and continuing problem of major importance. Sorokin clearly documents the embarrassment of riches in the diversity of schools of thought, research procedures, priorities as to the relevant topics for investigation, and judgments as to the centrality or marginality of various opinion leaders and spokespersons for sociology as a science. He also makes clear that none of these schools of thought subscribe to any explicit criteria by which to evaluate or reconcile these competing perspectives, procedures, priorities, and judgments. This matter is usually ignored not only in symposia at professional meetings but also in anthologies dealing with the current state of sociological theory; it is generally not perceived as a problem by participants in any domain in which the fashion process is operative. But to those sociological theorists committed to the principles of rationalism on which they believe the discipline should rest, this matter is seen as a crisis and a cause for apprehension. Instead of admitting a full-fledged crisis – an admission which could be construed as an endorsement of the position of such ostracized figures as Sorokin, Lynd, Mills, and Ernest Becker – the apprehension of these theorists is expressed in a more subtle and less alarmist manner. They call for the arrival of a new opinion leader, a charismatic figure who can unify all the bewildering varieties of schools of thought into a new and reassuring perspective behind which all interested parties could rally.

For example, in The Nature and Types of Sociological Theory, one of the most widely used and respected surveys of the history and recent development of the discipline, Don Martindale candidly concludes:

> It is possible to offer neither easy solutions for the integration of theory nor utopian hopes for sociology as a boon to mankind. . . . In the cooperation of reason and energy, when the tinder is at hand and the sparks are struck from mother wit, sociology may yet find the ingredients for its synthesis. Sociology may yet produce a Newton or a Maxwell who will take the materials cast up by chance and worked up with patient labor, clarify them in the crystalline formations of his logic, and fuse them in the fire of his love.[6]

Despite the fact that Martindale thoroughly surveys the logic and the assumptions of fourteen major schools of thought in sociology and many offshoots or variations within each of those schools, he finds no basis on which to indicate the criteria for adopting one perspective over another or integrating all of them in a larger synthesis. He gives no indication of the criteria for ascertaining who the true "Newton" of sociology might be or how imposters might be exposed or censured.

The call for a new leader who can save the discipline from itself, although it has not been definitely answered, has been echoed by other sociologists. In *The Mosaic of Sociological Theory*, Alvin Boskoff advises that

> serious students of society and human behavior would welcome alternative theoretical frameworks that promise to give better or more extensive explanations. Other disciplines have had their crucial "paradigmatic" shifts. While current candidates for that role are less than adequate, I believe sociological theory will have its equivalent of a Newton or an Einstein, and I look forward to that epiphany.[7]

Boskoff similarly gives no indication of the criteria for ascertaining who the true "Newton" of sociology might be, although he is clearly not satisfied with the present contenders for this vanguard role. He is avowedly opposed to "the various intellectual fads that masquerade as theorizing or that impede the business of developing and refining sociological theories"[8] although he offers only the following means of differentiating the "fads" from the "theories":

> The future of sociology rests on continuing constructive criticism and additions to specific theoretical problems. The "proper study of mankind" includes disciplined description, careful comparison, responsible explanation, and, *when founded on all of the preceding*, detailed criticism of the functioning of specific social processes and tentative suggestions for improved functioning. (264)

On the one hand, Boskoff insists upon disciplined, careful, responsible, detailed, and constructive study of the social order and of the theoretical perspectives developed to explain it. On the other hand, his own characterization of recent alternatives to the conventional approaches to sociological theory is an example of the facile and derogatory posturing he claims to oppose:

> We can also resist the insistent siren call for the renunciation of theory in favor of ideologies, passions and assorted literary-philosophical entertainments. Sociology possesses a rich and sometimes confusing heritage. (265)

Boskoff does not attempt to indicate the criteria for identifying these "entertainments," which, he believes, are distinguishable from works to be judged as "serious business." He is of little help in coping with the "confusing heritage" in the discipline, for, unlike Horton, he clearly regards the work of Sorokin as central rather than marginal to its development.[9] Without reviewing the substantive content of the perspectives he wishes to condemn, Boskoff designates such works as Alvin Gouldner's *Coming Crisis of Western Sociology*, Deutsch and Howard's *Radical Perspectives in Sociology*, and the 1970 issue of *Sociology Inquiry* devoted to radical studies as illustrative of the fads, ideologies, and entertainments that, in his judgment, must be eliminated from the discipline.[10]

Boskoff ignores the fact that some sociologists have already come to perceive Gouldner as the new and proper leader of the discipline while others consider Marxist or other varieties of radical sociology as the best explanation of the social order. Boskoff's repudiation of these trends as fads, ideologies, passions, and literary-philosophical entertainment unworthy of serious attention is nevertheless instructive. Like Horton, he is giving expression to the collective tastes of the profession as a whole: he singles out for denunciation and ostracism those who have threatened the underlying assumptions and rules of the game (that is, the rules of fashion process itself) by which the various schools of thought can negotiate and legitimize their status in the competition for preeminence. Boskoff does not examine the possibilities that he himself might well be caught up in the fashion process and that the unwitting acceptance of this process leads to the selection of certain models over others in an orderly manner that nevertheless excludes or minimizes any reference to rational criteria in making one's choices.

The debate between Sorokin and Horton indicates that objective criteria of validity are not being employed to resolve questions regarding the selection of competing models of the discipline of sociology itself. The absence of such criteria is fertile soil in which the fashion process takes root as well as a symptom of the process itself. The widespread and avowedly felt need to find a modern "Newton" for the discipline, as expressed by such articulate sociological theorists as Martindale and Boskoff, also paves the way for an uncritical and even zealous reception for a savior who might reveal a new perspective for the employment of such criteria or, failing to deliver such a testament, at least a new interpretation of the present state of intellectual disarray as though it were a virtue rather than a vice. The work of three of the most prominent saviors, the enthusiastic reception they have individually and severally received and the instructive points of similarity in the influence of Kuhn, Friedrichs, and Merton are next to be examined with an eye toward identifying the play of fashion in modern sociology.

Is the grave concern for the future of sociology declared by Martindale and Boskoff indicative of crises festering not only in the discipline but also in the larger society? By what means can the discipline be extricated from the seemingly endless parade of new concepts and specializations, the embarrassment of riches, the Tower of Babel, in which it appears to be lost? Is the parade as endless as it seems? How have the crises in sociological inquiry been interpreted by leading sociologists of science? Has the call for a Newtonian sociologist to rescue the discipline from these crises actually been answered? Have these interpretations and answers solved the problems arising from the fashion process in sociological inquiry? Have they been a manifestation of the fashion process in the discipline? To answer these questions, a critical analysis of the efforts by Thomas Kuhn and Robert Friedrichs to investigate the scientific community is now in order.

CHAPTER 3
AMBIGUITY AND THE FASHION PROCESS
IN KUHN'S STUDY OF SCIENTIFIC
REVOLUTION

The background of Kuhn's approach to the study of scientific revolutions must be taken into account when evaluating his influence on the sociology of science.[1] Despite the widespread impression that his work is highly innovative, Kuhn himself recognizes that his approach is by no means original. He observes that fifteen years before he wrote *The Structure of Scientific Revolutions*, he had already

> . . . encountered Ludwig Fleck's almost unknown monograph,
> *Entstehung und Entwicklung einer wissenschaftlichen Tatsache*,
> an essay that anticipates many of my own ideas. Together with a
> remark from Francis X. Sutton, Fleck's work made me realize
> that these ideas might require to be set down in the sociology
> of the scientific community.[2]

At a very early phase of his research, Kuhn was admittedly puzzled by the high level of disagreement over the nature of legitimate research problems and methods in the social sciences compared to the much lower level of disagreement over these questions found in the physical sciences:

> Both history and acquaintance made me doubt that practi-
> tioners of the natural sciences possess firmer or more perma-
> nent answers to such questions than their colleagues in social
> science. Yet, somehow, the practice of astronomy, physics,
> chemistry or biology normally fails to evoke the controversies

66

over fundamentals that today often seem endemic among psychologists or sociologists. (x)[3]

Kuhn concluded that this disparity between the natural and social sciences could be explained in terms of differences in the degree of consensus over the cognitive apparatus or what he calls the recognition of scientific achievements embodied in one paradigm over against others. With this conclusion now firmly in mind, it remained only for him to elaborate the full meaning of models in physical science in *The Structure of Scientific Revolutions*:

> Attempting to discover the source of that difference led me to recognize the role in scientific research of what I have since called "paradigms." These I take to be universally recognized achievements that for a time provide model problems and solutions to a community of practitioners. Once that piece of my puzzle fell into place, a draft of this essay emerged rapidly. (x; emphasis added)

Since this conclusion became the major point of departure for all of his subsequent and far-reaching investigations into the history of science, the logical arguments and evidence that led him to it deserve close scrutiny.

The Nature of Paradigms: The Match between Experiment and Tentative Theory

Kuhn draws a sharp distinction between a speculative theory and a paradigm theory and asserts that the latter arises only when the most rigorous experimentation and formal hypothesis are demonstrated to be in close correspondence:

> But not all theories are paradigm theories. Both during preparadigm periods and during the crises that lead to large-scale changes of paradigm, scientists develop many speculative and unarticulated theories that can themselves point the way to discovery. Often, however, that discovery is not quite the one anticipated by the speculative and tentative hypothesis. *Only as experiment and tentative theory are together articulated to a match does the discovery emerge and the theory becomes a paradigm.* (61; emphasis added)

Kuhn's definition of a paradigm here is unequivocal, and it is consistent with the widely held view that a hypothesis can be considered verified only when the relevant data support it. Although he assumes that the establishment of a paradigm is an expression of highly formalized logic in the design of research and that it is attainable only in the phase of "normal" science, he does not specify the historical conditions under which a scientific community in the "pre-paradigm" stage of development progresses to the next or more advanced stage. Despite his lack of historical specificity about when and how the transformation of the scientific community takes place, he is most explicit about the match between an experiment and tentative theory as the defining characteristic of the paradigm in the advanced or normal stage of science.

What happens to normal science when there are disagreements over the selection of paradigms?

> Since no two paradigms leave all the same problems unsolved, paradigm debates always involve the question: Which problems is it more significant to have solved? Like the issue of competing standards, that question of values can be answered only in terms of criteria that lie outside of normal science altogether, and it is that recourse to external criteria that most obviously makes paradigm debates revolutionary. (109)

One difficulty with Kuhn's portrait of paradigm debates is his arbitrary designation of certain aspects of communication within a scientific discipline as "outside" or "external criteria." He does not explain why the criteria of significance in the selection of problems for investigation are "outside" or "external" to normal science. One might argue that a discipline in which there are no guidelines concerning the puzzles to be investigated would be in a state of chaos in which the scholarly resources for deployment would be aimlessly dissipated or even impossible to mobilize at all. Although Kuhn does not wish to advocate such an unsettling state of affairs, his notion that the criteria for significance in problem solving are "external" to normal science is conducive to this implication. Moreover, he ignores the possibility that the language and logic of a normal science do include such criteria even though they are only implicitly accepted rather than explicitly recognized. Kuhn gives no historical evidence to support his claim that such criteria are external to normal science in any case; he uncritically relegates to the status of "external criteria" or "outside considerations" those aspects of scientific inquiry that he arbitrarily excludes from his own research. But since the attainment of consensus is a feature of normal science, according to Kuhn, one might reasonably expect that consensus on the criteria of significance would be just as "internal" to normal science as the consensus on the criteria of validity would be. Kuhn gives no logical justification for classifying the former criteria as "external" and the latter criteria as "internal" to science in its normal or revolutionary stage of development.

The Importance of Anomalies for the Sociology of Science

A provocative suggestion in Kuhn's research is that

> the manner in which anomalies, or violations of scientific expectations, attract the increasing attention of the scientific community needs detailed study, as does the emergence of the crisis that may be induced by repeated failure to make the anomaly conform. (109)

An immediate difficulty with this important suggestion is that there is no intrinsic quality of the anomaly that causes a scientist to take note of it or to reject a given paradigm because of its appearance in the course of normal research. Unless the scientist is sensitized to the possibility of negative evidence for a given paradigm, unless he is prepared to recognize it as a serious problem calling for his attention, the anomaly does not exist for him so far as his line of inquiry is concerned.

How are anomalies recognized and interpreted in actual practice within the scientific community? When do they lead to the emergence of a crisis for the individual scientist or the entire scientific community? One cannot answer these questions by defining the characteristics of anomalies as though they automatically lead to the recognition of negative evidence for a paradigm. These questions can be answered only by conceiving of the anomaly as a social object toward which the scientist is prepared to act on the basis of the meaning of that object from his own subjective standpoint.

For purposes of sociological investigation, then, an anomaly must be conceived in terms of its relevance or irrelevance, seriousness or triviality, universality or peculiarity as interpreted by the scientist himself. The scientist's interpretation of this object is the product of his participation and communication in the scientific community as it actually exists[4] and not as it is abstractly defined (e.g., as a "mature science" allegedly governed by the rules of formal logic or pure reason). To ascertain why one group of scientists gave increasing attention to an anomaly while another group denied its existence, one would therefore have to empathize with the scientists under study in light of their interests and relationships as they emerge in their actual social setting. To explain such orientations or decisions in terms of the alleged essence of the anomaly or of the scientific community, as Kuhn has sketchily proposed, is to engage once again in the kind of psychological reductionism we have already seen in the work of Simmel and Kroeber.

The meaning of anomalies in the scientific community is a crucial topic for investigation because the recognition by that community of negative evidence for a prevailing paradigm is a major indication of whatever intellectual integrity and capacity for improving the fund of knowledge it may possess. Although Kuhn suggests inappropriate means by which anomalies can be investigated, the fact that he points out the need for such investigation at all is in its own right a useful contribution to the sociology of science.

If one wished to study anomalies in the social sciences, a series of problems to which Kuhn is insensitive must be solved. The paradigm of social order or equilibrium, for example, continues to be uncritically taken for granted in (1) the proliferation of empirical studies and techniques for the adjustment or rehabilitation of deviant persons,[5] and (2) the preoccupation with new concepts and strategies for predicting and controlling the behavior of deviant groups in the larger society and in the rest of the world.[6] This paradigm is used by functionalists to articulate and legitimize the beliefs that a socially disruptive person has pathological tendencies,[7] that sudden and drastic change in society is unnatural,[8] and that any major social crisis is temporary, accidental, and containable through ameliorative reforms.[9] Social disruptions, drastic changes, and major crises are therefore perceived as exceptions to the rule, as worthy of study only insofar as they illuminate and render more efficient the systemic laws that have been violated. They are perceived not so much as anomalies but rather as unnatural disturbances to be eliminated: they are seen as occasions for restoring order, minimizing change, and rationalizing a crisis.[10]

This search is carried out on the macrosociological level through continuing innovations in the concepts for counterinsurgency research abroad and domestic pacification at home;[11] it is carried out on the microsociological level through new techniques in counseling and encounter group approaches to personal adjustment as well as experiments with brain surgery, drug therapy, psychosocial isolation, role playing, behavior modification, and various combinations of these measures.[12] This constant search for new concepts and techniques to predict and control behavior is often justified on the grounds that "we don't want to be caught standing still," "there is always room for improvement," and "progress is the name of the game."[13] Older concepts and techniques are discarded as obsolete or irrelevant and newer ones are heralded in the professional literature as well as the political centers of power that utilize them. Older ideological justifications for American society as the best of all possible worlds are discarded as newer ones are similarly heralded as "the latest thing," "prophetic discoveries," "revolutionary new perspectives," and so forth. This emphasis on new discoveries and new justifications to deny or eliminate the appearance of anomalies takes for granted the validity of an ideologically given but theoretically and empirically questionable sociological perspective; it cannot be equated with progress in science unless the validity of the perspective itself is first granted.

Methodological Implications of the Study of Anomalies

In Kuhn's view of anomalies there are two assumptions that, although only vaguely, tacitly, and tentatively advanced, lead to highly misleading sociological approaches to the study of these phenomena. The first assumption is that anomalies have a causal impetus of their own in the scientific community; the second is that anomalies are objectively determined by the perceptions (or consensus) of scientists. These assumptions, their implications for the study of scientific revolutions, and an alternative to both of them are now examined.

What is the methodological significance of Kuhn's insight into the study of anomalies? Can anomalies as they actually exist be distinguished from the various interpretations they are given as social objects? What lessons can be learned from Kuhn's oversights in the service of understanding the fashion process in the scientific community?

Although the sociologist who wishes to study anomalies in the scientific community must be able to understand how scientists perceive anomalies in practice, he cannot allow the objective criteria for ascertaining their presence to be equated with the beliefs, collective tastes, and conventional wisdom of those scientists at a given time. If he were to equate the criteria by which an anomaly is identified with whatever criteria scientists happen to accept, the sociologist becomes (1) uncritically encapsulated by the language and customs of the participants under study and (2) dependent on a potentially vacillating social situation to produce reliable indicators of phenomena that the participants themselves may find unpleasant or impossible to recognize. Anomalies may be so threatening to the individual and collective self-image of scientists as to be discounted conceptually or targeted for destruction through new social policies; the scientists who do insist on highlighting the anomalies may themselves be condemned for acting in bad taste, speaking irresponsibly, or causing their own disqualification from membership in the scientific community. For example, Mills, Sorokin, and Lynd attempted to highlight various anomalies that the prevailing sociological paradigms of order and value-neutrality could not explain; the collective reaction to their efforts consisted largely of ostracizing these men and ignoring or ridiculing their outspoken publications. Similarly, other sociologists have more recently attempted to demonstrate that the trends toward revolution in the Third World and internal crises in American society are anomalies that cannot be explained by the paradigm of order and consensus; their efforts have not been greeted for the most part with approval or even begrudging acknowledgment in the major journals of the discipline.[14] By taking these organized responses to anomalies into account, one may begin to answer the questions posed above.

The sociological study of anomalies requires not only the fullest possible empathy with scientists who interpret (or ignore) them but also a conception of negative evidence that is not in the first instance defined by the shifting collective tastes of participants under study. If one tests hypotheses concerning anomalies only on the basis of observations that are filtered, classified, approved, and conveyed by participants to the researcher, one has hopelessly gone native and succumbed to the ethnomethodological notion of "consensual validation." Such a culture-bound approach, however much it is currently enjoying prominence in the discipline, ignores the importance of reflective intelligence (in Mead's sense) and critical transcendence (in Marcuse's sense); it relegates the researcher to a status of participant, creature, and carrier of social definitions but denies his capacities as observer, critic, and creator of those definitions. Although this ethnomethodological approach is frequently represented as "pro-people," "participatory radicalism," and in the vanguard of symbolic interactionism,[15] it dulls the sociological imagination, offers only a caricature of Mead's conception of inquiry, and precludes any objective study of anomalies in the scientific community.

Mead makes clear that a prevailing consensus in the scientific community must not be automatically equated with a bona fide model of social or physical reality:

> Continuous advance in science has been possible only when analysis of the object of knowledge has supplied not elements of meaning as the objects have been conceived but elements abstracted from those meanings. That is, *scientific advance implies a willingness to remain on terms of tolerant acceptance of the reality of what cannot be stated in the accepted doctrine of the time, but what must be stated in the form of contradiction with these accepted doctrines.*[16]

The scientist is not merely a creature and observer of nature, but also a critic of allegedly timeless doctrines about it and an active participant in its transformation as new human needs and problems arise. Scientific method, for Mead, is therefore *centrally* concerned with the recognition and explanation of anomalies and the progressive determination of the world through a critical understanding of it:

> Scientific method is indifferent to a world of things-in-themselves, or to the previous condition of philosophic servitude of those to whom its teachings are addressed. It is a method not of knowing the unchangeable but of determining the form of the world within which we live as it changes from moment to moment. It undertakes to tell us what we may expect to happen when we act in such or such a fashion. (225)

In Chapter 2, I suggested that one indication of the fashion process in any domain is insensitivity to negative evidence and the absence of explicit criteria to evaluate competing models under consideration for possible adoption. Another means of ascertaining the presence of the fashion process in science is to examine those anomalies that are in collision with the prevailing paradigm and the responses to them in the scientific community. Although the denial of anomalies is not conclusive evidence that the fashion process is operative (for it may stem from separate and heavy-handed political or cultural influences in the discipline), it does suggest the distinct possibility that this process is operative and deserving of further investigation.

Precisely because Kuhn ignores the different subjective meanings of anomalies to the advocates of competing paradigms and the possible discrepancy between the subjective perception and the objective reality of these anomalies, he is at a loss to explain the failure of these advocates to agree on the ground rules for debate when new proposals are introduced. He candidly admits he is puzzled by the

> . . . most fundamental aspect of the uncommensurability of competing paradigms. In a sense that I am unable to explicate further, the proponents of competing paradigms practice their trades in different worlds. One contains constrained bodies that fall slowly, the other pendulums that repeat their motions again and again. In one, solutions are compounds, in the other mixtures. One is embedded in a flat, the other in a curved, matrix of space.[17]

Despite the fact that Kuhn's research is meant to describe and explain paradigm conflicts and the structure of scientific revolutions, he concedes that he is "unable to explicate further" this crucial observation about the different worlds in which competing paradigms are developed and proposed. He admits that he is unable to explain why a paradigm self-evident to one scientist may be totally unacceptable to another, why the relationships among elements and forces in the physical universe may be seen in a given way by one scientist and in the opposite way by another. His failure to investigate empirically the subjective and objective aspects of anomalies helps to explain this serious inadequacy in his work.

The sociological study of anomalies in the scientific community is, as Kuhn notes, essential to an understanding of how that community persists, responds to crisis, and changes. The empathetic approach just proposed is a sketch of the steps to be taken toward this end. It is an alternative to the mechanistic notion that anomalies themselves have an intrinsic propensity to cause scientific revolutions as well as the equally misleading ethnomethodological notion that the existence of anomalies is entirely contingent on the shifting perceptions and tastes of scientists as conveyed to the researcher.

Implications of Kuhn's Research for the Play of Fashion and the "Generation Gap" in Paradigm Debates

Whether or not the criteria of validity and significance of a given paradigm are internal to normal science, it is clear that the paradigm itself is internal to it. But what are the conditions under which it rises to or falls from prominence? How is a consensus formed around it? Kuhn tends at times to assume that new paradigms exert an influence upon the thinking of scientists as if paradigms generally were independent variables with a life of their own; that they naturally become objects of consensus in the scientific community; that the major obstacle to their adoption is the resistance from some older scientists who still adhere to traditional paradigms. The evidence on which these assumptions are based and the implications to which they lead are now examined.

Kuhn maintains that normal science does not allow for the play of fashion and that it proceeds to assimilate new ideas on the basis of the match between evidence (or the experiment) and the theory (or tentative hypothesis):

> Normal science does not aim at novelties of fact or theory and, when successful, finds none. New and unsuspected phenomena are, however, repeatedly uncovered by scientific research and

radical new theories have again and again been invented by
scientists. History even suggests that the scientific enterprise
has developed a uniquely powerful technique for producing
surprises of this sort. (52)

Exactly why a successful science is one that neither seeks to discover
novelties of fact or theory nor finds them is not explained. Since the
characteristics of a given set of phenomena (in the physical or social universe) are always subject to the possibility of change under certain conditions, one might expect that normal science would have a paramount
interest in (1) observing those phenomena under various conditions and
(2) corroborating, refining, rejecting, or reevaluating the paradigms, as
appropriate, in light of such observation. The actual reason for Kuhn's
view that normal science is not concerned with "novelties of fact" is that
he avowedly envisions it as though it were governed by uniform and infallible laws of reason in the formulation and adoption of new paradigms. Although he does acknowledge that new and unsuspected
phenomena are discovered within the context of normal science, he
does not explain why the rate and pattern of such discovery varies
greatly from time to time, place to place, and discipline to discipline.
Similarly, he does not explain why certain types of scientists rather than
others are responsible for these discoveries within this context. To say
that young or marginal scientists are among the most enlightened or
productive in this regard is misleading (150), since they are often the
most insecure and cautious about "rocking the boat" in their profession;
some scientists, on the other hand, make their most important discoveries in the latter part of their career.

What prevents new paradigms from gaining the full acceptance of all
members of the scientific community? Kuhn believes that obstacles to
the recognition of new discoveries are almost entirely traceable to old
scientists who identify with traditional views even in the face of compelling refutation against them. But Kuhn gives no evidence to support this
belief. He goes so far as to argue that no evidence is really necessary to
support it because (1) "these facts are too commonly known to need further evidence (150), and (2) Darwin and Planch also accepted this belief
as self-evident (150). According to Kuhn, young scientists must always be
prepared to use whatever means are available to convert the older ones
to the new paradigm; this conversion of the older generation to the
prevailing consensus is essential to the progress of normal science:

Lifelong resistance, particularly from those whose productive
careers have committed them to an older tradition of normal
science, is not a violation of scientific standards but an index to

the nature of scientific research itself. . . . Though some scientists, particularly the older or more experienced ones, may resist indefinitely, most of them can be reached in one way or another. (150)

Kuhn ignores the fact that scientists do not always or necessarily resist new ideas because of allegedly ingrained intellectual habits or needs for a traditional self-image. To explain the resistance to new ideas in such terms is to advance a psychologically reductionist conception of scientists as the mere creatures of their own motives. Such an explanation ignores the importance of the structure of the scientific community in which there are constellations of vested interest, changing centers of power, and fierce struggles for prestige that influence the selection or rejection of certain paradigms. These constellations of interest are not determined by their members' ages; they cannot be explained away in the mechanistic terms of a conflict between old and young scientists. But what does Kuhn's thesis about a "generation gap" tell us about revolutions in the scientific community?

Kuhn himself does not consider his formal treatment of scientific revolutions to have been adequate, for he is acutely aware that the model of normal science advanced throughout his study does not approximate the actual operation of the scientific community. Toward the end of his investigation, he realizes that the question of how scientists convert from one paradigm to another has still not been answered:

We must therefore ask how conversion is induced and how resisted. What sort of answer to that question may we expect? Just because it is asked about techniques of persuasion, *or about argument and counter-argument in a situation in which there can be no proof*, our question is a new one, demanding a sort of study that has not previously been undertaken. We shall have to settle for a very partial and impressionistic survey. (151; emphasis added)

Kuhn at this point argues against what he considers extraneous and psychological factors that might affect the conversion process and even grants the possibility that individual scientists might be less than perfectly rational:

Individual scientists embrace a new paradigm for all sorts of reasons and usually for several at once. Some of these reasons—for example, the sun worship that helped make Kepler a Copernican—lie outside the apparent sphere of science entirely. Others must depend upon the idiosyncrasies of autobiography and personality. Even the nationality or the prior reputation of the innovator and his teachers sometimes plays a significant role (151–52)

One difficulty with Kuhn's admittedly impressionistic survey of the conversion process is the manner in which he poses his question; he assumes that the process necessarily and exclusively emerges "in a situation in which there can be no proof" without considering the possibility that implicit criteria for adequate proof are in fact operative. The further possibility that such criteria may not speak well for Kuhn's image of normal science is hardly a reason to ignore an investigation into their scope and consequences for scientific revolutions. A second difficulty with his survey is that the *seemingly* idiosyncratic and psychological factors in the conversion process might well be the systematic consequences of the organizational and cultural constraints of normal science itself. Although Kuhn might wish to discount these factors as external or extraneous to the scientific community, his logic is equivalent to the belief that mental illness is a psychological condition that can be explained apart from the social context in which it arises. One cannot assume that seemingly irrational or idiosyncratic behavior is produced apart from its normative context—whether one is studying deserters in a given army, drug addicts in a given neighborhood, streakers on a given campus, or "idiosyncratic" scientists in a given scientific community. One must *investigate* these seemingly aberrant performances and ascertain whether they are meaningful and patterned responses to the social environment. This kind of investigation is not carried out, recommended, or even acknowledged by Kuhn as essential to his survey.

Aesthetic Criteria and the Selection of Paradigms: Collective Taste and Normal Science

From the standpoint of formal logic, a paradigm is adopted because it is strongest where competing or older paradigms are weakest and able to predict what older ones ignored:

> Probably the single most prevalent claim advanced by the proponents of a new paradigm is that they can solve the problems that have led the old one to a crisis. When it can legitimately be made, this claim is often the most effective one possible. . . . Claims of this sort are particularly likely to succeed if the new paradigm displays a quantitative precision strikingly better than its older competitor. . . . Particularly persuasive arguments can be developed if the new paradigm permits the

prediction of phenomena that had been entirely unsuspected while the old one prevailed. (152–53)

However, Kuhn's own evidence to the contrary makes clear that his idealized account of normal science does not actually approximate concrete developments even in the history of physical science with which he is most familiar and from which the most favorable case for his account can be made. He observes, for example, that

> Copernicanism made few converts for almost a century after Copernicus' death. Newton's work was not generally accepted, particularly on the continent, for more than half a century after the *Principia* appeared. Priestley never accepted the oxygen theory, nor Lord Kelvin the electromagnetic theory. (149–50)

Kuhn further reports that any consideration of formal logic in the evaluation of a paradigm can be suspended altogether in favor of the prestige of the advocate. He gives an instructive example of this tendency in normal science:

> For the role of reputation, consider the following: Lord Rayleigh, at a time when his reputation was established, submitted to the British Association a paper on some paradoxes of electrodynamics. His name was inadvertently omitted when the paper was first sent, and the paper itself was first rejected as the work of some "paradoxer." Shortly afterwards, with the author's name in place, the paper was accepted with profuse apologies. (152 no. 10)

Whether or not Kuhn considers the reputation of various scientists to be a *desirable* characteristic of normal science, he should have investigated (1) the degree to which it is an inherent part of the operation of the scientific community and (2) the possibility that it facilitates rational debate concerning the scientists paradigms under certain conditions and hinders such debate under other conditions. Kuhn's assumptions that the reputation of scientists is extraneous to normal science and to the consideration of competing paradigms, and that a consensus is naturally formed around the paradigm that best solves a stated problem are brought into the most serious question by his own further observations:

> All the arguments for a new paradigm discussed so far have been based upon the competitors' comparative ability to solve problems. To scientists those arguments [based upon formal logic and debate] are ordinarily the most significant and persuasive. . . . *But they are neither individually nor collectively compelling.* Fortunately, there is also another sort of consideration

that can lead scientists to reject an old paradigm in favor of a new. *These are the arguments, rarely made entirely explicit, that appeal to the individual's sense of the appropriate or the aesthetic—the new theory is said to be "neater," "more suitable," or "simpler" than the old. . . .* By the time their full aesthetic appeal can be developed, most of the community has been persuaded by other means. Nevertheless, the importance of aesthetic considerations can sometimes be decisive. Though they often attract only a few scientists to a new theory, it is upon those few that its ultimate triumph may depend. (154–55; emphasis added)

Kuhn ignores the possibility that the aesthetic appeal of a paradigm might itself be greatly increased by the prestige of its advocates; he ignores his own evidence that a paradigm initially considered unacceptable to a scientific association was suddenly considered entirely acceptable when the presitigious author's name was correctly divulged. He fails to explain both why the criteria of formal logic are not in themselves "individually or collectively compelling" in the operation of normal science and how the criteria of aesthetic appeal are established in the process of selecting one paradigm over others. If the aesthetic criteria of "neatness," "suitability," and "simplicity" are in fact as decisive as Kuhn suggests they are, then they are presumably (1) internal to the operation of normal science and (2) in correspondence with such criteria of formal logic as the new paradigm's ability to solve problems and predict events beyond the scope of older paradigms. But Kuhn offers neither evidence to show that aesthetic criteria are internal to the operation of normal science nor any logical explanation concerning the correspondence between formal and aesthetic criteria. Indeed, there is no intrinsic reason to believe that such a correspondence would necessarily or usually prevail in any field of science in any stage of development.

Certain orders of phenomena in the physical and social worlds, for example, are extremely complex and cannot be explained in terms of an appeal to "common sense," conventional wisdom, or intuitive feelings about the nature of reality. Hence, the theories that most adequately explain these phenomena may not be either "simple" in scope or "suitable" to the subject matter under study. Einstein's theory of relativity is more complex and less directly applicable or suitable to an understanding of the physical universe, from the standpoint of intuitive or commonsense perceptions, than older models. Mead's theory of the self is more complex and less directly suitable to the solution of immediate problems of salesmanship than Carnegie's popular manual on how to win friends and influence people. But relativity theory and symbolic interactionist theory are hardly to be jettisoned because they fail to satisfy a given set of aesthetic criteria that in turn can be interpreted in a variety of ways within normal science. Kuhn ignores the possibility that the application of aesthetic criteria might lead to the adoption of one paradigm, while the application of formal criteria might lead to the selection of the very opposite paradigm.

In the last analysis, Kuhn concludes, debates over the relative success of competing paradigms to solve problems are actually debates over a very different set of issues with little or no reference to the criteria of formal logic:

> But paradigm debates are not really about problem-solving ability, though for good reason they are usually couched in those terms. Instead, the issue is which paradigm in the future should guide research on problems many of which neither competitor can yet claim to resolve completely. A decision between alternate ways of practicing science is called for, and in the circumstances that decision must be based less on achievement than on future promise. . . . A decision between alternate ways of practicing science is called for, and in the circumstances that decision must be based less on achievement than on future promise. . . . A decision of that kind can only be made on faith. (156–57)

Kuhn now maintains that paradigm debates really deal with the relative importance of some problems rather than others and some solutions rather than others on the agenda for the scientific community. Clearly this is an instance of recourse to the allegedly external criteria that, as Kuhn earlier noted, make a paradigm debate revolutionary. Kuhn does not investigate the conditions under which aesthetic criteria become salient in determining the relative importance of some problems rather than others and, by implication, the probable adoption of one paradigm rather than others for the guidance of research into those problems. How is a paradigm actually evaluated on the basis of "future promise" and "faith" in the preparadigm, normal, or revolutionary stage of development in the scientific community?

Professional Allegiances and the Adoption of a New Paradigm

Kuhn attempts to answer this question in terms of the tastes of a few scientists in the vanguard of scientific community:

Something must make at least a few scientists feel that the new proposal is on the right track, and sometimes it is only personal and inarticulate aesthetic considerations that can do that. Men have been converted by them at times when most of the articulable technical arguments pointed the other way. (157)

Kuhn does not articulate the possibilities that the collective tastes concerning aesthetic criteria can have a creative role in scientific discoveries and revolutions; that their very nature (vagueness, restlessness, concern over suitability to changing circumstances) may under certain conditions actually facilitate the study and appreciation of new paradigms that would be otherwise suppressed indefinitely; that they may even be necessary to move a discipline out of a period of stagnation in which traditional paradigms and normal science have led to crises that cannot be solved or even defined by the usual procedures. Although he ignores the possibilities, they would be another compelling argument against his view that a sharp distinction can be drawn between "internal" and "external" criteria in the scientific community.

Kuhn himself at one point suggests that the scientific community is neither more nor less rational than any other community in connection with the resolution of major debates:

But if a paradigm is ever to triumph it must gain some first supporters, men who will develop it to the point where hardheaded arguments can be produced and multiplied. And even those arguments when they come, are not individually decisive. Because scientists are reasonable men, one or another argument will ultimately persuade many of them. But there is no single argument that can or should persuade them all. Rather than a single group conversion, what occurs is an increasing shift in the distribution of professional allegiances. (157)

What are the implications of such "professional allegiances" when the scientific community is in its normal or revolutionary stage of development? Kuhn ignores the potentially grave consequences of accepting a paradigm on the basis of "professional allegiances" rather than objective judgments about its validity. If the shifting of professional allegiances is the determinant of success in a paradigm debate, then the scientific community is an arena for the operation of factionalism, cronyism, the pursuit of vested interests—for the operation of the very forces that Kuhn would consider extraneous to the scientific community. Kuhn offers no reason to assume that such allegiances are necessarily or usually in correspondence with the criteria of formal logic.

The nature of the conversion process is rendered unclear by Kuhn's argument that it consists of "an increasing shift in the distribution of professional allegiances"; this implies a slow and gradual evolution in the thinking of the scientists who reflect and reinforce a consensus based upon factional grounds and vested interests. But he earlier argues that the conversion process is never gradually accomplished, and that it leads to a consensus "all at once" on the basis of a selection of one set of standards rather than others:

> Just because it is a transition between incommensurables, the transition between competing paradigms cannot be made a step at a time, forced by logic and neutral experience. Like the gestalt switch, it must occur all at once (though not necessarily in an instant) or not at all. (149)

Since Kuhn does not specify the time span he has in mind for the gradual shifting of professional allegiances on the one hand or the rapid transition between competing paradigms on the other hand, it is difficult to know whether the former or the latter is empirically accurate. It is even possible that both periods refer to the same time frame, although Kuhn's lack of specificity here renders such speculation hazardous.

Despite his vagueness about the transition period, some of Kuhn's remarks about the vanguard of the scientific community merit more emphasis and appreciation than he or his admirers have accorded them. His own descriptions of the conversion process indicates that shifting professional allegiances in the scientific community correspond far more closely to the dynamics of collective behavior than to the rules of formal logic.[18] He notes, for example, that a few scientists must "feel that the new proposal is on the right track"; that "personal and inarticulate aesthetic considerations" are responsible for this shared feeling; that arrival at a given consensus takes place at different times and in different ways among scientists because "one or another argument will ultimately persuade them"; that a heightened sense of uncertainty, a groping for some new definition of the situation, a milling process are set into motion as the established model is threatened by a new and unfamiliar one;[19] that the many participants in doubt about how to proceed are watchful of the signals conveyed by respected opinion leaders; that the growing consensus around the new model is itself perceived as an inducement to accept it by those still vacillating yet seeking to remain in step with the latest developments. These observations are undermining to Kuhn's earlier and unqualified assertion that a paradigm is adopted only on the basis of a rigorous matching between evidence and theory and an even more searching comparison of the ability of competing models to solve a set of puzzles or explain some anomalies. It is also true that he advances these observations so unsystematically as to invite unduly severe criticism for this shortcoming alone. Nevertheless, Kuhn must be all the more commended for observing on an empirical basis these important features of collective behavior in the scientific community because his abstract vision of paradigm debates in the mature sciences, whether in the "normal" or "revolutionary" phase, does not allow for these observations and is indeed directly refuted by them.

The Insulation of Science from Society: Value-Neutrality and the Free-Floating Intellectual

The aspect of professional life in the sciences of most interest to Kuhn is the insulation of the individual scientist as well as the scientific community as a whole from the pressures and surveillance of society. He emphasizes the

> . . . unparalleled insulation of mature scientific communities from the demands of the laity and of everyday life. That insulation has never been complete — we are now discussing matters of degree. . . . Just because he is working only for an audience of colleagues, an audience that shares his own values and beliefs, the scientist can take a single set of standards for granted. He need not worry about what some other group or school will think and can therefore dispose of one problem and get on to the next more quickly than those who work for a more heterodox group. (179)

While Kuhn does acknowledge that the "mature" scientific community is never completely insulated from the pressures of society, he does not even cursorily attempt to explain why it should be considered any more insulated than art or philosophy from these pressures. Although it is true that many scientists subjectively perceive themselves as immune to or aloof from these pressures, there is no reason to assume that their perceptions are necessarily accurate and reliable. Max Weber, for example, was a social scientist especially committed to the goals of critical self-awareness and value-neutrality in the study of social issues; but there is ample evidence to indicate that a number of ideologies concerning the liberal state, the growth of modern capitalism, the effect of higher education, and fear of Russia, tended to inundate and distort many of his important scholarly investigations.[20] Karl Mannheim, another sociological advocate of this insulation from the pressures of everyday life, went so far as to consider himself a free-floating intellectual capable of transcending all concrete values and vested interests in the society; but his writings became increasingly imbued with social democratic ideology and a faith in Western Christianity even as he declared himself to be an enlightened synthesizer of the major ideological and utopian views in the modern world during his tenure at the London School of Economics.[21] If highly sophisticated and rigorous students of ideology could not attain the goal of insulation from social pressures despite their intensive efforts to do so, then physical scientists unfamiliar with the sociology of knowledge and uninterested in launching any special efforts to recognize and overcome those pressures in their own discipline are hardly likely to succeed where Weber and Mannheim failed. If Kuhn had investigated this alleged insulation from social pressures as problematic rather than self-evident, he might have discovered a vast array of structural, ideological, and social-psychological forces that give shape and direction to modern science. Had he done so, he would have been able to explain seemingly bizarre and "unreasonable" responses to major new paradigms in sociological terms rather than advancing a psychologically reductionist view of elderly and aberrant obstructionists who blindly stand in the way of progress.

Still another difficulty with Kuhn's view of the insulation of the scientific community from social pressure is his neglect of the difference between *apparent* and *short-term* insulation on the one hand, and *actual* and *long-term* insulation on the other. One reason that corporate and government sponsors of research choose to refrain from day-to-day meddling in the scientists' laboratories or "think tanks" is that scientists tend to be more productive of the ideas and techniques desired by those sponsors when they enjoy a sense of entrepreneurial autonomy and academic freedom to carry out their research.[22] Another reason for the absence of such meddling is that most scientists, especially those whose research is so sponsored, are already so thoroughly socialized into the prevailing ideologies of the day as to render any surveillance of their academic or political endeavors superfluous.[23] Finally, corporate and government sponsors of research find that they benefit considerably from the establishment of a diversity of research centers and academic environments in which alternative solutions to complex problems can be developed and compared by those in actual control of the larger enterprise or program.[24] The Manhattan Project, for example, was organized on many vertical and horizontal levels of research culminating in some sound discoveries and some unsound ones for the construction of an atomic bomb. Federal funds to universities to study riot control and student unrest also allow for a wide array of research proposals for the solution of a given set of problems.[25] But these and other instances of apparent autonomy from social pressures should not obscure the fact that the nature of the problems to which the diverse and seemingly insulated scientists address themselves may be imposed by the centers of power in the larger society upon the scientific community. Moreover, the uses to which the solutions are put may also be determined by vested interests in the society and not by the allegedly autonomous or free-floating scientists who developed them.[26]

Yet another difficulty with Kuhn's view is the failure to make the crucial distinction between the scientific community in an abstract sense and the constellation of vested interests and groups of scientists who actually control much of that community's resources. Although no government agency or multinational corporation can possibly control the abstract vision of the scientific community to which most or even all scientists might subscribe, they do control (1) the flow of funds for advancing or inhibiting the development of one paradigm rather than another as well as (2) the appointment of many of the most prominent scientists to direct powerful government agencies and great tax-exempt research foundations and therefore (3) the influential sectors of the audience to which a scientist presents his discoveries and paradigm proposals. Kuhn's assumption that a physical scientist addresses his work freely to all of his colleagues as though they were equally committed to knowledge for its own sake, as though they valued one another's judgments on an egalitarian basis with pure reason as the sole arbiter, is not empirically or logically supported by any discussion in the text or reference material cited in The Structure of Scientific Revolutions.

The same assumption leads Kuhn to believe that individuals in the applied and social sciences are doomed to engage in intellectual work that is far less enlightened than individuals in the physical sciences are destined to carry out:

> The insulation of the scientific community from society permits the individual scientist to concentrate his attention upon problems that he has good reason to believe he will be able to solve. Unlike the engineer, and many doctors, and most theologians, the scientist need not choose problems because they urgently need solution and without regard for the tools available to solve them. In this respect, also, the contrast between natural scientists and many social scientists proves instructive. The latter often tend, as the former almost never do, to defend their choice of a research problem—e.g., the effects of racial discrimination or the causes of the business cycle—chiefly in terms of the social importance of achieving a solution. Which

group would one then expect to solve problems at a more rapid rate? (163)

Let us consider Kuhn's last question at once, for it is a key to the difficulties he encounters in attempting to explain progress in science. First, he does not acknowledge that the rapid rate at which problems are solved in a given discipline may be correlated with their triviality or strictly technical rather than substantive scope.[27] Trivial and technical problems tend to be easily and rapidly solved, but the preoccupation with them may be retrogressive for the discipline regardless of the number of successful solutions that are produced. Second, the pressure to solve a problem because of a social crisis involving racism or unemployment, for example, may actually be an inducement to engage in persistent, resourceful, innovative research because the scientist feels he has a tangible stake in developing an effective solution (or paradigm).[28] The absence of such pressure may lead to the selection of routine or trivial problems and the investment of a bare minimum of energy in their solution by scientists who feel alienated from the product of their intellectual work and from the society in which their work seems irrelevant or inconsequential.[29] Although it is also possible that social pressures will undermine the scope and integrity of what would otherwise be a promising line of investigation, Kuhn ignores the need to distinguish among the types of pressures that will facilitate or hinder scientific progress. Many opinion leaders within the scientific community have deliberately encouraged certain social pressures in the larger society in order to increase the funding for new and massive programs of pure and applied research—especially in the 1950s and 1960s. Kuhn disregards the fact that the enormous expansion of programs and funding in theoretical physics after the Sputnik crisis was defended in terms of "national security" by scientists themselves in testimony to federal and state legislatures. Even seemingly abstruse or esoteric areas of scientific inquiry are often deliberately funded because they are considered to have some ideological, technological, or economic value by those in positions of political power despite the perception of individual scientists that such research is value-free or "science for its own sake."[30]

The Professional Socialization of the Scientist: The Role of Standard Textbooks in Normal Science

With this view of the alleged superiority of the physical sciences in mind, Kuhn argues that the physical scientist has no need to study the history of his discipline because there is already in its present state an abundance of wisdom to ensure the guidance of future research. One need not understand how a paradigm was originated and what obstacles and crises may have affected it, for an acquaintance with it as presented in modern textbooks is all that matters:

> Why, after all, should the student of physics, for example, read the works of Newton, Faraday, Einstein or Schrödinger, when everything he needs to know about these works is recapitulated in a far briefer, more precise, and more systematic form in a number of up-to-date textbooks? Without wishing to defend the excessive lengths to which this type of education has been carried, one cannot help but notice that in general it has been immensely effective. Of course, it is a narrow and rigid education, probably more so than any other except perhaps in orthodox theology. But for normal-scientific work, for puzzle-solving within the tradition that the textbooks define, the scientist is almost perfectly equipped. (164–65)

There is, however, considerable evidence *in the physical sciences* of increasing imprecision in the basic units of measurement and increasing vagueness in the concepts and logic of inquiry; one of the most influential textbooks, *The American Institute of Physics Handbook* (fifteen hundred pages in length), is among the standard works most imbued with these serious defects.[31] As M. King Hubbert points out in his critical survey of the alleged rigor and creativity in modern physical science:

> About 35 years ago the preoccupation of physicists with nuclear phenomena became so great that there occurred a wholesale abandonment of interest in classical physics, and that with this abandonment the intellectual foundations of the whole structure of physical theory were lost sight of. As a result of this abandonment it is possible that within recent decades they have not learned classical physics and that now those same students have become authors of textbooks.[32]

Although Kuhn maintains that the loss of interest in the founders of physical science and the current emphasis on simplified textbooks has been "immensely effective" in leading physical scientists to solve problems rapidly, he offers no criteria by which this alleged effectiveness can be ascertained. He further neglects the possibility that such a narrow and rigid education might actually stifle both the expression of (1) the discovery of new paradigms as well as (2) the recognition of negative evidence for the prevailing paradigm. Although he is quick to point out how orthodoxies in prior generations of physical science were often irrationally hostile to the acceptance of a new paradigm, he does not acknowledge that an ahistorical and complaisant view of progress in the present generation may lead to similar or even greater authoritarianism in suppressing new discoveries and negative evidence concerning the paradigm about which a consensus has formed.

Kuhn's uncritical exaltation of "up-to-date textbooks" and his defense of the current indifference to the serious study of the history of physical science in the education of the scientist are themselves symptoms of the fashion process at work. He does not prove or even casually illustrate the superiority of new textbooks to old ones—he simply assumes it. He does not prove that an indifference to the founders of a given discipline ensures more rapid and effective solutions to the problems facing a given discipline—he assumes it. He does not prove that the problems currently perceived as important in the discipline by virtue of a consensus are in fact the most important and fruitful ones which could be investigated—he simply assumes it. As we have seen, however, there is not only the possibility that these and related assumptions are misleading but also some evidence to indicate that the very opposite of them may be true.[33] With regard to the social sciences, Kuhn's assumptions become still more questionable, because introductory sociology textbooks, for example, are often superficial sources of information about the discipline; so-called revised and up-to-date editions rarely differ in any significant way from the "old" or "obsolete" editions except in the increased price students are forced to pay for them. The massive advertising campaigns by large and influential publishers carried out on behalf of "up-to-date" textbooks and the glamour associated with new reference books and teaching devices, however much they accelerate or reflect the fashion process, hardly prove the superiority of such products.

Kuhn nevertheless argues that the modern approach to the professional socialization of the physical scientist ensures that

> he is well-equipped for another task as well—the generation through normal science of significant crises. . . . Scientific training is not so well designed to produce the man who will easily discover a fresh approach. But so long as somebody appears with a new candidate for a paradigm—usually a young man or one new to the field—the loss due to rigidity accrues only to the individual. Given a generation in which to effect the change, individual rigidity is compatible with a community that can switch from paradigm to paradigm when the occasion demands. (165)

What does Kuhn mean by the "loss due to rigidity"? How does he know that it "accrues only to the individual"? Again and again he seeks to explain irrational and authoritarian tendencies in modern science as though they were individual aberrations, as though they have little or no significant impact on the discipline, as though they will be neutralized or overwhelmed by the inexorable forces of progress. Although Kuhn speaks of the transition from one paradigm to another as requiring as long as a whole generation to complete, he ignores the possibility that a given discipline is thereby deprived for a considerable period of time of a proposed paradigm that might be far superior to the prevailing one. This would certainly be a loss accruing to the scientific community itself and not merely to a few of its individual members. Without proving that the scientist in the "normal scientific" community is well equipped to generate crises within his discipline, Kuhn proceeds to assume that there are certain universal qualifications for membership in the scientific community and to make clear the kinds of individuals who are ineligible for admission to it.

Criteria for Membership in the Scientific Community

According to Kuhn:

> The scientist must, for example, be concerned to solve problems about the behavior of nature. In addition, though his concern with nature may be global in its extent, the problems on which he works must be problems of detail. More important, the solutions that satisfy him may not be merely personal but must instead be accepted as solutions by many. The group that shares them may not, however, be drawn at random from society as a whole, but is rather the well-defined community of the scientist's professional compeers. (167)

Let us grant Kuhn the benefit of the doubt and assume for the moment that all persons recruited into the scientific community possess these characteristics. If this were the case, then the fact that some scientists oppose new paradigms for antiquated reasons while others accept new paradigms for transient aesthetic reasons would be impossible to explain. Why would scientists act against their own reasonable psychological and intellectual nature when their possession of this nature is what enables them to join the scientific community in the first place? Although Kuhn's vagueness and ambiguity about these criteria make it difficult to answer this question, his unqualified insistence on the development of solutions only when they are "accepted as solutions by many" would clearly bar from membership in the scientific community such men as Darwin, Newton, Galileo, and Einstein, whose ideas (or paradigms) were the object of bitter hostility at the time of their original presentation. When Kuhn speaks of the need for a "well-defined community," he clearly intends to exclude from it those who resist or question the latest trends in a given discipline as well as those who might introduce new paradigms that threaten to shatter the prevailing orthodoxies, the tendency toward self-celebration and complaisance, which he chooses to ignore in his account of it. As Hubbert cogently observes, the scientific community is all too well-defined and stifling as it now stands:

> It is also urgent that universities abandon their preoccupation with trivial "research" and its bookkeeping based on the number of papers published per year, and attempt to achieve an atmosphere in which a Galileo, a Kepler, a Newton, a Darwin, or a J. Willard Gibbs would find it congenial to work. (890)

There is still another group that Kuhn wishes to exclude from his well-defined scientific community:

> One of the strongest, if still unwritten rules of scientific life is the prohibition of appeals to heads of state or to the populace at large in matters scientific. Recognition of the existence of a uniquely competent professional group and acceptance of its role as the exclusive arbiter of professional achievements has further implications. The group's members, as individuals and by virtue of their shared training and experience, must be seen as the sole possessors of the rules of the game or of some equivalent basis for unequivocal judgments. *To doubt that they shared such basis for evaluations would be to admit the existence of incompatible standards of scientific achievement. That admission would inevitably raise the question of whether truth in the sciences can ever be one.* (167; emphasis added)

How is this consensus in the scientific community ever to come about in view of the intellectual ferment usually associated with science? To ensure that no question will be raised concerning the fundamental assumptions, criteria of validity and the purposes of inquiry within the ranks of the scientific community, Kuhn has found it necessary to make even more stringent the requirements for membership in this exclusive and well-defined community. For example, public officials are to be excluded from membership and interested laypersons, however scholarly and enlightened they might be, are also categorically declared *persona non grata.* With the exclusion of public officials, laypersons, skeptical or "stubborn" scientists, and charismatic or creative scientists from this community, the road to an unchallenged consensus on the prevailing paradigm of the day is paved and secured. However, Kuhn's vision of the scientific community would also preclude any serious intellectual ferment and any but the mildest exchanges concerning the means of consolidating the prevailing orthodoxy. This would seem to be too high a price to pay for the establishment of a consensus; it would undermine the very processes of communication that are necessary for the existence of science itself. But this grave consequence of Kuhn's vision as well as the implication that he wishes to ostracize everyone he considers out of step with the times (e.g., his own identification with the fashion process in science) are both ignored in his research.

Why is Kuhn so strongly opposed to communication between interested citizens and members of the scientific community? He assumes that laypersons are incapable of any intelligent participation in the decisions concerning the priorities for scientific research. But his assumption is really a self-fulfilling prophecy: if citizens are denied the necessary information and experience in evaluating the relative importance of paradigms and problems for investigation because the grounds of "scientific privilege" or "executive secrecy" or "academic freedom" have been invoked, then they are likely to lack the wisdom and self-confidence essential to such participation. There are many fields of physical and social science that would benefit in their own right from the elimination of unnecessary jargon, which could then be explained simply and clearly to the public, and which might then be guided by an agenda of research priorities of a more ambigious scope and enjoying far more public support than would otherwise be possible. When Kuhn asserts that scientists alone must possess "the rules of the game," including unwritten rules of admission to the scientific community, he is saying that the guardians of collective taste in the discipline must be authorized to sanction anyone who questions the elitist and secretive mode of inquiry he believes is necessary for the complete insulation of science from social pressures.

Kuhn's Image of Reasonable Men in the Scientific Community

Kuhn's remark that scientists are "reasonable men" is of great significance because it is this alleged fact that he uses as an explanation for the receptivity to new paradigms. What social conditions, internal and external to "normal science," are conducive to making scientists into "reasonable men?" Are all scientists inherently more reasonable than laypersons? Are all scientists in all disciplines equally reasonable? Are the criteria for "being reasonable" themselves an expression of aesthetic tastes in the scientific community? How did Kuhn come to the conclusion that all scientists are reasonable when he also pointed out that Copernicus's work was flatly rejected by most scientists for nearly a century after he died and Newton's *Principia* was generally rejected for over a half-century after it was published? On what basis could one find Kuhn's own conclusions reasonable in view of his own evidence to the contrary?

Kuhn himself maintains that the only scientists who might be occasionally unreasonable are the "elderly hold-outs" in the way of a consensus for a new paradigm and that even they should eventually become enlightened through one or another means of persuasion:

> Gradually the number of experiments, instruments, articles and books based upon the new paradigm will multiply. Still more men, convinced of the new view's fruitfulness, will adopt the new mode of practicing normal science, until at last only a few elderly hold-outs remain. . . . Though the historian can always find men—Priestley, for instance—who were unreasonable to resist for as long as they did, he will not find a point at which resistance becomes illogical or unscientific. At most he may wish to say that the man who continues to resist after his whole profession has converted has *ipso facto* ceased to be a scientist. (158)

Kuhn is holding that old scientists are alone in resisting a new paradigm and that, in the event they persist too long in their obstructionism, they are to be drummed out of their profession. But he ignores the possibility that a consensus may form around an incorrect paradigm, in which case the few who resisted would be logical and those who acquiesced in the new paradigm would be illogical. In this event, Kuhn's criterion for membership in the scientific community would exclude those who were logical and include those who were illogical. The fallacy in his reasoning is his uncritical assumption that a consensus regarding a given paradigm is necessarily evidence of its objective validity. Kuhn himself gives ample reason to be most suspicious of any paradigm that suddenly rises to prominence without careful scrutiny, and points out the many aesthetic considerations of taste and the preoccupation with the status of the author of a paradigm that might very well lead to a hasty or unwarranted consensus concerning a new paradigm.

To say that only "elderly hold-outs" can ever be in opposition to a new paradigm and that mere numerical consensus is the necessary and sufficient indication of its validity is to ignore Kuhn's own evidence regarding the formation of a consensus in the first plce. To say that a member of the scientific community who disagrees with the "whole profession" is ipso facto no longer a scientist is to resolve a scientific debate by the repressive use of institutional power rather than by the process of rational argument and counterargument. Similarly, to equate the validity of a paradigm with the number of experiments, instruments, articles, and books devoted to its advancement is to equate the truth-content of an idea with its aesthetic appeal and popularity at a given time.

Kuhn's view that opponents of a popular paradigm have automatically ceased to belong to the scientific community is tantamount to the application of the fashion process to those who fail to keep in step with the times: scorn, ostracism, and the classification of the obstructionists as unreasonable, old-fashioned, or even senile are among the sanctions used against those who are felt to stand in the way of progress.

The intellectual lens used by Kuhn to study new paradigms is itself clouded by the assumptions that take for granted the legitimacy of the fashion process. His uncritical acceptance of these assumptions helps to explain why he is unable to recognize the play of fashion in any of the instances of normal science and scientific revolution reported in his historical investigations. This same myopia may also help to explain why he repeatedly claims that "normal science does not aim at novelties of fact or theory" and that it always proceeds on the basis of formal logic in making comparative judgments about alternative paradigms:

> The act of judgment that leads scientists to reject a previously accepted theory is always based upon more than a comparison of that theory with the world. The decision to accept another, and the judgment leading to that decision, involves the comparison of both paradigms with nature *and* with each other. (52, 77)

As already shown, however, Kuhn himself offers much evidence to support a far less optimistic view of these allegedly rational acts of judgment. He also offers some insightful observations concerning the presence of aesthetic criteria and collective taste in the scientific community. This evidence calls into question his idealized account of the degree to which formal logical considerations determine the selection of a new paradigm.

Whatever the inadequacy of his account of a single paradigm shift or scientific revolution, Kuhn is still left with a puzzle of his own: How do revolutions in general bring about progress in science? How and why is there progress in science? Is there some teleological meaning behind the pattern of scientific revolutions? These are the crucial questions to which his conclusion is addressed; the answers proposed therein warrant close scrutiny, for they are a potential framework for a sociological theory of science.

Creativity and Progress in the Social and Physical Sciences

Kuhn now ambiguously argues that progress in such fields as art and philosophy may not be so different from progress in science as he has previously held. He becomes entirely relativistic at this point and suggests that participants in *all* fields of endeavor are the ultimate arbiters of "creative work" and the "progress" to which it must lead:

> With respect to normal science, then, part of the answer to the problem of progress lies simply in the eyes of the beholder. Scientific progress is not different in kind from progress in other fields, but the absence at most times of competing schools that question each other's aims and standards makes the progress of a normal-scientific community far easier to see. (162)

The most striking aspect of this new argument is that it completely reverses the view Kuhn had just previously seemed to defend without qualification—that progress is "a perquisite reserved almost exclusively for the activities we call science." Another difficulty with this argument is that competing schools of thought are not always or usually present in other fields of endeavor. The Catholic Church, for example, tends to have a monolithic worldview, and internal assaults upon it are quickly suppressed. But this does not prove that the Catholic Church is therefore either scientific or in a period of great progress. Moreover, the presence of competing schools of thought may actually be highly conducive to the searching debate over fundamental assumptions, the clarification of concepts, and the efforts at synthesis that can in fact lead to substantial progress in a given discipline. The absence of serious discussion and debate can lead to the very stagnation Kuhn wishes to avoid in his vision of the normal-scientific community.

In his search for the impetus to progress in science, Kuhn assigns to the paradigm a causal influence that allegedly moves the scientific community to go forward:

> Once the reception of a common paradigm has freed the scientific community from the need constantly to re-examine its first principles, the members of that community can concentrate exclusively upon the subtlest and most esoteric of the phenomena that concern it. Inevitably, that does increase both the effectiveness and the efficiency with which the group as a whole solves new problems. Other aspects of professional life in the sciences enhance this very special efficiency still further. (163)

Kuhn does not state how the acceptance of a paradigm or any inherent feature of the paradigm per se can liberate the energies of the scientific community. One might reasonably expect that acceptance of a single paradigm leads to such a constriction of intellectual vision and a stifling of meaningful criticism within the discipline as to promote ritualistic demonstrations of foregone conclusions rather than new research into subtle and esoteric phenomena. Although it is logically possible that the adoption of a single paradigm will lead to the results Kuhn suggests, it is also logically possible that the very opposite result might obtain. Kuhn gives no evidence to justify the assumption that the logical possibility desirable *to him* is also the empirical case in the history of science. Although it is true that certain aspects of professional life in the sciences do allow for the concentration of resources to solve a problem efficiently, it is also true that other aspects of professional life, such as extreme specialization and fragmentation of intellectual interests, can produce major obstacles to such problem solving. Again, the mere identification of one or another logically possible contingency cannot substitute for the actual demonstration of outcomes in various disciplines under concretely specified conditions. Although this is the kind of essential demonstration that Kuhn's research does not provide, he does offer some suggestions concerning those aspects of science that might fruitfully be studied.

Kuhn's View of "Progress through Revolutions"

Kuhn's initial formulation of the puzzle sets the stage for a far-reaching inquiry into scientific progress:

> Why should the [scientific] enterprise move steadily ahead as, say, art, political theory or philosophy does not? Why is pro-

gress a perquisite reserved almost exclusively for the activities we call science? (159)

An immediate difficulty in this formulation is the absence of any evidence that scientific progress is steady or that art and philosophy are relatively stagnant fields of endeavor. Unless Kuhn can demonstrate empirically that science alone marches forward while other fields stagnate, his line of inquiry is bound to be misleading because he would then be trying to explain the advent of a phenomenon that has little or no basis in reality. The key to his explanation is the concept of progress, which becomes the defining characteristic of science itself:

> Part of our difficulty in seeing the profound differences between science and technology must relate to the fact that progress is an attribute of both fields. It can, however, clarify, not solve our difficulty to recognize that we tend to see as science any field in which progress is marked. (160–61)

Does the fact that we subjectively perceive progress in a given field necessarily prove that progress has taken place? Since the criteria of progress may vary from the considerations of formal logic to those of aesthetic appeal, and since some judges of progress may wish to take into account the reputation of individual scientists or the stature of the discipline as a whole, such perceptions would seem to be a most unreliable indicator of actual progress in science. Moreover, many students of philosophy, for example, might perceive that immense progress has been made in linguistics in some respects and in aesthetics in other respects. Does this constitute evidence that linguistics and aesthetics are now part of "science" (in Kuhn's sense of a paradigm that matches an experiment with a theory)? Kuhn's aforementioned attempt to clarify the puzzle would seem to permit no alternative but an answer in the affirmative.

Kuhn's further attempt to clarify the puzzle actually deepens the difficulty from which he must eventually extricate himself:

> Does a field make progress because it is a science, or is it a science because it makes progress? . . . Normally, the members of a mature scientific community work from a single paradigm or a closely related set. Very rarely do different scientific communities investigate the same problems. In those exceptional cases the groups hold several major paradigms in common. Viewed from within any single community, however, whether of scientists or nonscientists, the result of successful creative work is progress. How could it possibly be anything else? (161)

Kuhn's own definition of progress is therefore whatever the scientists "within any single community" wish to say it is; the successful creative work of scientists necessarily leads to progress because scientists so perceive it. However, Kuhn previously indicates major episodes in which significant discoveries and creatively inspired paradigms were condemned, suppressed, or ignored for decades or even an entire century within the ranks of the scientific community. His own evidence calls into question the notion that creative and varied discoveries automatically lead to progress in science.

On the Passage of Time and the Stages of Development in Scientific Progress

Kuhn's analysis of scientific revolutions rests heavily on the distinction between the preparadigm and postparadigm stages of development in a given discipline. Although he maintains that it is only in the latter stage of development that a rational consensus becomes possible and "normal," he also concedes that the distinction may be conceptually crude and empirically unsupported in certain instances:

> My distinction between the pre- and post-paradigm periods in the development of a science is, for example, much too schematic. Each of the schools whose competition characterizes the earlier period is guided by something like a paradigm; there are circumstances, though I think them rare, under which two paradigms can coexist peacefully in the later period. (xi)

Despite Kuhn's perceptive effort at self-criticism here, he still takes for granted a dubious and unproven assumption that pervades his analysis: he assumes that a scientific discipline becomes more rationally disposed to recognize the merits of alternative paradigms as a consequence of the inexorable passage of time. This is why he consistently speaks of the "normal" consensus over a paradigm in a discipline being reached in its "later period" rather than in its presumably turbulent origins. In view of the fact that Kuhn's analysis is often regarded as central to the contemporary interest in the sociology of science, one must examine the reasons for such an arbitrary and mechanistic version of progress in science.

As Kuhn himself points out, he decided at the very outset of his research to exclude from consideration all of the social, cultural, and historical forces that might influence the rate and pattern of scientific progress. Although he fails to recognize exlicitly the potentially grave consequences of this decision, he clearly had little choice but to invoke time itself as the only remaining "variable" with which such progress could be correlated:

> Mere possession of a paradigm is not quite a sufficient criterion for the developmental transition [in the route to normal science]. More important, except in occasional brief asides, *I have said nothing about the role of technological advance or of external social, economic and intellectual conditions in the development of the sciences.* (xi–xii)

Kuhn ignores the subject matter that would be of central importance to the sociology of science because he candidly avoids the substantive questions associated with this area of investigation. He mentions only in passing that such an investigation might be valuable for other scholars to explore, although he himself does not intend to do so on a systematic basis:

> External conditions may help to transform a mere anomaly into a source of acute crisis. [They could] illustrate the way in which conditions outside the sciences may influence the range of alternatives available to the man who seeks to end a crisis by proposing one or another revolutionary reform. Explicit consideration of effects like these would not, I think, modify the main theses developed in this essay, but it would surely add an analytic dimension of first-rate importance for the understanding of scientific advance. (xii)

The evidence on which Kuhn's view of scientific revolutions is based, then, is obtained

> from the history of biological as well as of physical science. My decision to deal here exclusively with the latter was made partly to increase this essay's coherence and partly on grounds of present competence. (xi)

If, however, Kuhn's view were applicable to all of the "natural" sciences, then the coherence of his research would be enhanced rather than undermined by demonstrating precisely this range of application. If his "present competence" is as confined to physical science as he himself admits (and the limited scope of source materials in his study further corroborates), then one wonders how he could possibly engage in the sweeping claims about paradigms, anomalies, puzzle solving, and "normal science" as though they were universally applicable to all scientific disciplines at all times.

Social Darwinism and Progress in Science

None of Kuhn's characterizations of science thus far examined has really solved the central problem of his entire work: why is there progress in science? Since he wishes to rule out the effects of social pressure on science and even argues that scientists solve problems rapidly and effectively only when they are insulated from such pressures, he cannot answer this question by examining the influence of ideologies and the social structure on the scientific community. Since he wishes to rule out the play of fashion in science, he cannot answer this question by examining concrete circumstances that intensify or inhibit the emphasis on finding new paradigms in the scientific community. Just before he reveals the ultimate answer to this question, Kuhn reaffirms his idealized conception of the paradigm:

> First, the new candidate must seem to resolve some outstanding and generally recognized problem that can be met in no other way. Second, the new paradigm must promise to preserve a relatively large part of the concrete problem-solving ability that has accrued to science through its predecessors. Novelty for its own sake is not a desideratum in the sciences as it is in so many fields. (168)[34]

With these qualities of the paradigm and of the scientific community in which it is adopted now explicitly defined, Kuhn speaks of the endless growth in the list of problems science has solved, in the precision of solutions developed, in the depth and proliferation of scientific fields of specialization established:

> Though science surely grows in depth, it may not grow in breadth as well. If it does so, that breadth is manifested mainly in the proliferation of scientific specialties, not in the scope of any single specialty alone. . . . The nature of such communities provides a virtual guarantee that both the list of problems solved by science anad the precision of individual problem-solutions will grow and grow. (169)

Although Kuhn believes that the proliferation of specialties in science is ipso facto evidence of progress, this tendency can also be a manifestation of increasingly compartmentalized and myopic areas of inquiry, and might well be part of the fashion process in science. Conventional fields of study (e.g., social psychology) can be reintroduced as though they were a new diversity of fields, such as "group dynamics" and "interpersonal communication," for the purpose of appearing glamorous, attracting large numbers of students, securing research grants for "experimental projects," and so forth. One might argue that such proliferation of new specialties renders increasingly difficult the pursuit of interdisciplinary research and of a unified theory in the physical or social sciences. Kuhn's unqualified approval of such proliferation as though it were evidence of progress is another indication of the extent to which he has uncritically incorporated the play of fashion in science into his own thinking about the scientific community. He fails to consider the possibility that the proliferation of specialties itself is an indication more of the play of fashion in the scientific community than of the attainment of significant new realms of inquiry.

Since Kuhn's general thesis is that a scientific revolution comes about as a result of a crisis generated in normal science, it is instructive to note that the internal logic of his own view (or paradigm) of the scientific community in itself leads to a crisis. On the one hand, it presumes to explain the structure and progressive nature of scientific revolutions. On the other hand, most of the social forces, internal as well as external to the scientific community, that might help to serve as a basis for his paradigm are explicitly ruled out for possible consideration. In his assertions that the list of problems solved and the precision with which they are solved by the scientific community will "grow and grow" and that the "nature" of the scientific community is indeed a "virtual guarantee" of such growth, Kuhn shows an awareness of this crisis and the need for a dramatic solution to it.

His allusion to natural, endless, progressive growth is the first explicit clue to his real paradigm for explaining scientific revolutions: *progress in science is caused by the inherent force of evolution in the scientific community itself.* Kuhn leads up to this view by posing a new question to which evolutionism is the only conceivable answer:

> Can we not account for both science's existence and its success in terms of evolution from the community's state of knowledge at any given time? . . . If we can learn to substitute evolution-from-what-we-know for evolution-toward-what-we-wish-to-know, a number of vexing problems may vanish in the process. . . . *The Origin of Species* recognized no goal set either by God or nature. Instead, natural selection, operating in the given environment and with the actual organisms presently at hand, was responsible for the gradual but steady emergence of more elaborate, further articulated and vastly more specialized organisms. Even such marvelously adapted organs as the eye and hand of man—organs whose design had previously provided powerful arguments for the existence of a supreme artificer and

an advance plan—were products of a process that moved steadily *from* primitive beginnings but *toward* no goal. (171)

Kuhn solves his paradigm crisis, a result of trying generally to explain
scientific progress in history without the use of historical and sociological data, by positing an ahistorical analogy between the scientific community and the living organism:

> The analogy that relates the evolution of organisms to the evo-
> lution of scientific ideas can easily be pushed too far. But with
> respect to the issues of this closing section, it is very nearly per-
> fect. The process described . . . as the resolution of revolu-
> tions is the selection by conflict within the scientific community
> of the fittest way to practice science. The net result of a se-
> quence of such revolutionary selections, separated by periods
> of normal research, is the wonderfully adapted set of instru-
> ments we call scientific knowledge. (171)

Although Kuhn mentions that this organic analogy should be used with
caution, he also asserts that "it is very nearly perfect" as a paradigm to
solve the crisis of his own position. This evolutionist paradigm assumes
that progress is the unfolding of potentialities for growth inherent in the
organism (or scientific community) and that it comes about naturally,
gradually, and continuously to ensure increasingly perfect adaptations
to the environment. Any given stage of development is therefore necessarily superior to those preceding it, and destined to be replaced by an
even more perfect stage with the passage of time. The introduction of
new ideas is, pursuant to the same logic, part of this all-embracing and
inexorable progress, and anyone or anything impeding its realization is
an unnatural or pathological obstacle to be removed from the system.
This, then, is the argument by which the preoccupation with new ideas
as an end in itself and the traditional faith in social Darwinism are fused.
Kuhn is by implication clearly arguing that the many foes of progress in
the scientific community, all of whom should be hermetically isolated
from its vital processes in his judgment, are not only unreasonable but
also *unnatural* or *accidental* factors to be ignored or discounted accordingly.

Even if the organic analogy were as tenable as Kuhn supposes, one
must question the arbitrary interpretation of "science as an organism"
advanced in this paradigm. No organism, for example, can possibly survive without adapting to and deriving sustenance from the environment. But Kuhn ignores the patterns by which science does adapt to and
derive sustenance from an environment often inhospitable to it. He also
ignores the fact that scientists, unlike the parts of an organism, can plan

and redefine their goals and that they can actively attempt to transform the larger environment itself. To depict the scientific community as an arena in which biological processes of adaptation and stimulus-response relationships mechanically prevail is to make a caricature of the very institution Kuhn wishes to celebrate.

There are still other difficulties with this organic analogy as an explanation of progress in science. In the biological world, the processes of adaptation and stimulus-response activity are ongoing; they do not erupt at some times and disappear at others. But Kuhn has already argued that the scientific community is in its "normal" state at some times and its "revolutionary" state at others. What are the biological equivalents of "normal" research and "revolutionary" development? Kuhn does not attempt to answer this question. Moreover, one can envision an organism in terms of birth, maturity, and death (leading to a cyclical paradigm for a given species) or of cumulative growth of the species to which a particular organism belongs and contributes in its relatively short lifetime (leading to a unilinear paradigm for the evolution of the species). There is no logical reason to assume that either model applies a priori to the history of science or to the indefinite future of this institution. Kuhn arbitrarily chooses the unilinear paradigm for this purpose as though there were laws of development operating outside the scope of human activity and reason to vindicate his choice.

The concept of "survival of the fittest" assumes that there is intense struggle among the competing paradigms or among the scientists who wish to propose or question them in the scientific community. But Kuhn's avowed insistence on the exclusion of skeptical, creative insiders as well as meddling outsiders from the scientific community would virtually eliminate the possibility of such intellectual struggle. Kuhn's invocation of ahistorical laws to explain the development of science also implies that progress takes place regardless of the deeds of living men and women, regardless of their intellectual competence or incompetence, regardless of their acceptance or rejection of a given paradigm, regardless of any empirical evidence that might seem to call into question this optimistic view. Scientists become merely the acquiescent creatures of history, the passive beneficiaries of cosmic, immanent laws of progress. The prevailing paradigm in a given discipline must be the best of all possible paradigms, for it has, by Kuhn's definition, proved itself to be most successful in the process of natural selection. For Kuhn, it must follow that to question a prevailing paradigm is to question the revealed laws of evolution that produced it. Although Kuhn frequently insists that the scientific community must be free from authoritarianism and that any view of progress in the scientific community should be open-ended and judiciously based on the actual historical evidence, one would be hard put to imagine a more dogmatic and empirically unfounded view of science than the one Kuhn offers.

His own concluding remarks in his study are an accurate assessment of the failure of his evolutionist paradigm to explain progress in science or the relationship between the scientific community and the society of which it is a part:

> It is not only the scientific community that must be special. The world of which that community is a part must also possess quite special characteristics, and we are no closer than we were at the start to knowing what these must be. That problem— What must the world be like in order that man may know it?— was not, however, created by this essay. On the contrary, it is as old as science itself, and it remains unanswered. (172)[35]

There are, however, a vast number of studies in the sociology of knowledge and science that help to clarify the conditions under which the growth of knowledge is facilitated. These studies, whatever their areas of disagreement or differing emphases, make clear that scientific progress is neither the automatic product of an insulated, encapsulated group of persons who are alone in possession of true reason nor the expression of timeless laws of evolution that work themselves out with the mere passage of time. If Kuhn had been at least dimly aware of them, he would not have needed to resort to spurious organic analogies to explain the subject matter of his research.

Kuhn ignores the fact that evolutionist thought is already deeply ingrained in the social sciences and that its most conservative implication, that human beings are the creatures or agents of immutable laws in the social system, is taken for granted both in structural-functional theories of society and in microsociological theories of personality adjustment. Kuhn has permitted these ideological tendencies to join hands by defining science as equivalent to a social organism and relegating the scientist to a role of witnessing the great drama of evolution unfold on its own; the scientist is seen as having neither the powers of reason nor the qualities of a social self that might question the already flawless script. Although Kuhn does not explicitly recognize the policy implications of his vision of the scientific community, he is in the camp of those functional theorists of deviance who perceive disruptive behavior as though it were a disease to be cured, a germ to be destroyed, a cancer to be removed from the normal, healthy, self-correcting social system.

Despite Kuhn's insistence on the insulation of the scientific community from the fashion process, he not only observes manifestations of this process in his analysis of paradigm debates but also permits much of the analysis he himself carries out to be under its influence. The new ingredient in his approach is neither his denial that the fashion process is operative in science nor his judgment that challengers to the prevailing orthodoxy should be ostracized from the community. The new and important feature of his approach is the explicit invocation of the laws of evolution (1) to justify a doctrine of progress in the modern scientific community; (2) to defend the play of fashion in science ideologically as the unfolding of potential for newer, better, more sacrosanct paradigms; and (3) to equate the appearance of these paradigms with proof of progress in that same community.

Kuhn and Friedrichs on the Meaning of Proliferation: Operant Conditioning and the "New Look" in Social Psychology

Kuhn does not consider that the proliferation of areas of specialization may actually reflect the continuation of orthodox lines of inquiry that are embellished as though they were major new developments in a discipline.[36] For example, traditional studies of juvenile delinquency can be represented in terms of group dynamics (in the operation and breakdown of agencies of social control); such studies can thus be adorned with the more modern guises of studies in "deviance," "social psychology," or "political sociology" as fields currently enjoying popularity in the discipline. The glamorization of customary assumptions, perspectives, and methods of inquiry is most vividly illustrated in the case of theories and techniques of social control and personality adjustment. What had once been the vigorously contested doctrines of behaviorism and positivism in sociology, especially as embodied in the views of George Lundberg, have now been reanimated in the guise of behavior modification as envisioned by B. F. Skinner.[37] This allegedly "new look" in sociology is represented not only as the most advanced research under way in social psychology but also as the sure road to utopia for all mankind. As Robert Friedrichs himself has most recently and approvingly observed:

> Skinner's life-long marriage to an austerely natural scientific epistemology is as self-evident as his fathering of an operant behaviorism that focuses immediately upon the change that can be brought about through positive reward. The very anomaly that was the fatal plan of the "system" presumption—change—

becomes operant conditioning's fundamental aim. Furthermore, the posture is graced by a proper claim to extreme conceptual parsimony, to logical adequacy, and to at least provisional experimental success with subject-settings (psychotics in hospitals and children in ghetto schools, among others) that have largely eluded the sustained efforts of social and behavioral scientists employing other modes. And *Walden II* and *Beyond Freedom and Dignity* clearly register Skinner's "prophetic" commitment.[38]

With Kuhn's image of the autonomous development of the scientific community in mind, Friedrichs maintains that this new version of social psychology is a promising field of specialization because of the reputation of opinion leaders who now endorse operant conditioning:

> Skinner's foremost advocate within sociology is, of course, George Homans, strategically placed as he has been of late as chairman of Harvard's Department of Sociology. Even the departure of the program from the umbrella of "Social Relations" created by Parsons would seem to encourage the possibilities of which I speak, for it has allowed Social Relations' center of gravity to slip towards a psychological perspective in which Skinner has been afforded a privileged place and has granted Homans freer rein within the Sociology Department itself. (4)

Friedrichs also maintains that this new specialization will further serve to confirm the disappearance of turmoil in the discipline during the 1960s and, indeed, to consolidate the belief that the radical assaults upon the discipline were only temporary, frivolous, and symbolic gestures that can be henceforth ignored:

> What one may expect is that *synonyms* of such terms as "positive reinforcement," "reward" and "non-aversive control" will find their way increasingly into the sociologist's vocabulary. One of the intriguing aspects of a shift from a Parsonian to a Skinnerian-inspired orthodoxy is that it would reflect a measure of underlying continuity as well—just as, for all the highly touted (yet largely symbolic) "revolutions" of the 1960s, the ethos that undergirds the public expression of our larger culture's norms has remained remarkably stable. This should not be altogether surprising, for the ethos not only has deeply imbedded within American history, but is evidenced in Parsons' and Skinner's biographically formative years as well. (7)[39]

How can one evaluate the degree to which operant conditioning is an advancement for sociology as a science? Does its very existence or the endorsement of opinion leaders constitute evidence for this purpose?

Does its ability to manipulate and deny the subjectivity of the self consti-tute appropriate evidence for this purpose? Does its convergence with prevailing paradigm in the discipline of sociology constitute relevant evidence? Can its many failures, even within its own terms of reference, be taken into account? Can its avowed indifference to the historical, structural, and biographical dimensions of the human condition be fairly included in such an evaluation? Does its exclusive preoccupation with the here-and-now serve somehow to recommend it for adoption by the scientific community? The consequence of defining progress in science in terms of the *number* of problems solved and the *number* of specializations produced is that such questions are given only a passing nod or ignored altogether. The substantive content of paradigms, the priorities for investigation, the relative merits of competing fields of in-vestigation, the social impact of conventional and new fields of investi-gation on the larger society are not seriously examined by those who es-pouse this quantitative conception. These matters are considered only insofar as they can be interpreted to illustrate the unfolding of an al-ready postulated line of progress. Such an indicator of progress renders Kuhn and those who accept his paradigm insensitive to the possibility that the play of fashion rather than the identification of major new prob-lem areas may be responsible for the proliferation of new fields of specialization.

A serious methodological problem arises from Kuhn's decision to equate the rate at which problems are solved with the level of progress in the discipline. One should again recall the considerable evidence, es-pecially in the social sciences, that the priorities for investigating one set of problems rather than another and the systematic use of certain as-sumptions and data rather than others are a response to the pressures from the dominant sectors of the larger society.[40] Hence, the rate at which problems are solved might well be an indication of the degree to which a discipline has acquiesced to the demands of powerful sponsors and utilized the funds given by those clients to solve externally imposed problems. When a discipline accepts a set of problems as given or self-evident, develops a system of language and logic to clarify and solve those problems, and depends for its very existence on the degree to which those problems are considered central to its intellectual life, those problems have been incorporated into the internal culture of the scientific community; those problems are clearly no longer external, marginal, or superficial to the discipline. In sociology, for example, the paradigm of functionalism prevails not because it was ever proved to be the most valid explanation of human nature but rather because of its ideological and strategic value in legitimizing and obscuring the present structure of domination in American society.[41] Similarly, the rate at which the problems of alienation, exploitation, and militarism are defined and solutions are proposed in terms of transforming the class structure through social revolution is not seen as progress by those in the mainstream of American sociology; such problem solving is viewed as a step backward, as a symptom of ideological fanaticism, as diversionary from the real and allegedly scientific concerns of the discipline.[42] The possibility that the sociologist can advance the science of society by formulating approaches to assist oppressed peoples in their political struggles rather than producing new models for the prediction and control of their behavior is seen as heretical and is rarely even acknowledged in such mainstream publications as the *American Sociological Review*, the *American Journal of Sociology* and the *American Sociologist*.[43]

Large numbers of publications, research centers, graduate training programs, and fields of specialization are devoted to the solution of various problems and crises facing the existing agencies of social control in American society. New solutions or approaches to such problems as black radicalism, student activism, union militancy, and Third World uprisings are produced at an increasingly rapid rate as government, corporate, and university research centers perceive these matters as problems and furnish the resources for the sociological investigation of them.[44] Some of these solutions are effective; others fail and are repudiated or "placed on the back burner"; still others are supplanted by even more innovative solutions as the need arises.[45] Substantial resources are placed at the disposal of those sociologists who specialize in developing models for the prediction and control of the disruptive behavior in question.

Under these conditions, the rate at which problems are solved would be an indicator of the penetration of the discipline by those with a vested interest in maintaining social order. Although Kuhn *assumes* that the rate of problem solving is a reliable measure of maturity in the scientific community, his own empirical indicator for this characteristic can be a measure of susceptibility to external social pressures. Under certain conditions, the rate at which problems are solved might well indicate "scientific maturity" in Kuhn's sense; but under other conditions, such as those just outlined, this same measure can indicate the degree to which economic, political, and ideological forces in the larger society have been incorporated into the language and logic of the scientific community.

The methodological problem of interpreting this measure of maturity and progress is made especially difficult not only because of Kuhn's own insistence that susceptibility to external pressures is an unmistakable sign of immaturity but also because of his more recent claim that his paradigm applies in essential respects to such fields as literature, music, art, and politics:

> To the extent that the book portrays scientific development as a succession of tradition-bound periods punctuated by non-cumulative breaks, its theses are undoubtedly of wide applicability. But they should be, for they are borrowed from other fields. Historians of literature, of music, of the arts, of political development and of many other human activities have long described their subjects in the same way. Periodization in terms of revolutionary breaks in style, taste and institutional structure have been among their standard tools. If I have been original with respect to concepts like these, it has mainly been by applying them to the sciences, fields which had been widely thought to develop in a different way.[46]

Kuhn thereby reverses the position he had originally and consistently argued that the natural sciences differ from the arts, humanities, and social sciences in their basic nature and form of development; far from resolving the ambiguity in his paradigm concerning maturity and progress in the scientific community, his revised statement compounds it. This reversal can be explained in terms of the operation of the fashion process itself.

Kuhn's paradigm of the scientific community "caught on" so rapidly in a variety of fields that he himself concurred in the new belief that most and perhaps all disciplines are governed by the principles in this reassuring model of endless progress. This transformation of his own assumptions illustrates some important features of the fashion process. First, an opinion leader can only propose a style or model for possible adoption and cannot control the varying interpretations to which it may be subjected by the public while it is being considered. Second, even a highly influential opinion leader is susceptible to the ongoing interpretations of a style he himself may have introduced.

The Ambiguous Meaning of "Revolution" in Science

Although Kuhn's study is nominally about the structure of revolutions in science, he ignores entirely the changing structure of power in the scientific community in its normal and revolutionary stages of development; he refers only incidentally to some of the ideological changes (in the expression of aesthetic criteria) associated with these phases. Nor does he examine the extent to which the structure of domination in the larger society is reproduced in the structure of domination in the scientific community. He similarly ignores the relationship between revolution in the larger society and revolution in the scientific community despite the long-term and reciprocal patterns of influence that might have been historically investigated in this connection. He does not acknowledge that the very usage of the term "revolution" has become fashionable in the academic world just as it has in the new symbolism of Madison Avenue. Even slight alterations in a given commodity are extravagantly represented as revolutionary and sensational developments; social science textbooks on the "new" history, "revolutionary" psychiatry, and "radical" sociology have been flooding the academic marketplace for over two decades despite the fact that many of their assumptions, pedagogical uses, and even their source materials are often similar to the more conventional products. In Kuhn's own discussion of the invisibility of paradigm revolutions,[47] for example, one could often realistically speak of a moderate and gradual shift to a paradigm that (1) incorporates much or all of the old model in a limited reformulation of existing knowledge and (2) is neither perceived as a revolution by members of the scientific community nor intended as such by its architects. Had Kuhn been aware of the play of fashion in his own area of interest, the history and philosophy of science, he might have been better prepared to guard against the tendency to use extravagant terms that happen to be in vogue but are nevertheless sometimes misleading in the characterization of a given subject matter.

Despite Kuhn's realistic and repeated observation that *The Structure of Scientific Revolutions* is not a definitive or adequate explanation of the structure of revolutions in science, his publisher, the University of Chicago Press, nevertheless boldly states on the cover of the original edition that it is "a brilliant, original analysis of the nature, causes and consequences of revolutions in scientific concepts." The ambiguities in the meaning of "revolution" in science and the systematic inattention to the structural features of the scientific community are symptomatic of a wide range of ambiguous claims found in Kuhn's model of the scientific community. These claims are examined here in terms of the sociology of knowledge to explain the remarkably successful reception his model has enjoyed in the academic world.

Ambiguities in Kuhn's Paradigm and Their Appeal to the ` Scientific Community

One should consider the extent to which the ambiguity in Kuhn's thesis helps to explain its great popularity. On the one hand, he claims that a paradigm is by definition a rigorous match between evidence and theory; this appeals to those committed to the ideals of formal logic in the philosophy of science and to social scientists preoccupied with modern systems theory. On the other hand, he claims that a paradigm is whatever the consensus in the scientific community says it is at a given time and place; this appeals both to those committed to a relativistic and situationally determined view of truth and knowledge and to those who identify with the ethnomethodological doctrine of consensual validation.

On the one hand, he claims that scientific revolutions take place all at once or not at all and that they constitute fundamental and irrevocable transformations in how the world (or some aspect of it) is to be approached. This appeals to those committed to Popper's conception of the crucial experiment and critical debate in scientific discovery as well as to those who agree with the abstract dialectical conception that any given worldview necessarily leads to its opposite in all spheres of thought and action. On the other hand, he claims that new paradigms are often adopted only slowly and reluctantly by the influential circles in the scientific community and that they incorporate whatever was of value in the older paradigms. This appeals to those committed to the view that the scientific community is essentially similar to most other communities in dealing traditionally with the selection of new proposals, and that in this significant sense it falls far short of its rationalist ideals. (One could hypothesize that the renewed countercultural movements against technology and science may eventually "discover" Kuhn as they already discovered McLuhan and Roszak.)

On the one hand, Kuhn claims that any paradigm that hopes to explain the progress in modern science must approach this matter in a historical light; scientists must intensively study the Copernican revolution, for example, and other major foundations of Western thought. This appeals to those committed in traditional academic departments to the advancement of classical education and the appreciation of the rugged individualists and persons of genius in the heyday of the industrial revolution. On the other hand, Kuhn argues that the members of a scientific discipline should read only the up-to-date textbooks that summarize the consensus about the prevailing paradigms in their discipline, and that any consultation of classical or original source material is likely to be tedious and counterproductive. This appeals to those committed to the advancement of the modern image of science in terms of appearing to look forward rather than backward, to keep abreast only of the latest developments, and to standardize the ideas in a discipline as though they should be considered timeless and infallible in the eyes of its newly socialized members.

On the one hand, Kuhn claims that the conventional wisdom in science is never finalized or perfect because the normal-scientific community is always refining the current paradigm and even uncovering anomalies that cannot be explained by it. This is attractive to those committed to the belief that science is always changing, open to new discoveries, or that science and nature are together changing in an ever-increasing number of progressive directions. On the other hand, Kuhn claims that the conventional wisdom in a given discipline is necessarily the outcome of an evolutionary process of adaptation and that it is, by definition, the most fit for survival of all competing paradigms. This appeals to those committed to the belief that "what is, is good" in the scientific community and that reverence (or at least complaisance) toward the existing state of knowledge is an appraisal justified by the laws of evolution.

On the one hand, he claims that for progress in science to take place, "the world of which that community is a part, must also possess quite special characteristics." This appeals to (1) those committed to the view that science is a social product to be explained chiefly or exclusively in terms of the sociology of knowledge as well as (2) those who believe that scientific ideas individually and the scientific community as a whole are the mechanistically determined expressions of pressures and vested interests in the larger society. On the other hand, he claims that the scientific community is perfectly insulated from social pressures and that scientists decide on the problems they wish to investigate without any concern for moral or political issues in the larger society. This appeals to those who feel that (1) the sociology of knowledge has little or no value in the social sciences, that it should be relegated to a peripheral or less than legitimate status as an area of special study, and that all scientists are automatically capable of transcending their cultural and political biases by virtue of their membership in the scientific community.

On the one hand, Kuhn claims further that authentic paradigm debates and scientific revolutions can take place only in the "mature" or natural sciences and never in the "immature" or social sciences, that the natural sciences are devoted to the explicit testing of hypotheses while the social sciences, like the humanities and fine arts, are confused over the criteria of validity and the priorities for research on their agenda. This makes sense to those committed to the doctrine that a permanent chasm exists between the physical and social sciences; that the physical sciences are legitimate and objective while the social sciences are illegitimate and subjective; that the social sciences are little more than the expressions of metaphysical speculation and undeserving of recognition in higher learning. (Although most public universities in the United States no longer share this seemingly antiquated doctrine, some of the most prestigious and conservative universities in Western civilization have only recently and begrudgingly recognized sociology as a field in which an advanced degree can be earned and for which a minimal academic staff should be recruited.) On the other hand, Kuhn also claims, however, to know so little about the social sciences as to leave open the possibility that much or all of his proposal regarding the structure of scientific revolutions might eventually be applied to these disciplines. This appeals to those seeking some means by which (1) to capture some of the high prestige enjoyed by the physical sciences, (2) to demonstrate that the two worlds of intellectual development are governed by the same laws of progress, (3) to represent the social sciences as a mature and respectable field deserving of government funding and academic certification on a par with the physical sciences. (We have already seen that this possibility has been vigorously exploited by many scholars in recent years.)

On the one hand, he claims that the prevailing consensus and aesthetic tastes are the actual arbiters of debate over competing paradigms in the scientific community. This appeals to those who believe that the winner of a debate is ipso facto the possessor of truth, that a minority opinion is by definition in error. On the other hand, he claims that any sign of authoritarianism is out of place in the scientific community—that its appearance in a paradigm debate means that such a debate has irretrievably lost all pretense to being scientific:

> If authority alone, and if particularly non-professional authority, were the arbiter of paradigm debates, the outcome of those debates might be revolution, but it would not be scientific revolution. The very existence of science depends upon the vesting of power to choose between paradigms in the members of a special kind of community. (166)[48]

This appeals to those who are convinced that each member of the scientific community is in fact free to make intellectual judgments entirely on the basis of his concern for truth and without any fear of surveillance or censorship by any internal or external authority.

Kuhn's own academic background also helps to explain the great appeal of his work for the discipline of sociology. First, his scholarly credentials were established at Harvard University, and his present academic appointment as professor of the history of science at Princeton University adds still more luster to his reputation and the legitimacy of his paradigm for scientific revolutions. Second, he began his academic studies not in history or philosophy, but in the far more prestigious domain of theoretical physics. Third, he takes no explicit position on the ominous crises facing modern science and the larger society, and hence has caused no offense to radical or conservative sectors of the scientific community.

It is in the very weaknesses of Kuhn's work that the strength of its appeal can be explained: through the systematic emphasis on one side of his ambiguous and vague claims and the neglect of alternative interpretations to which his work is just as amenable, a case for almost any conceivable paradigm of how the scientific community operates can be reasonably derived from a most prestigious source. Marxist sociologists and conservative philosophers, classical absolutists and modern pluralists, rugged individualists and consensual teamworkers, eager young scientists and entrenched experts in grantsmanship can and do find in *The Structure of Scientific Revolutions* substantial justifications for whatever conception of science they wish to advance.

The Career of Kuhn's Paradigm in the Selection Process: The Filtering and Screening of Timely Models in the Discipline of Sociology

In view of the tendencies toward *ad hominem* debate in much of sociological inquiry, one should be cognizant of Kuhn's exemplary intellectual integrity before making any final appraisal of his research. Few if any writers in the sociology of knowledge or the philosophy of science have ever even attempted such realistic and searching self-criticism as Kuhn has done.

Kuhn's unprecedented and unquestioned rise to prominence cannot be explained in terms of a psychologically reductionist view of his personal aspirations or needs. It can only be explained in terms of the historical context in which his ideas were formed and eventually submitted for possible adoption. The major features of this historical context, insofar as they are essential to such an explanation, are suggested as follows. First, certain crises in the scientific community existed before and during the publication of Kuhn's research, and the traditional means of coping with them were proving ineffective. Second, many groups were competing with each other in a number of disciplines, and a number of disciplines were themselves competing with each other for such resources as prestige and research funds, as well as general academic recognition; the value of science was increasingly being questioned as part of a conservative drift in American politics, and the climate of competition and apprehension within the scientific community was exacerbated accordingly. Third, there was an amorphous groping for some new response to overcome or at least to rationalize and contain the scope of these crises; some of the most prominent opinion leaders in sociology especially were calling for the arrival of a Newton or a Kepler who might lift the crushing weight of these crises from a discipline in distress. Fourth, Kuhn proposed a model that seemed immediately to articulate and reconcile the many competing interests, ambiguous themes and amorphous tastes in American sociology. Fifth, these crises were grave and of potentially revolutionary consequence because they were produced by (a) the overwhelming embarrassment of riches in the number of theoretical and methodological models competing for adoption; (b) the absence of criteria by which to ascertain the relative validity of these models; and (c) the political and intellectual assaults on the traditional authority of the sociological profession to prescribe legitimate areas of research and to suppress radical activism on the part of its members. Sixth, regardless of his own intentions and perceptions, regardless of severe shortcomings in his research, Kuhn has been heralded as the Promethean savior whose ideas have settled these potentially explosive crises and enabled the discipline to regain its composure by (a) denying the existence or importance of these crises in the scientific community; (b) defining crises merely in terms of anomalies that develop gradually and immanently from that community; (c) leading the discipline ideologically back to the road of normal science.

One might at first glance be puzzled to note that these crises have not really been solved by the adoption of Kuhn's paradigm, that Kuhn himself never claimed to solve or even recognize these crises; that no discernible revolution in thought or action (theoretically, ideologically, or organizationally) has taken place since the adoption of his paradigm, and that Kuhn has nevertheless continued to receive the highest praise from influential members of the discipline as though these crises were in fact solved. However, the criteria for identifying an authentic savior or synthetic paradigm are never spelled out by those who have called for a sociological Newton; the center of the stage, as previously shown, remains open and vaguely defined. One therefore should not be surprised to find that the *appearance* of a solution to these crises has been equated with its substances. Through the adoption of Kuhn's paradigm, the discipline of sociology takes on the appearance of a stable, "mature," "normal," and noncontroversial science with a secure future of endless progress in store. Through its adoption, the discipline also incorporates into its professional identity a sophisticated rationale for ostracizing from the scientific community those who might still question this public image. In short, Kuhn's paradigm has been adopted because it provides the appearance of a credible solution to far-reaching intellectual and social crises—largely by the categorical denial of their existence—and not because it is a fundamental solution to them or a valid account of any scientific community.

The Constructive Role of the Fashion Process in Sociology

One might at first glance suppose that the climate of orthodoxy and consensus surrounding Kuhn's paradigm would be debilitating to the scientific community. On closer inspection, however, one might consider that this model can be accepted, rejected, or modified on many different grounds; that it can serve as an object against which one may develop an alternative, empirically based, and rigorous model of the actual progressions and retrogressions in science; that the high integrity of its architect and the accolades it has enjoyed as the alleged key to "our professional nature and destiny" offer a positive example as well as cautionary lessons the scientific community would do well to heed. If Kuhn's model is seen in this light, an alternative and more viable conception of the scientific community might specify the following ingredients:

(1) the conditions under which scientists can individually and collectively attain the level of critical self-awareness exemplified by Kuhn and incorporate this virtue into discussions and debates concerning the substantive validity of competing paradigms;

(2) the conditions under which a consensus formed over a new paradigm will correspond to the substantive validity of the paradigm rather than the amorphous collective tastes and vested interests of that community;

(3) the requirements for the rigorous education of scientists so that they will not only know of the past errors, discoveries, and struggles in their discipline but also constructively take

this knowledge into account when formulating and testing new paradigms;

(4) those political, economic, and ideological pressures conducive to sound scientific research and those obstructive of it as well as a blueprint of what scientists and laymen can do to promote the former and oppose the latter pressures;

(5) those aspects of the fashion process that facilitate and those that retard the search for important new solutions to the crises facing the scientific community and the larger society;

(6) the social, ideological, and epistemological consequences of selecting one paradigm over another so that scientists become constantly aware of their responsibilities as privileged citizens and their objective interests as intellectual workers in the class structure.

But how can the formidable task of applying these specifications be launched? An instructive point of departure would be to examine critically the achievements, the shortcomings, and the rise to prominence of Kuhn's paradigm about the structure of scientific revolutions. The preceding case study indicates the degree to which the success of his paradigm is a product of the fashion process in science. It suggests the value of the sociology of knowledge in implementing these specifications by taking into account the positive example and the cautionary lessons gleaned from a critical review of Kuhn's paradigm.

One should at this point recall the cautionary note emphasized earlier in the present study. The evidence thus far presented to indicate the play of fashion in Kuhn's paradigm and the enthusiastic reception it has received in modern sociology is reasonable and plausible rather than exhaustive and conclusive. It is meant chiefly to accomplish the first two steps in the demonstration of the fashion process in a particular scientific discipline and should not be taken for the demonstration of it in toto. It also suggests other aspects of the fashion process, especially the high probability that the implementation of all steps in the larger investigation of the fashion process would show that Kuhn's ambiguous paradigm reflects and reinforces the collectively felt "needs" and amorphous tastes in many sectors of American sociology,[49] and that his influence is far more attributable to this resonance with these needs and tastes than to any substantive validity his work might possess. This evidence paves the way for the further investigation of the fashion process along the lines suggested in the section entitled "Some Cautionary Methodological Considerations: Criteria of Validity and Tentative Assumptions Made in the Present Study" as well as in the conclusion, "The Tasks Ahead in the Study of the Fashion Process in Science."

Limitations on the Fashion Process as an Explanatory Concept

Although the most important insights in Kuhn's paradigm of the scientific community have already been emphasized, they do not explain the widespread and rapid acceptance of this paradigm in the discipline of sociology. These insights, especially those concerning the dynamics of collective behavior among scientists and the study of anomalies, remain largely ignored by the sociologists who are most enthusiastic about this paradigm. The elements of vagueness and ambiguity in this paradigm render it especially vulnerable to the play of fashion in a discipline nurturing this process in the era of Simmel and Kroeber. The insights as well as the myopia in this paradigm continue to be unduly ignored, not because sociologists are irrational, but rather because they have adopted it in terms of the fashion process with consequently little regard for the positive and negative evidence on which it could otherwise be evaluated.

Because of the focus in the present study on the fashion process, one might be tempted to conclude that this process alone is sufficient as an explanation for the adoption of Kuhn's paradigm. Such a conclusion would be misleading, however, for it would obscure a number of crucial questions. Why did the fashion process lead to the adoption of Kuhn's vague and ambiguous paradigm rather than another and still more vague and ambiguous paradigm among the many from which a selection might have been made? Why was the fashion process so intensely operative on this particular paradigm in the late 1960s and early 1970s rather than at an earlier period? Why has this paradigm been so much more rapidly, widely, and uncritically adopted in sociology than in any other discipline? To answer these questions, one must examine the concrete setting in which major theoretical issues were defined and debated during this crucial period of sociological scholarship. By taking into account the political and ideological forces operative in the discipline and in the larger society at the time, one realizes that the fashion process was a necessary but insufficient condition for the adoption of Kuhn's paradigm. It remains to be shown that these forces together with the fashion process serve as an adequate explanation of this phenomenon and that they tend to reinforce one another in the same direction of adopting the paradigm and reviving traditional appeals to value-neutrality under the new banner of such modern symbols as "progress" and "revolution" in the scientific community.

In attempting to explain the major forms of social change and control in modern science and society, one is led astray just as much by neglecting the importance of the fashion process as by imputing to it a causal propensity in excess of its actual influence and thereby discounting other historical forces that cannot be reduced to any timeless process or propensity. Although the present study emphasizes the importance of the fashion process, any misguided inclination to view it ahistorically as a universal or single-factor theory of human behavior can be corrected by an analysis of the historical evidence of its useful but limited applicability. The evidence presented in later chapters on Friedrichs, Merton, and Alexander indicates that some of the impetus behind the fashion process in science derives from political and ideological forces in the larger society and that these forces must be examined empirically if one wishes to ascertain the degree to which they and the fashion process influence one another.

Much of the crisis in the identity of professional sociologists, as already noted, stemmed from a mounting concern over the embarrassment of riches in theoretical models, fields of specialization, methods of research, criteria or validity, and an increasingly proliferating spectrum of cults, factions, and rivalries cutting across each of these other tendencies. A subdued but occasionally acknowledged sense of alarm over this state of affairs was expressed in the 1950s and early 1960s by prominent spokesmen in the discipline. This growing sense of alarm was suddenly and sharply exacerbated by those organizational, ideological, and theoretical conflicts in the discipline that reflected the political polarization erupting in the larger society by the mid-1960s. Ramifications of the antiwar movement, student activism, black power, and women's liberation were felt throughout the discipline. Caucuses and perspectives of black sociologists, feminist sociologists, and the Sociology Liberation movement challenged the existing centers of authority, not only on a theoretical and symbolic level, but also on an ideological and political level by demonstrating at scholarly conventions, sometimes disrupting the usual course of business at these usually staid and innocuous meetings, and publishing a variety of irreverent articles, journals, and anthologies that attracted considerable attention. The Sociology Liberation movement, though itself internally divided and short-lived, succeeded in recruiting into its own organization large numbers of sociologists from the ranks of the American Sociological Association. It at first even attracted some recruits from the faculty and graduate student body at such elite universities as Harvard, Columbia, the University of Chicago, and Berkeley. The growing intensity and ferocity of the debate over the legitimacy of Marxism and political activism inside and outside the classroom, the research institute, and the jurisdiction of the profession reflected the escalating level of crisis in the discipline and in the larger society. Was there some means by which the crisis could be resolved or at least contained? Could the situation be redefined so that the image of sociology as a science might still retain its credibility in the eyes of government agencies and corporate foundations that traditionally sponsored its research enterprises and enhanced its prestige? These questions themselves were being posed, debated, and answered in an endless variety of ways, publicly and privately, in the scholarly journals and the organizational proceedings of the profession. Political compromises and epistemological syntheses were suggested by some while hard-line policies of political condemnation and ideological suppression were suggested by others in an attempt to respond to the worsening crisis in American sociology.

Kuhn's Influence and Stature in American Social Science

The cover of the original edition of *The Structure of Scientific Revolutions* features one reviewer's claim that "this is probably the most important contribution to the historiography of science since Butterfield's *Origins of Modern Science*" and another reviewer's claim that it "will raise the whole level of discussion about the nature and true character of science." Robert Friedrichs quickly adapted Kuhn's vision of physical science to the study of sociology itself; a growing number of equally enthusiastic scholars in the various fields of social science carried out similar applications in the study of their respective disciplines between 1965 and 1970. In the revised edition of his monograph, Kuhn in turn announced a shift in his original paradigm: he acknowledged and agreed with the rapidly forming consensus that the "less mature" sciences do approximately follow the general scheme of growth and revolution already chartered for the "more mature" sciences. Illustrative of the intense excitement generated by Kuhn's work is Friedrichs's remark:

> The argument Kuhn has fabricated has not only captured the imagination of sociologists of science, but have moved beyond into the realm of general speculation concerning our professional nature and destiny.[50]

Kuhn is considered not only to have advanced a definitive model or paradigm for the sociology of science but also to be the oracle of the "professional nature and destiny" of modern sociology.

But the analysis of Kuhn's view of the scientific community in the present study demonstrates that he is accurate and candid in observing some serious limitations of his own research. His admission that he knows very little about the social sciences, for example, is corroborated by the evidence presented here showing that he is unfamiliar with the intimate relationship between science and society and that his original research was completed without reference to the vast literature on this matter. His further admission that he remains puzzled by the conditions responsible for the operation of collective tastes (or "aesthetic criteria") in scientific inquiry is corroborated by the evidence showing that he categorically denies the existence of the fashion process in science and yet offers no empirical basis for this sweeping denial. His most candid and striking admission at the conclusion of his study is his concession that he has no idea whatsoever of the social conditions conducive to the growth of scientific knowledge—to the creation and adoption of new paradigms that are the essence of scientific revolutions. This admission is supported by the evidence here showing that he offers only spurious and ahistorical "laws of nature" to account for progress or growth in the scientific community. Although there are other and even more serious deficiencies in his work than those Kuhn recognizes, the accurate admissions he does make would seem sufficient to warrant a far more tempered appraisal of his work than the glowing terms in which *The Structure of Scientific Revolutions* is usually acclaimed. Although his own capacity for self-criticism and candor is admirably high, none of his admirers refer to this rare virtue in his work. In view of the ambiguities and fallacious claims advanced by Kuhn concerning the nature of paradigms and the scientific community, one might at first glance suppose that the task of explaining his sudden and uncontested rise to prominence in the academic world is elusive.

If one applies the sociology of knowledge to this task, however, the ambiguities and fallacies in Kuhn's work can be understood in the context of crises in American science at a time when the society in which it develops is also facing a series of economic, ideological, and political crises of a magnitude unparalleled since the 1920s. One can in this light examine how these ambiguities and fallacies help to define and legitimize new ameliorative responses to these crises, how the interests of powerful sectors of the scientific community are well served by these responses, and how Kuhn's ideas have thereby come to be heralded as timely revelations for the benefit of future generations of natural and social scientists.

Kuhn's writings about the nature and destiny of modern science first came to prominence in the mid-1960s. Even at Harvard University, where his thoughts began to crystallize, the attacks upon the bastions of higher education were escalating. Such organizations as Students for a Demo-

cratic Society, the Black Panther Party, and large antiwar coalitions during the regime of Lyndon Johnson challenged the use of university facilities for war research and counterinsurgency programs; they were particularly hostile to those social and physical scientists who acquiesced in
or expressed neutrality over such forms of oppression as racism, sexism,
economic inequality, and the denial of civil rights within the academic
community. Many students involved in these and similar challenges
were suspended or expelled from their campuses, some were arrested
and imprisoned, and still others were beaten or killed by police and National Guardsmen for their efforts. During this same turbulent period,
a growing number of scholars in physics and mathematics, in biology
and medicine, in foreign languages and the humanities, in the social
sciences (especially sociology and political science), and even in history
and philosophy—the fields on which Kuhn's own interests were
centered—came to organize radical caucuses *inside the ranks of their*
own disciplines, to voice intense criticisms of universities, research
agencies, professional associations, and to express limited public
solidarity with the movements and coalitions that were already launching attacks on those same institutions. The Stanford Research Institute,
one of the most influential and prestigious agencies engaged in "pure"
and "applied" research for the Department of Defense, was forced to
curb its range of operations substantially and its ties to Stanford University were severed in the wake of these assaults. Classrooms normally under the jurisdiction of a professor and annual conventions normally under the jurisdiction of a profession also became arenas in which the
political and ideological role of science in American social policy was intensely debated and various disruptions of customary proceedings were
carried out. Whatever the vision of value-neutrality or insulation from
social pressures in the scientific community, the empirical realities were
making clear the crises in the system were erupting in a forceful and
threatening manner. By the late 1960s and early 1970s, the national political response to these assaults was clear: the sweeping electoral victories
of such conservatives as Richard Nixon and Ronald Reagan, with their
outspoken platforms of "law and order," confirmed the largely successful attempt to silence or neutralize the individuals and organizations
responsible for the eruptions. The indiscriminate use of the apparatus
of state power to silence the antiwar movement in the cities culminated
much later in the sabotage of the moderate presidential campaign of
George McGovern by a group of FBI, CIA, and anti-Castro agents under
White House direction and the intimidation of vast numbers of news
reporters critical of foreign and domestic policy. Although the extreme
version of this repressive policy led eventually to a sense of national

revulsion, one should keep in mind the marked success and popularity it enjoyed as well as its counterpart in the scientific community: progressive and liberal university administrators were forced to resign their positions, faculty members actively involved in the aforementioned demonstrations and challenges were dismissed and in some instances subjected to blacklist campaigns, and many radical students were facing harsh prison sentences. The scientific community had, in short, a period of crisis unparalleled in the annals of recent scholarship; the new and massive social pressures exerted upon it were neither anticipated nor welcomed by the entrenched and powerful sectors of that community. In one discipline after another, prominent spokespersons declared that the professor must be answerable only to his own conscience and his scholarly peers regarding his research and views in matters of public importance, that the scientific community can solve only the problems that are given to it, and cannot ethically judge whether one or another set of problems is worthy of attention. It was also stated that scientists who raise questions about the underlying ideological assumptions and social consequences of research are engaging in polemical debates that are out of place in the community of scholarship. There was during this period a limited revival of interest in the work of Max Weber, whose advocacy of value-neutral inquiry was relatively sophisticated and useful to those who wished to support such declarations by invoking one of the most revered names among the founding fathers of sociological inquiry. Although Kuhn gives no indication of any familiarity with Weber's work, he nevertheless rediscovers and reaffirms the theme of value neutrality not only for sociology as a science in the twentieth century but for *all* of the sciences and for all time.

Kuhn's thesis of "insulation from social pressures" has been welcomed by that sector of the scientific community that subscribes to the elitist mystique of the autonomous intellectual—to that sector of the community whose goal of keeping protesters and meddlers at a healthy distance from one's own work is defended under the banner of "science for its own sake." More significantly, Kuhn's thesis holds that such insulation and value neutrality are absolutely essential to the realization of scientific progress, to the creation and solution of new paradigms, to the very goal of scientific revolutions.

What is the ideological importance of this thesis? In many disciplines, there was a vague search, an uneasy groping for a new and more compelling justification for Weber's position. Opinion leaders in these disciplines were increasingly distressed by the failure of the customary appeals to professional responsibility, restraint, and good judgment to convince radical and activist scientists of the error of their ways. Indeed, the radicals were heeding opinion leaders of their own—including C. Wright Mills, Noam Chomsky, Irving Louis Horowitz, Alvin Gouldner, Marlene Dixon, David Colfax, Ernest Becker—in attacking and developing alternatives to Weber's position and the appeals based upon it; whatever the disagreements among the radical caucuses and their opinion leaders, it was clear that their perspective and allegiances were moving increasingly to the left, and in some cases were becoming avowedly Marxist in their critique of American social science. *Since Kuhn's thesis holds that insulation from social pressures and value neutrality are absolutely essential to scientific progress and scientific revolutions, the search launched by the scientific community for a new defense of Weber's thesis was successfully concluded.*[51]

The ascendance of *The Structure of Scientific Revolutions* to a stature unprecedented in modern scholarship and the consensus surrounding its applicability to all scientific disciplines have become virtually invulnerable to criticism for several reasons. First, it is not merely an entrenched and conservative group in the scientific community that endorses Kuhn's work; social scientists associated with radical, critical, and humanistic perspectives are also enthusiastic about it because they see the concept of "revolution" being freely expressed in circles that once found the term in bad taste.[52] Radical scholars can also cite Kuhn in justification of the claim that "establishment science" (or normal science) is indeed under the sway of some irrational forces that obstruct the adoption of new ideas (because of elderly holdouts) and allow for the adoption of erroneous ideas (because of illogical aesthetic criteria).

CHAPTER 4
THE FASHION PROCESS AND THE SCIENTIFIC COMMUNITY
ROBERT FRIEDRICHS AS AN OPINION LEADER AND CREATOR OF COLLECTIVE BEHAVIOR

A *Sociology of Sociology* by Robert Friedrichs is of great interest in the present study because this work is (1) generally regarded as a major and definitive account of substantial issues and developments in the discipline; (2) represented by Friedrichs himself as offering a paradigmatic solution to the conflicts and diversity in the discipline; (3) praised both by prominent radical scholars (e.g., Norman Birnbaum)[1] and by the powerful center of the profession (e.g., the American Sociological Association conferred the Sorokin Award on Friedrichs for this work); (4) one of the most far-reaching attempts to adopt Kuhn's paradigm of the scientific community in the service of understanding the discipline of sociology. Finally, an effective check against the excessive and irrational aspects of the fashion process is the exercise of critical and historical self-awareness when competing models are being considered in the selection process. A *Sociology of Sociology* is therefore especially important to examine because it is an indication of the level of self-awareness in the discipline of sociology at the present time.

In this analysis of Friedrichs's paradigm of dialectical and pluralistic sociology, evidence is presented to suggest that (1) the substantive content and assumptions of his *Sociology of Sociology* and the favorable reception it continues to enjoy are both manifestations of the fashion process operating in the discipline, and that (2) Friedrichs is himself so fully and uncritically caught up in this process as to be insensitive even to the remotest possibility of its presence in the discipline and its influence in the rapid elevation of his paradigm to great prominence. Again, the focus is on the many grave defects in the paradigm and their intimate association with those ideologies concerning the supposed virtues of modernity, consensus, and moderation that suggest the operation of the fashion process. Where this evidence suggests still other aspects of the fashion process germane to one or another of the steps in the investigation bracketed for the present purposes, reference to them will also be noted.

Transcending Order and Conflict: Friedrichs's New Conception of Dialectical Sociology

In criticizing Kuhn's puristic notion of value-neutral paradigms in the scientific community, Friedrichs maintains that the social sciences necessarily play host to paradigms at two levels of discourse because "such sciences are forced to encompass the scientist, his activity and his self-image as part of their subject matter."[2] He fails, however, to apply this epistemological insight to his own proposal for a

> . . . "dialectical" image [that] has been introduced as a possible basis for a cease fire between the two warring schools. . . . The system paradigm appeared to be a product of a prior commitment to a paradigmatic image of the sociologist as *value-free*; the conflict paradigm an outcome of the sociologist as *engagé*. (290)

Friedrichs then summarizes the perspective that allegedly reconciles these sharply conflicting images of the sociologist:

> As the realization grows that the substantive focus of sociology includes social research and the resultant awareness that the very precipitation and comprehension of past and present order will inevitably be to some degree fed back through social interaction to deny that order, a dialectical paradigm becomes increasingly tenable. Neither "system" nor "conflict" need be denied; rather they become necessary elements within a larger dialectical *gestalt*. Formally, system would still take cognitive priority over conflict simply because the former must be presupposed. But conflict is in principle a partial product, even though it in turn contributes, as in the classical formulation of the dialectic, to a new moment of stability. (297)

Friedrichs offers no logical justification or empirical evidence for the claim that order must have "cognitive priority" over conflict. Is conflict between the Democratic and the Republican parties, for example, to be investigated in the same terms as a struggle between workers and the ruling class? Is the kind of order imposed by the repressive policies of the cold war and the alleged requirement for national security to be investigated in the same terms as order created by equality of opportunity and the eradication of corporate domination of society? Does order automatically generate conflict? Does conflict automatically lead to order or the restoration of social equilibrium? Does the "dialectical *gestalt*" in which these tendencies oscillate have a life of its own? If so, what are the laws governing its development? What are the historical conditions under which revolutionary struggle (or "conflict") might lead to a reactionary backlash (or "order")? What are the historical conditions under which severe repression (or "order") might lead to the radicalization of consciousness and revolutionary struggle (or "conflict")?

The need to clarify these concepts and to answer these questions must be underscored because Friedrichs claims that his dialectical paradigm is an explanation of order and conflict in the scientific community as well as in the larger society. The fact that he does not attempt to answer or even acknowledge the centrality of these questions suggests that this paradigm, like the one Kuhn advances, has enjoyed a rise to prominence for reasons other than its intellectual candlepower. Although the more sophisticated spokespersons for various conservative and radical perspectives have undertaken in recent years to define their concepts rigorously and to specify the conditions under which their hypotheses hold, Friedrichs is content to treat the concepts of "order" and "conflict" in a simplistic manner reminiscent of the most pedestrian functionalism and vulgar Marxism found in the discipline. He takes for granted the ahistorical, vague, and grandiose interpretations of "systems" theory and "conflict" theory, and claims to have synthesized them as though the resulting paradigm yields a valid approach to sociological inquiry and a means of preventing the discipline from relapsing into

> . . . an intellectual adolescence that has been outgrown. All speak to the idiographic in human experience when it is in dynamic relationship to the nomothetic, the disjunctive linked with the functional, conflict harnessed with system. Although reaching beyond the traditional language of science, the metaphors they offer point toward a presumptive base for sociology that is itself interactive. If the dialectic does not seriously challenge conflict and system for paradigmatic status in the 1970s, it will not be because of inadequate formal credentials. (297)

Regardless of one's misgivings about the substantive merit of this dialectical paradigm, Friedrichs's own aspirations for its success are abundantly clear. He suggests that the generally esteemed origins and credentials of his dialectial paradigm will facilitate its adoption and that a bandwagon effect on its behalf will take hold in the discipline. His aspirations are well founded in light of the fashion process, for they illustrate some important features of its operation. A proposal likely to succeed, first of all, seems dramatically to overthrow traditional practices while nevertheless faithfully adhering to the collective tastes of the public and appearing to reflect many or all of the divergent and popular styles associated with older and competing proposals, and second, is packaged in a seemingly "relevant" and "up-to-date" manner designed for immediate expression and conveyance to the now-generation.

The Prophetic, the Priestly, and the End of Ideology in Friedrichs's Paradigm

Friedrichs loosely defines the "prophetic mode" in sociology as analogous to the divinely inspired visionaries who appear in the Old Testament, and the "priestly mode" as analogous to the faithful witnesses to order, continuity, and the sacred past revealed in the same document.[3] These are the concepts he uses to account for oscillations between periods of crisis, restlessness, and disarray on the one hand, and order, tranquillity, and consensus on the other hand. Whatever their aesthetic appeal, these vague and far-fetched analogies to the role of prophets and priests lead Friedrichs to discuss the conflict between the views of Mills and Parsons on the nature of sociology as though it were an abstract, moralistic, epistemological debate only distantly if at all related to real struggles for power in the larger society.[4] These analogies similarly lead him to neglect the need for analyzing the actual effect of political confrontations and theoretical debates in the discipline upon the consciousness of sociologists as members of professional societies.[5] One concrete and increasingly evident effect of such confrontation and debate, for example, is the gradual democratization and partial radicalization of the membership of the American Sociological Association. This effect was manifested by the election of Alfred McClung Lee as president of the Association. Although Lee was an active supporter of the Union of Radical Sociologists and an outspoken critic of ahistorical scholarship, one would be unable to describe, anticipate, or explain his victory in that strongly contested election if one were restricted to the claims and tools of analysis found in *A Sociology of Sociology*. However, it is precisely in the failure of Friedrichs's analysis that the clues to its success can be discerned. He does not discuss the lingering and haunting issues of confrontation that many members of the profession hoped to forget.[6] His imagery of "crisis" in modern sociology—as though it could be ended by a semantic reconciliation of the concepts of order and conflict into a new paradigm of dialectical theory, as though prophets and priests can resolve their differences through incantations of a revealed pluralism—offers reassurance to those who fear for the future of their discipline and their identity within it.[7]

The crisis in the professional identity of American sociologists, as already noted, stemmed from a well-founded alarm over the embarrassment of riches in the competing theoretical models, research methods, fields of specialization, priorities for research, criteria of validity, and polarized schools of thought (including factions and cults forming around individual opinion leaders, ideological and regional differences) in the discipline. Intense conflicts erupted over the legitimacy of Marxism and political activism inside and outside the classroom, inside and outside leading research centers, inside and outside the jurisdiction of the profession itself; these conflicts tended to reflect and exacerbate the growing sense of alarm already felt throughout the discipline in the 1960s and early 1970s. Kuhn's image of the scientific community readily allows for the interpretation (1) that "pluralism" in the scientific community may well be a sign of intellectual maturity and professional wisdom; (2) that polarization and the embarrassment of riches are no longer the symptoms of a chaotic and relativistic potpourri of largely irreconcilable assumptions; and (3) that even the struggle between conservative and radical views is not a sign of crisis as long as its overt manifestations are modulated through the customary channels of debate and deference to the sovereignty of professional canons of good taste. What had appeared as a terrible liability to the profession, a real threat to its credibility and legitimacy, was now reinterpreted as an asset. Robert Friedrichs quickly seized upon the opportunity to adopt this interpretation of Kuhn's model as though it were a conclusive, authoritative, and forward-looking justification of this pluralism:

> When one begins to perceive sociology as concerned fundamentally with the "puzzles" centered about the compulsive hold of given social constructions and "normal" science (and thus sociology) wed immediately to a dialectical epistemology, then Kuhn's exclusively natural scientific claim to the crucial role of "exemplars" also dissolves.
>
> Of more general interest, I suspect, was my conclusion that

the sociology of the 1970s would evidence an increase in paradigmatic options, and that we would begin to tolerate that pluralism as a measure of our scientific maturity. (xxvii)

Friedrichs proceeds to make explicit an argument pervading much of his own work as well as that of other prominent sociologists who wish to minimize or dissipate the appearance of the crisis facing the discipline without resolving its underlying political and theoretical causes:

> The phrase "orthodox sociology" is rapidly disappearing from our seminars and learned papers, except when offered within an historically descriptive context. Both undergraduate and graduate students are reading Goffman, Skinner, Lévi-Strauss, the Marx of the "Grundrisse," "West Coast" and "East Coast" phenomenology, classic and contemporary Anarchism, Merleau-Ponty, Sartre, and Hegel, whether or not they have been assigned. A new Black Ibn Khaldun has been rediscovered. (xxvii)

Friedrichs ignores the possibility that this new eclecticism has become an orthodoxy in its own right. How can one decide whether this panoply of new interests in the discipline is evidence of intellectual maturity and creativity or a sign of growing incoherence, self-indulgent eclecticism, and what Sorokin has menacingly called the "fads and foibles of modern sociology"? What theoretical perspective might serve to distinguish the more valid ideas from the less valid ones, the important from the trivial, the scholarly from the dilettantish in this flood of unreconciled ideas, interests, and cults surrounding Goffman at one extreme and a "new Black Ibn Khaldun" at another? It was precisely because these questions were urgent and no clear answers were in sight that influential and prestigious sociologists felt impelled to call for the arrival of a Newton to show the way out of intellectual anarchy, a Prometheus to burn down the Tower of Babel and offer an eternal light in its place. Friedrichs argues that the questions themselves are in error; that his own receipt of the coveted Sorokin Award, bestowed upon him by a newly enlightened profession, is proof of the scientific status of sociology; that intellectual diversity is inherently a virtue and not a vice:

> There may be, however, less unanimity over a concomitant growth in pluralistic "tolerance" on the part of those on either side of the lectern. Still, if the publishing houses stand, as I believe they do, as indicators of a discipline's consumptive tolerance range, they offer an encouraging sign. And to discover the American Sociological Association honoring Oliver Cox, Harrison White, and the present author with its highest purely symbolic honors has at least convinced the latter that his projection

of the likely extension of the profession's (to be distinguished from the discipline's) pluralistic tolerance had been considerably underestimated both in speed and in breadth. (xxvii–xxviii)

Friedrichs makes clear the ideological importance of Kuhn's paradigm in the task of appearing to solve the crisis of modern sociology by (1) institutionalizing its scope within manageable boundaries and (2) redefining it as the "coming of age" of the new sociology:

> Indeed [Kuhn] is quite explicit in contending that a science must have reached a level of maturation beyond the mere eclectic assemblage of competing "schools" to qualify for inclusion beneath the umbrella he raises. But if one were to apply Kuhn's posture to the behavioral sciences, it would be possible to conceive of the divisive struggle currently being waged within sociology not as humiliating proof of the discipline's relative immaturity but as evidence of its coming of age. It might enable us to ignore the incessant demand that we profess ourselves worthy of the label "scientific" and instead get on with both the routines and the revolutions that are thereby our nature. Rather than running in embarrassment from evidence of fundamentally competitive models, we might find we were justified by them. (2–3)

Friedrichs's Modification of Kuhn's Paradigm and the Uses of the Sociology of Knowledge

Friedrichs's major modification of Kuhn's paradigm is to take issue with the customary meaning of intellectual pluralism and to propose that such diversity should be newly interpreted as a sign of normal as well as revolutionary science at an advanced stage in the development of sociology.

> Revolutions by definition imply the overthrow of the orthodox and the acquisition of supreme power by the victorious combatant, while the revolutionary model itself was projected as infinitely repetitive. Kuhn's error is precisely where one might expect it to lie: with the fact that, trained in the physical sciences, he brought to his task the assumption of recurrence native to that province. . . . For in an exercise such as his own the very knowledge we gain of the periodic cresting of paradigmatic revolutions may be fed back as a new and unique factor in sciences' communal life, enabling the latter to break with the compulsive routines that would lead once again to monopoliza-

tion of orthodoxy by a single paradigm. As a result, "revolution" may, after a time, no longer be the appropriate image. (324–25)

Friedrichs does not specify the conditions under which a knowledge of prior revolutions in a given discipline will affect its communal life. He does not explain why such knowledge is more likely to halt the infinitely repetitive process of paradigmatic revolutions in one discipline rather than another. He does not explain how this final and permanent stage of diversity in the range of approved paradigms can be distinguished from a tendency toward "compulsive routines that would lead once again to monopolization of orthodoxy by a single paradigm." He ignores the possibilities that a pluralistic paradigm can become just as orthodox as a monolithic one; that it too might be ritualized for reasons other than its substantive merit in the scientific community; and that the mere awareness of prior debates and revolutions is hardly adequate to guard against yet another tyranny. He ignores the fact that such historical self-awareness is extremely rare in the social and physical sciences, and that Kuhn, from whom Friedrichs avowedly draws so much inspiration,[8] flatly opposed educating physical scientists in the history of their discipline. Moreover, such self-awareness would be attainable only if the sociology of knowledge were considered central to the appraisal of one's discipline and one's own identity as a scientist. This would enable one to recognize the ongoing interplay between the ideological and theoretical elements in competing paradigms. Otherwise, one would not know what is changing into what in the course of paradigm debates.

How does Friedrichs approach the sociology of knowledge in order to accomplish the formidable and admirable goal of translating an awareness of past paradigmatic revolutions into an appreciation of the "communal life" of science? He goes to considerable lengths to make clear his approach to this area of study:

> One final note: For those who would reduce sociology to the sociology of knowledge, the present volume has been—and cannot help but continue to be—a disappointment, for the author is among the overwhelming majority within the discipline who presume it to be a science, however dialectical in nature. This means that it must assume that there *is* something "out there," accessible to public verification which, though socially constructed, cannot be reduced at any given moment to mere phenomena projected by a prior though "bracketed," perceptual "reality," and rooted in a completely relativized substratum that is "social class," "vested interest," or some other form of "false consciousness." (xxxi)

Exactly why the sociology of knowledge in any way denies the world "out there" Friedrichs does not explain; he further fails to explain why this field of study leads sociologists astray by virtue of its focus on social class, vested interests, and the false consciousness that may produce, reflect, or reinforce definitions of social reality in the discipline of sociology. Friedrichs also does not clarify why claims made by the sociologist of knowledge are or should be exempted from the requirements of proof through "public verification." He does not explain how the "overwhelming majority" of sociologists who may share Friedrichs' impressions can in itself constitute evidence in favor of their accuracy or credibility. But why would a sociologist addressing himself to "the sociology of sociology" ignore precisely those matters, which would appear to be central to his own line of inquiry? Friedrichs answers this question in a most revealing manner:

> Thus, the present venture is in the tradition of the sociology of science, not in that of the sociology of knowledge, as the latter developed on the classic foundations laid by Karl Mannheim. Science condemns itself to normative and descriptive criteria, as Thomas Kuhn has been among the latest of a lengthy lineage to testify. There is "good" scientific practice and "bad" scientific practice . . . and this exercise must be judged accordingly. It must not be judged on the assumption that all that is of concern to sociology—or to a sociology of sociology—simply reflects the relativized interests of a given stratum or biography. (xxxi–xxxii)

Friedrichs does not consider that the sociology of science and the sociology of knowledge are neither logically nor empirically separable in anything like the hard-and-fast terms he takes for granted and that little is gained by arbitrarily bifurcating still further the specializations and subspecializations in the scientific community. Indeed, his conception of the "prophetic" and "priestly" modes, although ahistorical and often ambiguous in its own right, is strikingly similar to Mannheim's conception of "utopian" and "ideological" modes of thought.[9] (His brief and incidental references to Mannheim's work miss this instructive convergence entirely.) If Friedrichs had recognized the extent to which he was working in the sociology of knowledge and exhuming categories of analysis that long ago were delimited historically and rigorously by other sociologists of knowledge, he might have utilized these substantial intellectual resources instead of overlooking them, undertaken to examine critically the ideological assumptions of his own worldview instead of denying them, and illuminated the oscillating modes of thought in his dialectical paradigm instead of myopically identifying them in terms of "the sociology of science."

Friedrich's confusion about the means by which self-awareness is achieved is symptomatically expressed in his decision to damn the sociology of knowledge with faint praise:

> Yet to acknowledge a firm and crucial place to a sociology of knowledge that roots itself in a Mannheimian relativism is not to reduce sociology itself or this exercise in the sociology of science, in solipsistic fashion, to it. Exceedingly persistent "order" in human action over time is available to public verification by the perceptive and trained craftsman, as is the opportunity to contribute to its dialectical denial as awareness of that order is bent back upon the site from which it was precipitated to permit and encourage its transcendence. (xxxii)

For Friedrichs, then, the failure to recognize exceedingly persistent order in human affairs is tantamount to solipsism. How did he discover this allegedly universal order? Did he employ intuitionism or accept the prevailing ideological bias in favor of order as self-evident or devise some new system of thought that yielded this discovery? There is no special reason why his version of "dialectical theory" should lead to it, for such a paradigm might just as well favor conflict over order or simply assume endless cycles of order and conflict, persistence and change, social statics and dynamics, with no meaning or purpose behind all this oscillation. Friedrichs's paradigm is subject to an infinite range of logically possible interpretations in this regard, and the arbitrary one he chooses to advance deserves careful review.

Although he repeatedly insists on the need for objectivity and the public verifiability of all sociological claims, Friedrichs does not indicate the reasoning or the data by which other scientists might verify his own sweeping assertion about the nature of social order. His exhortations in defense of a "hard" sociology of science are hardly sufficient to satisfy the need he himself emphasizes. Some sociologists, for example, do not see the scientific community in general or the discipline of sociology in anything like the pluralistic, consensual, and orderly state of armistice that Friedrichs takes for granted. Still others see the "order" in the political system as a largely coerced, manipulated, and temporary outcome of underlying contradictions not only within a single society but also in the context of advanced capitalist societies and the Third World. Are their observations about socialist trends in Greece, Portugal, Turkey, and Italy, as well as in Latin America and Southeast Asia, and about the often violent struggles of the Irish Republican Army, the Vietnamese National Liberation Front, the once-active Front for the Liberation of Quebec, the Thai Student Movement, and similar movements to be classified as "solipsistic" because they fail to see the "exceedingly persistent order" prescribed by Friedrichs? These sociologists would, according to Friedrichs's criteria, fail to measure up to the standards of "perceptive and trained craftsmen" in the discipline.

Friedrichs's approach to the sociology of knowledge is plainly to repudiate it and all that it implies for purposes of investigating the scientific community. He fails to acknowledge that the innuendo he heaps upon this field of study—with accusations that it is solipsist, relativistic, antiempirical, impressionistic—is for the most part a distortion of Mannheim's work in the sociology of knowledge and a caricature of the forms of investigation carried out in this field as a whole.[10] He seems equally unaware that his impatience with this field might be symptomatic of an institutionalized reluctance to examine the prevailing tendency toward self-celebration rather than self-criticism in sociology as well as an uncritical faith in the mystique of "hard science" in a discipline still deeply apprehensive about its security and respectability in the academic world.[11]

Despite the alleged synthesis of "conflict" theory and "system" theory in his dialectical paradigm, despite the alleged transcendence from the postures of engagement and value-neutrality he believes he has achieved, Friedrichs concedes that this paradigm is singularly unhelpful in providing any guidelines to ascertain the validity of competing claims in the discipline's embarrassment of riches:

> It is with the social sciences, however, that one should expect the pluralistic motif to come to the fore initially. Hard evidence in support of one paradigm to the exclusion of another is too difficult to come by to dull the social scientist's appreciation of the long-range value of "peaceful" paradigmatic co-existence. . . . For sociology, the candidacy of the "dialectic" would be immeasurably strengthened. For it, like the paradigm of "democracy" in the truly pluralistic state, grants a place to competing paradigms, if but a secondary place. Loyalties to competing paradigms within either the "dialectical" or the "democratic" frames play active and fruitful roles. (325)

But who shall be the arbiter of various claims concerning the "active and fruitful roles" of one perspective rather than another? Does the alleged existence of a pluralistic social order necessarily justify the notion that a pluralistic scientific community is the highest stage of development for all disciplines? Friedrichs maintains that only those who are committed to the "larger *gestalt*" are competent to serve as arbiters in answering these questions and judging whether a given perspective is "fruitful" or harmful for the discipline. He implies that any future attack on pluralism in science is tantamount to an attack on pluralism in modern civilization itself:

> With the growing realization that all specific conceptual and empirical activity within a science is dependent ultimately upon a larger "given" *gestalt*, scientific communities may themselves come to accept a fundamental pluralism as an appropriate style of life of scientific mind just as much of the larger populace of the West has come to accept pluralism in civic and religious life as an appropriate response to an awareness of the repetitive nature of revolutions in the history of the civic sphere. There is, indeed, some slim evidence available that this has in fact already begun to occur within the natural sciences. (325)

Friedrichs does not document the "slim evidence" of this trend toward pluralism in the natural sciences. Even if such evidence were available, however, it would not be an argument in favor of a similar trend for sociology. Friedrichs himself goes so far as to insist repeatedly on the fundamental disparity between the social and natural sciences:

> I have never claimed that there was complete symmetry between the biography of a social science such as sociology and any of the natural sciences; indeed, *the nature of their fundamental disparity is the central message of my book.* Paradoxically, however, I have found it necessary to *posit* their identity in order to establish the conditions under which their distinctive epistemological features may be precipitated. (xxvi–xxvii; emphasis added)

Although he does find it necessary to perceive the natural and social sciences as fundamentally irreconcilable for some ideological purposes and identical for other purposes, the fact remains that a system of language and logic for one discipline cannot be assumed a priori to be suitable for another discipline having an entirely different subject matter and set of problems. Such suitability is problematic and must be critically investigated, evaluated, and documented in each case rather than arbitrarily "posited" and taken for granted when convenient for a rhetorical purpose. One should recall that Kuhn emphasized in his *Structure of Scientific Revolution* that he refrained from applying his paradigm for the physical sciences even to the biological sciences, much less the social sciences, because of the complexity of these fields and his insufficient command of their history.

Can one ascertain the validity of competing paradigms by examining their relative success in solving major problems that have been defined as such by past and present scientists? Can one ascertain their validity by examining the major shortcomings and failures of these paradigms in the historical development of the discipline? Can one take into account the insights, oversights, struggles, and lasting contributions of the most profound scientists who created and consolidated the discipline? Friedrichs answers these questions by praising the writers of survey textbooks in sociology and echoing Kuhn's answers to these same questions:

> The writers themselves now see the discipline's history *through* the new paradigm, and in all good faith select, rephrase and emphasize as the main current of the discipline that thread of research and theory, among the many threads that had been spun, which indeed led most directly to the new *gestalt*. The rest, like forms of pre-hominid man-ape that succumbed to the vicissitudes of geological change and biological competition, are simply dropped from the lineage, although their ancestries and successes were, to a crucial moment, just as significant as those that survived in the new paradigm. *A science that hesitates to forget its fathers, Whitehead warned us, is lost.* . . . With each revolution the discipline re-draws its family tree. (10; emphasis added)

Friedrichs therefore answers the aforementioned questions in the negative. Since his dialectical paradigm and the advent of pluralism have withstood the test of time and witnessed the demise of other paradigms, they are, according to his reasoning, the prevailing *gestalt* in which lesser paradigms may be privileged to come and go; he asserts that they represent the survival of the fittest truth, the ultimate and most inviolate stage of development for sociology as a science:

> Within the context of that lineage we may be in a position to claim only that one paradigm is more satisfactory than another. *The ultimate paradigm stands inviolate.* The general thesis that Kuhn proffers, then, stands in the highest tradition of the sociology of knowledge and its more youthful progeny, the sociology of science. (10; emphasis added)[12]

Friedrichs's arguments against serious consideration of the sociology of knowledge should be recapitulated. First, sociology is an empirical science rather than a solipsistic philosophy, and the sociology of knowledge leads to solipsism and introspection rather than objective and empirical inquiry. Second, the "good" and "bad" aspects of inquiry must themselves be judged by normative criteria; since these normative criteria are given as presuppositions, no useful purpose would be served by critically examining them. Third, the logical and empirical verification of Friedrichs's dialectical view and his espousal of pluralism would especially be hindered rather than facilitated by an application of the sociology of knowledge, for this would be tantamount to an exercise in solipsism.

Instead of giving evidence to support his dialectical and pluralistic image of sociology, Friedrichs offers his impression of a conversation with a Soviet sociologist:

> The author himself was witness to the suggestion by a prominent Soviet colleague in the context of an informal discussion that system theory might well be appropriate for the analysis of social structure while dialectical theory was reserved for the analysis of social dynamics. (326)

Friedrichs is suggesting that one should be a functionalist when American society is stable and a Marxist when it is unstable, and that this situationally determined posture is validated because it was recommended by an unnamed Soviet colleague. This suggestion is substantively untenable because these perspectives entail vastly different sets of assumptions, methods of investigation, and conceptions of the historical role of the researcher himself as a participant in the reality being investigated. A Marxist perspective, for example, does not allow for American society to be seen as an inherently self-stabilizing social structure while the functionalist perspective not only allows for this view but actually requires it as the point of departure for the study of "moving equilibrium." Without making some kind of rigorous evaluation of these perspectives, one would not be able to tell whether the society in question was "static" or "dynamic" at a given time or whether the functionalist or Marxist perspective was appropriate to the study of that society. Even more striking than the substantive untenability of Friedrichs's suggestion, however, is that he repeatedly denounces all forms of relativism only to conclude that his own choice of theoretical models should be determined by the immediate social situation from time to time, from place to place, from static to dynamic period, ad infinitum.

Friedrichs all but concedes this extreme relativism by observing that he is in doubt over not only the relevance of the system and conflict models to the investigation of concrete problems and situations but also the merit of a social-psychological ("prophetic" and "intrasubjective") orientation versus a sociological ("priestly" and "intersubjective") orientation for enhancing the image of the discipline:

Informed by the dialogical nature of the relationship between intra- and intersubjective experience, I would both expect and encourage a pluralism at the level of substantive paradigm. Although the prophetic and the priestly modes enlighten one's image of the fundamental nature of sociology's subject matter, the former is rooted in a sensitivity to the intrasubjective, the latter in a preferential response to the intersubjective. (327)

Whatever Friedrichs's pretensions to originality and his vagueness in the treatment of his basic concepts, one should note again that the prophetic mode corresponds in some important respects to what Mannheim meant by "utopia" and what Kuhn meant by "revolutionary" science;[13] the priestly mode corresponds to what Mannheim meant by "ideology" and what Kuhn meant by "normal" science. He ignores the fact that a given mode of thought has no intrinsic properties or a life of its own, and that it has meaning only insofar as it is conveyed, used, and interpreted by social participants. What may seem to be "psychological" may actually be a social transaction; what may seem to be a highly structured and ritualized situation may actually be a product of strong sentiments on the part of one or more participants and have little or no meaning apart from their definition of it. In the context of the scientific community or any other sphere of group life, for example, social interaction can take place by way of self-reflection on an "intrasubjective" level. Individual sentiments may inspire and be produced by social interaction on an "intersubjective" level.

Review of Friedrich's Modification of Kuhn's Paradigm: On Permanent Revolution and Maturity in American Sociology

Kuhn's image of the scientific community assumes that competition among many assumptions and worldviews takes place in the revolutionary period of paradigm debates; that these assumptions and worldviews emerge in the long run as a consequence of anomalies in normal research; that such competition is evidence of the scientific maturity of a given discipline. This image of the scientific community allows for the interpretation that an endless array of competing paradigms, questions, and answers in the scientific community is a necessary or natural stage of development in the progress of the community itself. If what Kuhn sees as just one phase in the cycles of progress (from normal to revolutionary and back to normal science) could be reinterpreted as a new and permanent stage of progress (revolutionary science at all times), then it follows that intellectual pluralism is prima facie evidence of the maturity of the discipline. By virtue of such a *tour de force*, the discipline of sociology could represent itself simultaneously as a mature as well as progressive science, as a normal as well as revolutionary science, as having whatever image or thrust its otherwise warring factions might wish to behold.

What had once appeared as a terrible liability to sociology as a science might yet be reinterpreted as a vital asset, as a sign of the rebirth and new maturity of American sociology. If only the appropriate criticisms and modifications of Kuhn's paradigm would be made and the restyled paradigm certified as the true representation of the discipline, then what had appeared a Tower of Babel could be conceived anew as though it were the embodiment of scholarly ferment, freedom for all points of view, and scientific maturity in its final and most advanced stage of development.

Robert Friedrichs quickly seized upon the opportunity to elaborate just such a model as though it were a conclusive justification and, indeed, even a celebration of intellectual pluralism. He received the coveted Sorokin Award for articulating a paradigm that not only legitimizes this pluralism but also implies that there is no need ever to reconcile or choose among the countless treasures in the discipline's embarrassment of riches. Kuhn's emergence as an esteemed figure in American sociology is partly to be explained by virtue of his answer to the call for a Newton who would reconcile the polarized views in the discipline and rescue its members from the uncertainty, apprehension, and turmoil festering within it. The many possibilities for the interpretation of his vague and ambiguous paradigm and Friedrichs's articulation of precisely the one that could symbolically appear to extricate sociology from its crises thus served to transform doubt and fear about the future of the discipline into a source of pride and confidence about its newly revealed maturity. This is why Friedrichs's paradigm is hailed as a major breakthrough in keeping abreast of or just a step ahead of latest developments, and even "internationalizing" the level of debate by transcending the provincial concerns of sociology.

Regardless of the empirical and theoretical difficulties arising from the adoption of this paradigm, it served to end the milling process and to create the appearance of a daring solution attractive to most sociologists and offensive to none. To declare one's endorsement of it is to ensure oneself of displaying good taste in the eyes of one's peers in the higher as well as the lower circles of American sociology.

Friedrichs' interpretation of the widespread view that sociology was in a "crisis" or "at the end of its tether" is open to serious question. He occasionally treats the "crisis" of modern sociology in the 1970s as a prior assumption or point of departure for the elaboration of his allegedly dialectical and pluralistic synthesis of competing models. At other times he presents it as a conclusion of his research, as a culmination of other crises in the 1950s and 1960s. At still other times he vacillates in depicting the crisis as ominous, only to suggest that it could be readily overcome by the adoption of his own modified version of Kuhn's paradigm of scientific revolution. At yet other times he suggests that since sociology is a science, and since Kuhn asserts that every normal science must naturally go through its share of revolutions or crises, the turbulent times are to be settled by a new era of tranquil introspection:

> System theory, particularly the Parsonian variety, was seen simply as providing justification for the conservative impulse dominating the post-war period. The stubborn anomaly that resisted solution was "change"—*fundamental social change.* . . . The significance of the flood of critical pieces is impossible to deny. Seen within the framework of Kuhn's image of the development of a scientific discipline over time, they signaled the breakup of the consolidation that had been occurring since World War II around the system paradigm and an almost random search for an alternative.
>
>   . . . Clearly, both the *ad hoc* adjustments and the stubborn resistance that Kuhn sets forth as characteristic of the early stages of a scientific revolution were abundantly evident as sociology moved from the consensus of the 'fifties to the division of the 'sixties. As frustration over a fundamental anomaly lengthens into crisis, the scientific discipline involved, Kuhn notes, becomes archly self-conscious.[14]

In his textual exegesis of Kuhn's monograph, however, Friedrichs presents little actual evidence to support either Kuhn's or his own view of the disciplinary crisis. Exactly how and when opinion leaders in the mainstream of the discipline became "archly self-conscious," for example, remains unspecified. In view of Friedrichs's lack of critical self-awareness in most of his own research, moreover, it is most difficult to discern just what criteria he might have in mind in referring to the "self-consciousness" with which any scientific discipline responds to an alleged crisis.

   Although the image of the scientific community advanced by Kuhn and Friedrichs does not substantively resolve the issues besetting the discipline, it should not be lightly dismissed as though it were an altogether misleading and unhelpful conception of sociology today. It is unique among paradigms about the nature of modern sociology insofar as it does by implication recognize that the discipline is prepared at best to acknowledge these issues on a level of abstract permissiveness and that the day of reckoning will have to be postponed until such time as they can be seriously debated and settled.

Despite its appeal, this image obscures the importance of these festering issues and falsely implies that the crisis of Western sociology can be resolved or dissipated under the banner of intellectual pluralism. But it nevertheless permits a discipline allegedly at the end of its tether as it approached the 1970s a respite from the eruption of struggles based on real political, ideological, and theoretical differences that could not be reconciled. Those radicals who had not yet been drummed out of academia could welcome the attendant decline in overtly repressive measures; conservatives could all the more welcome the de facto armistice in a battle they were not certain of winning; and moderates could welcome the opportunity to pursue the kind of uncontroversial, banal, middle-range research that had been the mainstay of the discipline during its stage as a "normal science" (i.e., prior to the polarization of the discipline).[15] We will see later that the image of the scientific community advanced by Kuhn and Friedrichs helped to establish a suitable ideological climate for the adoption of an even more "mature" version of dialectical sociology in the work of Jeffrey Alexander, that the collective tastes in a crisis-ridden discipline continued to call for new saviors and new mystifications to enter center stage well into the 1980s.

CHAPTER 5
SOROKIN, MERTON, AND THE MANY FACES OF THE FASHION PROCESS

Sorokin's *Fads and Foibles in Modern Sociology and Related Sciences* is an indictment of the social sciences for their failure to establish rational criteria for evaluating the many schools of thought that compete for acceptance; the evidence he assembles in support of this indictment is massive. Although two decades have passed since this work was originally published, most social scientists still respond to it with studied indifference or outspoken denunciation rather than serious acknowledgment. Although Sorokin must be credited for raising fundamental questions about the current state of the social sciences, his indictment is really just a preamble to his major arguments on behalf of the philosophy of integralism — his approach to the intellectual and moral rehabilitation of the social sciences in the twentieth century. His indictment must be taken into account in any informed appraisal of the social sciences. But the hostility and anti-intellectualism with which prominent scholars continue to refer to some of his work, especially *Fads and Foibles in Modern Sociology*, have already been shown in the analysis of Horton's review of it; such vitriolic responses have helped to drive the book out of print and increasingly into the oblivion for which Horton and others agitated all along.[1] But the further implications of Sorokin's indictment and the ultimate solution he wishes to advance are by no means self-evident. His major arguments must be critically examined to ascertain whether (1) he successfully explains the fashion process in the social sciences; (2) he, like Kroeber and Simmel, is himself unwittingly caught up in the fashion process; (3) both of these possibilities are true; or (4) neither of them is true.

Sorokin argues that chaos now prevails in the social sciences in general and sociology in particular; that it can be eliminated only by the adoption of his integralist perspective; that it is so pervasive, so taken for granted, as to be unrecognizable by the vast majority of sociologists who are themselves the naive creatures of the sensate culture responsible for this chaos in the first place. Sensate culture, he maintains, is nothing less than the decadence of Western civilization and its various institutions (particularly including the social sciences): its defining characteristics are relativism, eclecticism, cynicism, dehumanization, egoism, sensualism, and scientism. Sorokin further argues that modern civilization is already beginning to move away from this still-dominant sensate culture and that a rebirth of absolutist, sublime, and altruistic culture is insight. Integralism, his own synthesis of these "sensate" and "ideational" extremes, is the perspective that he believes can rescue sociology from the chaos in which it is floundering.

Sorokin's arguments rest on the premises that chaos reigns unchecked in the social sciences and that it is caused by the sensate culture, which is allegedly internalized by social scientists and in turn translated into nonsensical jargon by them. But does Sorokin's own evidence of fads and foibles in the social sciences really support his interpretation of this chaos? To maintain that sensate culture is the necessary and sufficient cause of the Tower of Babel is to assume that the edifice exists in the hopelessly chaotic state alleged by Sorokin. Let us examine this assumption more closely.

First, the demonstration of a vast number of ambiguous and even patently absurd doctrines abounding in sociology does not necessarily prove that chaos prevails therein. For example, members of the discipline give far more weight to some doctrines competing for acceptance than others; moreover, some doctrines endure far longer than others as serious competitors in the academic marketplace. Sorokin himself points out that many doctrines come and go, often in rapid succession but sometimes only slowly and after bitter internecine struggles are waged; that only a few of these doctrines (e.g., functionalism and positivism) are salient to the prominent journals and opinion leaders in the discipline; and that very powerful orthodoxies and sanctions operate to exclude any perspectives that are deemed too "far out" or offensive in the eyes of those in the mainstream of various disciplines. The denunciations as well as the silent treatment accorded to some of Sorokin's own writings further serve to illustrate that the chaos is more apparent than real, that a filtering and screening process is indeed operative to elevate some doctrines to remarkable success and to suppress others with an equally chilling efficacy. In short, the fact that the selection process is not governed by any rational and explicit criteria does not mean that the process operates in a chaotic or random manner.

Second, most of the seemingly sudden and drastic "revolutions" in the social sciences in recent decades have really been efforts to adorn traditional models (e.g., Lundberg's positivism and Pareto's equilibrium theory) in new and more glamorous styles (e.g., Skinner's operant conditioning and Parsons's functional analysis). Most instances of apparent anarchy and flux in social science are really efforts (1) to add minor embellishments to major worldviews; (2) to display the wares of sociology as though the discipline were keeping abreast of the time and affirming its "modernistic" or even "futuristic" public image; (3) to quantify conventional assumptions and observations with greater technical precision; (4) to take advantage of the vagueness of the criteria for evaluating new models and the limited openness of the center of the stage to new opinion leaders; (5) and, most revealingly, to establish the glittering appearance of sensational and incessant changes for which, as Sorokin himself astutely observes, the ahistorical "pioneering Columbuses" are quick to take the credit. As Sorokin further documents in great detail, the idiosyncracies of the researcher, the vagueness of the concepts studied, and the ambiguities built into the methodology of a given investigation often lead to spurious novelties in the findings that are in turn heralded as though they were evidence of great "originality" and "serendipity." But regardless of whose notion of methodology is at the center of attention—for example, Lazarsfeld's metalanguage of mathematical sociology or Hyman's recipes for survey design or more evident variations on these or other themes—the tendency toward ahistorical and conservative theory also continues to gain momentum in American sociology. The appearance of chaos in these tendencies does have a certain reality in the sense that new variations constantly displace old ones on a given set of themes and new opinion leaders occasionally displace old ones in the center of the professional stage. But the orthodoxies themselves, however often they are reinterpreted by a changing cast of characters, are for the most part fixed by the collective tastes of participants in the scientific community; these collective tastes reflect and reinforce the dominant interests, values, and traditions in the discipline as they respond to new internal crises and to developments in the larger society. Indeed, the advent of concentrated fiscal and ideological resources in a few elite universities helps to explain why some of the opinion leaders who rise to great prominence tend to retain their status for decades; these opinion leaders not only work hard to keep their finger on the ever-changing pulse of the profession but also have the resources to enforce their particular interpretations of the latest developments with far greater efficacy than do colleagues with similar talents but less prestigious academic affiliations. Parsons at Harvard, Merton at Columbia, and Janowitz at Chicago are examples of the steadiness with which articulate, prolific, and orthodox opinion leaders can effectively crystallize the shifting tastes in American sociology. While peripheral rivals surface from year to year as aspiring candidates for center stage, they are soon displaced by other contenders who are themselves also destined to be quickly forgotten in the shadow of the major opinion leaders. Sorokin's characterization of an infinite variety of fads, foibles, opinions, and opinion leaders in the discipline is highly misleading and in need of further scrutiny.

On the one hand, Sorokin's name has been in part maligned and in part forgotten; some of his work has been actively and effectively suppressed. On the other hand, some of his ideas have become a highly influential legacy as his students, followers, and critics alike continue to devise increasingly sophisticated versions of his "theory of social systems" in accordance with the latest trends in mathematical formalization and ahistorical determinism. Sorokin's students and followers (many of whom stand accused of plagiarism by Sorokin himself) have been more sensitively attuned than their mentor to the tastes of an increasingly policy-oriented sociological profession and the exigencies of a programmed and orchestrated mass society.[2] Although the flux, the anarchy, the Tower of Babel in sociology might appear to take on a life of their own, although the proliferating concepts and fields of specialization might seem to be out of control, although the pretenders to the thrones at Harvard and Columbia and Chicago seem to rise and fall in dizzying succession, the fact remains that an underlying and remarkable continuity is maintained and opinion leaders embellish it with ever-changing styles of adornment.

Although Sorokin appears at first glance to be investigating the fashion process in the scientific community, the internal logic of his analysis rules out such an investigation. Let us examine this logic in terms of the causal sequences he has in mind:

(1) The sensate culture has placed modern sociology in the grip of irrational, anti-intellectual, dehumanizing, chaotic forces; its symptoms in the discipline are found in the endless range of fads and foibles displayed by its academic practitioners.

(2) Sociologists have internalized the sensate culture in toto; they are the unwitting agents or creatures of this cultural system.

(3) Only by a program of moral rearmament, a spiritual reconsti-
tution, and restoration of faith in absolutism and altruism,
can modern sociology and sociologists, and civilization itself,
be saved.

Sorokin's analysis ignores entirely the distant characteristics of modern
society leading social participants to feel apprehensive about the future,
to keep in step with the times, to seek to reconcile the appearance of
novelty and the reality of convention in everyday life; he ignores the milling process in the collective behavior of social participants, including sociologists, and is therefore led to the vague, abstract, and simplistic conclusion that sociologists are blindly driven by the sensate culture to act
in an irrational, idiosyncratic, and bizarre manner. Sorokin depicts sociologists as virtual automatons in the scientific community (or "sociocultural subsystem"), which is in turn predetermined by the society
(or "sociocultural system") as a whole. His refusal to acknowledge the
reflective intelligence of those who are ideologically offensive to him,
his failure to examine the degree to which the "foibles" of sociologists
are responses to the alienation of their intellectual labor in the knowledge factory, his neglect of the concrete historical conditions under
which scientists can and do transcend the constraints and folkways of
the scientific community are strikingly reminiscent of the myopia already shown in the works of Simmel, Kroeber, Kuhn, and Friedrichs. The
notion of a vast system governing the thoughts and actions of all participants, as though forces beyond human recognition and control inex-
orably unfold their potential or work themselves out in the social arena,
is tantamount to a denial of the very creativity Sorokin claims to cham-
pion in his philosophy of integralism. Although this notion enjoys a hallowed place in the conservative and ahistorical versions of evolutionist
thought, it is based on a false assumption that social participants are inherently the creatures rather than the creators of their environment, the
acquiescent cogs rather than the active producers of historical change,
the actors in someone else's script.

   Sorokin is quick to condemn his many students and, indeed, the entire profession, for their immorality and to exhort them (as well as his
many critics and enemies) to mend their ways, but he fails to consider
that his own work might also be very much a part of the dominant worldview in American society. He calls so much attention to the vast number
of fads (i.e., the frivolous, short-lived, episodic developments) in sociology as to obscure the great degree to which certain prior assumptions
and worldviews concerning functionalism and positivism enjoy
prolonged salience in the work of most sociologists. He is so preoc-

cupied with exposing the spurious novelties and eccentricities of individual researchers as to lose sight of the fact that many of these foibles
are given but little attention even when they are "in the running" and are
quickly forgotten in any case. Although he claims to have transcended
all of the biases in American culture by virtue of faithful adherence to
the philosophy of integralism, the fact remains that his obsession with
exposing wrongdoing and denouncing it on moral grounds as a sign of
hopeless decadence rather than explaining it in historically specific
terms is very much a part of the liberal muckraking tradition in American
journalism and scholarship. Whatever the contributions of muckrakers
to liberal reform movements, they tend to cultivate the dangerously misleading impression that the mere exposure of a given scandal (e.g.,
domestic counterintelligence by the CIA, graft, or plagiarism for that
matter) is somehow sufficient to eliminate or at least ameliorate the
problem. But because they ignore the underlying structural, ideological,
and social-psychological conditions that generate these practices, even
the most valiant efforts of muckrakers more often than not lead only to
an increased use of camouflage and subterfuge by the culprits rather
than a sustained struggle to eliminate the systemic causes of the scandals themselves.

Sorokin's analysis therefore distorts the stable as well as the change-
ful aspects of the scientific community. The excessively static bias is introduced by characterizing scientists as predetermined in their cognitive activity by the sensate culture and insisting that sensate culture itself
must rise and fall because of the allegedly universal "principle of limits"
that governs it. The excessively dynamic bias is introduced by depicting
the discipline of sociology as though it were inundated with ever-
changing fads and foibles that have supposedly gotten out of control
and that are on borrowed time because of the incessant operation of the
cyclical forces in history.

But what makes for this continuity in a context of apparently incessant change? What brings about this orthodoxy in a seemingly chaotic
Tower of Babel? Just how do the major opinion leaders manage to preserve their stature in the discipline of sociology? The prevailing orthodoxies and opinion leaders are clearly not selected by any public tri-
bunal of scholars abiding by rational criteria for the evaluation of
competing models and opinion leaders or "fashion dudes": Sorokin
demonstrates that no rational criteria for such selection are operative in
modern sociology. But to claim abstractly that the "sensate culture" is
responsible for this state of affairs, to prophesy that integralism will inevitably or automatically cleanse the discipline of its "decadent" orthodoxies and opinion leaders, is to ignore the evidence that specific

ideological configurations, class interests, modes of discourse, and collective tastes are represented by those opinion leaders who do occupy center stage. However faddish or whimsical they may seem, the usually ineffective thrusts and parries of erstwhile pretenders to stardom must be understood in this context. The opinion leaders who are most responsive and successful in making these representations are considered the "superstars" of the discipline, not because they necessarily impart objective sociological truth to the scientific community, but rather because they have managed to reflect, accommodate, reinforce, and crystallize the vague, ambiguous, amorphous collective tastes of the many individuals, groups, and strata constituting the discipline. Because Sorokin fails to examine or even recognize the fashion process in modern societies (and especially in the United States as an advanced capitalist society), his analysis of the fads and foibles in the discipline bogs down in a muckraking exposé of intellectual anarchy on the one hand and ideological orthodoxy on the other hand. However much Sorokin ridicules the anarchy and the orthodoxy, he never attempts to consider the possibility that these seemingly irreconcilable phenomena are actually manifestations of the fashion process; that the anarchy he documents is by no means as indefinite and random as it might seem to be; that the orthodoxy he also documents is by no means as permanent and rigid as it might seem to be; that the regulatory principle behind the oscillations of anarchy and orthodoxy in the scientific community derives not from the immanent workings of sensate culture but rather from the operation of the fashion process in a historically specific context:

> Fashion introduces order in a potentially anarchic and moving present. By establishing suitable models which carry the stamp of propriety and compel adherence, fashion narrowly limits the range of variability and so fosters uniformity and order, even though it be passing uniformity and order. In this respect fashion performs in a moving society a function which custom performs in a settled society.[3]

The major opinion leaders who manage to withstand challenges from aspiring members of the profession, then, are able to maintain their status not so much because they have prestige or coercive resources at their disposal (although such means of influence can indeed be helpful) but rather because they carefully keep abreast of the latest developments without seeming to be too "far out" or "behind the times." They are the most successful "fashion dudes" who adopt and articulate new styles that are collectively considered to be in good taste and that therefore ensure an ongoing continuity in the trends otherwise threatening to become anarchic.[4]

Some Orthodoxies in Sorokin's Own Study of the Fads and Foibles of American Sociologists

Sorokin did not investigate or even acknowledge the continuities between the movement for moral rearmament championed by Christian fundamentalist groups in American society and his own advocacy of integralism. His failure to display any critical self-awareness in the course of his zealous crusade can to some degree be explained in terms of the following circumstances.

First, Sorokin developed his worldview on the basis of a lifetime of personal crises and scholarly endeavors that were unrelated to any American church affiliations; his original affinities for the Russian Orthodox Church may well have blinded him to his actual proximity to domestic versions of revivalism in his adopted land. Second, he emphasized the empirical and secular aspects of altruism, and once had a fierce exchange with J. L. Moreno, the founder of "sociometry," about the comparative virtues and vices of their respective systems; Sorokin was convinced that his kingdom was of this world, and those who vindictively accused him of mysticism only reinforced his judgment that the work of his Center for the Study of Altruism and Creative Integration was an empirically based approach to social science. Although this failure at critical self-awareness is understandable, it ill befits a scholar who devotes himself to exposing and ridiculing the ideological blindness of others to be just as uncritical as they are concerning the easy acceptance of dubious doctrines.

Sorokin himself gives evidence to indicate that his appeal in the social sciences and the humanities was far greater than some of his claims to have been ostracized would indicate.[5] His eventual election to the presidency of the American Sociological Association also suggests that at least some of his work was well received even though his attacks on the sociological profession itself were actively suppressed. But can the limited and favorable reception he did enjoy in the social sciences and humanities be entirely explained in terms of the validity of his sociological studies alone?

Rather than enjoying some limited popularity because of its epistemological merit alone, for example, Sorokin's philosophy of integralism might have appealed in part to those conservative and theologically inspired sectors of the academic community that found the standard rhetoric of evangelicalism too crude, platitudinous, or offensive to their collective tastes. Although Sorokin eagerly and favorably compared his views with those of Kroeber, Spengler, Schweitzer, and other impressive scholars, he might also have considered the possibility of critically comparing his views with those of Billy Graham, Oral Roberts, Herbert Armstrong, and similar evangelists who attracted mass followings in the 1950s and 1960s. Had he done so, he might have been able to recognize the possibility that at least some of his appeal could be attributed to the satisfaction of collective tastes shared by a conservative audience having little or no interest in the objective validity of his sociological principles. Had he done so, moreover, he would have been pursuing in practice the lofty aim of critical self-awareness that, he so often pointed out, was ignored in the work of other sociologists.

Sorokin must be severely criticized for his failure to acknowledge the continuities between the work of Karl Mannheim and the philosophy of integralism.[6] That Sorokin is largely unfamiliar with Mannheim's writings is evident from his failure to note the striking parallels in the work of these two formidable scholars. For example, Mannheim attempted (1) to distillate and synthesize the major worldviews found in various historical epochs and to present the end product as a universal means of overcoming the partial or fragmentary truths of any single worldview; (2) to reaffirm the altruistic and socially cohesive values of Christianity in bringing about a newly planned world order; (3) to show that the manipulative, dehumanizing, stifling, violent order in Western societies must be fundamentally reconstituted rather than merely reformed; and (4) to argue that most of the seemingly objective and value-neutral research done in the name of social science is really the ideological expression of scientism, of the obsessive search for technical precision rather than theoretical comprehension of the human condition. Although Mannheim always cautioned against the dangers of an overdeterministic model of social behavior, he nevertheless endowed ideological and utopian modes of thought with the same kind of unidirectional causal primacy over human affairs[7] that Sorokin, who also polemically inveighed against simplistic single-factor models, imputed to the sensate culture. Mannheim's *Man and Society in an Age of Reconstruction*, *Ideology and Utopia*, and *Freedom, Power and Democratic Planning*, for example, have important themes in common as well as some differences with Sorokin's *Crisis of Our Age*, *Sociocultural Causality, Space, Time*, and *Forms and Techniques of Altruistic and Spiritual Growth*. If Sorokin had critically examined Mannheim's ambitious but abortive efforts to transform the world through moral exhortation and without regard for the necessity of a political constituency, he might have been able to apply the resulting lessons to his own work, to tighten up the arguments he wished to advance, to avoid the naïveté of his erudite predecessor. Sorokin's failure to do so not only detracts from the credibility of his own contributions to the sociology of knowledge but also deprives the scientific community of the opportunity to examine how one of the most articulate advocates of scholarship in the service of human betterment might begin to evaluate and improve upon his own views in light of the unsuccessful efforts of his major precursor. For all of Sorokin's calls for historical and critical self-awareness, then, his own practice as a sociologist of knowledge and his own analysis of irrationality in the discipline of sociology represent major errors from which we should learn rather than precedents on which we should rely in the study of fashions in science.

The Operation of the Fashion Process in Sorokin's Integralist Philosophy

From the discussion of Sorokin's analysis of the fads, foibles, and alleged chaos in the social sciences, one can reasonably infer that his explanation of these phenomena leaves much to be desired and that he failed to heed his own admonitions concerning the need for historical and critical self-awareness. Despite his abstract insistence on the need for the kind of theoretical model that recognizes the complexity of social forces and the subjectivity of the social self, Sorokin's account of fads and foibles in sociology rests on the mechanistic assumption that the sensate culture alone determines the pseudoscientific performance of sociologists who are, essentially, the mindless creatures of this historical epoch. Most damaging to Sorokin's analysis is his failure to investigate or even acknowledge the fashion process in generating and controlling the seemingly endless parade of fads and foibles in American sociology. But what can explain the failure of a sociologist of knowledge to examine his own premises in a critical and historical perspective? Why does Sorokin see fit to compare his work favorably to that of prominent social scientists, conservative philosophers, and internationally eminent theologians and to ignore the crucial similarities and differences between his work and that of the most prominent sociologist, Karl Mannheim, who shared many humanistic goals with him? Why does he consistently ignore the points of similarity between his philosophy of integralism and the varieties of fundamentalism in American society? Why does he assume that integralism will be any more successful in "cleaning up" the immorality and alleged chaos in American sociology than Christian fundamentalism has been in eliminating corruption in American society? In the following effort to answer these questions, Sorokin's own legacy in the sociology of knowledge will be put into perspective; this appraisal will further serve to introduce us to the work of Sorokin's most influential student, Robert K. Merton, a scholar who has also devoted many years to the sociology of the scientific community.

Sorokin might have considered the possibility not only of the fashion process as an impetus to the fads and foibles of sociologists but also of the influence of this process upon his own work. Although he succeeded in meticulously exposing and condemning the relativism and "eclectic hash" in the discipline, he was nevertheless caught up in the same trends he presumed to transcend. The ambitious scope of his integralist philosophy, for example, represents an assemblage of unrelated worldviews, assumptions, and methodologies that Sorokin himself seeks to advance not by demonstrating their synthesis in practice but rather by asserting it in an abstract and dogmatic manner:

> The integralist conception views psychosocial reality as a complex manifold in which we can distinguish at least three different aspects: sensory, rational, and supersensory-superrational. The sensory aspect is present in all psychosocial phenomena that can be perceived through our sense organs. The rational aspect is present in all the rational phenomena of the psychosocial universe; in logically and mathematically consistent systems of science, philosophy, religion, ethics, fine arts, up to the rationally motivated and executed activities of an individual or group. The supersensory-superrational aspect of psychosocial reality is manifested by the highest creative activities and created masterpieces of genius in all fields of cultural activity.[8]

It is significant to note that Sorokin makes no effort whatsoever to apply this allegedly comprehensive approach to the data he himself presents in great detail to document the fads and foibles in modern sociology. Is the "illusion of operationalism," for example, an instance of purely sensory self-indulgence on the part of misguided sociologists? Or is this "illusion" also in part an expression of the search for intuitional truth—especially in view of the mystifications and self-celebrations that Sorokin accurately identifies in the work of such writers as Cottrell, Dodd, and Bridgman? Or is this "illusion" in part an abuse of sensory and rational and supersensory-superrational modes of perceiving reality? If these three aspects of psychosocial reality do exist as a "complex mani-

fold," then how do they concretely influence one another in the instances of operationalism, sham-scientific slang, testomania, quantophrenia, mental mechanics, and so on? In a study over 350 pages in
length, in the very work in which he is most avowedly insisting that his
own theoretical perspective is altogether superior to all other approaches to sociological inquiry, Sorokin never attempts to use this perspective to analyze the fads and foibles that are his subject matter. One
might reasonably surmise that Sorokin does not attempt to do so precisely because (1) such an attempt would necessitate some kind of systematic answer to the aforementioned questions; (2) he has no answer
or even the barest guidelines for finding any answer to these questions;
and (3) these lacunae are the result of arguing that incompatible worldviews have been "synthesized" when they remain at loggerheads regardless of the vehement, arbitrary and unproved claims to the contrary.

In addition to being caught up in the same eclecticism and relativism
he so convincingly attacks, Sorokin is also so enamored with the mystique of modern science that he defends some of his most dubious conclusions by arbitrarily claiming that he and he alone is "in perfect agreement" with modern physics:

> In perfect agreement with modern physicists, we find statistical
> methods little applicable to "microphysical"—unique and rare—
> psychosocial phenomena, especially for the purposes of dis-
> covering statistical uniformities in their static and dynamic rela-
> tionship. In full agreement with modern physicists, we find, too,
> that the best field for statistical study of psychosocial
> phenomena is the realm of large aggregates or "vast dumps" of
> personal, social and cultural congeries. Finally, again in full
> agreement with modern physicists, we find that in regard to bio-
> logical, personal and sociocultural systems statistical methods
> are either inapplicable or are greatly limited in their service.[9]

Exactly why the views of physicists should persuade us that quantitative
studies of groups or individuals are "inapplicable" for sociological purposes is by no means clear. Exactly why the views of *modern* physicists
should take precedence over the views of classical physicists is also unclear. Indeed, classical physicists tended to be far more familiar with
epistemological problems than their more narrowly trained modern
counterparts, and their views might therefore be more deserving of serious consideration than those Sorokin chooses to cite. But Sorokin is
taken in by the ostensible convergence between his views and those of
"modern physicists," convinced that his utterance of a statement is
somehow sufficient to validate it, confident that his revelations about

the philosophy of integralism will extricate sociology and modern society from their present state of chaos and depravity; he does not pause to consider that his identification with the prevailing fashions of eclecticism, scientism, and "modern thinking" might prevent him from adequately carrying out the program of purification he wishes to undertake. Indeed, it is from Sorokin himself that the outcry against "eclectic hash"[10] and "the grand cult of social physics"[11] is most resounding; it is from Sorokin himself that the arguments in favor of a profound distinction between the subject matters of social science and physics are most compelling;[12] it is from Sorokin himself that the condemnation of the frenzied pace of sensate culture, of the ahistorical pursuit of novelty for its own sake, is most severe.[13] Sorokin describes and denounces these trends in principle only to be caught up in them in practice.[14]

Merton's Role as an Opinion Leader in the Sociology of Science

We now move on to the work of the most influential opinion leader in American sociology, Robert K. Merton, and especially to his contributions to the sociology of science.[15] This examination is to be carried out with an eye toward Merton's own contributions to the study of the fashion process in the scientific community.

Although he emphasizes the importance of recognizing continuities in sociological research,[16] Merton ignores the implications of Simmel's and Kroeber's research on the fashion process in his own investigations of such phenomena as serendipity, multiple discoveries, and styles of inquiry in the scientific community.[17] Indeed, one of the most striking aspects of Merton's voluminous writings in the sociology of knowledge and science is his failure to examine or even mention the fashion process as a possible characteristic of modern science in general or the discipline of sociology in particular. But he does make a serious effort to illuminate such phenomena as the shifting interests and fields of specialization in science, the ambiguous self-images and rivalries among scientists, the processes by which competing claims are evaluated, and the pervasive neglect of the sociology of science in the scientific community.[18] Although Merton does not explicitly identify these phenomena as possible manifestations of the fashion process, he nevertheless investigates them in detail and must be credited at least for his appreciation that they are deserving of serious study. He studies these phenomena, which, as we have already seen, are in some respects greatly influenced by the fashion process and in other respects integrally related to its operation. Since he brings to bear on these investigations all of the concepts and assumptions of sociological functionalism and develops middle-range theories of the scientific community based upon them, Merton's substantial writings on the sociology of science warrant the fullest consideration.

There are several additional reasons of particular importance for the present study to warrant such consideration. First, the prevalence of "structural-functional analysis" and "theories of the middle range" in current research on the sociology of science can be critically examined to ascertain whether this perspective is helpful in understanding those complex forces in the scientific community to which Kuhn, Friedrichs, and Sorokin have called attention;[19] Merton's own prominence in the literature on this subject renders a critical examination of his work into a case study of such analyses and theories. Second, Merton does at least implicitly discuss some of the manifestations of the fashion process [20]; his insights as well as his oversights can usefully be taken into account in the present effort to formulate an adequate theory of how this process operates in the scientific community. Third, in sharp contrast to Kuhn's admitted ignorance of the sociology of knowledge and Friedrichs's outspoken repudiation of it, Merton's erudition in and sympathy for this scholarly domain is well established; the degree to which he utilizes the sociology of knowledge (including his widely cited "Paradigm for the Sociology of Knowledge") by applying its lessons critically to his own investigations of the scientific community and thereby striving to resist the temptations of substantively dubious but fashionable trends in the discipline of sociology can prove to be most instructive for the present study. Fourth, an intensive examination of Merton's studies of the scientific community can illuminate the degree to which they are themselves (a) caught up in the fashion process; (b) guided by assumptions that whether or not they are exclusively signs of the fashion process, are taken for granted as though their mere utterance were sufficient to validate them; and (c) symptomatic of the myopic and ahistorical tendencies (e.g., vague, ambiguous, empirically unsupported claims) already seen in the work of such earlier figures as Simmel and Kroeber, and such contemporary ones as Kuhn and Friedrichs. Fifth, Merton is familiar with the writings of Sorokin, Friedrichs, and Kuhn, and he does undertake to evaluate their various contributions to our understanding of the scientific community; his evaluation of their efforts can itself be critically examined in terms of the intellectual lens through which he reviews them and the objectively valid or distorted conclusions he thereby reaches. Finally, a full consideration of Merton's investigations of the scientific community is ipso facto a case study of the most prominent opinion leader in the discipline of sociology at the present time; the degree to which the fashion process is found to be operative in his work is therefore a reasonable indication of the degree to which this process is generally operative in the discipline as a whole. It will be shown that the most plausible interpretation to which the evidence presented in this study leads is that the fashion process is actively operative in sociological inquiry and that the most important opinion leaders in the discipline are themselves unwittingly caught up in this process even as they attempt to investigate its various characteristics. One of the more immediate concerns in the following examination of Merton's work is to demonstrate that his failure to recognize explicitly the play of fashion in science and his tendency to celebrate or uncritically take for granted some of its features are a source of systematic rather than incidental distortion in his findings. Another and closely related concern is to demonstrate that the inadequacies of functional analysis and middle-range theory for an understanding of the scientific community tend to plague the work of even the most sophisticated and articulate spokesman for these dominant trends in American sociology.

Merton's Study of the Selection of Models in the Scientific Community

Merton begins his study of patterns of evaluation in science with this assertion:

> The referee system in science involves the systematic use of judges to assess the acceptability of manuscripts submitted for publication. [They] are charged with evaluating the quality of role-performance in a social system. They are found in every institutional sphere. Other kinds of status judges include teachers assessing the quality of work by students (and, as a recent institutional change, students officially assessing the quality of performance by teachers), critics in the arts, supervisors in industry, and coaches and managers in sports. Status judges are integral to any system of social control through their evaluation of role-performance and their allocation of rewards for that performance. They influence the motivation to maintain or raise standards of performance.[21]

Merton's account of the referee system is of value insofar as it highlights the extent to which the social control over the behavior of participants in a given organization is achieved by means of status judgments of competent or incompetent performance. Indeed, as Merton observes, the very survival of the organization is made possible through the enforcement of these judgments. But how do status judges evaluate the scientific ideas of those participants who provide arguments or evidence calling into question the legitimacy of the organization or the competence of the judges themselves? If these referees serve the "function" of ensuring the survival of the organization, then they are hardly likely to approve for publication those ideas that seriously threaten to annihilate it or to reject those ideas that legitimize it—even when the former are empirically verified and the latter are not. Although this problem would be thorny enough if one were only considering ideas in art or sports or kindergarten teaching, it becomes all the more grave in the case of the scientific community. On the one hand, scientists who serve as editors or "status judges" are presumably committed to the evaluation of competing models strictly on the basis of their substantive truth-content. On the other hand, editors or status judges who approve of models that tend to undermine the prevailing worldview or the legitimacy of a given discipline are opening the door to the possible downfall not only of a particular model but also of the system in which the model is produced in the first place. Although it would seem that the abstract commitment to truth for its own sake and the practical obligation to keep order in the system are likely to be irreconcilable, Merton's neglect to specify the concrete historical conditions under which these goals are complementary or antagonistic to each other leaves this matter in some confusion. We have already seen that Merton's own mentor, for example, painfully learned that the referees or status judges affiliated with the *American Journal of Sociology* did not hesitate to ridicule *Fads and Foibles in Modern Sociology* and to ostracize its author rather than consider this work on its merits. Regardless of the status judge's alleged commitment to high academic standards or pure reason, then, some members of the scientific community may (1) actively support struggles against oppression and the uses of knowledge for human betterment; (2) find that certain elements of a given scientific discipline or profession are themselves obstacles to such betterment;[22] (3) develop a model in which theory, research, and political practice are interwoven for the avowed purpose of advancing such struggles and elminating such obstacles; and (4) receive a hostile rather than a sympathetic or open-minded verdict from the status judge who is opposed to any model of this kind. Publications emanating from the Sociology Liberation movement and the Union of Radical Political Economists were routinely disparaged in the turbulent 1960s because they were "unprofessional" in the judgment of major spokespersons for the mainstream of sociology, political science, economics, and related academic discplines;[23] similar examples could be given concerning anthropology, history, and psychology to illustrate the conservative and controlling influence of referees in the evaluation process. Merton ignores the contradiction between role performance to defend the existing order in the scientific community by status judges and the articulation of theoretical and political challenges to that order by radically or critically oriented members of the same community. The notion that a referee can evaluate competing models for publication or adoption along some value-neutral dimension of "performance quality" under such conditions is untenable.

Although Merton's emphasis on the controlling influence of status judges in the evaluation process is well taken, he is vague about the direction of such influence and raises indirectly some questions obscured by his own focus. Do status judges approve or disapprove only of the models submitted for consideration? Or do they also reward and punish the designers who produce them? Do they seek strictly to upgrade the scholarly standards of their discipline even when radical or revolutionary proposals are under study and supported by considerable evidence? Or do they seek to reject or suppress such proposals even when the substantive evidence for them is clearly demonstrated? Who judges the status judges? To answer these questions, one must make the following qualifications and corrections to Merton's view of status judges in the scientific community.

First, "status judges" are essentially the designated personnel in charge of encouraging or discouraging not only the models that compete for adoption per se but also the designers who produce and submit them for consideration; they exercise a powerful determination over the fate of ideas and the participants who create them. They are the guardians of the standards and policies of the organization that so empowers them. They therefore serve to perpetuate the system by which privileges and inequities are distributed: they clearly represent the vested interests of privilege rather than the outcries against inequity in such a hierarchy.[24] They are not "value neutral" or indifferent to the interests they represent, and their official judgments consistently tend to reflect this fact.

Second, "status judges" are themselves placed in key positions for evaluating (rewarding, ridiculing, suppressing) competing models as the result of a selection process. Many members of the sociological profession are eligible to serve as editors of the *American Sociological Review*, for example, but only a handful are given serious consideration. The previously cited studies by Gouldner and Horowitz would seem to suggest that among those few candidates who are seriously considered, the final appointments in nearly every case are awarded to sociologists having (1) an academically functionalist and politically liberal perspective (itself represented as being "value neutral"), or (2) an outspoken "hard numbers" view of methodology, or (3) a combination of these approaches to the study of society. If Merton had recognized rather than ignored this selection process, then he might have identified at least the major characteristics by which some prospective status judges are chosen over others in the scientific community. Although the process by which status judges are selected is subtle, complex, and unduly ignored in the sociology of science, the following factors would seem necessarily to come in to play and to warrant study in their own right:

(1) the collective tastes and sentiments of social participants, with the voice of strategically located participants being more effectively heard than that of those less advantageously situated in the scientific community, concerning the most up-to-date and glamorous or appealing candidates for consideration as status judges;

(2) the vested interests in the structure of domination in the scientific community as well as the larger society being realistically concerned to ensure their fullest representation at all important levels of decision making, to support candidates who are sympathetic to them for sensitive positions, and to oppose those who are not so inclined;

(3) the efforts of prospective candidates themselves to engage in such activities and to display such a front as to be (a) most appealing to the collective tastes of the community insofar as they can be discerned, as well as (b) most deserving of political and ideological support from the most powerful interests and strata in the scientific community and the larger society.

But even these three factors do not adequately characterize the process by which status judges are selected: under certain conditions collective tastes may be decisive, under other conditions the structure of domination may be decisive, and under still other conditions the resources and imagery of the individual candidate may be decisive in the designation of status judges. Although it is probably true that a combination of all three factors usually tends to guide or determine the evaluation and selection of status judges, the causal relationships among them are not self-evident. The degree to which they jointly or individually affect the selection process must be historically specified rather than abstractly conjectured. Merton's conception of status judges is therefore useful only if one keeps in mind those crucial aspects of the selection process that he fails to examine or even acknowledge in passing.

Third, Merton's oversights are all the more disappointing because he argues earlier that the "existential basis" on which knowledge is produced and through which it is perceived must always be theoretically *and* empirically identified in its historical context.[25] But to discuss the role of status judges as though they were neutral referees, to ignore the situational and ideological context in which they are selected and within which they make their decisions about models competing for adoption, is to flout Merton's own guidelines for research in the sociology of knowledge. Although he abstractly subscribes to these guidelines and concretely invokes them in his criticism of shortcomings in the work of other investigators, Merton does not follow them in his own study of the evaluation process in science.

Finally, the selection process by which status judges are recruited into a decision-making body (whether a panel to judge a beauty contest or an editorial board for a scientific jounral) has a substantial effect in turn upon their tastes, perceptions, and priorities concerning the evaluation of models submitted to them. Status judges who exhibit indifference or insensitivity to the boundaries of propriety and the rules of the game are ostracized or penalized accordingly for their failure to go along with the latest developments on one hand or their hubris for going too far out on the other hand. Hence, they occupy positions of influence not so much because of their alleged commitment to scientific truth as an end in itself, but rather because of their actual responsiveness, accessibility, congeniality, and, ultimately, their loyalty to the powerful constituencies and interests that elevated them to these positions in the first place; their sobriety of judgment in the eyes of peers is largely evaluated in terms of these latter criteria. Such commitment might even be difficult and at times impossible to reconcile with the previously discussed factors operative in the selection process. Insofar as status judges are unaware of the forces behind the selection process by which they themselves are elevated and chosen, insofar as they uncritically believe that their decisions are inherently the value-neutral expressions of scientific judgment, the consequences for the scientific community are bound to be corrosive. Under these conditions, status judges are likely to be more rather than less susceptible to these forces and more rather than less myopic in achieving even a semblance of objective judgment over the models submitted for consideration.

Whatever the underlying forces that guide the process by which models are evaluated, one must ultimately face the question of whether the actual evaluation of models or manuscripts leads to the approval of sound scholarship and the disapproval of unsound scholarship. It is logically possible that the many aforementioned obstacles to an open-minded and objective evaluation of models do not deter truly principled status judges from living up to the highest academic standards in their editorial decisions. If such a possibility were the case, one would be obliged empirically to demonstrate it rather than take it for granted. What does Merton say about the realities of the evaluation process in modern science?

> With all its imperfections, old and new, the developing institution of the referee system provides for a warranted faith that what appears in the archives of science can generally be relied upon. As Professor Michael Polanyi in particular has observed, the functional significance of the referee system increases with the growing differentiation of science into . . . extensive networks and specialities.[26]

Although it is true that the referee system in its present form serves to buttress the growing number of specializations in the scientific community, these specializations tend to reinforce the compartmentalization and fragmentation of scientific inquiry to such an extreme degree that only partial and distorted findings are generated. To impute to the process of differentiation and specialization in science the inherent virtues of wisdom and progress is to ignore the attendant dangers in a decline of interdisciplinary research and to succumb to the temptations of a mechanistic evolutionism in the sociology of science. We have already seen that Simmel, Friedrichs, and Kuhn exalted the process of differentiation and specialization in modern intellectual life; we now see that Merton also champions this ideological cause in his defense of the referee system as it currently stands. Instead of offering evidence to support the sweeping claim that the referee system and modern science are moving progressively closer to a true understanding of the universe, Merton is plainly content to invoke the prestigious name of Polanyi (who provides no more evidence than Merton does for this claim) as though this were sufficient to validate it.

Exactly why Merton assumes that the "archives of science can generally be relied upon" is, moreover, never really explained: his criticisms of his own mentor's contributions to the sociology of science[27] – particularly in view of the vast amount of work by Sorokin found in the archives at Harvard – would seem to justify a verdict in opposition to the uncritically optimistic one he reaches. All of Sorokin's important theoretical views were published during his lifetime in journals and anthologies that were governed by the referee system of status judges and that

presumably certified the validity of the principles of integralism and cyclical change in history. But how is it possible that the status judges certified views that Merton has convincingly called into question? Did the
status judges lack the necessary competence to recognize the deficiencies in Sorokin's work? Did they permit or even endorse the publication
of Sorokin's views because they unwittingly or intuitively considered
those views to be consonant with prevailing fashions in social science
during the 1940s and 1950s, for example? Why did the status judges fail
to exercise the necessary vigilance in barring from the archives of
science a set of dubious theoretical views that have greatly influenced
sociology in particular? Merton does not come to grips with these
questions.

We have already seen that an accumulation of anomalies can produce
a crisis resolvable only by a paradigm shift or "scientific revolution."
When the scientific community is in such a state of crisis, the validity and
legitimacy of the scientific annals or archives are severely questioned
and subjected to far-reaching redefinitions or reexaminations. The notion that scientific archives are necessarily reliable merely because they
are endorsed by a given referee system is a misleading and ahistorical
view that ignores the conditions under which archives, like the referee
system itself, may be open to question in a state of crisis. Indeed, if the
archives or the referee system were inherently reliable, then there
would be no need for scientific revolutions and no evidence that they
have ever taken place.

Merton goes so far as to acknowledge not only the existence of scientific revolutions in the twentieth century[28] but also the onset of intense
theoretical and ideological debate within modern sociology itself.[29] He
clearly acknowledges elsewhere that

> much of the controversy among sociologists involves social
> conflict and not only intellectual criticism. Often, it is less a
> matter of contradictions between sociological ideas than of
> competing definitions of the role considered appropriate for
> the sociologist. Intellectual conflict of course occurs; an un-
> remitting Marxist sociology and an unremitting Weberian or
> Parsonian sociology do make contradictory assumptions.[30]

Just how the archives of sociology or any other discipline can be deemed
to have attained the stage of general reliability Merton takes for granted
becomes most puzzling in light of his own observations about "contradictory assumptions" in the major perspectives competing for
adoption.

Sorokin and Merton on the Evaluation Process in Modern Science

Before Merton's other contributions to the sociology of science are critically appraised, it will be useful to compare his view of the evaluation process to that of Sorokin in order to clarify the similarities and differences in their respective positions on this crucial matter.

Sorokin makes a number of far-reaching assumptions about the evaluation process in modern sociology. First, he assumes that there is no academic control or review whatsoever over the allegedly endless, random, chaotic array of "fads and foibles" in the social sciences, and that virtually "anything goes" in this pseudoscientific folly—especially as seen in the downfall of modern sociology. Second, he assumes that his eminence in learned societies and his numerous publications in reputable journals are evidence of the basic soundness of the evaluation process. Third, he assumes that the frequent denunciations of his work by influential reviewers are (a) deliberate strategies of ideological repression at the hands of "Tammany Hall cliques" in the discipline, (b) idiosyncratic and temporary aberrations by his rivals and former students who eventually adopt his views anyway, or (c) a combination of these two factors. We have already seen that his first assumption is empirically untenable; we now see that the other two assumptions are incompatible not only with each other but also with the first assumption as well. Merton adds to this confusion about the evaluation process by making yet another series of assumptions that are in opposition to those advanced by Sorokin but that he does not explicitly recognize as being at odds with those of his mentor. Merton assumes, for example, that the referee system of status judges guarantees the general reliability of the scientific archives, that status judges can and do exercise value-neutrality and objectivity in evaluating all models submitted to them for consideration, and that this system, which Sorokin held to be immersed in the anti-intellectual biases of sensate culture, should be preserved as it currently stands in the scientific community.

We have already seen that Merton's analysis of the evaluation or selection process is tantamount to a misleading celebration rather than a realistic investigation of the scientific community. Although Sorokin and Merton do have opposing views of this process, we cannot ascertain its true nature merely by attempting to reconcile their underlying assumptions: *their views of the evaluation process, however much they appear to be at loggerheads, are both ultimately based on the axiom that the fashion process does not operate in the scientific community.* Although this axiom might be regarded as a logical possibility, it cannot be defended if it is both the basis of sweeping claims about the scientific community and untenable in light of the available evidence about the system of controls operative in that same community. Insofar as the sociology of science is to be an empirically and historically rooted discipline, any of its axioms that are contradicted by the available evidence must be jettisoned regardless of their popularity or sanctity at a given time.

Had Sorokin and Merton recognized rather than denied or ignored the play of fashion in the evaluation process, they might have been able to avoid the fallacious arguments and distorted observations that pervade their respective studies of the scientific community. Had they recognized it, moreover, they might have examined the possibility that their ascendance in the sociological profession could be largely explained not so much because of the truth-content of their publications per se but rather because of the fidelity of their ideas to the collective tastes of an academic audience that only superficially evaluated their substantive claims in terms of their objective validity.

Merton's Evaluation of Opinion Leaders in the Sociology of Science

Merton on Sorokin

Sorokin's influence in the sociology of science is illustrated in several respects by Merton's efforts to evaluate his work. Although "Sorokin's Formulations in the Sociology of Science" originally appeared under the joint authorship of Merton and Barber,[31] its distinctive style (ingenious turns of phrase, wide-ranging citations, frequent use of aphorisms) would seem to indicate that Merton had the decisive role in its preparation.

Merton begins his analysis of Sorokin's view of the sociology of science with a characterization of the academic context in which Sorokin found himself initially at the University of Minnesota and later at Harvard University. According to Merton, there was a great deal of intellectual debate and diversity in higher learning during Sorokin's tenure as the founder and chairman of Harvard's department of sociology; this ferment, we are led to believe, was part of the intellectual life of students and faculty concerned with the sociology of science. He observes in addition that this ferment is a unique attribute of American universities, which are pluralistic, in contrast to the monolithic European universities in which a single professor usually holds a dominant chair and tolerates little or no dissent from students or colleagues:

> We should try the thought-experiment of imagining that Sorokin had gone not to Harvard but to some other important university—in Europe. He would have held "the chair of sociology" in that university. He would have had a number of assistants as well as students who, in accord with the cultural expectations of docility, would have become his disciples, echoing his words and thoughts as though they were their own. But in the American scheme of things academic, and particularly in a university such as Harvard, the social structure and culturally defined patterns of expectations . . . of the department were pluralistic rather than strongly centralized. There was not only *the* occupant of The Chair but members of the faculty who had equal access to students. Moreover, Sorokin's own personality and role behavior reinforced his tendency toward independence of mind among his students. . . . All this meant that the structurally defined role of Sorokin was primarily that of alerting students to intellectual alternatives rather than that of imprinting the particulars of his own theory upon them. And all this, we conjecture, helps to explain how it is that Sorokin's students have not hesitated to differ with him when, rightly or wrongly, they did not see matters just as he did.[32]

Merton's invitation to engage in a "thought-experiment" as a means of understanding the nature of Sorokin's academic community could be useful if the reconstruction into which readers are asked to project themselves has some correspondence with the actual historical setting. Merton does not demonstrate this correspondence on empirical grounds, however, and chooses instead merely to assume that European universities are monolithic while American universities are pluralistic. But this assumption is questionable for several reasons. First, for several decades many French universities have been supportive of a very wide spectrum of conservative, liberal, and even Marxist orientations in social science;[33] a number of German universities have legitimized various trends in the tradition of critical theory;[34] some Italian universities have hosted radical perspectives ranging from Maoism and Leninism to nonsectarian versions of militant socialism tied to the trade union movement.[35] There has never been a successful effort to establish American centers of scholarly ferment on anything like the scale found in Europe in recent decades.[36] There have been consistently successful attempts, however, to purge American universities of those scholars and programs that gave even the appearance of organized opposition to the legitimizing ideologies of state power: the instances of such monolithic intolerance at Washington University, the University of Connecticut, the University of California, San Francisco State College, and many other institutions of higher learning, especially during the 1960s, call into question Merton's image of pluralism in American universities in general and in the discipline of sociology in particular. Indeed, Merton cannot help but be familiar with the academic reprisals directed against C. Wright Mills for his views in *The Sociological Imagination* and Robert S. Lynd for his views in *Knowledge for What?* For these developments took place in the very same department of sociology in which he himself has been a faculty member. But there is one sense in which Merton's image of academic pluralism might be tenable. Although the reception accorded to Sorokin's, Lynd's, and Mills's work calls into question the claim that American sociology is "pluralistic" or even begrudgingly tolerant of serious theoretical and ideological debate, there may well be intellectual diversity *within* the boundaries of sociological functionalism: the successive stewardships of Sorokin, Parsons, and Homans at Harvard, for example, suggest that there is toleration of macro- and microsociological versions of functionalist thought. But such toleration within a narrow ideological spectrum cannot be construed as evidence of great ferment or pluralism at Cambridge or any other American university in recent decades.

What Merton represents as a "thought-experiment," then, is for the most part an empirically untenable assertion that he himself does not really defend. The available evidence would seem to suggest that the very opposite of Merton's image of the scientific community is probably closer to the truth. Moreover, the fact that the limited and belated radicalization of American sociology in the 1960s (with the emergence of activist caucuses and journals throughout the profession) was itself largely unprecedented would seem further to suggest that intellectual and ideological pluralism has not been a discernible academic tradition in American sociology.[37]

Two implications of Merton's view of academic pluralism in his appraisal of Sorokin's contributions to the sociology of science should be clarified. First, far from being the cognitive aberration of an individual scholar, Merton's distorted picture of the history of American universities seems attributable to his uncritical acceptance of the following ideological premises. Merton tacitly assumes that American universities are hospitable to diverse viewpoints; that they allow and even encourage each student to become his or her own master and to remain free of any obsequious ties to entrenched faculty; that their intellectual pluralism necessarily generates significant lines of scientific inquiry and new areas of intellectual or cultural ferment. These unproven assumptions, which Merton occasionally makes explicit in some of his other studies cited below, are illustrative of the tendency to praise one's own institutions (e.g., the scientific community) as though they were infallible. They are tantamount to the ahistorical celebration of the present, the abandonment of any real commitment to critical and historical self-awareness; they are further examined in a later section, "On Precedence for Contemporary Models of Sociological Pluralism," because they constitute a most shaky foundation on which to develop the sociology of science and the sociology of knowledge.

Second, Merton must be severely criticized for his failure to reconcile the absence of radical and Marxist views in American universities with his conviction that the academic world is highly pluralistic and progressive as it now stands or to clarify the meaning of "pluralism" itself. But one should not hastily conclude that all forms of radicalism and Marxism are alike or that all theoretical and ideological tendencies encompassed by pluralism are moving toward a final synthesis. Radical scholarship, for example, refers to getting at the root of things, pursuing knowledge in the service of human betterment and self-determination, demystifying structures of exploitation and oppression whereever one finds them, and therefore speaking the truth to power even at one's own peril; Marxism, as depicted by Marx, is itself devoted to these goals but nevertheless has been ideologically reconstructed by the Communist Party in the Soviet Union (and elsewhere) as a rationale for inhibiting the heightened political consciousness of the working class. As Colfax observes, many varieties of "radicalism" and "Marxism" in American universities are neither radical nor Marxist; his analysis of radicalism is highly suggestive of the possibility that these trends may well be caught up in the fashion process in their own right. Although the sense in which Merton refers to "pluralism" in American universities does take for granted the absence of radical and Marxist views, the many varieties of existentialism, phenomenology, psychoanalytic theory, functionalism, and determinism in the social sciences do allow for lively competition among many schools of thought for center stage: the ongoing competition among these legitimate views, in short, makes possible the advent of a selection process in the scientific community. But whatever the appearance of an endless range of models and an unlimited freedom to adhere to any criteria to which one feels rationally committed, the fact remains that (a) certain models are ruled out of consideration and (b) certain criteria, particularly those most consistent with the shifting collective tastes of the day, are given priority over other criteria in the selection of models for possible adoption. As Sorokin observes, the absence of objective criteria by which to evaluate competing models only contributes to the state of affairs in which efforts to reconcile the various models turn out to yield little more than what he aptly calls "eclectic hash" rather than a coherent theoretical synthesis of differing assumptions. Merton does not evaluate Sorokin's substantive claims regarding the development of eclecticism in modern sociology and therefore fails to recognize one of the most provocative points of emphasis in his mentor's contributions to the sociology of science.

Merton is nevertheless critical of some epistemological assumptions in Sorokin's view of scientific knowledge:

> Sorokin has explicitly adopted an idealist and emanationist theory of the sociology of science. Unlike the theories of a Marx or a Mannheim, which seek primarily to account for the character and limits of knowledge obtaining in a particular society in terms of its social structure, Sorokin's theory tries to derive every aspect of knowledge from underlying "cultural mentalities." . . . This has also been noted by Stark, who observes that "It is essential for the understanding of the whole theory to realize that it considers the ontological convictions prevailing at a given time not so much as cultural contents but rather as cultural premises, from which the culture proceeds and emanates as a whole."[38]

Merton immediately seizes upon this weakness in Sorokin's position by asking:

> How can he escape from the self-contained emanationism of the theoretical position he adopts? For it would appear tautological to say, as Sorokin does, that "in a Sensate society and culture the Sensate system of truth based upon the testimony of the organs has to be dominant." For, sensate *mentality*—that abstraction which Sorokin makes ontologically basic to the culture—has already been *defined* as one conceiving of "reality as only that which appears to the sense organs." . . . Sorokin seems to vacillate between treating his types of culture mentality as a defined concept or as an empirically testable hypothesis.[39]

Merton's trenchant critique of Sorokin's position can be summarized as follows. (1) Sorokin's explanation of modern science is at bottom an emanationist, idealistic, deterministic, single-factor model. (2) Sorokin insists that since culture is the only important variable responsible for the development of modern science, the study of the social structure and personality takes on relatively little importance. (3) Sorokin argues at some times that the assumption of cultural determinism is a logical construction or "analytical proposition" and at other times that it is a substantive claim subject to empirical verification or refutation. (4) Sorokin's view of the sociology of science is therefore vulnerable to the criticism that it is (a) overdeterministic and even mechanistic, and (b) exceedingly vague about the logical status of its essential assumptions, which cannot possibly be both unprovable axioms *and* empirical claims at the same time.

But Sorokin is hardly alone in his vacillations over the "analytical" and "empirical" aspects of such a model: the expedient characterization of an arbitrary or dubious model as "analytical" when the available evidence would refute it and as "empirical" when the evidence would serve to illustrate it has become de facto tantamount to an academic tradition in its own right in American sociology. Merton's well-known scheme of means and ends as the sole determinants of behavior, for example, also represents an emanationist model with an equally ambiguous "analytical" and "empirical" status. According to his scheme, virtually all forms of conformative and deviant behavior are derived from the various logically possible combinations of structurally established means and culturally prescribed ends.[40]

		E N D S	
M		+	−
E A	+	Conformity	Ritualism
N S	−	Innovation	Retreatism

To depict "innovation" as the acceptance of a given set of ends and the inaccessibility to the established means of their realization, for example, is to use two factors (the culture and social structure) where Sorokin would use only one (the culture) to explain such a contingency. Regardless of the number of variables or factors one might add to the list of alleged properties or elements in the "action system," however, the logic of Merton's model is in principle identical to that of Sorokin's. Where Merton speaks of the "interaction" between cultural ends and social means or opportunities, Sorokin speaks of the "interaction" among cultural themes in the study of integralism. Just as Merton presumes thereby to explain the origins and nature of anomie in modern society, Sorokin presumes in the same manner to explain the decadence of modern science and the disintegration of modern civilization. Both explanations suffer from the same weakness of overdeterminism, ahistorical distortion, and gross neglect of the capacity of the social self to redefine the meaning of these allegedly omnipotent forces or variables.

Although Merton's criticisms of Sorokin's position are well taken, they are also misleading because they neglect the theoretical foundations on which the emanationist perspective ultimately rests. Merton implies that Sorokin's perspective is in error because of shortcomings in the philosophy of integralism or aberrations in the thought of its chief architect. But Sorokin's theoretical perspective and his methdology for the interpretation of data are, as he himself has pointed out, avowedly functionalist in the concepts and ideological assumptions about social change in the system of action. The internal logic of Sorokin's model of immanent cyclical development, far from being unique or eccentric in American social science, rests squarely on the evolutionist doctrine of the inexorable "unfolding of potential" or the "working out of forces" inherent in the system of action. According to this view, social developments take place as they do because they are bound to happen in just that way. Although Sorokin's model of cyclical change differs from Parsons's more clearly organicist notion of ongoing, unidirectional evolution (i.e., adaptation, specialization, differentiation) and subsequently endless progress in modern society, the ahistorical, emanationist, deterministic thrust of this model is fully in the tradition of modern sociological functionalism. Indeed, Merton, Parsons, Davis, Moore, and other prominent functionalists were inspired in their appreciation of classical versions of "action system theory" by virtue of serving for many years as disciples or colleagues of Sorokin at Harvard. The criticisms advanced by Merton against Sorokin's conception of the sociology of science are really an indictment of the functionalist worldview to which Merton himself is devoted.

Merton offers a number of noteworthy and specific criticisms of Sorokin's research in the sociology of science. In a searching analysis of the methodology employed in Sorokin's *Social and Cultural Dynamics*, Merton contrasts Sorokin's sweeping repudiation of social statistics as expressed in *Fads and Foibles in Modern Sociology* with his abundant use of quantitative data in studies of intellectual and cultural trends.[41] He also questions the extreme relativism that pervades Sorokin's approach to the sociology of science.[42] Merton further observes that Sorokin ignores the selective accumulation of scientific knowledge in sensate culture:

> Sorokin summarizes his judgment of [fluctuations of scientific theories over time] in these words: "as far as oscillation is con-

cerned, there probably has been no scientific theory which has
not undergone it, and, like a fashion, now has been heralded as
the last word of science, and now has fallen into disrepute."
This judgment leads us to ask in what sense recurrent sets of
ideas constitute one and the same theory that now finds
general acceptance and later rejection, only to be accepted
again, still later.[43]

Unfortunately, Merton does not pursue the far-reaching implications of
his observation about the changing meanings of a fashionable theory
from the subjective standpoint of those who adopt, discard, and redis-
cover it under various historical conditions. But his point is well taken
and cannot be too strongly emphasized: any scientific theory or procedure that is caught up in the fashion process becomes a salient object
to those who seek to be in "good taste" and in step with the times. As
previously indicated in the discussion of anomalies under conditions of
crisis in the scientific community, the meaning of any object caught up
in the fashion process is a product of (1) the context of modernity in
which new trends and opinion leaders compete for acceptance, and (2)
the ongoing redefinitions of and readjustments to that context by the social participants who are the creatures, carriers, and creators of culture.
A major oversight in Sorokin's research, then, is his neglect of the possible shifts in the meaning of such concepts as "equilibrium" and "social
energy" as they are hailed, forgotten, and resurrected by the pioneering
Columbuses of American sociology. Although Merton's criticism of
Sorokin's research in this connection is couched in the form of a fleeting
query that is never elaborated, he nevertheless deserves credit for identifying a major weakness in Sorokin's approach to the study of fashions
in the "social and cultural dynamics" of modern science.

Just as Sorokin chooses to corroborate some far-fetched assertions by
invoking the banner of "modern physics," Merton equally yields to the
same temptation. He questions Sorokin's view of the decadence of modern science because, in Merton's own judgment, science today is more
revolutionary and productive than ever. He defends this judgment not
by giving any systematic evidence for it or even any criteria by which it
might be independently evaluated. He resorts instead to the invocation
of the illustrious name of

. . . C. P. Snow, speaking of what happened in science during
two decades at Cambridge University: "I was privileged to have
a ringside view of one of the most creative periods in all
physics." He then goes on to describe "a much louder voice,
that of another archetypal figure, Rutherford, trumpeting: This

is the heroic age of science!" [Snow] expresses his conviction that this is a revolutionary time for science, a time to take joy in science.[44]

Although Merton is quick to condemn the impressionistic and intuitionist aspects of Sorokin's work in the sociology of science, the disciple far surpasses the mentor in the use of such dubious reasoning. Exactly why Snow's vague reminiscences about his "ringside view" at Cambridge University should be taken as evidence that science in general is in a period of great creativity is nowhere explained. Indeed, the many physicists who founded the *Bulletin of the Atomic Scientists* had a very different and better-informed judgment of the importance of developments at major research centers, but Merton ignores their views entirely. Exactly why Rutherford's exclamation about an allegedly new "Elizabethan age" in modern physics should be taken at face value or construed as an authoritative contribution to the sociology of science is nowhere explained. The intensive and successful efforts by British scientists to emigrate to Canada, the United States, Australia, and other countries in more recent decades can hardly be testimony to an "Elizabethan age" for scientists in a society that has in fact been increasingly reluctant to support existing levels of research and unable to generate new or expanded programs in the physical sciences.[45]

What is the significance of Merton's effort to evaluate Sorokin's approach to the sociology of science? What lessons can be learned from this evaluation for the purpose of illuminating the sociology of science and the sociology of knowledge and applying both to the study of the fashion process in the scientific community?

Although Merton ostensibly launches his analysis of Sorokin's contributions to the sociology of science *from the perspective of the sociology of science*, he does not attempt to explain the serious weaknesses in Sorokin's model by invoking that perspective. Merton ignores the ideological and structural forces in American society that might be responsible for the shaping of Sorokin's fallacious assumptions. We see once again that Merton flouts the many useful guidelines for research in the sociology of knowledge he himself advocates in his "Paradigm for the Sociology of Knowledge." Since he does not acknowledge the intimate connection between Sorokin's emanationist theory of science and the logic of functional analysis, Merton is all the more unable to examine the possibility that his mentor successfully inculcated this very logic into the thinking of many disciplines, including Merton, who would eventually promulgate it throughout the social sciences in American society.

This lack of critical self-awareness, this studied indifference to the historical context in which sociologists themselves are participants, cannot be interpreted as though it were a defect peculiar to Merton's approach to the sociology of science and knowledge. Merton neither invented nor consciously endorsed this myopia: he acquired it from his mentors at Harvard, especially from Sorokin, who unwittingly but effectively exemplified it. But the castigation of Sorokin as though he were the primary culprit in bringing about this myopia would be equally misleading. This lack of self-awareness is itself reinforced by a tendency to celebrate rather than critically and historically examine the scientific community in which one is a participant; it is a pervasive, dominant, and rarely acknowledged tradition in American social science. This ahistorical orthodoxy has been taken for granted by virtually all of the influential social theorists and sociologists of knowledge in recent decades, and the ascendance of "system building" and "general theory construction" remains largely unchallenged. So long as this orthodoxy goes unquestioned by those scholars who might be expected to study and seek ways of eradicating it, so long as sociologists of knowledge ignore the extent to which they might be the creatures of it, misleading assumptions, oversights, and imaginary experiments of the kind found in Merton's effort to evaluate Sorokin's view of modern science are likely to continue to plague the discipline of sociology. Of still greater concern to the present study is the fact that this orthodoxy serves as fertile soil in which the fashion process in science can be cultivated.

Merton on Kuhn

Norman Storer's introduction to Merton's research in the sociology of science calls attention to the convergence and complementarity between Kuhn's and Merton's views on the scientific community:

> Since the emergence of the Mertonian paradigm in the early 1960s, most research in the field appears to fit Kuhn's definition of "normal science." Not only Merton's own work but that of many others in the field have focused on problems which, once elucidated, turn out to be directly relevant to questions explicit or implicit in the paradigm. In short, the sociology of science has matured to the point where much research involves "puzzle-solving."[46]

The semantic usages of Storer's characterization of Merton's research call for close inspection. The "emergence" of the Mertonian paradigm in the 1960s is depicted as though it were equivalent to the "authentication" or "verification" of its hypotheses. The "relevance" of Kuhn's and other studies of the scientific community to this paradigm is represented as though it too were a verification of its hypotheses. The fact that "research in the field" often fits Kuhn's definition of normal science is taken as evidence that such a definition has been thereby corroborated. The "elucidation" of problems that are "relevant" to the Mertonian paradigm is construed as though it were proof that the sociology of science has therefore "matured." But far from verifying any hypotheses in the Mertonian paradigm, these developments only illustrate the acceptance of an arbitrary definition of the scientific community by a large number of investigators in the sociology of science. These developments indicate the degree to which certain assumptions are commonly taken for granted. Although they do indicate that these assumptions are regarded as self-evident or legitimate, they are not evidence of their validity. To equate a social consensus with a demonstration of the validity of a paradigm is to make a travesty of scientific method. Storer's representations about the importance and validity of Merton's paradigm rest essentially on the same doctrine of consensus among reasonable persons already examined in the previous discussion of Kuhn's image of the scientific community. Although Storer exalts Merton's paradigm because it has allegedly ushered in a new era in which "the sociology of science has matured to the point where much research involves 'puzzle-solving,' " he nowhere specifies any criteria by which to ascertain whether the puzzles are trivial or important, whether the solutions are true or false, whether the puzzles are to be solved for their own sake, for the purpose of social betterment, or for no reason at all.

We have already seen that pretentious and fallacious assertions have been made by Friedrichs and other contributors to the sociology of science; Storer's dubious logic, though hardly unusual, is instructive because he is also prominent as a sociologist of science and an articulate spokesman for Merton's contributions to this field. How can fallacies of such magnitude be explained?

Storer's uncritical comparison of Kuhn's and Merton's models of the scientific community is revealing because it not only foreshadows Merton's own interpretation of Kuhn's work but also illustrates the extent to which Storer's thinking is caught up in the fashion process. Storer (1) depicts Merton's work as pioneering and Kuhn's as the "latest thing"; (2) notes the convergence between their respective paradigms; (3) adds enthusiastically that still more recent research in the field fits Kuhn's definition of "normal science"; and (4) concludes that the Mertonian paradigm is therefore substantively valid in its own right and vital to the newly discovered "maturity" of the sociology of science. What is new and popular is, in Storer's judgment, valid and important. But he ignores the possibility that the consensus around a given model designed by a given opinion leader may have taken shape more because of the operation of the fashion process than because of the validity of the model itself.

Merton commences his own evaluation of Kuhn's model of the scientific community by observing that

historical changes in the foci of scientific work are a matter of experience familiar to sufficiently long-lived scientists and a commonplace among historians and sociologists of science. But how these changes come about and how they are distributed through the community of scientists remains a long-standing and knotty problem, which has lately attracted a renewed interest. As much else in the history, philosophy, and sociology of science, this recent development is a *self-exemplifying pattern* in which workers in these fields are registering a sort of shift in research interests much like that of scientists whose comparable behavior they are trying to interpret or explain.[47]

But *why* are sociologists of science now interested in the shifting "foci of scientific works" rather than, for example, the long-range social consequences of prevailing assumptions and paradigms in the scientific community? In view of the large and growing number of scholars and the voluminous body of literature in this field of study, why is so central a problem as changing "foci of scientific work" so vaguely defined and inadequately understood? How can Merton's own observations about this long-standing, vaguely formulated, and wholly unresolved problem in the sociology of science be reconciled with Storer's sweeping assurance that "the sociology of science has matured to the point where much research involves 'puzzle solving' "? On what basis do sociologists of science *assume* that such shifts can be explained through Kuhn's model of a self-adjusting community insulated from social pressures? Are they responding in part to a tacitly felt but still unrecognized sense of apprehension or crisis concerning the direction of trends they presume to explain as well as the quality of scholarship in the sociology of science itself? Merton does not attempt to answer or even acknowledge the importance of such questions. The possibility that the fashion process might be operative in the sociology of science in general and his own research in particular is unduly ignored. Although Merton insightfully calls attention to the reality of shifting trends in the sociology of science, he does not investigate the structural and ideological forces that produce it or the ongoing contexts of collective behavior among scientists in which this reality takes shape.

Merton holds that Kuhn's research is a major step toward the solution of the "long-standing and knotty problem" of shifting interests in the scientific community:

> Both reflecting and deepening the renewed interest in this problem is Thomas S. Kuhn's book, *The Structure of Scientific Revolutions*, which in less than a decade has given rise to a library of criticism and appreciative applications. To judge from the assorted use of this book in just about every branch of learning, it has become something of a complex projective test, meaning all things to all men and women. (ibid.)

Although Merton recognizes the widely divergent uses to which Kuhn's research is put, he fails to pursue the lines of inquiry directly implied by this recognition that a sociologist of science and knowledge might be expected to consider. For example, what do the ranges of interpretation to which Kuhn's paradigm is subjected indicate about the ideologies, priorities, and collective tastes in the scientific community? Why is this particular paradigm rather than its many competitors the object of so much acclaim in recent years? Why is *The Structure of Scientific Revolutions* regarded as a major contribution to the sociology of science and the sociology of knowledge when Kuhn himself candidly and realistically admits his innocence of these domains, when his highly ambiguous paradigm is rooted in assumptions that are anathema to these domains, and when the logic of his actual analysis of scientific revolutions confirms his admission? What are the limits that have been established de facto on the ranges of interpretation sociologists of science have made of Kuhn's paradigm? What forces in the structure and collective behavior of the scientific community might be responsible for establishing the boundaries of permissible interpretations of its meaning? Why do these interpretations have in common a systematic insensitivity to Kuhn's exemplary efforts at realistic and critical self-evaluation? The seemingly extravagant interpretations given to Kuhn's paradigm by sociologists of science in short cannot be casually dismissed as psychological oddities or random hallucinations. Merton's hasty relegation of this phenomenon to the status of a "complex projective test, meaning all things to all men and women" is all the more disconcerting in view of his dominant role as an opinion leader in the sociology of science.

According to Merton, Kuhn makes three contributions to the study of shifting foci of interest in the scientific community:

> One, he joins Popper in a major concern with "the dynamic process by which scientific knowledge is acquired rather than the logical structure of the products of scientific research." Two, central to this kind of inquiry is an understanding of "what

problems [scientists] will undertake." And three, it "should be clear that the explanation must, in the final analysis, be psychological or sociological. It must, that is, be a description of a value system, an ideology, together with an analysis of the institutions through which that system is transmitted and enforced."[48]

Merton goes so far as to suggest that Kuhn reopens the question of investigating the selection process and collective tastes in the scientific community:

> Kuhn thus reinstitutes as a concern central to the history and sociology of science an understanding of the changing foci of attention among scientists; more specifically, the question of how it is that scientists seize upon some problems as important enough to engage their sustained attention while others are regarded as uninteresting. (554.55)

Merton does qualify this praise for Kuhn's position by observing that "exogenous influences upon the foci of research . . . from the environing society, culture, economy, and polity" (555) must also be taken into account when studying the causes of these changing foci. But he nevertheless carries out his own research in full agreement with Kuhn's position on narrowly conceptualizing the structure of the scientific community per se and investigating only "the social composition and relations [e.g., age differences] of scientists at work in the various disciplines" (555), in order to solve the problem of shifting interests in that community. Still more puzzling is Merton's contention that Kuhn has reinstituted a concern for this problem in the sociology of science for, as he earlier and more correctly notes, scholars in this field have never seriously investigated it (or, for that matter, even formulated it) as a central problem in the first place. Although the problem has often been noted in passing or tacitly acknowledged, neither Merton nor Kuhn, neither classical sociologists of knowledge nor contemporary sociologists of science, have systematically investigated it on anything like the scale Merton would have us believe.

Merton repeatedly stumbles upon aspects of the fashion process in science only to reduce them to the alleged manifestations of age differences, generation gaps, and similar clichés with which Kuhn and other sociologists of science concur:

> We begin with one well-worn assumption and one familiar fact. The assumption (which is also adopted by Kuhn) holds that the time in their career at which scientists encounter ideas will sig-

nificantly affect their responses to them. The familiar fact is the strong, and perhaps increasing, emphasis in science on keeping up with work on the frontiers of the field, that is, with new work. (557)

But how and why do scientists selectively encounter some new ideas rather than others at any time in their career? Are their responses to such encounters determined by their length of time in a professional career or the *stage of advancement* in that career? Or are their responses chiefly determined by forces in the scientific community and the larger society about which they have relatively little knowledge and still less control so long as they act as rivals in isolation from one another in that community? Is the strong and increasing emphasis on keeping up with new work a preoccupation that might be developing at the expense of appreciating the important discoveries of classical physics and the principles of scientific method itself in modern science? Is this preoccupation an indicator of the fashion process in science deserving of systematic investigation rather than being uncritically taken for granted as a "familiar fact"? Instead of answering or even posing these questions, Merton attempts to explain away the aforementioned "well-worn assumption" and "familiar fact" by resorting to a psychological assertion about the mental state of scientists "approaching middle age":

> As incoming cohorts move toward what in science is a swiftly approaching middle age, the work they had focused on in their youth has grown "old," as age of publications is judged in much of contemporary science. The problems, new or old, which members of the older cohorts are investigating will often reactivate memories of pertinent work in the literature which they had encountered as new in years gone by. . . . In this model, scientists in each successive cohort re-enact much the same citation behavior in the same phases of their career. (557)

In adhering to Kuhn's paradigm, Merton proceeds to examine the changing foci of interest among scientists in terms of "reactivated memories" allegedly produced by age differences. These psychologically reductionist arguments lead Merton to the conclusion that scientists are naturally or inherently doomed to "re-enact" the same judgments or "citation behavior" of their predecessors. This model is not only ahistorical and mechanistic in its view of the scientific community but also indifferent to the possibility that scientists can learn from their history, that they can reflectively take into account the errors and folkways of their predecessors. Although the citation behavior found under certain conditions conducive to "normal science" at times may well be as compulsive, repetitive, and mindless as Merton suggests, one cannot *assume* that such behavior is universal or inherent in the scientific community. Merton offers no systematic evidence to support such a sweeping assumption, and is instead content to refer selectively to a limited number of case studies which (1) examine scientific behavior only under conditions of "normal science" in Kuhn's sense, (2) are carried out on the basis of data from a single society during a single historical period, and (3) take for granted the same assumption and lead to the same foregone conclusions advanced by Merton himself.[49]

Merton on the Precedence for Contemporary Models of Sociological Pluralism

Despite the common impression that little or no intellectual ferment existed in American sociology during the "silent fifties," Merton calls attention to the many varieties of theoretical and methodological debate that had emerged well before the signs of overt political confrontation surfaced in the more recent and turbulent history of the profession.[50] According to Merton, the issues on which debate was focused during that period were microscopic versus macroscopic sociology, experimental versus naturalistic sociology, formal versus concrete sociology, bourgeois sociology versus Marxism, the lone scholar versus the research team, substantive sociology versus methodology, and sociology versus social psychology (62.68). He observes that

> perhaps the most pervasive polemic, . . . which underlies most
> of the rest, stems from the charge by some sociologists that
> others are busily engaged in the study of trivia, while all about
> them the truly significant problems of human society go unexa-
> mined. After all, so this argument goes, while war and exploita-
> tion, poverty, injustice, and insecurity plague the life of men in
> society or threaten their very existence, many sociologists are
> fiddling with subjects so remote from these catastrophic trou-
> bles as to be irresponsibly trivial. (59)

Merton takes issue with this particular argument by insisting, on the contrary, that:
> you can add at will, from the history of sociology and other
> sciences, instances which show that there is no *necessary* rela-
> tion between the socially ascribed importance of the object un-
> der examination and the scope of its implications for an under-
> standing of how society or nature works. The social and the
> scientific significance of a subject matter can be poles apart. (60)

Merton disavows any commitment to the notion that "there is no genuinely trivial work in contemporary sociology," however, and concedes that

> it may be that our sociological journals during their first fifty years have as large a complement of authentic trivia as the *Transactions* of the Royal Society contained during their first fifty years (to pursue the matter no further). (61)

To put into perspective Merton's arguments and concessions regarding the charge that sociologists engage in the study of trivia, at least three questions must be answered: (1) What exactly is the nature of the "trivia" to which Merton refers? (2) Why does he feel called upon to respond at all to the charge of trivial work in the discipline? (3) How does this response illuminate the play of fashion in sociological inquiry?

First, the forms of trivia lurking in the background of Merton's concern would appear to include

> the dominant trends of sociological work in the United States, which are periodically subjected to violent attacks from within, as in the formidable book by Sorokin, *Fads and Foibles in Modern Sociology*, and in the recent little book by C. Wright Mills which, without the same comprehensive and detailed citation of seeming cases in point, follows much the same arguments as those advanced by Sorokin. (55)

But Sorokin does far more than contend that some dominant trends in American sociology are trivial. He argues rather that the discipline as a whole and all of its major schools of thought are hopelessly infested with ill-conceived, inconsequential, and incompetently executed research; that the malaise comes from the plague of sensate culture; that the only remedy is the adoption of the redeeming principles of integralism. Merton's fleeting reference to Sorokin's study is striking in view of its clear relevance to the immediate question of "triviality" in sociological inquiry. Even more puzzling at first glance is his characterization of Mills's study as "the recent little book" that allegedly (a) is "without the same comprehensive and detailed citation of seeming cases in point" and (b) "follows the same lines of argument as those advanced by Sorokin."

Merton's contentions regarding trivia in sociological inquiry are open to serious question. Although it is true that there is no logically necessary relationship between the study of trivial topics and the potential significance of any resulting discoveries, the fact remains that the formulation of a trivial problem and the investigation of a trivial topic only rarely

C. WRIGHT MILLS: Assaulting the Bastions of Liberal Sociology at
Columbia

lead to important solutions and findings. Merton's opaque remark about
instances of trivial research that have led to important discoveries loses
sight of the extreme rarity of such instances, their status as exceptions
that prove the rule, and their familiarity to sociologists of knowledge
precisely because they are singled out as instructive case studies of ex-
ceptional developments yielding some insights into the systematically
prevailing pattern in the history of science: namely, *important discoveries tend to come from the study of important problems and important
topics.* It is logically possible and even on rare occasions empirically

tenable to assert, for example, that an interest in frivolous hypotheses or a search for technical precision per se might be a source of discoveries having some enduring value. But in view of the force of Sorokin's study as a refutation of it on empirical grounds, especially so far as sociology itself is concerned, Merton's advancement of this logical possibility in defense of the varieties of trivial scholarship abounding in the social sciences is hardly convincing. He loosely and repeatedly confounds what is logically possible with what is sociologically probable and empirically demonstrable.

In the context of his attempt to examine the nature of trivial and important problems in modern sociology, Merton's abrupt dismissal of Mills's work as "the little book" is ironic and instructive.[51] His caricature serves to illustrate the sanctions often used by opinion leaders to symbolize as trivial those ideas that would otherwise threaten the legitimacy of an academic discipline and, in effect, to represent the standards of collective taste operative at a given time. Such a caricature therefore illustrates a normative rather than idiosyncratic response to a violation of the social definition of propriety in the sociological profession. In open violation of the rules of the game, Mills "names the names" and singles out one of Merton's own mentors, Talcott Parsons, for severe personal, ideological, and theoretical attack. Mills argues in Sociological Imagination, for example, that the intellectual bankruptcy of contemporary social science is a symptom of massive capitulation to the ideologies of state power; that the goals of raising social consciousness and politically transforming the structure of wealth and power in society, not merely promoting moral rearmament through personal exhortation as Sorokin attempted, is an essential and proper task of sociologists in the present era. Mills's empirical focus on the "bureaucratic ethos" and the "higher immorality," his explanation of these conditions in terms of the "conservative mood," and his solution in terms of a radical and activist approach to the sociological imagination are all in sharp contrast to Sorokin's assault on the "pioneering Columbuses" and Sorokin's cultural explanation and moral solution to this problem. Although Sorokin and Mills both seek to expose, explain, and denounce a variety of trivial undertakings in modern sociology and although their efforts may be seen in part as complementary, Merton's judgment that Mills is simply echoing Sorokin's views is a gross distortion of the profound differences in their respective studies of the discipline.

Merton fails to investigate the concrete historical conditions under which seemingly trivial or frivolous research has actually culminated in an important discovery. Had he investigated the extraordinary conditions conducive to such a discovery, he might have seriously considered the following possibilities: (1) it comes about only when the logical nature of the problem under study (in contrast to the empirical data per se) is formulated in a profound manner: (2) the researcher is usually a most perceptive, imaginative, rigorous, and independent scholar with a background of unhurried, intensive, interdisciplinary study reflecting a high capacity for self-education and self-criticism; and (3) both of these foregoing circumstances are seldom if ever even remotely approximated in the increasingly standardized, compartmentalized, regimented, "collaborative," state-funded, and state-monitored research centers in modern society.

The history of the discipline with which Merton is most eminently associated, the sociology of knowledge and science, is a case in point. Merton himself acknowledges that many enduring and far-reaching contributions to this field have been made by such figures as Durkheim, Marx, Mannheim, and Sorokin. But just how did these contributions originate? They resulted in part from the study of seemingly minor aspects of society and culture (e.g., conventional wisdom about time and space, irrational beliefs about private property, myths about an impossible future, notions of virtuous behavior and success) in intellectual milieus that cannot even be replicated in the modern scientific community.

Apart from Merton's neglect of the historical context in which trivial research is carried out and of the fashion process through which such research might be elevated to sudden prominence, one may wish to consider his analysis of charges regarding trivia in modern sociology made by Sorokin and Mills as well as Merton's own effort to differentiate important and trivial modes of inquiry. Such consideration is thwarted, however, because Merton avowedly and without explanation dismisses this latter set of issues as "pervasive polemics":

> But much of the attack on alleged trivia in today's sociology is directed against entire classes of investigation solely because the objects they examine do not enjoy widespread social interest. This most pervasive of polemics sets problems for those prospective monographs on the sociological history of sociology. . . . *We are here not concerned with the substantive merit if the charges and rejoinders involved in any particular polemic of this kind.* (61; emphasis added)

Merton again seeks to neutralize the serious charges advanced by Sorokin and Mills by contending that they and other critics object only or mainly to the topics for study chosen by most sociologists; he thereby obscures the extent to which such critics are really engaged in a frontal assault on the assumptions, scope, sources, consequences, and empirical unreliability of most research performed under the banner of "scientific sociology." Although he claims to rise above these "pervasive polemics," he nevertheless enters the arena through a back door[52] only to cast far more heat than light on the possible outcome of the battle.

Even on purely descriptive grounds, Merton's portrait of trivia leaves much to be desired. He claims on the one hand that "there remains the task of finding out the social sources and consequences of assigning triviality or importance to particular lines of inquiry" (62); this task might be of great value in illuminating the presence of collective tastes in the scientific community. But he offers on the other hand only the briefest characterization of "the alleged cleavage between substantive sociology and methodology," for example, and virtually no account at all of the actual sources and consequences of this cleavage or the ways in which adversaries define one another's views as "trivial" (62.64).[53] The very task Merton himself designates as important, then, is nowhere carried out or even mentioned in the balance of his essay "Social Conflict over Styles of Sociological Work."

Merton neither distinguishes the kinds of trivial and important research that might exist in modern sociology nor evaluates the charge that the discipline is inundated with trivial studies. He fails to examine the sources and consequences of trivial research or to identify the expressions of collective behavior manifested by the stereotyping of certain problems as trivial and others as important. He does not investigate the historical contexts in which serious conflicts over "styles of sociological work" are intensified in some instances, obscured in others, and resolved in still others. He even goes so far as to suggest that there is no need to resolve the many debates about the presence of trivial scholarship in modern sociology or, for that matter, to settle any explosive issues facing the discipline: cleavage, he maintains, is an intrinsically healthy and desirable state of affairs for the scientific community. In seeking to corroborate this assumption, Merton invokes:

> the hypothesis, in the words of [Edward] Ross, that "a society which is riven by a hundred [conflicts] along lines running in every direction, may actually be in less danger of being torn with violence or falling to pieces than one split along just one line. For each new cleavage contributes to narrow the cross clefts, so that one might say that society is sewn together by its inner conflicts." (68)

Merton appears to be at least dimly aware of the possibility that this speculative utterance by Ross is inadequate to corroborate such a sweeping assumption, for he quickly adds:

It is a hypothesis borne out by its own history, for since it was set forth by Simmel and by Ross, it has been taken up or independently originated by some scores of sociologists, many of whom take diametrically opposed positions on some of [these] issues. (I mention only a few of these: Wiese and Becker, Hiller, Myrdal, Parsons, Berelson, Lazarsfeld and McPhee, Robin Williams, Coser, Dahrendorf, Coleman, Lipset and Zelditch, and among the great number of recent students of "status discrepancy," Lenski, Adams, Stogdill, and Hemphill.) (69)

But do testimonials to the consensus surrounding this assumption really constitute evidence in its support? Merton does not explain how Ross's vague assertion can possibly be construed as proof of *any* sociological hypothesis; he does not explain how the good name of Simmel, whose notions regarding diversity and differentiation we have already seen to be untenable, can do so either. Merton ignores the great number of prominent scholars, especially Marxists, who call into question this assumption. He ignores the need to distinguish between: a popular and sanctified assumption and one that can withstand intensive empirical and logical examination; an assumption regarded as self-evident because it is caught up in the fashion process and one that is evaluated on the basis of explicit and objective criteria of validity; and an assumption uncritically taken for granted by prestigious opinion leaders and one that is independently investigated and corroborated in the absence of cronyism and ideological self-celebration.

Merton's uncritical acceptance of this assumption leads him willy-nilly to the more implicit but also more perilous notion that trivia and debates about trivia in modern sociology should be cultivated for the future advancement of "heterodoxy" in the scientific community. We will see shortly that Merton makes an eloquent concluding statement that encompasses this very notion.

Moreover, the fact that the prestigious figures named by Merton do disagree on some issues is hardly reason to believe that any given view on which they do happen to agree must ipso facto be true.

The weakest link in the chain of Merton's logic, however, is one that would seem to have no place in the sociology of knowledge. Just as sociological theorists must not draw inferences about the nature of society from the properties of the human organism, sociologists of knowledge must not draw inferences about the nature of the scientific community from simplistic and ahistorical models of the "social system." To assume that cleavage is permanently beneficial for society is dubious enough in its own right, especially from the standpoint of those who are victimized by the oppression underlying the cleavage; to assume that endless conflict and diversity are *therefore* beneficial for the scientific community is all the more far-fetched and naive.

Merton's acceptance of this assumption and his characterization of research on the relationship between conflict and order deserve further scrutiny. This research does not demonstrate or suggest that cleavages, chronic conflicts, radical confrontations, or revolutionary situations are in any way beneficial for society. Most of this research is really devoted to the investigation of (1) ways to predict and control only certain kinds of "discrepant behavior" or deviance;[54] (2) chiefly those deviant persons and acts representing *moderate, occasional, short-lived, segmentalized,* and *readily controllable* disturbances or violations of rules;[55] (3) the advantages (or "functional consequences") of such deviance for the social system arising form (a) the attendant opportunities for the agencies of control to test out, exercise, and improve their sanctioning procedures and (b) the tendencies of other social participants to identify with these procedures and thereby to reaffirm their loyalty to the status quo;[56] and (4) the need for an appropriate paradigm and a resilient and efficient sanctioning apparatus to deal with more serious threats to the security and defense of the social order.[57] If the many authors of such research had the slightest intention of endorsing serious conflicts or cleavages in the service of social order, if they were remotely convinced that chronic crises or revolutionary situations might lead to social progress, then they would hardly be preoccupied with the task of predicting, controlling, and sometimes even denying the existence of such conflicts, cleavages, crises, and revolutionary situations in their own society. But this is the very preoccupation that does characterize most of the conventional sociological literature on deviance, change, and social control in modern society. This is one of the governing objectives around which the seemingly endless varieties of "theory construction" and "policy research" have proliferated in the mainstream of the discipline in recent decades. Merton's citation of the studies of prominent scholars as though they were enamored with the virtues of serious conflict or cleavage is a grave distortion of their assumptions, purposes, and empirical claims. In view of his fulminations against those critics of the functionalist literature who misrepresent even some of its minor aspects, Merton's extreme distortion of this same literature to suit his own polemical purposes is all the more unconscionable.

By treating this shaky, unproven, and ahistorical assumption as though it were self-evident, Merton arrives at the following conclusion:

> If individual sociologists have different combinations of position on these and kindred issues, then effective intellectual criticism can supplant social conflict. That is why the extent of hetero-doxies among the sociologists of each nation has an important bearing on the future development of world sociology. The het-erodoxies in one nation provide intellectual linkages with the orthodoxies in other nations. On the worldwide scale of sociol-ogy, this bridges lines of cleavage and makes for the advance of sociological science rather than of sociological ideologies. (69)[58]

Insofar as this conclusion is accepted at face value, it opens the door to the kind of platitudes about endless diversity previously examined in the present study in connection with Friedrichs's model of dialectical and pluralistic sociology. One could grant for the moment that the scientific community and modern sociology in particular are every bit as diversified and pluralistic as Merton contends. If American sociology were really so pluralistic, then one would expect, in accordance with Merton's conclusion, that serious criticism would be especially intense among the most articulate opinion leaders from opposing positions in the discipline. In this case, Merton's own writings would tend severely to cast doubt upon his conclusion because he consistently and avowedly *refrains* from trying to evaluate critically the substantive merits of competing theoretical models and political positions in Ameri-can sociology. Despite his generalizations about the alleged "advance of sociological science," the ways in which "intellectual criticism can sup-plant social conflict," and the role of American heterodoxy in the bounti-ful "future development of world sociology," the fact remains that nei-ther Merton nor the many opinion leaders he chooses to cite offer a shred of evidence to support his optimistic forecasts. Merton does not examine the possibility that his own writings in the sociology of knowl-edge and science are permeated by ideological presuppositions and foregone conclusions around which a massive consensus, a veritable or-thodoxy in the fullest sense, has been formed. He is equally insensitive to the possibility that the great esteem in which his contributions are held might be largely attributable to his success in crystallizing and ac-commodating a wide range of amorphous sentiments and collective tastes about the virtues of cultural pluralism, the prophecies of a glori-ous future for sociology as a science, and the apprehensions over politi-cal struggle and serious intellectual conflict in the scientific community. Merton's work has been consistently and impressively resonant with these sentiments and tastes for several decades even as their nuances of meaning have subtly shifted from time to time.[59] He is always in the vanguard of those who would later consolidate the doctrine that modern sociology has "come of age" as a result of interminable diversity, but he never makes so extreme an argument in behalf of this doctrine is to seem far-out or in poor taste in the eyes of peers. He is among the very first spokesmen for the mainstream of the sociological profession to conceptualize the crises resulting from trivial scholarship, radical assaults on the integrity of the profession, and increasing polarization along theoretical and political lines as evidence of scientific ferment and academic maturity; he manages for the most part to have rendered this *tour de force* without seeming to have any partisanship in these developments. Although he appears to be statesmanlike in his receptivity to all points of view, thereby reflecting and reinforcing the search for civility and reasonableness in crisis-ridden and rapidly changing times, he nevertheless deftly scorns those ideas and individuals generally perceived to be most offensive and threatening to the mystique of sociology as a "hard science."

Merton's Stature in Modern Sociology

In view of the many fallacies, oversights, ahistorical doctrines, lack of critical self-awareness, and failure to pursue systematically the occasional insights he does offer about the scientific community shown in the present examination of Merton's writings, his eminence in modern sociology in general and in the sociology of knowledge and science in particular cannot be explained in terms of the substantive validity of his contributions. But how can this eminence be explained?

Merton's most enduring and vital contribution is not to the growth of reliable knowledge about the scientific community but rather to the alleviation of collective misgivings and restlessness in the ranks of modern sociology arising from a number of trends and conflicts that call into question the image of the discipline itself. Merton depicts those unwieldly trends and conflicts that threaten the image and the substance of the discipline as though they were testimony to its present and future solidity. Although his success in seeming to extricate the discipline from these unsettling trends and conflicts is not the recognized or acknowledged reason for his unrivaled stature among his peers, although his assumptions and conclusions about "heterodoxy" do not really come to grips with the underlying issues he claims to transcend, his success

ROBERT K. MERTON: Solving the Problem of Trivia in World Sociology

in fostering the mystique of a discipline in good health today and about to leap into an even better future tomorrow helps to explain his sustained influence as an opinion leader in modern sociology. The sign of crisis becomes redefined, in short, as reason for professional self-celebration. The pluralistic image has been so enthusiastically promulgated and so subtly consolidated as to enjoy a hallowed place in the general heritage of the discipline. As indicated earlier in the present study, for example, this image serves as a point of departure for Friedrich's even more modernistic vision of a newly matured scientific community in his universally acclaimed *A Sociology of Sociology*. The internal logic of the assumptions in Merton's research and the sustained influence he enjoys as an opinion leader in modern sociology, then, are manifestations of the fashion process in a discipline whose practitioners systematically ignore and sometimes even deny the existence of this process in their own work.

CHAPTER 6
THE FUNCTIONAL THEORY OF INEQUALITY
THE PROBLEM OF REWARDING MERIT OR MEDIOCRITY

Instead of reviewing the extensive debates between advocates and critics of the functionalist theory of stratification, we can consider the historical context in the late 1940s and early 1950s in which the Davis-Moore paradigm originally appeared. Among the abstract ideas that unified the American people during the dark days of World War II were (1) the belief in equality of opportunity—the view that even the least among us can make it to the top by hard work and entrepreneurial vision; (2) the recognition that the Japanese and German enemy intended to conquer the world and stamp out this very ideal for all humanity; (3) the commitment to defeat this enemy at any price in the name of freedom and justice for all. Even though prosperity in this land seemed to reign supreme after the enemy was finally defeated, some Americans were still more "equal" than others, much more prosperous than others, much more privileged than others. And not every returning soldier found an attractive job; millions of women, moreover, were pressured into giving up their work clothes and putting on their aprons all over again. And millions of black Americans were excluded altogether from the new affluence. And the signs of increasingly serious economic recession in the 1950s, adversely affecting vast numbers of working Americans while leaving a wealthy few even wealthier than ever, did not help to shore up confidence in the ideals for which they thought they were fighting in the war just concluded. How to explain this inequality to the unemployed and underemployed, to ex-GIs and to women?

The functional paradigm answers this question straightforwardly. Society requires the execution of a variety of role performances and services. Some of these services are especially difficult and complex: they require high levels of skill and training, which are often prolonged and expensive to obtain. To make sure these services are in fact provided, society establishes a system of differential rewards to induce prospective candidates to undertake the necessary training especially in those fields that are most difficult and important. Differential rewards lead to inequality in the system of stratification, but they are necessary for the well-being of the system as a whole. Within the framework of this paradigm, those who receive the highest rewards therefore deserve them in light of their contribution to the needs of the system as a whole. The advocates of this paradigm considered differential rewards to be necessary for the meeting of socially important needs. Inequality, they concluded, is therefore universal and inevitable.

The fierce debates over the functional theory of stratification, especially heated in the 1960s and early 1970s, continue to center on questions of equity in the distribution of differential rewards and access to opportunities for social mobility. For whom is such stratification "functional" or useful? Does it really work for the benefit of everyone, for the progress of society as a whole? Or does it overwhelmingly enable the already wealthy to gain still greater privilege while allowing only a few crumbs to reach those who are truly deserving and in need of scarce resources? Historical materialists are quick to add that the unequal distribution of wealth is a consequence of class relationships; that private ownership of the means to produce wealth leads to effective control over its accumulation and maldistribution in capitalist society.

Extensive studies have been launched by all interested parties to answer these questions. There is an almost endless proliferation of techniques to measure income differentials and to describe correlations between education and income, religion and income, gender and income, prestige and income, age and income, political connections and income, election to public office and income, mental illness and income, and so forth. These measurements and descriptions are carried out by conservative and liberal as well as radical sociologists who are empirically inclined and trained for the purpose of bolstering their respective positions. But the data keep coming in, and the debates continue ad infinitum. Part of the reason for the apparent impossibility of resolving them may well be that the conservative and liberal advocates of functionalism already do enjoy professional and ideological hegemony and therefore do not need to accommodate or even communicate seriously with their radical critics. Another part of the reason may well be that all parties resent each other on ideological and other grounds, and talk past each other no matter what the evidence happens to indicate. But a major part of the reason for the apparent infinity of these debates is, as we will see, an underlying assumption to which all parties uncritically adhere and which, on closer inspection, turns out to be extremely dubious. Let us survey the landscape before we come to grips with the roots of the endlessly sprouting debate.

Functionalists have argued that income differentials are (1) "functional" or useful to society as a whole and (2) not excessive or oppressive to the vast majority of Americans in any case. Their critics have argued that what *seems* to be useful to society as a whole is actually useful to the already privileged, to the capitalist class; and that the inequities are excessive and oppressive in any case. But both sides in this debate tend to assume that differential awards are allocated for the most part on the basis of merit; that doctors receive more income than childcare workers, for example, because they have greater abilities to perform difficult and socially necessary tasks that can be mastered only through expensive and lengthy training; and that the differential rewards are necessary to ensure society of a sufficient number of capable occupants for the most necessary and demanding roles.

The view that rewards are and must be based on *competence* or *merit* is sacrosanct in American society. Like others ideologically conditioned by and socialized into it, conservative, liberal, and radical sociologists are inclined to accept one of its most pervasive themes: *rewards go to those who earn them throughout American society, throughout the scientific community, throughout the capitalist world.* Whether this is objectively true, however, is quite another matter.

Liberals and conservatives hold that those currently privileged deserve to be privileged because they are doing what is most socially necessary. (They do disagree on the level of taxation and the applicability of the graduated income tax to ameliorate income discrepancies and to redistribute some of the wealth, but we need not examine this point of contention here.) Radicals hold that many members of the working class contribute to the accumulation of society's surplus wealth, perform difficult and even dangerous tasks only to receive meager rewards for their labor, and that the rewards and life chances available to the working class in general should be greatly enhanced — a goal to be facilitated by socialist revolution. The debate continues on not so much because of disagreement but rather because of agreement: each side is in effect competing to bolster its own position by outdoing its adversary with more data and more descriptions and measures of association on behalf of essentially the same assumption about the actuality, desirability, or necessity of merit in the distribution of rewards. And liberals in the capitalist tradition agree with moderate socialists on the virtues of giving disadvantaged people what they need for survival – leading to the welfare state, or at least to welfare capitalism. The debate cannot possibly be settled because both sides agree about a seemingly self-evident assumption that in reality is highly problematic.

Let us consider such cases as the U.S. Department of State, American higher education, and vertical mobility in the Communist Party in the Soviet Union under concrete historical conditions. What are the actual criteria for the allocation of rewards, the prevailing rules for success, and vertical mobility in these domains?

Let us grant that a knowledge of other societies, mastery of foreign languages and intellectual grasp of global economic and political forces might here and there be taken into account in the promotion of State Department personnel. But the fact remains that rewards and promotions at Foggy Bottom have little to do with any objective standards of competence and much to do with considerations of "professional responsibility" and "maturity of judgment." What do these considerations really mean? What happens when a candidate for promotion is well established and *known* to be obedient and to have a reliable track record; to acquiesce and make no waves in the flurry of shifting and expedient policies conjured up by an empire undergoing decline and disintegration; to have neither the intellectual ability nor the self-confidence to raise serious questions, for example, about the U.S. invasion of Grenada, the goal of overthrowing the socialist regime in Nicaragua, the engagement in open wars and hidden machinations throughout the world on behalf of "free enterprise"? Such a candidate is most likely to be promoted. In short, it is not "competence" in any objectively demonstrable sense that governs the differential rewards and prospects for vertical mobility in the State Department: it is *mediocrity* that is the operative criterion for a candidate's success in the State Department, *mediocrity* that is the de facto consideration in the selection process used to screen candidates for promotion.

The ideological assumption that rewards are necessarily based on merit leads to a proliferation of ever-changing measurements and embellishments on the functionalist view of the relationship between income and other variables. But it short-circuits and undermines any potential investigation of *incompetence* or *mediocrity* as a basis for vertical mobility. If mediocrity is a decisive consideration in the allocation of rewards, then a thorny question must be raised about the functionalist paradigm: how is it possible that those who do not know what they are doing manage nonetheless to contribute to the maintenance of the social system, to the performance of needed services, to the benefit of all its participants in the long run? The assumption of rewards given for merit opens the door to an endless array of measurements and procedures ignoring the extent to which income may well be determined by mediocrity. Despite the increasing precision and refinement of these measures and procedures, they cannot be used to prove or disprove any hypothesis because they presuppose a doctrine of social utility that is not objectively tenable. They contribute to the flood tide of technical nuances in a sea of raw empiricism. What I have just suggested and will develop in the immediately following examples is that *some* candidates for vertical mobility are occasionally rewarded for their actual merit whereas *most* candidates are rewarded for their mediocrity and that this view is more adequate than the functionalist model of stratification. A defense of the functionalist paradigm might be proposed here: one might view mediocrity itself as useful for social order and therefore inevitably deserving of rewards in accordance with the system's prerequisites for survival. But such a defense begs the question of whether all sectors of society can possibly benefit from the incompetent or mediocre provision of essential services, including those in higher education.

Let us grant that candidates for such positions as department chairs, deans, and academic vice presidents are also here and there chosen for their record of superior scholarship and effectiveness in teaching as well as their executive talent or skill, and that those who make the final selection of candidates go to the extraordinary lengths of trying to measure or evaluate such skill in some rational and objectively demonstrable way.

When all of these contingencies are granted, however, it is still extremely difficult to cite examples, much less systematic evidence, to support such a possible scenario and extremely easy to cite examples to the contrary at virtually all institutions of higher learning. Again and again, the selection of candidates for these administrative positions is guided by considerations *other than* competence in any objectively demonstrable sense. We once again see such factors as "maturity of judgment" and "professional responsibility" alone looming large in the selection process for very good reason: a record of high academic competence on the part of a given candidate is actually an alarm signal indicative of the likelihood that he or she might have the self-confidence to challenge unjust educational policies, to feel an allegiance to the students or faculty, or, even more ominously, to the consumers and working people in the community rather than the wealthy and powerful interests typically in control of the university's board of regents or trustees. A major responsibility of university administrators, then, is to know what the marching orders are without the necessity of a trustee issuing any overt written or verbal commands at all. If a figure from the ruling class does find it necessary to tell an administrator what to do in any concrete sense, then some politically unpleasant consequences may well erupt when the commands are made public. The students and faculty alike might then recognize their de facto exclusion from the decision-making process, their extremely vulnerable place in the larger chain of command, their presence in a system of alienated intellectual labor rather than a democratically or consensually established academic community, their common interest in bringing about structural change with an eye toward making a nominal academic community into a real one. At the first sign of "immaturity," then, the university's decision makers do indeed dismiss their chief executive officer: the very fact that the administrator has to be told what to do is considered ample basis for his or her removal and replacement by a more mature candidate. This de facto selection process was brought into unusually sharp relief during the late 1960s and early 1970s, for example, in California's system of higher education: Governor Ronald Reagan and Superintendent of Instruction Dr. Max Rafferty, working in cooperation with university trustees and regents, dismissed large numbers of upper- and middle-echelon administrators who showed the slightest sympathy for student and faculty demonstrations against U.S. policy in Vietnam. A few of those abruptly dismissed administrators did have distinguished academic and professional records, but virtually all of those who were selected to replace them were chosen primarily and explicitly because they declared themselves to be and were considered "responsible," "reliable," and committed to the restoration of law and order on the campuses. One apparent exception to this trend was the designation of S. I. Hayakawa as president of San Francisco State College in the midst of fierce student and faculty antiwar demonstrations. Although he was regularly portrayed in the press as "the noted semanticist," he was called to serve on the basis of his early, frequent, and vehement condemnations of all participants in the uprisings. In his subsequent campaign for election to the U.S. Senate, his appeal was based on his success in restoring law and order to the West, not on his contributions to linguistics, semantics, or philosophy.

The same general pattern obtains in the other areas of personnel selection and the granting of awards in higher education. The granting of academic tenure is the most graphic case in point of de facto consideration of factors other than competence or merit in the filtering and screening process. By the time a candidate for a continuing or permanent appointment is finally evaluated, his or her track record is well established. But are scholarly achievements and teaching effectiveness the primary or secondary criteria in this process? These criteria are indeed taken into account, but only in terms of the candidate's known record of loyalties and behavior during the probationary years. Indeed, *entire academic departments*, including tenured and untenured faculty, are systematically dismantled on the ostensible grounds that they are "superfluous," "redundant," or "inefficient" when their stirrings of political activism and radical views begin to challenge the legitimacy of capitalist domination and imperialism. The fate of the School of Criminology at the University of California's Berkeley campus in the 1970s is, again, an example of the unwritten and usually unacknowledged criteria with which seemingly "permanent" decisions about individual faculty and entire academic programs are actually made: "reliability," "responsibility," and "professional maturity," characteristics of what C. Wright Mills calls the "cheerful robot," are the most important and most rewarded qualities in the academic selection process. Although the iron fist in the velvet glove of academic management is seldom obvious, its influence is always present. The usually subtle operation of these criteria and the unacknowledged presence of capitalist domination embedded in the academic decision-making process serve to explain why it is so rarely necessary for the velvet glove to be taken off, for the veneer of academic consensus and the "free marketplace of ideas" and "theoretical discourse" to be scratched or shattered. And to minimize the risk of such episodes actually taking place, it is essential to keep administrative hierarchies and academic departments staffed primarily with the mediocre, the unexceptional, the pedestrian candidates who can be counted on to do the right thing, to know what is expected of them even when no one gives them any marching orders. Those candidates who exemplify these latter qualities are praised for their "initiative," "leadership," and "vision," which are highly valued and rewarded; those who exhibit "irresponsibility," "recalcitrance," "impertinence," and, worst of all, sympathy for "mindless activism," are, by contrast, targeted for containment or removal from the groves of academe. The former are considered flexible, cooperative, and responsive; the latter are seen as inflexible, uncooperative, and unresponsive, and are classified as mortal enemies of the academic community.

Still another apparent exception that proves the rule about mediocrity as the prevailing norm in the academic distribution of rewards is the *Sputnik* crisis of the 1950s. Federal commissions and national security officials declared that Soviet superiority in science and engineering, as manifested by our inability to duplicate the feat of launching satellites into planetary orbit, was due to the Russian emphasis on high academic standards and the American emphasis on partying, sports, and the "gen-tleman's C." A new national policy was quickly established: high aca-demic standards and concentration on science, mathematics, and for-eign languages suddenly became signs of good adjustment and patriotism while goofing-off and joining fraternities and sororities be-came signs of backwardness and stupidity. By the 1960s, we too knew how to launch satellites; we even beat the Russians to the moon with a manned expedition in the extraterrestrial aspect of President Kennedy's widely hailed agenda for the New Frontier. By the mid-1960s, however, the very same students who had been socialized into the new mandate for studying hard in the liberal arts and sciences had shown that they had acquired a number of extremely dangerous skills: they had learned to investigate the statistical and political claims of government officials for themselves, to ask probing and volatile questions about U.S. war policy overseas and racial injustice at home, to formulate and produce political pamphlets and campus literature that systematically challenged the state itself, to call for unity among students and faculty and commu-nity residents—to become, in short, politically uncontrollable. By the 1970s, the Carnegie Commission on Higher Education and related cor-porate think tanks came to a number of important conclusions about the effects of high academic standards and the harmful consequences of taking scholarship too seriously: the introduction of high standards in the public universities and the emphasis on liberal arts and sciences were giving rise to undue "restlessness" and "unrealistic aspirations" among college youth, according to these appraisals, and should be phased out in favor of vocational and technical programs to encourage more "realistic" and "practical" attitudes in higher education. The conse-quences of this strategy are today evident. We find a new era of aca-demic mediocrity, grade inflation, ascendance of vocational and techni-cal training, widespread and lucrative "term papers for sale" enterprises, and the rapid revival of fraternities and sororities by the late 1970s and 1980s: social adjustment counts more and more, academic merit counts less and less, and the conservative mood becomes increasingly institu-tionalized and pervasive. Even if sociologists might wish to debate the intimate and long-term relationship between *academic merit* and *the potential for heightened political consciousness*, the capitalist class has no doubt about the need for *low* standards of competence and *low* levels of aspiration in the public universities and *high* standards of com-petence and *high* levels of aspiration in the elite private universities, where the sons and daughters of the ruling class learn to appreciate, ex-pand, and defend their class interests.

There is a profound and potentially ruinous contradiction built into the strategy of watering down academic standards in the service of a malleable and exploitable working class: if the next generation of college graduates is more knowledgeable about "Dallas," "Knots Landing," and video games than they are about science, mathematics, English, and foreign languages, then American capitalism will have neither a labor force able to keep up with the demands of a high-tech economy nor any prospect of competing effectively against other countries in world markets. This grim prospect is no longer just idle speculation. In recent years, even former President Reagan, although not known for his scholarly proclivities, found it necessary to insist that academic standards need to be drastically "beefed-up" so that American capitalism can prevail over Soviet, Japanese, and European competition; exactly how far the pendulum can swing toward higher standards in public universities without causing yet another period of heightened political consciousness and activism is unclear. Indeed, whether the pendulum can swing substantially or even slightly away from a comprehensive academic policy that has been institutionalized for nearly two decades is unclear.

The distribution of rewards on the basis of incompetence or mediocrity can also be seen in the history of the Communist Party in the Soviet Union. For all the talk of "de-Stalinization" in the era of Khrushchev and "openness" in the era of Gorbachev, the fact remains that the Communist Party's success in minimizing expressions of criticism and discontent was accomplished *only in part* by the use of terror and coercion. Particularly during Stalin's own reign, considerations other than competence or merit were uppermost in the selection of some candidates rather than others for advancement in the Party, for material and social rewards, and for deciding who would be spared from the firing squad, from a sentence in a concentration camp, from the ordeal of "rehabilitation" in a state mental hospital. Absolute loyalty to the Party in general and to Stalin in particular was the *sine qua non* for career advancement and often for survival; this criterion in turn was used to determine who was deserving of promotion and privilege, who was competent and meritorious, in the selection process. This criterion prevailed not only in the organs of state power and the Communist Party itself but also in the domains of art, literature, and science. Even the most gifted performing artists, authors, and scientists were relegated to obscurity, sometimes imprisoned, exiled, or forced into repressive psychiatric institutions, at the first sign of political insubordination or ideological unorthodoxy. Even the most capable Marxist social scientists, including Bukharin and Trotsky, were liquidated as enemies of the state without the slightest regard for their intellectual contributions or merit; their work was declared "worthless" and banished from the annals of Soviet social science. Neither their vertical mobility nor their survival was en-hanced by considerations of competence or merit. As in capitalist soci-ety, the systematic allocation of rewards to those who are mediocre rather than meritorious ensures a high level of obedience to the state, a high level of "political responsibility" and "professional maturity" on the part of those who gratefully receive privileges they have not earned.

We have seen that the pattern of rewarding incompetence is advanta-geous in any exploitive or repressive system of domination, for it en-sures the obedience of those who enjoy vertical mobility. But it has yet another advantage from the standpoint of maintaining social order: it sends a message to those who *are* truly competent and meritorious that there are virtues far more important than competence, that these virtues can *override* the issue of competence altogether and even determine the outcome of the selection process, that the state is endowed with a special omniscience and omnipotence to redefine at will the meaning and application of such terms as merit, competence, and worthiness. This pattern therefore has a chilling effect on the thought and behavior of the truly competent who might otherwise wish to speak out against injustice, oppression, scandals, or ruinous economic policies in their so-ciety. It helps to ensure what Talcott Parsons calls the "boundary-maintenance" and "tension-management" of the social system.

The assumption that rewards are universally or necessarily allocated on the basis of merit is an ahistorical and highly misleading view of American society. It short-circuits and undermines any systematic inves-tigation of *incompetence* and *mediocrity* as the basis for vertical mobil-ity. It also contributes to an intellectual setting in which measurements and procedures become increasingly refined, precise, varied, and in-capable of testing any hypothesis and from which the play of fashion in the pursuit of empirical data becomes increasingly likely.

Functionalism, Neofunctionalism, and the Ascendance of Jeffrey Alexander in Social Theory

By the late 1960s, the functionalist model of society had undergone se-vere criticism on logical and empirical grounds—particularly because of its ahistorical bias and its presuppositions about value-neutrality. A closely related and politically more immediate challenge to this model emerged in the amorphous radical sociology movement, which at-tracted substantial support by the early 1970s and culminated in the elec-tion of Alfred McClung Lee to the presidency of the American Sociologi-cal Association; an outspoken critic of functionalist ideology and articulate humanist was seated, albeit temporarily, precisely where the advocates of functionalism ordinarily enjoyed uncontested hegemony. But the ASA's political command structure not only endured these irreverent assaults on the bastions of "normal science" but also managed to close ranks with other professional associations and universities throughout American society by using co-optation where possible and repression where necessary for the pacification of the restless rank and file. Just as Richard Nixon quickly carried out his avowed executive mission of restoring "law and order" in the streets, the ASA managed by the late 1970s to restore the veneer of "normal science" in its annual conventions, its mainstream journals, its subtle grip over graduate education, its means of ideological reproduction. Kuhn's ambiguous image of the scientific community was selectively and judiciously invoked to help reaffirm a sense of legitimacy for the recently polarized ASA and its bruised functionalist paradigm. But even the most loosely conceived and caricatured invocation of Kuhn's image of "normal science" could not avoid the lingering difficulty arising from his occasional suggestion that *any* scientific community must be prepared to jettison a paradigm that cannot explain major anomalies – particularly as they become frequent and cumulative.

The problem with the functionalist paradigm was that its critics were using historical and comparative evidence against it and were going so far as to suggest that conservative ideological assumptions about "useful" institutions and the immanent need for social order were responsible for its shortcomings. Whatever the other features of Kuhn's image of normal science, his emphasis on empirical evidence and rational analysis was precisely the outlook that had allowed the earlier criticisms of the functionalist paradigm to gain an audience and that might set the stage for a recurrence of radical challenges to its legitimacy. Although the opinion leaders and strategists within the ASA were relieved to see the *Sturm und Drang* of radical sociology relegated to obscurity by the late 1970s, an ideology in the guise of a new paradigm was still needed for strategic purposes: to enable the functionalist enterprise to keep its "analytical propositions" intact and to protect the enterprise, as the arbiter of normal science, from future shock at the hands of irreverent critics. The search for a modified conception of theory, a modified conception of science itself, was on.

A "post-Kuhnian" paradigm of the scientific community was needed (1) to protect functionalism from empirical and logical attack; (2) to justify the dismissal of those who might introduce evidence that the "postindustrial" society had never arrived; and (3) to advance a plausible rationale for ignoring the decline of mature capitalism and the disintegration of the American empire as though these trends were irrelevant to social theory in general and functional analysis in particular. If such a "post-Kuhnian" paradigm could be conjured up, then functionalist sociology could be salvaged as a useful, heuristic, and ahistorical perspective for appreciating the utopian wonders of postindustrial society, shielded from any future trauma of the kind that had been nearly fatal to "normal science" in the uncomfortably recent past. Such a paradigm could define negative evidence and logical criticism as inconceivable, unnecessary, or irrelevant *in principle* and *in advance* of any future challenges. If such a paradigm were established in the mainstream of general social theory, it would be timely indeed. It would be, as Oliver North might say, a "neat idea."

By the late 1970s and all the more so in the 1980s, then, the emergent collective tastes in mainstream sociology were primed and ready for something like functionalism, something newer and better than functionalism, but without its drawbacks. They produced by the 1980s just the right ambience for the arrival of *neofunctionalism.* They set the stage for the rapid rise to prominence of the most articulate spokesman for this model, Jeffrey Alexander, as a refreshing new opinion leader in normal science.[1]

The rapid ascendance of Alexander as an opinion leader in sociology might seem at first glance to be explained on the basis of some substantive contribution or discovery about the nature of society with which he could be credited. But he does not offer or claim to offer anything equivalent to Weber's thesis on the rise of capitalism, Durkheim's on the origins of religion, Parsons's on the pattern variables, or Merton's on reference group behavior; indeed, Alexander sees his own work as *transcending* such concerns and advancing a new conception of social science in what he takes to be the era of postpositivism. There is no substantive observation, claim, or hypothesis in his work that appreciably extends or modifies contemporary functional analysis; his role as a founder of neofunctionalism therefore cannot be explained by or reduced to any critical synthesis of functionalist concepts within a positivist tradition. His distinctive contribution to and influence on sociological theory in general and neofunctionalism in particular are found in his image of the scientific community and his delineation of theoretical discourse within that community. Although previously implied by a variety of structuralist, humanist, existential, and phenomenological thinkers ranging from such deterministic Marxists as Althusser to such voluntaristic social psychologists as R. D. Laing, and suggested in some of Alexander's own earlier writings, his most recent manifesto, "General Theory in the Postpositivist Mode," is a clear, vigorous, and explicit presentation of what he means by the "scientific community" and the "discourse" anticipated within its boundaries. Moreover, Alexander presented this essay at a recent conference on general social theory and responded to numerous questions about his position, indicating that he said what he meant and meant what he said therein. Hence, we will concentrate on this essay to ascertain what he said, what he meant, and how his views reflect and reinforce the operation of collective tastes in the scientific community.

According to Alexander:

> It is precisely the perspectival quality of social science that makes its own version of foundationalism, its more or less continuous strain of general theorizing, so necessary and often so compelling. It is natural science that does not exhibit foundationalism, for the very reason that its access to external truth has become increasingly secure. *Commensurability and realism delegitimate foundationalism, not increase its plausibility.* In natural science, attention can plausibly be focussed on the empirical side of the continuum. In social science, by contrast, practitioners cannot so easily accept "the evidence of their senses." (46; emphasis added)

As the most recently and rapidly established opinion leader in sociological theory in the 1980s, Alexander's view of "discourse" merits our close attention. His equivocal and ambiguous endorsement of postmodernism in general and the work of Foucault, Habermas, and Rorty in particular lead him to an *intuitionist* view of scientific progress, an *intuitionist* faith in discourse as an end in itself:

> Discourse becomes as important a disciplinary activity as explanation. Discourse is general and foundational. It aims at thematizing the standards of validity that are imminent in the very practice of social science. Responding to the lack of disciplinary confidence in empirical mirroring, theoretical discourse aims to gain provisional acceptance on the basis of universal argument. It is, therefore, the very impossibility of establishing permanent foundations that makes foundationalism in the social science so critical. This is the postpositivist case for general theory. It is also a case for present reason. (62–63)[2]

Let us consider what Alexander means by progress in the scientific community in light of his reliance on discourse as the guarantor of reason. Since quantitative and comparative evidence cannot be trusted, since historical evidence is even more suspect, since the very act of studying objective reality is problematic and perhaps even illusory in the postpositivist view, Alexander must find some new feature of the scientific community, (1) to establish the credibility of postpositivism itself, and (2) to exclude from serious consideration such "inapplicable" and potentially disruptive criteria as commensurability and realism in the evaluation of competing paradigms. Alexander finds that "discourse" is the new methodology to be featured in general sociological theory and that adherence to "universal criteria" is the strategy for progress in this domain.

But how can neofunctionalist and postpositive models be validated or even appear to be validated in the new era of "historical practice" envisioned by Alexander?[3] Through what process can they be ideologically legitimized? Through the immanent process of discourse itself, he maintains, social science creates its own foundations and "foundationalism"; these naturally unfolding products of discourse render the pursuit of general theory necessary and compelling. For Alexander, the de facto meaning of "general theory" becomes coextensive with neofunctionalist and postpositivist theory; any other form of theorizing becomes illusory and retrogressive for the scientific community.

Like Kuhn and Merton, Alexander assumes that the scientific community progresses from particularist to universalist criteria of truth, from individual, proprietary, and partisan control over these criteria to a consensual, public, and neutral application of them in evaluating proposed models:

> The more individuals share conceptions of their impersonal worlds, the more individual practice can be subject to extra-personal control; the more practice is subjected to impersonal control, the more it submits itself to universal criteria of evaluation. The more shared ground, the more neutral this ground not only seems but is in fact. Not neutral in the sense of absent reason, but in the sense of an historical practice that neither party feels it can either own or control. (46)

But who will be the guardians, arbiters, and enforcers of this "impersonal control"? Alexander ignores the political and ideological consequences of his new image of science. Those vested interests already entrenched in the sociological profession, those scientists considered to be most responsible and responsive and reliable in the eyes of agencies of state power and the great foundations and corporate think tanks and publishers, those scientists perceived to be most "up-to-date" and "forward-looking" and endowed with good taste have an important destiny: they become the guardians of what he calls the "shared ground," the "neutral ground," the "universal criteria" by which new proposals or conceptions are evaluated. Alexander assumes that the scientific community is graced with an invisible hand of universal wisdom extended by a benign postpositivist umpire to ensure that all proposals are fairly evaluated. He offers neither empirical evidence nor logical justification for this assumption. Despite his assumptions and reassurances about the free play of ideas and the fairness and reason with which competing models are entertained in the scientific community, the fact remains that the command-and-control structure of this guardianship is in the hands of functionalists and neofunctionalists. The dominion already exercised by these vested interests is so effective that they seldom find it necessary to give even a passing nod to the criticisms voiced by advocates of the once-troublesome but now largely neutralized and co-opted movement of radical sociology. The former are "up-to-date"; the latter are "obsolete."

As noted earlier, those with the greatest fidelity to the collective tastes prevailing in the scientific community, those with the greatest support from and acquiescence toward agencies of state power, those in a position to award and withhold academic tenure, promotions, and research grants are likely to enjoy hegemony in cases of intuitional disagreement over what Alexander calls "standards of validity" and their "foundations" (however permanent or transient) in the discipline. If no one is willing or able to introduce force, coercion, co-optation, moralistic appeals, or an insistence on being modern (or postmodern) into the debate, then the only possible outcome is an endless diversity, a Tower of Babel, in which all intuitive models, paradigms, and "foundations" are granted equal status. Even if the opinion leaders and decision makers within the discipline were to allow this nebulous uncertainty to continue, the state requires a number of important services from the scientific community and is unlikely to stand idly by when confronted with the spectacle of intellectual paralysis in ideological production. The systematic outcome of Alexander's vision of "theoretical discourse" is therefore determined by the operation of collective tastes within the scientific community and by the structure of domination in the larger society.

The New Vocabulary of Postpositive Social Theory: New Guidelines and Collective Tastes for the Scientific Community

The intuitionist thrust of the postpositivist model is found more in its vocabulary than in its substantive claims about social structure. The ex-

istential, phenomenological, and pre-Marxist dialectical thought of Kier-
kegaard, Merleau-Ponty, Nietzsche, Hegel, and Kant are in effect rediscovered as the foundations of a seemingly new and revolutionary style
of discourse, a seemingly bold and daring science of society. Whatever
the protestations of the neofunctionalist and postpositivist theorists to
be seen as the resuscitators of these once-dominant and ahistorical views
of the human condition, the fact remains that their mission and allegiances are squarely in the philosophical traditions just noted. Indeed, we
are presented with what appears to be a liberating vocabulary that upon
closer inspection, is designed to facilitate academic dialogue as an end
in itself, as a ritualized exercise among free-floating intellectuals. We are
told, for example, about the importance of "grounding" in metatheory
rather than a class-based alliance witih those struggling against exploitation; "hermeneutics" for self-contemplation rather than historical self-
awareness and class-consciousness; "dialectics" in the study of any logically possible distinctions rather than the analysis of contradictions between productive forces and productive relations; "transcendence" for
the avoidance and even the evasion of responsibility to confront the oppressive aspects of capitalism rather than engagement in the theory and
practice of challenging it; "feeling the pain of others through language"
rather than developing strategies for effective participation and communication to eliminate the causes of alienated labor; "heuristic devices" to
illustrate "analytical propositions" rather than the formulation of concepts to identify the points of vulnerability in a structure of domination;
the pursuit of "discourse" or "dialogue" as a sacrosanct end in itself rather
than the dissemination of an interdisciplinary and historically informed
social science to facilitate the search for justice and self-determination;
the undertaking of academic "projects" within the framework of this
vocabulary rather than the investment of scholarly effort to bring about
progress in science or society. Even the terms "structuralism" and "structural analysis" now refer largely or entirely to the study of patterns of language and styles of discourse per se rather than investigations into the
apparatus of state power and the means of ideological reproduction and
the forms of class struggle under concrete historical conditions. The acceptance and use of this vocabulary already imply a certain conception
of society, a certain image of social science, a certain role for the
researcher especially well conveyed in the meaning of the "project."

The "project" typically envisioned within the guidelines of this new
vocabulary, however unhelpful it may be to the advancement of social
justice or the science of society, is by no means impractical or inconsequential.[4] It can be of service, for example, to the state in the search of

ideological mystification. It can also enhance the researcher's own prospects for being awarded tenure, promotions, and generous grants in return for his or her benign contributions to the newly refurbished scientific community. It is therefore "functional" for the system as a whole and for the individual actor. And the ostensible content of this vocabulary includes just enough seemingly bold, radical, and antiestablishment rhetoric so as to give the scientific community and, indeed, the capitalist society that sponsors and sustains it the appearance of novelty, open-mindedness, freedom of expression, and democracy in action. The fact that the language of progressive scholarship has been co-opted by and selectively integrated into the logic of postpositivist and postmodern social theory is graphic testimony to the prevalence of the conservative mood and the neutralization of the critics of functionalism in sociology.

Some trends in literary criticism and some opinion leaders in that domain are appearing in the mainstream of general sociological theory, complete with the ahistorical rhetoric and pedagogy of "postmodernism," "hermeneutics," "dialectics," and "transcendence." In turn, the more extreme positivists, modernists, and realists in sociological theory are increasingly defined as obsolete and out-of-step with the latest developments. Since these latter adherents to old-fashioned paradigms are considered to have a diminished claim to center stage in the drama of sociological theory, their fate becomes uncertain. One wonders whether Alexander might take it upon himself to help guide these prospectively uprooted positivists and realists in efforts at relocation to a new home — the world of literary or, perhaps, postliterary criticism. Such a relocation would allow for a mutual transfusion of personnel, a circulation of elites, and a reduced risk of future turmoil over the validity and primacy of the functionalist paradigm of the scientific community.

CHAPTER 7
REVIEW OF THE THEMES DEVELOPED IN THE STUDY OF FASHIONS IN SCIENCE

The present study begins with a discussion of the many lacunae in the conventional wisdom regarding the fashion process in modern society, and a criticism particularly of the exceedingly narrow and ahistorical conception of this process found in standard encyclopedias and sociological textbooks. A summary of the major arguments and findings presented thus far is now in order.

The fashion process refers to the preoccupation with keeping in step with the times; admiring proposals or models when they are in "good taste," compatible with collective sentiments, and regarded as new or modern; downgrading proposals when they are in "bad taste," offensive to collective sentiments, and regarded as old or obsolete; opposing the weight of tradition in general while rediscovering older models as though they were unprecedented, daring, sensational, or even revolutionary; condemning anyone who resists new and popular proposals on the grounds that he or she is "old-fashioned," "out-of-step," or "too straight"; and celebrating the present as though it were surely an open door to a bountiful and proximate future.

The first case study of a scientific opinion leader caught up in the fashion process examines the theoretical research of Georg Simmel. It concentrates on an examination of Simmel's extensive essay on fashion, reviews the many fallacies in his claims about the fashion process in modern society, traces these fallacies to the operation of the fashion process in Simmel's own thought, and highlights the great extent to which his dubious claims have become a myopic precedent for most of the research on the fashion process in sociological inquiry.

The second case study examines the empirical research of Alfred Kroeber. It concentrates on an examination of Kroeber's essay "On the Principle of Order as Exemplified by Changes of Fashion," demonstrates the extreme unreliability of most of his allegedly verified claims about the fashion process in modern society, traces the defects in his quantitative research to the operation of the fashion process in his own thought, and highlights the extent to which his dubious claims have also become a myopic precedent for most of the research on the fashion process in modern society.

A comparison of Simmel's theoretical research and Kroeber's empirical research on the fashion process indicates that the errors in each approach tend to complement one another, to obscure many of the important features of this process. It suggests that most contemporary studies of the fashion process are inadequate because of their uncritical acceptance or "rediscovery" of the precedents established by such prestigious opinion leaders as Simmel and Kroeber in the history of social science.

The analysis of a debate between Donald Horton and Pitirim Sorokin on the scientific merits of *Fads and Foibles in Modern Sociology* calls attention to the absence of objective criteria by which claims or hypotheses are verified in the mainstream of modern sociology. It concentrates on the tendency to employ personal and polemical arguments in place of objective or historical ones in resolving differences over the scientific status of the discipline itself. This analysis indicates that the seemingly endless array of models in the discipline of sociology, the lack of objective criteria by which they can be evaluated and to which sociologists are willing to subscribe, and the developing polarization in the discipline around a wide range of theoretical and ideological issues[1] have together created an objective crisis and a subjective sense of uncertainty over the future of the discipline itself. These objective and subjective conditions in the recent history of American sociology, it was shown, have brought about such a state of collective restlessness and insecurity as to prompt Martindale, Boskoff, and other influential sociologists to call for the arrival of a new opinion leader, a charismatic savior, who would unify the apparently irreconcilable models into a new and reassuring perspective behind which all interested parties could rally.

The next case study examines the influence and stature of Thomas S. Kuhn in modern sociology in general and in the sociology of science in particular. It concentrates on an examination of Kuhn's *Structure of Scientific Revolutions*, reviews the many fallacies and ambiguities in his claims about the scientific community in modern society, traces these defects to the operation of the fashion process in Kuhn's own thought, and emphasizes the great extent to which his eminence is more the result of his unwitting accommodation and articulation of the collective sentiments in the discipline than the objective validity of his research. It also calls attention to Kuhn's most important contributions to the sociology of science, his occasional efforts at critical self-awareness, and his recognition of the need to study anomalies on a systematic basis, which have been consistently ignored by the sociologists who acclaim his work.

The next case study examines the ascendance of Robert Friedrichs's model of dialectical pluralism – especially for modern American sociology. It calls attention to Friedrichs's tendency unwittingly to accommodate and reinforce the collective tastes shared by most American sociologists, his skillful modification of Kuhn's paradigm of the scientific community in the service of legitimizing the present and proximate future of modern sociology, and his eminence in the discipline as a result of this fidelity to the tastes and the ideologically defined "needs" of the profession rather than any objective validity his model might have. It emphasizes that the ahistorical assumptions and the caricature of the sociology of knowledge portrayed in his model lead to many grave misrepresentations, both theoretically and empirically, of actual developments in sociological inquiry; and that his work is still another instance of the unacknowledged but pervasive operation of the fashion process in the thinking of an opinion leader in the scientific community.

The next case study examines Pitirim Sorokin's charge that American sociology is floundering in a "Tower of Babel," his explanation of the irrationality in the discipline, and his great eminence as an opinion leader in the discipline for several decades. It emphasizes that Sorokin ignores the considerable degree to which the "chaos" in the discipline is in fact severely regulated, that the unrecognized play of fashion is responsible for limitations on this apparent chaos, and that its operation is largely ignored in his research on the "fads and foibles" in the discipline. It calls attention to the many points of correspondence between collective tastes in the sociological profession and Sorokin's own mode of discourse, between ideological assumptions in the larger society and Sorokin's worldview of integralism; it suggests that Sorokin's work has enjoyed great stature not because he played the role of a radical or a maverick, not because his substantive claims were carefully evaluated and shown to be objectively valid by other scholars, but rather because his work has been for the most part also caught up in the fashion process. It finally emphasizes that Sorokin's fall from grace in the scientific community came about largely as a consequence of his publication of

Fads and Foibles in Modern Sociology and that he was condemned accordingly for violating standards of good taste and civility in the profession. It suggests that the success of vested interests and individually outraged sociologists in the movement to drive this book out of circulation is testimony to the coercive power behind the stamp of orthodoxy and the glamorous mystique of self-celebration in modern sociology, that the effective denunciations against him were carried out selectively so as to preserve those aspects of Sorokin's work that do enhance the image of the discipline.

The next case study examines the role of Robert K. Merton as the most influential opinion leader in modern sociology. It calls attention to the fact that while Merton shares with other opinion leaders a tendency to neglect or trivialize the operation of the fashion process in the scientific community, he does at least indirectly recognize its existence by dealing with such issues arising from the investigation of it as the patterns of evaluation, the function of "status judges," and the shifting fields of interest in that community. But this analysis demonstrates that Merton's efforts at characterizing these phenomena lead to a shaky use of evidence and a dubious set of conclusions systematically resulting from the unacknowledged yet recurrent operation of the fashion process in his own sociological thought. It emphasizes that his towering stature in modern sociology in general and in the sociology of science in particular cannot be explained in terms of the substantive validity, logical rigor, or originality of his writings in view of the many serious deficiencies found in these areas of his work. It further emphasizes that his stature can largely be explained in terms of (1) his general fidelity to collective tastes in favor of value-neutrality and moderation in debates, (2) his ingenuity in conceptualizing the preoccupation with trivial topics as well as the political and theoretical polarization of the discipline as proof of a secure and bountiful future for "world sociology" rather than as a threat to its very existence, and (3) his efforts, partly unwitting and partly deliberate, to play the dual role of the charismatic savior who professionally appears to *reconcile opposing factions* and extricate the discipline from crisis and of the elder statesman who personally appears to *transcend all sectarianism* on behalf of a bona fide social science in its alleged victory over ideological strife and fanaticism.

The final case study examines the rapid rise to prominence of Jeffrey Alexander in the recent waves of "neofunctionalism," "postpositivism," and "postmodernism" in contemporary social theory. It suggests that the relative stature of Merton in the 1950s and 1960s, Kuhn in the 1970s, and Alexander in the 1980s is indicative of the uneasiness and, at times, the panic behind the search for opinion leaders who might rescue the discipline from one crisis after another, from real and imagined threats to the image of a scientific priesthood. It suggests that shifting collective tastes in the discipline govern the selection process by which one savior rather than another gains the greatest acclaim, the latest stamp of orthodoxy, the role of chief designer of the most "exciting" and "refreshing" paradigm of the day. It further suggests that the absence of objective truth-content in Merton's claims about "modern science" and "world sociology," Kuhn's claims about "scientific revolutions," and Alexander's claims about "postpositivism" in social theory, far from being a deterrent to their acceptance, is ignored altogether in the collective behavior governing their celebrated destiny in the selection process. It finally suggests that the ostensibly daring language of "structural analysis" and "theoretical projects" in the service of "dialectical" and "transcendental" sociology serves to accommodate the ongoing disciplinary appetite for the illusion of radical commitment and the reality of conservative practice and cynicism in the scientific community.

There is much to learn from the history of social science. One can, for example, learn to stand "on the shoulders of giants" and savor the timeless insights of sages from every era.[2] One can also learn from the mistakes of those who believed they had discovered timeless insights that, on closer inspection, turn out to be in error. One can, finally, learn from the most common and serious mistake of all, the chronic mistake so stifling to the advancement of modern science: the doctrine of infallibility. This doctrine in its own right nurtures the fashion process in the scientific community each time the stamp of orthodoxy is imprinted on the model that happens to be ascendant at a given time. It must be overcome if science is to survive the danger of self-celebration when there is little to celebrate and much to reevaluate.[3]

Although well beyond the scope of the present study, several considerations might be mentioned as fruitful areas for subsequent research into the fashion process. First, the play of fashion in science does from time to time facilitate the discovery and adoption of innovations that go beyond merely superficial variations on a contemporary orthodoxy or a "rediscovered" traditional model. Perhaps this progressive feature of the fashion process might be deliberately accentuated to encourage substantially new lines of inquiry and debate in those scientific disciplines that are in the grip of a given orthodoxy and display intellectual stagnation in general. The conditions under which this task could be accomplished would seem to be most deserving of careful study.

Second, the fashion process, as already shown in the present study, does not emerge or endure in a political, economic, or historical vacuum. It tends to be intensified by certain structural, ideological, and

subjective conditions and inhibited by others. It can even render the social self into an object that becomes caught up in the mystique of
glamor, modernity, and "keeping in step with the times." It can lead to
the notion that the social self has merit or worth only insofar as endorsed by prevailing collective tastes over which the self has little control. It may contribute to the formation of the "marketplace personality"
(in Fromm's sense) and therefore to the socially prescribed attitude that
"I am as you desire me." To whatever degree these possibilities are tenable, then, the study of the fashion process might be far more relevant
to an understanding of alienation in modern society than would appear
to be the case at first glance. Such study might illuminate the impact of
the forces that generate commodity fetishism, including the "packaging"
of personalities, ideas, and scientific expertise in the most glamorous
and novel guises available. These possibilities are deserving of separate
investigation because they lead to a progression from merely describing
the play of fashion in science to explaining it in structural and historical
terms. They are explored in the following section, "The Fashion Process,
Science, and Society."

Third, the fashion process may be more operative under conditions
of relative stability, both in the society as a whole and in the scientific
community, than under conditions of revolutionary transformation. Although there are acute contradictions in American society and major
crises in modern sociology that might well erupt into one or another
type of revolutionary situation, the fact remains that little if any structural change in modern society or science has taken place in recent
years. Hence, one might consider the different kinds of opinion leaders
in the larger society and in the scientific community likely to arise in
revolutionary situations as compared to the kinds intensively examined
in the present study. In doing so, one must keep in mind that the opinion leaders in the scientific community examined here came to prominence under conditions of organized insecurity and restlessness in a
discipline that barely acknowledged the underlying crises responsible
for much of the alarm; that their various efforts to define the basic nature
of these crises in palatable terms served to obscure the trivial scholarship, ideological conflict, and political struggles within its corridors; and
that these struggles remain just below the surface of professional dialogue and tend to erupt only in seemingly transient, isolated, and aber-
rational symptoms of confrontation.

These considerations can help to develop the comparative, historical,
and social-psychological perspectives needed for the study of the fashion process in science. Although some aspects of the foregoing topics
for investigation are occasionally and briefly discussed earlier in this

book and are relevant to the central purpose at hand, it must again be emphasized that they deserve the most careful attention in their own right.

This study sets forth a perspective and an empirical basis for future research on the fashion process in modern science by demonstrating the great degree to which prestigious social scientists are caught up in this process. To remain faithful to the cautionary methodological considerations emphasized in the Introduction, however, one must keep in mind the limitations concerning what is assumed and what is actually demonstrated herein.

One should recall that the six remaining steps entailed in a complete investigation of all aspects of the fashion process in just one scientific discipline, sociology, were deliberately bracketed for the sake of close attention to the first two (and most formidable) steps in such a venture. To attain a definitive closure to this investigation, I intend subsequently to carry out these remaining steps by analyzing: (1) the records of intensive interviews with prominent sociologists at elite universities, typical sociologists at ordinary universities, and graduate students at both types of institutions regarding their subjective perceptions of the fashion process in their own and related disciplines; (2) the contents of the official journals published by the American Sociological Association in order to ascertain the degree to which the findings already demonstrated are applicable to everyday scientific happenings in the vineyard; and (3) the collective behavior of sociologists at professional conventions when they (a) applaud, condemn, or ignore various addresses that serve as "trial balloons" to foreshadow new standards of acceptable and unacceptable conduct, (b) look for certain new source materials and teaching devices sold by the more glamorous publishers at the book exhibitions, (c) assemble at "crisis sessions" to define the issues they regard as threatening to their discipline, and (d) stereotype certain views rather than others as "obsolete" or "in bad taste." A theoretical framework to guide such descriptive tasks is elaborated in the section here entitled "The Fashion Process, Alienation, and Social Evolution."

The present study suggests points of departure for the fullest inquiry into the aforementioned topics as well as the implementation of those steps in the investigation of the fashion process bracketed for the methodological reasons discussed in the Introduction. These various foci for study, it should be further noted, need not be seen as mutually exclusive. A theoretical and historical perspective that is inclusive of these foci is still needed. Although I advance such a theoretical framework in the following section, the implementation of the first two steps of this investigation can be considered to stand on its own.

With these stipulations in mind, we can investigate the complex relationships among the scientific community, alienated intellectual labor, and social evolution.

The Fashion Process, Science, and Society

We can now proceed from a description of the fashion process in science to an explanation of its origins and dynamics, its interplay with the structure of modern society. We have seen that major theorists in such disciplines as sociology and anthropology can become opinion leaders unwittingly caught up in the fashion process. We have also seen that they remain heavily influenced by this process even when they directly attempt to study fashions in modern society. But what are the factors that might explain the origins of this process in science and society as a whole? Can this process help to explain, for example, the rapid succession of scientific discoveries in the seventeenth century? Even as we undertake to answer these questions, still more pointed issues about the fate of modern science arise. What is the connection, for example, between the fashion process and the ideal of "knowledge as an end in itself"? Does the fashion process affect the way in which the scientific community responds to dubious or bogus paradigms? How, if at all, can the play of fashion be reduced or eliminated? How does an understanding of this process illuminate the granting of honors and awards to scientists whose work is in good taste but not necessarily meritorious on objective grounds? In view of the extent to which this process contributes to the appearance of technological progress through scientific ferment, does it have any bearing on the legitimacy of corporate and state power in modern society? Are fashions in science and fashions in costume adornment produced by the same forces in capitalist society? Could the fashion process serve as a means by which the scientific community copes with its lack of control over the decision-making agencies of state and corporate power? Finally, is the significance of this process found in accelerating discoveries under certain conditions and retarding them under other conditions on an evolutionary scale? Could the play of fashion in science serve as a catalyst for social progress in one era and as a brake on the rapid growth of uncontrolled technology in another? I shall address each of these questions, offer some preliminary answers, and suggest directions for future research to conclude this study.

Searching for the Causes of the Fashion Process: "Weak Character" and "Knowledge for Its Own Sake"

To explain the readiness with which scientists are caught up in the fashion process, one might attribute this complaisance to their "weak character." Even if such an ahistorical explanation had some validity, one would still have to account for the conditions under which this presumed psychological weakness is produced. Unless such specification is made, the presumed weakness must be explained in terms of an affliction in human nature—tantamount to a genetic defect—constantly and universally subverting the rational endeavors of the scientific community. Since the fashion process is demonstrably variable in its operation from time to time, from discipline to discipline, and from scientist to scientist at a given time within a given discipline, such a possible explanation must be considered untenable. In the context of psychological reductionism in American academic culture, such explanations lead to little more than moralistic condemnations of individual scientists or groups of scientists. The serious shortcomings in these explanations have not dampened the enthusiasm of those who, like Sorokin and Mills, have chosen to advance them. An equally misleading notion is that scientists can somehow rid themselves of any moral character at all, strong or weak, merely by declaring themselves to be "value-neutral" or "value-free" in their research.

Controversies surrounding the possibility of value-free science were especially heated in exchanges between conservative and radical sociologists in the 1960s. They usually centered on the question of whether scientists should pursue knowledge as an end in itself. This question leads inevitably to the moral dilemma over responsibility for the consequences of scientific inquiry. Is the discoverer of nuclear fission responsible for the incineration of Hiroshima and Nagasaki? Is the discoverer of a viable model for predicting and controlling deviance responsible for its use by a fascist regime determined to crush a popular revolution? Is the discoverer of laser rays responsible for the escalation of the arms race at an ever-increasing level of terror in an age of renewed militarism and "Star Wars"? Dilemmas of this type lead in turn to fierce arguments over the need for patriotism by scientists on the one hand and the belief that scientists should ignore political and economic constraints imposed by the larger society on the other. An ambiguous combination of both positions is also at times advocated. These arguments might appear to be tempered by Kuhn's article of faith that any authentic science is inherently insulated from social pressures and that scientific knowledge is and must be pursued as an end in itself or for the sake of curiosity. When the dust settles, however, the protagonists emerge as convinced as they were before about the reprehensible nature of their opponents. Even stickier questions then arise about the wisdom of doing research on behalf of a repressive but somewhat democratic society (e.g., the United States in the 1940s) on the grounds that a still more repressive one (Germany in that same era) had to be defeated at all costs. How does it happen that these controversies continue to attract the attention of radical as well as conservative scientists, "pure" as well as "applied" researchers? Is it possible that even such seemingly polarized adversaries have a common interest in using the doctrine of "value-free" science as a point of reference in a debate that seems to rage inconclusively?

We can answer these questions by calling attention to the link between the fashion process in the scientific community and the alienation of scientists as intellectual workers: *How does it happen that a doctrine that invites the exercise of whim and caprice (including one's own perception of collective taste) comes to receive so much interest and even sanctity in the scientific community?*

How is it possible for such a doctrine to exist side by side with the practice of doing scientific research for virtually any corporation, any nation-state, any organization at all, and rationalizing this practice in terms of "professional growth," "expert consultation," "academic entrepreneurship," "clinical sociology," "applied psychology," or, more generally, "science in the public interest"?[4]

The widespread appeal of the doctrine of "knowledge for its own sake" is far stronger and more compelling than can be found in the need for protection from repressive authority alone. It is true that this doctrine can serve as an ideological buffer to insulate or at least appear to insulate scientists from the prying and repressive eyes of church, state, and corporate authorities.

Just what *is* the underlying source of the doctrine of "value-free science" and the "free-floating intellectual"? How and why do so many scientists espouse the belief that research should be value-free even when it might serve as an invitation to pursue intellectually self-indulgent and collective behavior that in turn readily becomes part of the fashion process in science? How and why do scientists adhere to this doctrine even when Max Weber, its chief architect, was himself an actively partisan supporter of the liberal capitalist state in the early 1900s and a sociologist who generously and one-sidedly used the tools of his trade on its behalf?

Because of the institutionalized perception that mental labor is superior to manual labor and that intellectual work is not really work at all, most members of the scientific community do not consider themselves part of the working class in any sense. They often perceive themselves to be in a privileged elite, a well-respected "middle class" insofar as they might be in any class at all. Indeed, Thorstein Veblen went to great lengths to argue that engineers and scientists have the special talents and destiny to inherit the reins of power and run the productive system of society. With such lofty and ahistorical self-perceptions, it is understandable that scientists employed by some corporations (e.g., IBM) refuse in principle to join labor unions and that when they join unions, they often refuse to go on strike even when their own ranks are decimated by political purges, economic retrenchment, or both (e.g., during the McCarthyism of the 1950s and the academic retrenchments of the 1970s).

Scientists subjectively perceive themselves as autonomous professionals, as free-floating intellectuals, and their research as a detached quest for truth. However illusory these perceptions might be, scientists remain an important sector of the working class that is objectively responsible for the development of social products (paradigms). These paradigms are then used directly in the production of commodities or indirectly in plans for expanding the political and economic system in which production is organized. Still other paradigms are needed on an ideological level to promote the appearance of legitimacy for the system as a whole. And yet other paradigms are needed to help agencies of state power in the prediction and control of disruptive behavior, to promulgate the belief that social order is a natural tendency inherent in the normal human condition, or both. For scientists to carry their weight and receive the coveted awards for which they are in competition, they must generate an ongoing array of new, improved, and useful paradigms that are incorporated directly or indirectly into the prevailing system of production, command, and control.

Although the present line of analysis suggests that powerful forces in the social structure guide the direction and content of the search for new paradigms, it also leads to a question previously noted but thus far unanswered: Why are so many paradigms produced, approved, certified as self-evident and orthodox, and displaced by other paradigms with little or no regard for the objective truth-content of the old or new products? And why are these products submitted and sometimes adopted when there is an objective basis to believe that they are neither valid nor new? (We have already seen that many of the most important paradigms advanced by Simmel, Kroeber, Sorokin, Merton, Kuhn, and Friedrichs, for example, have been regarded as major discoveries eventhough there were substantial grounds all along to view them in an extremely skeptical and tentative manner.) Are scientists willing to submit and approve of dubious paradigms that are useless for the actual operation of the larger capitalist system? Are they willing to adopt paradigms that cast doubt in the long run on the integrity and credibility of their own discipline?

One of the important achievements for which a scientist is rewarded is the discovery of a paradigm that is *considered* new as well as useful in increasing the productivity or rate of profit for the capitalist class. Scientists are therefore under great pressure to "deliver" on new and useful paradigms, not because of intellectual curiosity or science for its own sake, but rather because of the requirements of capitalist development in general and the translation of those requirements into the "theoretical challenges" and the reward structure of the scientific community in particular.

This steady pressure to generate new, improved, and useful paradigms is an underlying structural source of the fashion process in the scientific community. But since scientists have widely varying abilities, training, motivation, and unequal personal, professional, and political connections, it is not possible for all of them to produce such *bona fide* paradigms on a regular basis. Many scientists are incapable of hammering out a single useful paradigm or even a small part of one, no matter how much they try. But the rewards and career mobility for which they strive are still attainable: it turns out that scientists, like other members of the working class, do not always need to have the actual skills required of them or to make substantive contributions on any level at all provided that they are able to act *as if* these skills and contributions were in hand or on the horizon. If a worker or a corporate executive is badly trained and administratively incompetent but capable of talking, dressing, and acting as if he were well trained, competent, and successful, if he appears to display the appropriate signs of organizational fidelity and corporate imagery, then he may well be granted the rewards ostensibly reserved for successful candidates. By carefully avoiding radical or controversial ideas, by appearing to be fully "in step with the times," by showing one's peers and superiors a "forward-looking" posture, by dutifully going through the motions of fabricating or imitating those paradigms most in tune with collective tastes, some of the rewards earmarked for the most capable candidates will also be conferred on those with the greatest dramaturgical and marketing skills. How do these customs and rituals in the world of work in general apply to the scientific community in particular?

Scientists do not own or control such means of intellectual production as the laboratories, academic offices, libraries, survey research centers, hardware, and software necessary for generating, testing, and packaging new paradigms. They do not own or control the decision-making agencies that establish priorities for "urgent" research and allocate resources for wages, salaries, prizes, and awards. They are just as much under pressure to produce new ideas as are the advertising personnel on Madison Avenue to produce new commercials. Let us suppose, for example, that a newly submitted paradigm is not really new, improved, or useful at all, but only a facsimile of one with these qualities. Let us suppose that a paradigm is represented as "the latest thing" and a "breakthrough" with only the imagery and trappings of novelty and significance. In such circumstances, and we have seen that they are especially common in the social sciences, the paradigm itself may be worthless and the scientist himself may be mediocre; but the paradigm is heralded and the scientist is rewarded.[5]

The need for new paradigms by the capitalist system on the one hand and the presentation of bogus paradigms by alienated scientists competing for rewards and recognition on the other hand are a driving force behind the play of fashion in science. The two sociologists who most strongly condemned the intellectual manifestations of this process in the discipline of sociology, Pitirim Sorokin and C. Wright Mills, contented themselves with denunciations of individual culprits. In launching their tirades, they singled out the most prominent opinion leaders (e.g., Parsons, Merton, Lazarsfeld) in a spirit of zealous muckraking. Sorokin labeled them as "pioneering Columbuses," "pirates," and "numerologists." Mills employed more arcane language by calling them "abstracted empiricists" and "grand theorists." The former's *Fads and Foibles in Modern Sociology* and the latter's *Sociological Imagination* did serve to document the operation of conservative ideology and collective behavior in recent sociological thought. Their observations also made clear that paradigms in this discipline typically rise to and fall from prominence with little concern by peers for their possible truth-content. Although their criticisms eventually served as ammunition in the arsenal of young radicals conducting a frontal assault on the citadels of "establishment sociology" in the 1960s, they did nothing to identify the causes of the fashion process or to specify the conditions under which its influence could be minimized in the scientific community.

The Appearance of Solutions to Social Crisis: Heroism in the Temple of Science

These opinion leaders are not merely exemplars and trendsetters: *these opinion leaders are in reality the collectively perceived heroes of their day*. Opinion leaders are perceived as heroes not because they engaged in some bold and daring act of sacrifice on behalf of scientific truth, and certainly not because they martyred themselves by attacking false prophets or sacrosanct paradigms in the scientific community. Indeed, opinion leaders perceived as heroes tend to exercise a great deal of prudence in their personal and professional demeanor, to articulate (or "capture the essence of") mainstream doctrines and paradigms and to avoid "going too far out" or "staying too far behind" vis-à-vis the conventional wisdom of the day. What *is* significant about the status of such heroes is that their work is perceived within the scientific community as though it were "prophetic," "revolutionary," "the greatest breakthrough of the decade," ad infinitum. How is it possible that such thinkers as Lipset in sociology or McLuhan in communications are viewed as heroes one day and all but forgotten the next? And how is it possible that few if any voices within the scientific community are raised to question what might appear to be the symptoms of over generous applause at one moment and collective amnesia at the next? What is the driving force behind the tenacity, even the ferocity, with which opinion leaders and their paradigms are defended against the few skeptics who do come forward here and there to challenge their prominence?

When new theories of social control are needed to predict and control the behavior of restless populations in the Third World, scientists must be willing and able to meet this demand. When the working class in an advanced capitalist society becomes actually or potentially poised to rise up against the structure of domination, new paradigms to promote law and order, to co-opt radical leaders, to make the system *appear* as though it were working fairly and legitimately, must be rapidly produced; scientists must be willing and able to meet the demand for same. When competing corporate sectors of the capitalist system cannot agree on the most advantageous and profitable direction for the use of energy resources (with various factions struggling over the development of oil, coal, natural gas, solar heat, and nuclear energy), decision makers in the agencies of state power require the advice and expertise of scientists who can produce recommendations, options, and contingency plans for the management of such an issue; scientists must be willing and able to meet this demand. Even when there is no objectively possible solution to the problem that scientists are called upon to solve, it is nevertheless important for political and corporate decision makers to promote the *appearance of a solution* either already in hand or on the horizon so that voters, taxpayers, and shareholders are led to believe that progress is being made. For this reason, it is not always necessary for scientists to produce paradigms that are objectively valid or ever likely to be adopted; it is not even necessary that the paradigms being produced are really new or different from the older ones. All that *is* necessary is that the production of paradigms creates the *impression* of new and significant research activity, the *illusion* that the crisis is being well managed and that everything is in good hands.

Toward this same end, even the appearance of diverse and multiple discoveries, research projects, and "scientific ferment" is helpful and expedient to those who wish to promote confidence in a political or corporate regime; scientists must be willing and able to contribute to the image of intense research activity, "intellectual ferment," and great discoveries or breakthroughs soon to be made in the service of solving all manner of crises. Since the public guides its behavior by what it believes to be true rather than what is objectively true, the creation and maintenance of this latter image is an overriding necessity for the system as a whole.

Scientists who contribute to this image do not need to have any great measure of creative talent; they do not need the highest quality of academic training; they do not even need to take their own credentials, projects, proposals, and paradigms seriously—so long as they keep on producing new ones from time to time. Indeed, they do not need to know what they are talking about so long as they keep on talking. This is why scientists with little talent, poor training, and weak motivation nevertheless contribute to both the confidence of the public in its leaders and the support that society as a whole provides to the scientific community. So long as untalented or poorly trained scientists are busily at work or at least give the appearance of staying busy, they are contributing to the appearance of legitimacy in the social structure in which they live. They can then dazzle themselves and the public with all manner of "academic projects" and exciting dialogue.

We can now observe two types of scientists who participate in the fashion process within the scientific community: (1) opinion leaders (including serious rivals and contenders rising to and falling from prominence), and (2) opinion followers (including those who are unable to make good imitations and variations on popular styles but give the appearance of proficiency, "new projects," and "intellectual ferment" just the same). Even though the followers may often lack the proficiency to develop paradigms with slight variations on an approved style, they can and do contribute to the image of scientists busily at work solving the nation's and corporation's latest problems.

Just what is the nature of the products introduced by this large and amorphous sector of the scientific community? What patterns or trends in the collective behavior of the scientific community can be attributed to the large number of mediocre participants in its ranks? Since they are not capable of producing *fashions* in the shape of new paradigms, it might seem at first glance that they are not part of the collective behavior in that community. But on closer inspection, we can discern a short-lived and all too easily ignored product that these scientists do steadily introduce: fads and whims, destined for early oblivion because they are out of touch with prevailing tastes, are nevertheless helpful to the larger play of fashion because they enhance the image of diversified, exciting, novel, and daring lines of investigation under way throughout the scientific community. The result is that an otherwise skeptical, even begrudging or potentially rebellious, audience is reassured that all is going well (or soon will be) in a crisis-ridden system.

Although opinion leaders and followers make important contributions to the appearance that all is going well in the scientific community, they are equally concerned about disseminating an image of science that has allegedly lofty origins, perhaps emanating from divine wisdom itself. The widely accepted view that modern science gained its impetus from the Protestant ethic is now examined.

Opinion Leaders and Critics Debate the Origins of Modern Science: Merton and Becker Appeal to the Court of Collective Taste

In Merton's view, English Puritanism and German Pietism are the elements of the Protestant ethic most responsible for the rise of modern science. But we have already seen that some opinion leaders in the dawn of modern science made observations about the cultural setting in which they worked suggestive of the fashion process as an impetus to their bold and daring experiments, their revolutionary paradigms. These opinion leaders did not consider it necessary or relevant to explain the setting for their research in terms of ascetic Protestantism stemming from English or German sources. A separate but equally serious challenge to Merton's thesis is that authorities representing Pietism, far from serving as champions of Prussian science, were typically hesitant, ambiguous, fearful, and at times actively hostile to the emergence of scientific thought in *any* discipline. For example, in a closely argued study George Becker points out that many of Merton's own citations are unhelpful to and, in some crucial instances, even in direct opposition to the thesis linking German Pietism to the rise of modern science.[6] Becker observes that Merton's real defense of this thesis has little to do with reliance on any historical evidence (which, he shows, is sorely lacking in any case). He observes that Merton's real defense rests on the conviction that a "great master" (in this case, Max Weber) set the stage for and would surely give an endorsement to the thesis in question. Merton's own reply to Becker's criticisms ignores the documentary lapses and substantive weaknesses in the historical data found throughout the former's writings on the asceticism-science connection.[7]

Indeed, Merton's reply evades virtually all of Becker's specific and telling criticisms. Becker's response is in turn marked by indignation and anger over Merton's ritual invocation of Weber's name, over his misrepresentations of evidence, over his evasions of the specific issues at hand in defense of a spurious thesis.[8] Becker then expresses alarm over the fact that the subterfuge and obfuscation employed by Merton in this exchange are corrosive to the intellectual foundations of sociology as a science. In addition to his well-founded anger and alarm, however, Becker also reveals a measure of embarrassment in the face of a challenge astutely posed by Merton: if we discard the thesis that German Pietism was the spark that ignited the flame of modern science on the European continent, then we should await Becker's submission of a new paradigm to replace the one under attack. Becker concedes that he has no viable hypothesis to offer in place of Pietism, but nevertheless insists that no explanation at all is preferable to a fallacious one. Both Becker and Merton fail to address the most urgent question arising from their exchange: how and why is a paradigm so dubious as the Pietism-science thesis readily acclaimed by the scientific community in the first place and tenaciously defended by its opinion leaders even after the paradigm's weaknesses are publicized in a major journal? What process might be operating to explain this apparent anomaly?

Although Becker and Merton fail to recognize the reasons behind the inconclusiveness of their exchange about the origins of modern science, they are nevertheless participants on the stage of a social drama. In effect, a certified opinion leader (Merton) is being told by an unrecognized Young Turk (Becker) that a paradigm is objectively unsound, that the evidence used to support it is spurious and suspect at every turn. Moreover, the opinion leader is told that the good name of and presumed endorsement by a great master (in this case, Max Weber) is not sufficient or even appropriate as a defense of the thesis and that even the most tasteful variations on and embellishments of the great master's teachings, even the most judicious revisions conjured up periodically to maintain the appearance of ongoing ferment and occasional breakthroughs in the discipline, cannot protect the paradigm from close scrutiny.

What is an opinion leader to do under these conditions of siege? How can the temple of science (or at least its image) be defended against infidels? To preserve the appearance of a discipline in scholarly ferment and the aura of an opinion leader guided by the highest standards of collective taste in the scientific community, he welcomes the criticisms in principle and ignores their substance in practice. Yet the very process by which the adversaries thrust and parry for advantage in the quicksand of collective taste—Merton invoking the name of Weber, Becker appealing to the iconoclasts and partisans of formal rationality—indicates the play of fashion in the scientific community. Their exchange illustrates such key features of the fashion process as keeping in step with the latest developments (e.g., the latest nuances in the work of opinion leaders on behalf of an acclaimed paradigm); ignoring or discounting explicit criteria by which some models are judged superior to others; ignoring or suppressing questions about the historical and evaluative processes themselves and the social forces that shape and govern them; and pitting an Old Guard against Young Turks now advancing and then retreating in cycles of paradigmatic revolution and orthodoxy. This is the process in which the adversaries are unwittingly engaged. This is also the process that, if its participants were to recognize its potency and pervasiveness, might have enabled them to develop a viable explanation for the rise of modern science. Thus, we can discount the role of Puritanism and Pietism as the main or only explanation for scientific thought in the seventeenth century; we can also advance the hypothesis that the unduly ignored play of fashion may well have helped significantly to nurture it, and thus to facilitate the rise of a new capitalist era so thoroughly dependent upon its guideposts to the mastery of nature.

Before this hypothesis is elaborated, we should closely examine the structural and ideological conditions under which the play of fashion is likely to be most prevalent. We will then resume this exploration of the origins of modern science in the section entitled "The Protestant Ethic and the Fashion Process in Modern Science: Weber and Merton Reconsidered."

The Alienation of Mental and Manual Labor: Origins of the Fashion Process in Science and Society

Just what is alienated intellectual labor? How does it lead to the fashion process in science? How does it lead to plagiarism, piracy, facades of busywork, and other acts of intellectual dishonesty in the scientific community? How does it lead to complaisance and cynicism in the face of collective irrationality and scandal in the temple of science?

In addition to the ongoing requirement for new paradigms (to predict and control deviance, to increase productive efficiency, to legitimate a system in crisis) and the intense peer pressure to generate them (or at least bogus products) in the scientific community, another structural source of the fashion process is the pattern of control over labor exercised by the capitalist class. Let us first consider the effects of exploitation for profit upon *manual* workers and in turn examine their bearing upon *intellectual* workers in order to make sense out of the seemingly opaque fashion process.

For the capitalist class to make effective use of its private ownership over the means of production, it must have the sovereign right to make plans about the allocation of profits, the consolidation or expansion of productive facilities, the divestment of unprofitable or inefficient units, and the establishment of special access to the resources and decision-making functions in the agencies of state power. Without such sovereignty, the capitalist class ceases to be the master of its own destiny; without it, the capitalist class is no longer the dominant or ruling class. Hence, the maintenance of this sovereignty over the decision-making process is absolutely essential and not merely desirable for the purpose of keeping the structure of capitalism intact. The steps that must be taken by the capitalist class to ensure its sovereignty over this decision-making process give rise to the alienation of labor in general. These steps, sometimes deliberate and sometimes unwitting, sometimes obvious and sometimes subtle, profoundly affect the self-image and life-style of all participants in the working class.

Once the location of scientists in the class structure is identified, once the scientist is seen as an intellectual worker performing mental labor in exchange for wages, the subtle forces that shape the consciousness and life-style of the working class in general can be explicitly recognized as having a corresponding impact on scientists in particular. The key features of the relationship between the capitalist class and the working class are as follows. (1) The fruits or products of the worker's labor are transformed into commodities for sale at a profit by the capitalist; the worker is separated or alienated from the social and economic value of what he has produced, and only receives a wage or salary having no systematic connection to its value. For example, even if the capitalist can make an enormous profit, say 500 percent, on the sale of the commodity, the worker's wages may not increase at all. Or the profit may well reach such a high level as to enable the capitalist to invest in automated plant and equipment, leading to the pauperization of the worker. Or the commodity may well represent some new health product that cures grave illnesses and is in great demand; the capitalist may well take all the credit (and all the profit) when making such a commodity available for sale. Even though the worker wants to see the product made available at a low price or at no charge to the public, the capitalist alone has control over the price, availability, and destiny of the product. (2) The worker is excluded from the decision-making process and culturally conditioned to believe that such exclusion is a universal or natural condition inherent in civilized society. Toward this end, the worker is actually conditioned to believe that he is undeserving of and unfit to exercise the right of decision-making in society in general and the workplace in particular.

Among the most important preconditions for the maintenance of wealth and power in the hands of the capitalist class is the internal disunity and lack of political consciousness in the working class: it is possible to engage in virtually unlimited oppression and exploitation of the masses only to the degree that they lack the organizational capability and consciousness to act in their own interests. A most telling and widely employed strategy for promoting just this disunity is to implement the doctrine of "divide and conquer." And the most successful method of bringing this strategy to fruition is to convince members of the working class that they are not in the working class at all, that they are in the "middle class," the "intelligentsia," the "technocracy," the cultural elite, or some other privileged group without any allegiance to or roots in the working class. One cannot join labor unions or go on strike if one defines him- or herself as being in the "middle class" or as belonging to no class at all.

Manual workers are conditioned to see themselves increasingly as "middle class"; they are politically neutralized accordingly. Intellectual workers are conditioned to see themselves as belonging to a privileged elite or to no class at all; they are politically neutralized accordingly. Manual workers and intellectual workers in turn see themselves as having few, if any, class interests in common.

Even when scientists do belong to labor unions, as in the case of college professors in the American Federation of Teachers, they usually frown upon proposals for holding strikes or other job actions (even when faced with retrenchment and reductions in salary or fringe benefits) on the grounds that such tactics are "unprofessional." This concern with "professionalism" is the result of a widespread and subtle conditioning process whereby intellectual effort is defined as though it were not an expenditure of labor power or labor time at all. Since many scientists do enjoy their work and since "working for a living" is widely regarded as an unenjoyable activity—something one *must* do to pay the grocery bills—they are all the more inclined to believe that they cannot possibly be oppressed or exploited or in any way a part of the working class. With the artificial distinction between mental labor and manual labor strongly institutionalized and with "intellectuals" and "hard hats" viewing each other with contempt, the fact that scientists subjectively perceive themselves as having no allegiance to the working class becomes understandable.

Perceptions and Realities of Power in the Scientific Community

Although scientists do enjoy a good deal of prestige in the eyes of most working people, the fact remains that they have far less autonomy and "clout" in their conditions of employment than is commonly believed. Indeed, scientists usually must accept the priorities and definitions of "significant" research as imposed by the organization that employs them, the profession that judges them, the state that funds them, and the class structure that enables them to enjoy some limited privileges (sabbatical leaves, travel grants, occasional honors, and material rewards). During periods of political repression (e.g., McCarthyism in the 1950s) and economic crisis (e.g., the depression of the late 1920s and 1930s), the dispensability and vulnerability of scientists to purges, blacklists, and all manner of denunciation and ostracism can be most clearly recognized. Scientists themselves usually have at least an implicit awareness of their essentially powerless position: they are usually cynical about the fact that they can offer all the expert advice and consulting services in the world to those in positions of real command (in corporations, in state power), but their advice turns out to be indeed advisory—subject to whatever discounting, revision, or reinterpretation might suit the convenience of actual decision makers.

They also have at least an implicit awareness of their dispensability when they are expected to produce findings, concepts, or paradigms that will be satisfactory to their employers, superiors, or peer reviewers. It is no accident that scientists working for the Tobacco Institute find that cigarette smoking is a safe habit; those employed by the construction and shipbuilding industry seldom admit that asbestos dust is carcinogenic; those working at public health agencies routinely find that talc dust exposure entails no risk to the consumer or that the subject is "too complex" or "too controversial" to warrant any regulation. Researchers working for the State Department or the CIA routinely develop "paradigms of social change" designed to predict and control "native unrest." Scientists who fail to produce the expected results or at least to fabricate bogus paradigms to promote the illusion of scientific ferment find that they are readily replaced by other scientists who are prepared to be more "cooperative" and "responsible" toward their employer.

There are two levels of organized insecurity facing scientists. (1) As individual participants in a given profession, scientists are largely (often entirely) excluded from decision making regarding access to lines of internal command and control (e.g., over the main journals, planning of conferences and conventions, and such points of interface between state power and academia as election to the National Science Foundation). Whatever the appearance of professional autonomy associated with such organizations, whatever the belief that they are insulated from external pressures, the fact remains that very few scientists are effectively consulted or even know about these lines of command and control within their own discipline. *The criteria and direction of decision making are subject to change, revision, or outright repudiation at any time; members of the rank and file must be ready to adjust to the new orthodoxies on pain of being declared "out of touch," "senile," or just professionallly incompetent.* This endless need for vigilance in and of itself generates a good deal of anxiety, for the scientist never knows exactly where he stands or just how long he may be standing there as a sentinel on behalf of an opinion leader or paradigm subject to rapid displacement and obsolescence. (2) As participants in a profession believed to be a scientific community insulated from social pressures, scientists collectively find themselves in practice having little or no leverage in controlling the uses or misuses of scientific resources and the formulation of the central problems requiring paradigmatic solution in their discipline. Despite opposition to the current plans for a "star wars" system of defense against nuclear attack, despite misgivings voiced by large numbers of prominent scientists throughout the nation, for example, plans for this venture continue to be implemented. With advertisements and petitions appearing in the *New York Times*, with the full endorsement of scientists well known in their own disciplines and even familiar to audiences of prime-time television (e.g., Carl Sagan and his popular "Cosmos" program), scientists collectively find again and again that their concerns and expert advice are heeded only when it is expedient for those in state power. The scientific community is not only vulnerable to social pressures but also largely impotent to exert pressures of its own against the structure of domination and decision-making process in the larger society.

The organized insecurity with which scientists live on a daily basis therefore has a dual source: first, the individual scientist is excluded from decision making within his own profession and is highly vulnerable to the pressures and constraints it exerts on him; and second, the scientific community has little or no access to the mechanisms of command and control in the state and is also highly vulnerable to the external pressures (awards, threats, surveillance, coercion, and terror) in the state's arsenal of persuasive techniques whenever a scientific paradigm is required or dutiful opinion leader is displaced.

The organized insecurity in which scientists are caught up has profound psychological consequences as well: it leaves the self-image of the scientist fragile and uncertain from one moment to the next. *The organized insecurity operating on a structural level is manifested as basic anxiety on a psychological level.* This basic anxiety, commonly manifested as cynicism within the scientific community, is essentially what Karen Horney meant by "neurotic detachment."

Even with recognition of the need for new paradigms in capitalist society and the pressure on anxiety-ridden scientists to produce them (or at least to appear as if they were doing so), a question remains about the unfolding of the fashion process in the scientific thought: How and why does it happen that participants in the scientific community would engage in collective rituals suggesting the debasement of their own discipline? Why would they collaborate or acquiesce in cultural antics that are incompatible with the principles of rationality? To understand why scientists might collaborate in the debasement of their own field, we must examine still further the structural origins and consequences of alienated intellectual labor.

This insecurity and anxiety are more than merely unpleasant or disconcerting to the self: the fact that they are usually felt on a subtle and unconscious level does not make them any less threatening and unbearable. One of the few subjective compensations for this sense of insecurity and anxiety is to conjure up the idealized image of a hero who is larger than life and capable of being quoted in raptures of textual exegesis. The names, faces, and paradigms do have cycles of prominence and obsolescence in accordance with the political requirements of the state, the industrial requirements of the economy, and the corresponding shifts in the ideological themes of the larger culture; but the very fact that heroes and their doctrines can be cited at all helps to reassure the scientific community that it is an orderly and secure one, that it is insulated from external social pressures. After all, a community legitimized by the pattern variables of Parsons, the political man of Lipset, the reference groups of Merton, the social dynamics of Sorokin—even though these paradigms and their makers come and go from time to time in ongoing cycles of discovering and rediscovering new "breakthroughs"—is a community that can be perceived as having its own traditions and sanctity. That these traditions and sanctity are more apparent than real, that the opinion leaders may well be disavowed and even forgotten with little fanfare, does not diminish their importance in giving members of the scientific community a sense of stability and continuity even when that same community is objectively fragile and vulnerable to all manner of external pressures. *The presence of opinion leaders therefore is a crucial resource for the maintenance of a perception of legitimacy and security within the scientific community.*

Scientists as Free-Floating Intellectuals: Alienation and the Fashion Process

In the absence of any loyalty to the working class and in the belief that their professionalism somehow insulates them from the demands of the capitalist class and the state in general, scientists understandably develop a value-free or value-neutral outlook toward their own work. One's own career mobility and professional self-interest about questions to be investigated and paradigms to be advanced take precedence over finding solutions to the crises in the social structure, questions about the physical universe or the scientific community itself. Indeed, the term "crisis" then becomes increasingly defined by the social pressures exerted on the scientific community by the dominant capitalist class in search of more efficient ways of obtaining profits, more effective ways of maintaining social order, and more persuasive ways of making the system as a whole appear to be operating legitimately for the benefit of all sectors of society. In the social sciences, for example, strategies for economic growth, the control of inflation and recession, the prediction of crime and the maintenance of order, and the superiority of capitalism over other economic systems are regarded as "projects" deserving of the highest priority in the construction, refinement, and approval of new paradigms.

Precisely because scientists are workers performing mental labor in return for wages essential to their own access to food, clothing, and shelter, they must be excluded from the decision-making process: as part of the working class as a whole, scientists do not have the same objective interests as the ruling class, whose source of income is *profit* rather than wages or salaries. Scientists are hired so that the fruits of their labor can be efficiently utilized in the service of profit accumulation and to help maintain the prevailing structure of domination. The ruling class does not hire them for the purpose of reallocating profits in the hands of the working class or transferring command and control over the productive system to those having interests (and, potentially, allegiances) antagonistic to private ownership of that system. Scientists are therefore excluded from the decision-making process because the ruling class does not actively or consciously seek its own downfall. They are confronted with a *fait accompli*, an awesome fact of life in capitalist society: whatever stirrings of moral concern they might express in the *Bulletin of the Atomic Scientists* or journals devoted to professional ethics, whatever prizes and awards they might receive for their discoveries, the fact remains that they have no control over the ultimate applications or profits resulting from their paradigms. How do scientists respond to this dilemma?

Scientists formulate an appealing rationalization to offset the anguish of powerlessness over decisions about the uses, misuses, and nonuses of their discoveries. *Since scientists cannot control the uses and consequences of their own paradigms in any case, they proceed to make a virtue out of their common plight: by declaring that "we must pursue knowledge for its own sake," scientists are acknowledging (if only on an unwitting and tacit level) that they do not and cannot control the fruits of their intellectual labor in a capitalist society.* This doctrine is a begrudging and implicit acknowledgment that they do not own or control the means of production; that they do not have effective access to the decision-making apparatus in the larger society; that they are only consultants to the heads of corporate and state power at the latter's discretion, convenience, and pleasure. The doctrine of "knowledge for its own sake," then, is an ideological means by which scientists can rationalize and cope with the otherwise distressing and even humiliating condition of alienated intellectual labor. Since scientists do not control the destiny of their paradigms or their own destiny as a sector of the working class under capitalist domination, it is understandable that they cling to an ideology that appears to make a morally redeeming virtue ("value-free inquiry") out of a structurally imposed necessity (only the dominant class decides the fate of new paradigms).[9]

The alienation of intellectual labor has an impact far beyond promoting the fashion process and the consequent proliferation of new paradigms per se. Alienation in the larger society leads workers to see themselves as weak, isolated, and inept consumers rather than producers, to become preoccupied with making themselves into attractively packaged images attuned to the vicissitudes of collective taste, to use the right deodorant, the right hair style, the right cosmetics, the right clothing as a means of gaining social acceptance. It leads, in short, to an orientation toward others tantamount to what Erich Fromm calls *the marketplace personality*: "I am as you desire me." A main purpose of the advertising industry is to exacerbate and take advantage of the organized insecurity of the working class as a whole, to encourage the masses to feel all manner of inferiority, rejection, weakness, aches, and pains for which the only remedy is the latest consumer product hawked on TV.[10] Indeed, getting a job and holding onto it usually require that the candidate convincingly present him- or herself as the embodiment of the marketplace personality. Workers engaged in mental labor in the scientific community, like those engaged in manual labor, are equally caught up in the organized insecurity generated by the forces of alienation. Scientists are therefore just as preoccupied with packaging their ideas, their energies, their very existence in keeping with the image of the marketplace personality. This orientation, objectively an indication of anguish and powerlessness, is commonly passed off and saluted as a sign of "intellectual flexibility," "professional adaptability," "scientific versatility," "academic entrepreneurship," "cooperativeness" and "congeniality."

The scientist understandably becomes eager to design his intellectual wares as attractively as possible, for he can thereby receive a handsome price (a bonus, promotion, grant, paid leave) for his product. This enthusiastic sensitivity to the nuances in the marketplace of ideas, this eagerness to please the audience of prospective buyers, should not be considered a sign of psychological weakness or "other-directedness" on the part of the lone scientist. This outlook should rather be understood as a sign of successful adaptation to the structural requirements of the larger society in which science is sponsored: the internalization of cultural definitions of "professional maturity" and "good judgment" is taken for granted in the scientific community. More systematically stated, the personality type of the "eager-to-please" scientist is a normative consequence of structural and ideological conditions over which the scientist as an individual has no control and of which he seldom even has any explicit awareness. The scientist therefore becomes a creature and carrier of the pressures and ideologies in his environment rather than its critic or creator. What happens to the working class in general happens to the scientist in particular: the well-adjusted manual worker and the well-adjusted scientist equally represent the marketplace personality. They equally give expression to its main symptomatic message: "I am as you desire me." The consequence for the scientific community is that its rank-and-file participants view themselves and each other in terms of this even more far-reaching message: "*my ideas, my paradigms, are as you desire them.*"

The play of fashion in the scientific community, then, is made possible not because scientists are themselves inherently susceptible to the shifting tastes and styles of their discipline but rather because the powerful and usually unacknowledged forces in the marketplace of ideas (itself an extension of the capitalist marketplace) effectively condition and transform the personality structure of the scientist in the service of maintaining the system as a whole.

Valid and Bogus Paradigms: The Play of Fashion in the Search for Profit and Power

It would be all too tempting to conclude that opinion leaders are themselves the source of or impetus for the fashion process. Another tempting but equally misleading notion is that the fashion process is necessarily the underlying cause of any irrational behavior found in the scientific community. The weakness of these notions consists in their neglect of the structural and historical conditions under which science evolved in advanced capitalist societies. It is to these conditions that we must direct our attention if the causes of the fashion process in science are to be more fully identified.

First, the rise of science is attributable to the ongoing requirement to grasp and exploit the forces of nature in the service of efficient production, profit maximization, and imperial conquest. Those who own and control the means of production have prudently encouraged and bankrolled all manner of scientific inquiry.[11] Second, members of the scientific community, regardless of their stature or income, are also intellectual workers who experience the same conditions of alienated labor found in other areas of commodity production. Scientists subjectively perceive themselves as members of a professional elite far removed from the drudgery and doldrums of working-class life. But they are objectively located in a highly exploited sector of the working class. A further analysis of this contradiction between subjective perception and objective reality for the scientist can illuminate the production, packaging, submission, and adoption of bogus as well as valid paradigms.

Little purpose would be served by citing a litany of misdemeanors in various disciplines and academic institutions in which plagiarism, piracy, all manner of cheating, fraud, and contrived busywork are exposed in what would appear to be major scandals only to be ignored and forgotten soon after they are made public. Whether the episode involves "lapses in documentation" in a social theory textbook, evidence-stacking in a grant application for cancer research, fraudulent credentials from a diploma mill passed off as earned doctorates, or the latest cheating scandal at West Point, the fact remains that little change in the peer review and evaluation process is usually forthcoming (or even seriously advocated) in the wake of such circumstances. Seldom, if ever, is more than a passing nod given even to the idea of soul-searching in response to such dirty linen cluttering the temple of science. This nonresponse to scandals corrosive to the image of science, this complaisance and cynicism in the scientific community toward collective irrationality and corruption within, is symptomatic of alienated intellectual labor.

In the face of the individual scientist's impotence within his professional community and that community's own impotence in the shaping of national policy, the designation and defense of opinion leaders through the granting of ceremonial honors (e.g., the MacIver Award, the Sorokin Award) are a means by which at least the *appearance* of professional autonomy and integrity can be maintained. The fact that the recipients of these awards are soon forgotten, the even more striking fact that the figures for whom these awards are named are themselves soon dismissed as "dated" and irrelevant to the scientific mainstream, does not diminish the ideological importance of making such designations within the scientific community. *The ritual processes by which this or that creator of a mainstream paradigm is honored help to maintain the illusion that this is a community with power and authority over its own affairs.* The reason for the proliferation of awards named after opinion leaders whose own work is readily forgotten, then, is not that the number of authentic scientific heroes has increased. The reason for the proliferation of such awards is not that the discipline is enjoying a renewal of historical appreciation of its "founding fathers." The reason for the proliferation of these awards and ceremonies is that the scientific community has very little else at its disposal to assert its competence and authority either to its own rank and file or to the larger society. Since it makes little difference to those in positions of state and corporate power whether there are MacIver Awards, Sorokin Awards, Lipset Prizes, Bendix Buttons, or Weber Medallions, *so long as the required paradigms are produced and made readily available as needed*, the scientific community can continue to engage in these rituals without fear of incurring the wrath of or causing an inconvenience to the larger structure of domination. The scientific community can therefore proceed with this ritual process of conferring awards without fear of being vetoed, questioned, or otherwise embarrassed by the forces that do shape the course of history.

This absence of any substantial reevaluation of the processes by which opinion leaders rise to prominence in the scientific community even when they are found to be blatantly corrupt (e.g., Sir Cyril Burt) is indicative of the intensely felt need for opinion leaders within that community. For example, one of the most coveted awards in the sociological profession is the MacIver Award, which was conferred on proponents of the ideologies of pluralism and structural-functionalism in the late 1950s and early 1960s. A much-heralded recipient of that award during the heyday of what C. Wright Mills called "the conservative mood" was Seymour Martin Lipset. Among other key arguments in his widely acclaimed *Political Man*, Lipset held that the most serious problem facing American democracy was that the satisfaction of socioeconomic needs among various interest groups was leading to a disappearance of issues around which public debate could be generated; with this lack of public debate to keep the mechanisms of democracy in working order, he contended, they would become rusty and atrophied. In that era of celebration of and deference toward the doctrines of pluralism and functionalism, there was virtually no sustained challenge to Lipset's celebration of the *pax Americana* or serious call for the reevaluation of the criteria and processes by which such a work could be considered the most distinguished sociological scholarship of that era. None of the movements, events, and uprisings of the immediately following years—including the black insurgencies in the inner cities, the student power movements on the nation's largest campuses, the antiwar militancy that began to spread even within the white middle class—induced the leadership and the scientific audience of ordinary sociologists to question the process by which leaders were (and still are) certified and legitimated. Although there have indeed been criticisms of Lipset's paradigm per se, the fact remains that *no* serious criticism has been raised against the processes by which it came to occupy center stage.

The ongoing creation of new awards, prizes, and honors named after some opinion leaders and the ever-increasing allocation of these awards to other opinion leaders are ritual processes that serve a vital purpose. These processes enable the scientific community to compensate for or at least appear to cope with alienation prevailing on the structural level and organized insecurity and basic anxiety felt on the social-psychological level. Precisely because these ritual processes are essential to the facade of legitimacy produced by the scientific community in posturing itself and adapting to the demands and degradations imposed by the larger society, their irrationality is generally not investigated or even recognized. The processes themselves and the substantive criteria by which awards are conferred, then, are therefore not subject to critical scrutiny by the scientific community.

To appreciate why the rules of scientific rationality are so often subject to loose or opportunistic interpretation, to understand why so many scientists at some times deliberately and at other times unwittingly participate in the fashion process, let us consider some normative responses to the discovery or perception of plagiarism. In plagiarism, we have the kind of incident that directly and gravely violates the "code of ethics" in the scientific community. We might expect that an incident of flagrant intellectual piracy or "ripping off" of a scientist's work by someone else would result in strong sanctions against the culprit. However, our expectation would not be borne out. For example, I know a colleague who happened to discover a case in which a book was published with significant amounts of material culled from other sources without any citation of same; the material was, he observed, misrepresented as though it were an original intellectual effort. This colleague then innocently published his discovery and expected that his documentation of it would be considered a meritorious deed in his field. But he was instead given "flack" for washing dirty linen in public. He took the message to heart and did not pursue his indiscretion any further. In the case of Sorokin's accusations that Parsons had pirated numerous concepts from the former's books and lectures, allegations circulated verbally and later in writing with documentation in the late 1950s and early 1960s, there was clearly no outcry in the discipline of sociology to investigate or take seriously the thrust of his charges. With one of Sorokin's circulars on this saga in hand, I asked a few prominent sociologists who had studied under both Parsons and Sorokin just what their own reaction might be.[12] Their advice was to *ignore* the charges because (1) Sorokin showed poor judgment by sending hundreds of these circulars to social theorists all over the country; (2) he was becoming isolated, embittered, getting on in years, and should be discounted accordingly; and (3) "so what else is new"? Sorokin had gone so far as to argue that Parsons's model of society, culture, and personality was among the major areas expropriated from one or another of his voluminous works. But why was nothing done about all this?

The readiness with which scientists shut their eyes to plagiarism and the enthusiasm with which they participate in the fashion process in their discipline, then, cannot be explained in terms of anti-intellectualism or moral degeneracy allegedly operating in their discipline. Even if such mental and moral defects did exist in a given discipline, one would still have to specify the structural and historical conditions under which these patterns appear and disappear over time as well as the circumstances that lead some scientists to be more and others less susceptible to their influence. To whatever degree these defects might be present in a given discipline, they can be more adequately understood as social symptoms or manifestations of the underlying forces behind the fashion process than as signs of a supposed moral decay or evil inherent in scientists or the scientific community.

Scientific Dialogue and the Granting of Awards to Opinion Leaders

The appearance of "scientific dialogue," the illusion of hustle and bustle represented as "scholarly ferment," is most vividly dramatized at the annual conventions of such professional groups as the American Sociological Association. At these meetings, the ritual processes of conferring awards on newly certified heroes in the scientific community can reach fever pitch. The rituals take on a high degree of sanctity as a solemnly convened audience of opinion followers (the rank and file of the profession) gives a standing ovation to the latest recipient of this or that honor. At the present time, such conferences serve primarily as avenues for career mobility—for making connections with federal and corporate "soft money" brokers, for adding a notch or two to one's résumé, for anointing and befriending transient opinion leaders, for celebrating the supposed scholarship of the discipline, for job interviews with prospective employers, and for virtually every purpose other than promoting serious intellectual exchanges of the kind advertised. All too often, what are represented as "symposia" and "panels" are little more than the transparent playing out of the buddy system through which miscellaneous and mediocre cronies go through the motions of politely praising and respectfully disagreeing with one another.

Although sociologists represent themselves as having the capacity for "sociological self-awareness," hundreds of them gathered in the same auditorium are still unwilling and unable to call for an investigation of the ritual processes by which awards are given out. Such an investigation could not be tolerated precisely because these ritual processes are a vital part of the scientific community's adaptation to an alienating environment. These ritual processes are a means by which powerlessness and humiliation can be obscured with the halo of new awards, the glitter of new medals, the glare of collective self-celebration.

Causes of Irrationality in the Scientific Community

Historians of science have been just as myopic as Sorokin and Mills when attempting to explain the origins of (1) irrationality and collective behavior within the scientific community and (2) the outcome of collisions involving new scientific paradigms and prevailing institutional forces in the society as a whole.

Illustrative of the many well-written and highly regarded histories of scientific thought in this regard is A History of the Sciences by Stephen F. Mason. Like most historians of science and sociologists of knowledge, Mason assumes but never attempts to prove that values are in themselves the necessary and sufficient cause of irrational behavior in the scientific community. He fails to recognize that the values to which he attributes this causal primacy are themselves reflections of underlying structural requirements in a given society. With such narrow assumptions of cultural determination over irrationality in science to guide his analysis, we should hardly be surprised to see that he is forced to explain one set of ideas (in science per se) by pointing to another and larger set of beliefs (in the culture as a whole):

> Throughout history scientific theories have been favored or opposed, apart from considerations based upon the criteria of the scientific method, according to the degree to which those theories have been congruent, or at variance, with the generally accepted beliefs of their time and place. Such judgements and the actions based upon them have been particularly conspicuous during those periods of history when two major movements of comparable strengths have stood in opposition to one another.[13]

The two sources of irrationality neglected by Mason are the structure of domination and the play of fashion.

There are two sources of irrationality in the scientific community. The first is the overt imposition of extralogical (ideological) criteria and the direct intervention of external political agencies (spies, censors, lackeys of the state in positions of academic or scientific command and control)—all at the behest of those in state power. The second, and more subtle, factor is the operation of the fashion process, including the influence of opinion leaders, the preoccupation with modernity and "keeping in step with the times," and the organized insecurity of scientists disposed to produce paradigms congruent with the vicissitudes of collective taste.

The first source of irrationality is readily observed and widely documented in the history of scientific thought. The systematic suppression of Mendelian genetics in the Soviet Union during the 1930s and 1940s, including the torture, imprisonment, and liquidation of biologists unwilling to recant their heresies, illustrates the deliberate imposition of ideological criteria on the scientific community. The readiness with which leaders and ordinary scientists alike became enamored with the production of statistical concepts and measures of significance (along with measures of association based on tests of significance) during the 1950s and 1960s in the United States illustrates the operation of the fashion process in the scientific community in an equally graphic manner.

The important distinctions between these sources of irrationality warrant emphasis: in the former case, noncooperation with the prevailing orthodoxy is likely to result in the shutting down of a laboratory or institute and the imprisonment or exile (or worse) of dissenters. In the latter case, noncooperation is likely to evoke a label of "backwardness," "rigidity," or "senility" attached to the image of the dissenting group or individual; grants and soft money usually dry up, at least temporarily. As a result of this latter sanction, employment is likely to be harder to find for those stigmatized as "too stubborn" to accept the latest trends.

Still another important distinction is the ease with which the standards of truth, orthodoxy, and ideological discretion can be ascertained in cases where ideological criteria are politically imposed on the scientific community. The standards of truth and good taste are often only implicit and open to a finite but somewhat flexible range of interpretations where the fashion process is operating. This range of interpretations is commonly taken for granted as self-evident; it is not consciously acknowledged by those caught up in those same standards in cases where the fashion process is operating.

A third notable distinction between politically imposed orthodoxy and the play of fashion as sources of irrationality is that the former is usually recognized as just one concrete sign of totalitarian domination permeating the society as a whole, while the latter is perceived by most members of the scientific community as the "free play of ideas," "the quest for new discoveries," and "intellectual ferment in a dynamic marketplace." In the former case, scientists usually have few or no illusions about the fact that they are required to make their choice of problems and production of paradigms subservient to the demands of the state. In the latter, scientists usually see themselves as having virtually unlimited options as to the research priorities and paradigms they can freely pursue; seldom if ever do scientists in this latter regard see themselves or their discipline as under the heavy-handed control of overall social and economic forces or as under the scrutiny of the state. (In this latter instance, the fact that scientists perceive themselves to be free from external constraint—indeed, free from any pressure to endorse a given doctrine—does not necessarily indicate that such freedom objectively exists.)

With these substantial differences between politically imposed orthodoxies and the influence of the fashion process on the scientific community, with differences in both the objective nature of these sources and the subjective perceptions of them by their key participants, we might conclude that they have little or nothing in common. But such a conclusion would ignore the fact that both sources of irrationality in science do, upon closer inspection, turn out to have striking features in common. First, *both sources of irrationality are marked by the systematic exclusion of scientists from the decision-making process in the structure of domination in the larger society and as well as the lines of real command and control in their own disciplines and professional organizations.*[14]

Second, both sources of irrationality lead to normatively patterned and systematic consequences for the development of scientific thought: they do not lead to random, accidental, or intellectually anarchic trends even though they both lead to irrational ones. The influence of political and ideological irrationality over scientific thought, like the influence of opinion leaders upon it, should not be considered random or bizarre activity. More generally stated, both sources of irrationality have a variable yet systematic influence over the scientific community from time to time, from place to place, in accordance with the historical conditions under which they take shape; the range of this variation is predictable in both cases. For example, innovations in costume adornment are judged according to their fidelity to the latest styles of opinion leaders in the larger society. Such judgment corresponds to the evaluation of research proposals in terms of their adherence to the most recently approved paradigms of opinion leaders in the scientific community.

Third, both sources of irrationality can and do affect each other. Politically imposed orthodoxy and the fashion process influence each other even as they contribute to the overall degree of irrationality in the scientific community. In the seemingly precise field of labor statistics, for example, an ever-increasing number of variables are used to measure "job satisfaction," "workers' consciousness," and "labor militancy." The proliferation of new concepts and techniques in labor statistics and, more generally, in industrial sociology is kept within the boundaries of collective taste: some terms rise to prominence while others fall by the wayside. But an underlying politically imposed orthodoxy establishes the ground rules within which the fashion process can operate at all: the prior assumption is made that the militancy of the American working class has declined. With this assumption taken for granted, the trend-setting Bureau of the Census has dictated that the criterion for a "strike," for purposes of record keeping and analysis, is that it must have a duration of three days of longer. The new criterion is justified under the guise of budgetary reductions for research staffing and methodological efficiency; strikes that last one or two days or just a few hours are no longer counted as such. That strikes may occur now as frequently or be as militant as before is thus statistically and ideologically suppressed. The conservative grip of a Republican administration over federal agencies that supposedly describe but in reality obscure trends in labor militancy therefore shapes the boundaries for new research into (1) the *causes* of reduced militancy and (2) the *magnitude* of declining political consciousness in labor unions and throughout the working class in general. The proliferation of new research, inspired by "hard" data from the Census Bureau and the Department of Labor, is then published in academic and professional journals to display new measures of political apathy in the working class and to spread the message that the labor movement is weak and in disarray. This spurious information is in turn selectively cited and quoted in the mass media of communication (including the latest sociology textbooks) to reflect and reinforce the ideologies of cultural withdrawal and privatization useful to a conservative political regime hoping to keep the lid on working-class consciousness.

Fourth, both sources of irrationality are personified and actualized by opinion leaders commonly regarded as "larger than life," as though they were prophets or giants in their own lifetime. Where politically imposed doctrines weigh heavily on the scientific community, the figure of Stalin or Mao, for example, is likely to pervade the scientific community. Where the fashion process operates in the scientific community, such figures as Weber, Durkheim, Freud, or Skinner are likely to dominate. The presence of these figures, usually heralded as though they were immortal, is by no means incidental to the normative pattern of irrationality in the scientific community: the names and guises of opinion leaders may change from time to time (so that Marx gives way to Lenin or Mao and Weber might give way to Parsons or Merton). But their ideological significance and legitimacy remain absolutely essential to the maintenance of irrationality in the scientific community. For example, when Stalin fell from grace in Soviet economic theory, a reemphasis on the more classical images of Marx and Engels was rapidly promoted; when Parsons and Merton came to be perceived as increasingly "dated" and "irrelevant," some of the mainstream works of Sorokin were quickly re-discovered, reaffirmed, and republished as major events in the social sciences.

Fifth, in both cases of irrationality, we find that opinion leaders are usually given all manner of awards and deference in their own lifetime, that they are *assumed* to exercise an enduring and profound impact on the development of major concepts within the scientific community, and that the processes by which these awards and honors are conferred are themselves not examined. The influence of these leaders usually wanes markedly after their death. At times, some of their most influential work is found to be extremely unsound or even altogether fraudulent (e.g., the research of Sir Cyril Burt in the field of psychological testing and measurement).[15] Or their influence is recognized to have been based on the use of censorship, blackmail, torture, and terror. But even in instances in which irrationality is clearly recognized in terms of the inappropriateness of this or that opinion leader as an exemplar for the scientific community, *nothing is done to disavow or even examine the processes and criteria by which such leaders came to prominence in the first place.*

The Protestant Ethic and the Fashion Process in Modern Science: Weber and Merton Reconsidered

The rise of modern science is usually attributed to the critical thought associated with the Protestant ethic. But its stirrings and growing acceptability to secular (and, occasionally, to religious) authority in the seventeenth century may also be attributed to the emergent play of fashion throughout society in general and scientific communities in particular. The new mercantile class had a need for innovation and improvement in industrial planning and intercontinental travel; its grip on wealth and power was also predicated on knowing how to harness (even if not always with full comprehension) the forces of nature to be used in the service of efficient production. Maps had to be made; the ocean winds had to be understood; all available sources and forms of energy had to be tapped; weapons of war had to be improved so that colonies could be secured for the maintenance and expansion of empires. These and related tasks necessitated that all manner of conventions, problems, and solutions in science and society be examined afresh; new and better ways of doing things were eagerly entertained. However much "Puritanism and Pietism" derived from selective interpretations of Calvin's and Luther's teachings, however much Weber and Merton assumed that the Protestant ethic was the major impetus to modern science, we can hypothesize that *the fashion process itself increasingly operated to accelerate the rate at which scientific ideas were proposed. It helped to facilitate procedures, priorities, and even the substantive content of science by the seventeenth century.* But why is there such a widespread insistence among sociologists that the Protestant ethic should receive all or most of the credit as the impetus to the growth of modern science?

At the time of the establishment of sociology as a separate discipline in the nineteenth century, a preponderance of its founding fathers and opinion leaders were themselves religious. Often, their backgrounds were deeply religious even though they at least nominally gave up such sentiments as they immersed themselves in the new "Science of Society." Their loyalty to the rising capitalist state was so great that they set forth sociological interpretations of capitalist enterprise in general and capitalist science and technology in particular, suggesting that these institutions were created, graced, and legitimized by nothing less than Christian faith itself. Capitalism, the working class was told, arose not because of any ruthless use of weapons for conquest, genocide, and colonialism, but rather because of "the Protestant ethic." Science and technology, in the same light, were developed rapidly, not because of ruling-class interests in ruthlessly exploiting physical resources and human labor power as efficiently as possible, but rather because of the critical and creative intelligence unleashed by the same Christian faith. The message of Weber and his countless supporters, with Merton as the most recent and influential among them, has been unwavering: the Protestant ethic is the fountainhead of Western civilization in general and modern science and technology in particular. Stripped of its ideological embroidery, the thrust of this message is that the power of prayer can do wonders right here on Earth, that obedience to the will of God and the rule of law is the responsibility of every mortal being. It is not significant here to ask whether all founding fathers and opinion leaders themselves seriously believed in these exhortations to obey the state and revere the growth of science in the hands of the state; it *is* significant to note that the impact of their doctrines has been to promote an uncritical obedience to the state, a sanctification of the capitalist system, and a reverence for the mystifications associated with modern science. Is it possible that factors other than the Protestant ethic may have set into motion the rise of modern science? Has too much credit been given to the Protestant ethic and too little to the fashion process by those who presume to explain the origins of modern science?

As early as the seventeenth century, before fledgling scientists were consciously aware of the intimate linkages among state power, capitalist expansion, exploitation of physical and human resources, innovative scientific research, and the need for ideological legitimacy, some scientists were already able to recognize the nascent and increasingly decisive fashion process itself as an impetus to the rise of science. Perhaps the most explicit and realistic acknowledgment of the fashion process in the dawn of modern science, all the more significant because divine inspiration and the power of prayer were then still considered the ultimate driving forces behind scientific discoveries, occurred as early as 1667, in Thomas Sprat's *History of the Royal Society of London*, in which he offers a revealing defense of the Reformation in religious and philosophical thought. The new "Religion" and the new "Philosophy" (especially including scientific inquiry), according to Sprat, have

> . . . taken a like course [through] passing by the corrupt copies, and referring themselves to the perfect Originals for their instruction; the one to the Scripture, the other to the huge Volume of Creatures. They are both accused unjustly by their enemies of the same crimes, of having forsaken the Ancient Traditions, and ventured on Novelties. They both suppose alike that their Ancestors might err; and yet retain a sufficient reverence for them. *They both follow the great Precept of the Apostle, of trying all things*. Such is the harmony between their interests and tempers.[16]

Sprat was certainly aware that the scientific ethos of his own day had already become open to "trying all things," venturing into "novelties," and taking a dim view of "ancient traditions." Even though he was oblivious to the origins and consequences of the fashion process per se, Sprat was secure enough in the knowledge that scientific inquiry had become sufficiently respectable to enable him to make a bold assertion: he declared that the scientific community has only a limited reverence for its intellectual "ancestors" and a great enthusiasm for entertaining as many newly proposed paradigms as possible.

While a complete reevaluation of the "Protestant ethic" thesis is beyond the scope of the present study, one could reasonably argue that the fashion process, itself generated by the forces of alienation in laissez-faire capitalism, had far more to do with the rise of modern science than previously recognized. Indeed, the culturally induced sense of innovation in science and appreciation of diversity in the natural world, preconditions for the rise of modern science, could and probably would have shaped seventeenth- and eighteenth-century philosophy even if "Puritanism and Pietism" were far less prominent than they were in that era. The play of fashion promotes not only its own orthodoxies and ritualized collective behavior but also some emancipating tendencies to scientists who might otherwise be caught up in tradition for its own sake. The impact of the fashion process on the scientific community therefore depends on the concrete historical conditions under which it operates. One cannot understand this process or trace its outcome unless its structural and historical context is specified.

Any effort to attach relative causal weight to the play of fashion and the Protestant ethic in explaining the rise of modern science can all too easily be led astray if one neglects the forces within late feudal society and early laissez-faire capitalism that required and promoted a rationalist approach to a host of increasingly urgent problems. In order to maintain and expand the scope of empires needed for trade and raw materials, for example, the most adequate, reliable, and intelligible maps had to be produced and made available to ocean navigators. And the maps themselves were useless unless methods could be devised to ascertain one's location on the high seas over long periods of time. Such seemingly mundane exigencies could be met only with revolutionary developments in astronomy and mathematics as well as in models reflecting the size and shape of the Earth. Without these developments, it would not have been possible to make sense out of such practical problems as the correction of the compass indicating true North—a matter of life-and-death importance to a ship's captain out of sight of land. Without them, the conquest and commercial exploitation of newly discovered continents would have been impossible. Hence, the introduction, discussion, and adoption of new disciplines—a trend accelerating on a dramatic scale by the seventeenth century—can be understood as an ongoing response to the needs of the dominant classes consisting of royalty and embryonic mercantile interests of that era. *One could reasonably argue that the need for such scientific development was so urgent, so acutely felt, that if the fashion process and Protestant ethic had not existed by the seventeenth century, the dominant social classes of the time would have been forced to create them in the service of expediting solutions to the awesome problems of the day.*

Whatever the political advantages of having the masses believe in the myths and superstitions of the Church, the ruling class could no longer afford to promulgate or even acquiesce in scriptural doctrines and conventional wisdom about the structure of and methodology for investigating the universe. The play of fashion and the secularized interpretations of Lutheran and Calvinist ideology did indeed expedite the proliferation and toleration of new scientific paradigms. A case can be fairly made that the fashion process had a more substantial impact than the Protestant ethic on the rise of modern science; but the fact remains that the fashion process and the secularized versions of Luther's and Calvin's teachings reflected and reinforced the dominant interests of laissez-faire capitalism rather than acting as its causal impetus. Both the fashion process and Protestant ideology, in turn, served to legitimize the search for new theoretical models and the all-important spirit of mutual independence, criticism, and rivalry among scientific opinion leaders and schools of thought. But neither of these forces can be credited with being the exclusive impetus to the rise of modern capitalism in general or science in particular. *To cope with the crises of late feudalism and early laissez-faire capitalism, the dominant classes promoted both the fashion process and Protestant ideology, which in turn served to legitimize and further accelerate the growth of what eventually became mature capitalism and modern science.* Does this hypothesis suggest that the process or the ideology are unimportant in the evolution of science?

The contributions of the fashion process and the Protestant ethic to the rise of modern science should not be minimized; the present study does not suggest that either one of these factors should be given short shrift in a comprehensive account of the proliferation of models in the scientific community. A possibility deserving of careful investigation beyond the scope of the present study is that the fashion process warrants recognition for being a major factor in the rise of modern science, that it may well be far more influential in expediting its growth than the Protestant ethic per se, and that both factors can be fairly seen more as products of early capitalism rather than first causes of same. We can view the fashion process and the Protestant ethic, then, as *expeditive* rather than primary causes of capitalist development. Both factors helped especially to hasten the development of modern science. A further possibility deserving of investigation beyond the scope of this study is that this process and ideology may well have worked in tandem all along to accelerate the pace at which new scientific paradigms have proliferated and new opinion leaders and schools of thought have challenged one another's authority at every turn. An indication that they could have been jointly operating in the rise of modern science is that by the seventeenth century many scientists were driven by such goals as (1) daring to make original and critical views known to the scientific community (suggestive of the intellectual self-reliance and inclination to break with authoritarian doctrine linked to the Protestant ethic), as well as (2) keeping in step with the latest developments and taking a dim view of traditional beliefs and practices (suggestive of the collective behavior linked to the fashion process).

How the Fashion Process Accelerates and Retards Scientific Discoveries

It required considerable courage for such figures as Darwin and Newton to publish discoveries that were widely perceived as menacing to the conceptual foundations of Western society: they faced bitter opposition at the hands of such powerful detractors as Louis Pasteur and Bishop Berkeley. Freud encountered ideological and religious enemies throughout Europe. His paradigms of infantile sexuality and unconscious motives also incurred the wrath of American behaviorists and symbolic interactionists who, for all the disputes they had among themselves, had no patience for the new and startling ideas he advanced. Why were their proposals given any attention at all in the face of such strong opposition?

It was not Puritanism or Pietism that enabled radical ideas to be entertained here and there by scientific audiences. It was the newly emergent and increasingly pervasive fashion process that allowed a parade of strange and interesting paradigms to be introduced into the arena of scientific discussion. Although many new ideas so introduced were outlandish, and many that enjoyed adoption were objectively untenable, the fashion process was a vital element in the historical context that allowed a broad spectrum of new paradigms to surface and stay afloat despite the best efforts of nay-sayers to sink them.[17]

From the seventeenth to the nineteenth century, the play of fashion in science and society throughout Europe was constrained by the entrenched forces of royalty and the church as well as by the barriers to upward mobility imposed even in the best of times on uprooted peasants and the new working class. Even though the fashion process was always limited in its reach, its partial emergence in the seventeenth century did help to promote an atmosphere of cultural toleration and, in some cases, even to turn the tide in favor of what were considered shocking substantive discoveries and revolutionary conceptual paradigms.

New concepts and techniques are introduced for possible adoption through the rapid acceleration of trial-and-error episodes and the intensification of rivalry among opinion leaders. These circumstances allow for a great deal of experimentation with new styles in clothing as well as scientific paradigms: they facilitate the identification and utilization of nature's delights, oddities, and peculiarities. The fashion process is admirably suited to promote this outcome. One might even hold that the delights of nature and the play of fashion in science seem to be "made" for each other. Even though the fashion process expedites the identification and enjoyment of nature's delights, it also generates an enormous number and range of worthless models, duds, and apparent novelties that are just variations on styles once in vogue but soon discarded as obsolete. More significantly, the fashion process does not itself ensure that discoveries of nature's most important secrets will be made at all. Indeed, there is much in the fashion process that militates against the kind of long-term investigation of unpopular or unconventional hypotheses often essential to the solution of a major theoretical problem. The play of fashion is a deterrent especially to any research that might be "too far gone" in terms of heavy dependence on traditional knowledge; it is equally a deterrent to any research that is "too far out" because it anticipates future trends not yet considered plausible, realistic, or within the boundaries of collective taste.

The value of the fashion process at crucial historical moments in protecting the exercise of critical intelligence and the interests of humanity as a whole should not be underestimated. In the seventeenth century, scientists needed an ideological defense against the repressive tactics of church and state aimed at stifling independent or unorthodox thought. In the twentieth century, humanity as a whole needs defenses against the utilization of scientific discoveries by one nation after another to exploit and oppress its own citizens. The fashion process protected scientists in past centuries by helping to legitimize the claim that new ideas, daring experimentation, and critical thought are intrinsically desirable; it protects all humankind in the present era by helping to slow down the rate at which nature's secrets are uncovered and incorporated into national policies of domination and terror.

Fashions in Science and the Protection of Humankind

The fashion process may be seen as a two-headed sledgehammer in the development of scientific thought. On the one side, it can help an unorthodox researcher to smash through the rituals, traditions, and illusions that are customarily taken for granted. On the other side, it can enable an opinion leader to smash the career as well as the paradigms of a daring scientist who proposes ideas that are seen as "too far out." It can also lead to the indiscriminate adoption of objectively untrue paradigms that happen to fit in with prevailing collective tastes or to the rejection of valid paradigms incongruent with those same tastes. One can fairly conclude that the proper time to see the disappearance of this process in science and society is when those conditions of alienation responsible for producing it are themselves eliminated.

One might even argue that the fashion process served humanity well by facilitating discoveries that made possible a deeper understanding of and mastery over the physical and social universe; material and social progress far beyond the wildest dreams of seventeenth-century scientists were thereby made possible. One might also argue that the fashion process now serves humanity even better than before by acting sometimes as a moderate damper and sometimes as a severe brake upon the search for nature's social and physical secrets. The orthodoxies imposed on scientific research by the operation of collective tastes and the mindset of rival opinion leaders can help to slow down the rate at which awesome knowledge becomes available to corporations and nation-states lacking the wisdom or capacity for social justice to use that knowledge safely or responsibly. One might speculate that the fashion process served at one point in history to enable humanity to gain some measure of control over the forces of nature; however, the resulting progress left the few with excessive wealth and privilege and the many with only modest improvements in the conditions of daily toil and struggle. At the present point in history, this same process may well be keeping humanity from arriving at knowledge that would, if introduced and adopted by the scientific community and then utilized by the prevailing political and corporate forces, bring life on Earth to extinction.

Preventing the Play of Fashion in Science

Are there any measures that might be taken to prevent or reduce the play of fashion in science? If the fashion process is viewed narrowly as an aberration in an otherwise rational scientific community, then corrective measures could be readily formulated on a strictly cognitive level. For example, rigorous and *explicit* criteria could be established for the acceptance or rejection of paradigms; special emphasis could be placed on the inadmissibility of "novelty" or "obsolescence" as considerations in the evaluation of such criteria. Only after extensive *public* debate in the scientific community would it be considered appropriate to decide on the merits of competing paradigms; scientists who question the validity of a new model must not be dismissed as senile or irrelevant. The proliferation of opinion leaders and the magnanimity with which they are designated as prophets, geniuses, or heroes would be brought to a halt through an intense debate over the criteria used to confer honors and awards on them.

Although the aforementioned measures would seem ample to eliminate or sharply reduce the play of fashion in science, it should be recalled that its operation in the scientific community does help to keep the door open for the entertainment of new paradigms that might not otherwise be tolerated at all. Hence, even if the fashion process could be brought to an end, some provisions would have to be made so that new models could be allowed into the intellectual arena for a fair hearing. A case could be made that some of the profession's resources should be earmarked for the support of journals and conferences in which new models, together with their most articulate advocates and critics, can openly and thoroughly air their views *and have access to the scientific audience as a whole.* It would be of little value to arrange for such conferences, for example, unless provisions were made to enable all members of the scientific community to have easy and uncensored access to the proceedings.

Unless the structural and historical forces that generate the fashion process are first addressed, however, cognitive measures of the kind suggested earlier have no chance of being adopted or even being seriously considered. Indeed, it is unlikely that the play of fashion in science can be explicitly acknowledged at all unless these forces are addressed. Only when the conditions responsible for the alienation of intellectual labor, including the rise of organized insecurity and basic anxiety in the scientific community, are publicly identified as the source of malaise among scientists can there be any prospect of dealing with the fashion process. It must be remembered that this process is itself but a coping mechanism, a means of responding to the individually and collectively felt pain of alienation, produced by the community of scientists. For scientists to have any realistic prospects of success in overcoming these powerful forces, they must also recognize that they are indeed engaged in the offering and selling of their intellectual labor—just as a much larger sector of the working class offers and sells its manual labor. Only when those who provide mental and manual labor are willing to recognize their mutual class interests, their collective social worth, and their contributions to the progress and wealth of society as a whole, can they become a unified force in their own right. Only when they collectively recognize the great harm they sustain psychologically, culturally, and socially as a result of their exclusion from the decision-making process will the symptoms of their malaise, including the play of fashion in which they are at present caught up, be amenable to a final remedy.

Themes for Future Research

The Fashion Process, the Protestant Ethic, and the Rise of Modern Science Reconsidered

It must be kept in mind that Darwin as well as his rivals in the annals of early evolutionist literature could never have survived the bitter denunciations to which their work was subjected unless there had been a widespread belief that intellectual diversity, new proposals (whether right or wrong), and competition among scientists for recognition and acceptance were virtues within the scientific community and, increasingly, in Western social thought in general. On the one hand, the fashion process produces a deadening pale of orthodoxy at certain junctures and a slightly stagnating effect at other junctures, especially through the proliferation of models and the deployment of scientific talent to conjure up new paradigms without considering the validity of old ones; on the other hand, its facilitating and legitimizing influence in the service of rapid and radical breakthroughs in scientific inquiry has been unduly ignored. The present study may hopefully serve as a point of departure for future investigations of the hypothesis that the fashion process was as influential, and perhaps even more influential, than the Protestant ethic in the rise of modern science. One may note in passing that recent reevaluations of Weber's thesis on the supposedly decisive influence of this ethic on the rise of capitalism have raised serious methodological questions about its viability. The assumption that this ethic is the only or major impetus to the rise of modern science is still taken for granted by researchers following uncritically in Merton's Weberian footsteps; it may well be in need of significant revision.

The Play of Fashion and Antiestablishment Domains: Radical Sociology and the Health and Fitness Movement

To what extent does the fashion process operate in areas of radical social science not directly examined in the present study? On the agenda for future investigation are several recent trends often heralded as "radical scholarship":

(1) the emergence of an antiestablishment literature in "the politics of madness" (e.g., Goffman, Szasz, Laing, Scheff, Ernest Becker) and the American reception accorded the work of Foucault in particular;

(2) the American reception accorded the work of structural and analytic Marxists in general and the work of Althusser in particular;

(3) the American reception accorded critical theory in general and the work of Habermas in particular;

(4) the American reception accorded the work of Wilhelm Reich with special reference to the proliferation of depoliticized "bioenergetics" therapies in clinical psychology.

The research already completed, together with the tasks on the agenda for investigation, will hopefully stimulate others to pursue analyses in these and related domains of the scientific community. There is all too much self-celebration and obscurantist rhetoric within the ranks of radical scholarship, especially in sociology, which, upon closer inspection, distorts or denies altogether Marx's own unified vision of theory and practice. A long-term value of the proposed undertakings can be to promote the historical, critical, and collective self-awareness needed to render that vision coherent and credible in the social sciences.

Still another seemingly antiestablishment domain in which the fashion process operates, here with often grave consequences for its participants, is the health and fitness movement. Its rapid commercialization, impact on conventional medical practice (e.g., the rise of "sports medicine"), and proliferation through the mass media have contributed to dramatic increases in such disabling injuries as knee and shoulder dislocations, shin splints, "tennis elbow," and gastrointestinal disorders. How can the socially and physically beneficial aspects of this movement be nurtured while its harmful consequences are minimized? By calling public attention to the dynamics of collective behavior in this movement and the circumstances surrounding the rise to and fall from prominence of its major opinion leaders (e.g., Jane Fonda and Adele Davis, Jack LaLanne and Jethro Kloss, Lelord Kordell and Carleton Fredericks), an important factor compounding the national health care crisis can be constructively addressed. The same focus can be applied to the analysis of conventional or mainstream medicine as well. The play of fashion is usually present and sometimes even decisive in areas of medical research that directly threaten public health and safety. I recently completed a study of opinion leaders and collective tastes in the glamorous arena of AIDS research, for example, in keeping with the approach outlined above. That study indicates the potentially tragic consquences of the fashion process when it is unrecognized in clinical settings.[18]

The Play of Fashion and the Role of Science in Bringing about Social Progress

Nature gives us its delights freely and with great abandon; its secrets, however, are yielded reluctantly and only after great struggle. And this is as it should be. For the delights and dalliances of nature give us some joy, some material and aesthetic sustenance, to make us human. But nature's secrets are of a fundamentally different order: even the discoveries about nuclear energy, for example, now constitute a clear and present danger to life on Earth. Suppose that a grasp of other secrets of nature, comparable in magnitude to those of nuclear energy, were easily acquired and rapidly utilized by a few fortunate countries (or just one or two powerful ones). Suppose, for example, that the secrets of immortality or antimatter were *now* in the hands of a single social class or group of nations. The forms of extortion, blackmail, economic exploitation, and military terror likely to arise from such control are incalculable. Life on Earth, perhaps even the physical existence of the planet itself, would be in immediate peril. It is far safer that the illusions, fancies, and indulgences associated with the play of fashion are still the major product of intellectual activity in much of the scientific community.

No nation or group of nations is currently organized to offer a socially accountable strategy for handling major new secrets of nature in a safe and responsible manner. We can therefore take comfort in the fact that the fashion process at the present time does help to prevent or at least slow down major scientific discoveries. The absence of such strategies is symptomatic of a world ill-equipped to handle even those secrets already unlocked. Only when the social organization of contemporary societies is changed so that no one is alienated from the decision-making process will it be safe to jettison the play of fashion in science. Only when no one is alienated from the fruits of his or her mental and manual labor will it be objectively possible and historically safe to allow for the displacement of the fashion process by rational modes of discourse in the scientific community. When the latter modes of discourse are established, the secrets of nature can be discovered and used in the service of human betterment. Although such a day is not immediately in sight, it is a goal, a vision, a possibility against which we can measure our progress from day to day with an eye toward the realization of the full potential of the scientific community and the human condition itself.

This would seem to be the appropriate point at which to end the present exploration into the scientific community, to await the benefit of any criticism, and to suggest that a sound platform on which to launch further efforts in the study of fashions in science is now established.

NOTES

NOTES

1. Introduction: Scope and Precedents for the
Study of Fashions in Science

1. Although there are several works that critically examine the problem of transcending a society's definition of itself and some that even examine the problem of transcending a discipline's definition of itself, there has been no substantial effort to solve the problem of self-celebration in a society or in a given scientific field. One might under these circumstances hope for a revival of interest in Sumner's insightful treatment of *ethnocentrism*; this concept could prove helpful in illuminating the sources and consequences of the extravagant praise with which scientists often refer to each other and their discipline in general. For a well-informed, but often ahistorical and tedious, effort to approach these problems from a philosophical standpoint, one might wish to see Alasdair MacIntyre, *Against the Self-Images of the Age: Essays on Ideology and Philosophy* (New York: Schocken, 1971), "The Idea of a Social Science," 211–29, especially 229; "Psychoanalysis: The Future of an Illusion?" 27–37; "Is a Science of Comparative Politics Possible?" 260–79. The real but obscured issue in many of MacIntyre's otherwise rigorously argued essays in this volume is whether a discipline that is encapsulated by its own rhetoric and epistemological assumptions can transcend its limitations by virtue of an abstract commitment to rationalism alone. He goes so far as to assume that what will rescue sociology from the error of its ways is to allow philosophers the right to redefine and transform this discipline in a new (and philosophical) image. MacIntyre fails to examine the possibility that he is perilously enamored with his own version of philosophy and encapsulated by his own polemical cause and ahistorical assumptions. Cf. 258–59. What can explain the arousal of collective tastes in sociology for the ideologies of postmodernism, postpositivism, and, indeed, postrationalism? What can explain the recent arrival of expatriates from philosophy and literature into this discipline? Why are these ideologies viewed as though they were

a breath of fresh air? These questions are examined later through an analysis of Jeffrey Alexander as a new opinion leader on center stage in a crisis-ridden scientific community.

2. Herbert Blumer, "Fashion," *International Encyclopedia of the Social Sciences*, vol. 5 (New York: Macmillan, 1968), 341–45; Blumer, "Social Movements," in Alfred McClung Lee (ed.), *Principles of Sociology* (New York: Barnes & Noble, 1967), 199–220, especially "Fashion Movements," 216–18; Edward Sapir, "Fashion," *Encyclopedia of the Social Sciences*, vol. 6 (New York: Macmillan, 1931), 139–44. The perspective for the present study generally and for the critical appraisal particularly of Simmel's and Kroeber's contributions to the study of fashion is indebted to Herbert Blumer, *Symbolic Interactionism: Perspective and Method* (Englewood Cliffs, N.J.: Prentice-Hall, 1969), especially "The Methodological Position of Symbolic Interactionism," 1–60.

3. Everett M. Rogers and F. Floyd Shoemaker, *Communication of Innovations: A Cross-Cultural Approach* (New York: Free Press, 1971), 1.

4. Earl Raab and Gertrude Jaeger Selznick, *Major Social Problems* (New York: Harper, 1964), 435.

5. A prominent example of this recognition is the recent statement by Maurice Valency, "Fashion," in *Encyclopedia Americana*, vol. 11 (1973), 40–41. However, another widely accepted source still equates the play of fashion with customs in costume adornment and makes no substantive distinction between traditional styles of dress and the selection process in the play of fashion characteristic of modern society. See Bernice Gertrude Chambers, "Fashion and Clothing," in *Collier's Encyclopedia*, vol. 9 (1966), 577–86; Jack Freeman, "Fashion and Clothing in the Nineteenth and Twentieth Centuries," ibid., 586–89. Another leading encyclopedia even omits the topics of "fashion" and "style" altogether, and offers a discussion of the clothing industry in strictly utilitarian and commercial terms with no clear recognition of the forces responsible for fashions within the industry. See John A. Blackburn, "Clothing Trade," in *Chambers' Encyclopaedia*, vol. 3 (1967), 655–59.

6. Valency, "Fashion," 40.

7. Ibid., 41. Valency's factual information here is also questionable: the young people who in the 1960s most fiercely revolted against the "establishment" came from relatively permissive middle-class families rather than regimented working-class families. Cf. Richard Flacks, *Youth and Social Change* (Englewood Cliffs, N.J.: Prentice-Hall, 1970). Valency's own advertising campaigns reveal more insight into the operation of collective tastes than that shown in his encyclopedia article. In his TV commercials, he portrays himself as a vigorous, forward-looking world explorer and mountain climber who leaves no stone unturned in the endless search for unique furniture for upscale customers. The image of always finding new things, always keeping busy, always being driven by restlessness, always making progress is what makes these commercials effective. The fact that no progress is objectively taking place or being demonstrated is of no consequence so far as the success of the commercial message is concerned: so long as opinion leaders and followers *believe* that progress is taking place, the fashion process governs their behavior. Valency the businessman and fashion designer seems to understand this process far better than Valency the author and social commentator.

8. In recognizing the development of such a conservative mood, however, one should not assume that it is a permanent feature of modern society or that human nature is inherently in need of opinion leaders to dictate what is in good taste or in the public interest. Cf. Robert Cirino, *Don't Blame the People* (New York: Random House, 1971), especially "The Role of the Mass Media," 27–31. A theoretical analysis of the concrete historical conditions under which this conservative mood arises is advanced by Erich Fromm, *Escape from Freedom* (New York: Avon, 1965), "Automation Conformity," 208–30; "The Emergence of

the Individual and the Ambiguity of Freedom," 39–55; "Character and the Social Process," 304–27.

9. Valency, "Fashion," 40.

10. Reinhard Bendix, Max Weber: An Intellectual Portrait (Garden City, N.Y.: Doubleday, 1962), especially "Max Weber's Image of Society," 469–94; C. Wright Mills, The Sociological Imagination (New York: Oxford University Press, 1967), "Uses of History," 143–64, especially 149–51; for a critical discussion of some precedents to ahistorical thought in social science, see Frederick J. Teggart, Theory and Processes in History (Berkeley: University of California Press, 1960), especially "The Idea of Progress and the Foundations of the Comparative Method," 82–98. Cf. Don Martindale, The Nature and Types of Sociological Theory (Boston: Houghton Mifflin, 1960), especially "Sociology and History," 11–12. It will be seen later in this study that this ahistorical bias is, more precisely, in part a cause and in part a manifestation of the play of fashion in sociological inquiry.

11. Georg Simmel, "Fashion," International Quarterly, 10 (October 1904): 130–55; reprinted in American Journal of Sociology, 62 (May 1957): 541–58. Citations of Simmel in text refer to the latter reprinted article by page number.

12. Simmel does briefly suggest that the imitation process has its origins in early socialization, but then loses sight of this matter and adds: "The imitator is the passive individual, who believes in social similarity and adapts himself to existing elements; the teleological individual, on the other hand, is ever experimenting, always restlessly striving, and he relies on his own personal convictions" (543). Simmel does not use these remarks to explain the fact that some persons are inclined toward imitation and others toward "teleological" experimentation, that there is more personal experimentation displayed in some societies rather than others.

13. For Simmel, the antagonisms in society derive not from conflicts between organizations or between persons but rather from such principles as collectivism and individualism.

14. Later I will show that some schools of thought within the discipline of sociology seek to maintain their prestige and professional image by displaying certain concepts and procedures that appear to be "the latest thing" and symbolize the exclusiveness of the in-group over against competing schools of thought.

15. Medicine and psychiatry are among the fields of endeavor in which practitioners tacitly agree to regard one another's work as above reproach at all times. The higher learning, especially through the tenure system in each academic department, often encourages cronyism, sectarianism, complaisance, and compartmentalization of knowledge. Scientific interests in such a context can hardly be expected to be "objectively determined" on a universal basis. See William R. Keast (ed.), Faculty Tenure: A Report and Recommendations by the Commission on Academic Tenure in Higher Education (San Francisco: Jossey-Bass, 1973), especially "Academic Tenure Today," 1–20; Robert A. Nisbet, "The Permanent Professors," in Charles H. Anderson and John D. Murray (eds.), The Professors: Work and Life Styles among Academicians (Cambridge, Mass.: Schenkman, 1971), 105–21; Thorstein Veblen, The Higher Learning in America: A Memorandum on the Conduct of Universities by Businessmen (1916; reprint New York: Hill and Wang, 1957), "The Academic Personnel," 124–39. Veblen has most clearly recognized the effects of the tenure system on the organizational and personal insecurity of academic life; the effects of such pervasive insecurity on the self-image of professional sociologists will be examined later in this study.

16. Fred Block, "Expanding Capitalism: The British and American Cases," Berkeley Journal of Sociology, 15 (1970): 138–65; Richard C. Edwards, "The Logic of Capitalism Expansion," in Richard C. Edwards, Michael Reich, and Thomas E. Weisskopf (eds.), The Capitalist System (Englewood Cliffs: Prentice-Hall, 1972), 98–106; Martin Glaberman and George

P. Rawick, "The Economic Institution," in Larry T. Reynolds and James Henslin (eds.), *American Society: A Critical Analysis* (New York: David McKay, 1973), 25–65. The demise of feudal aristocrats did not lead to the growth of a stable economy: "In their place arise new men, courageous and enterprising, who boldly permit themselves to be driven by the wind actually blowing and who know how to trim their sails to take advantage of it, until the day comes when, its direction changing and disconcerting their maneuvers, they in their turn pause and are distanced by new crafts having fresh forces and new directions"; Henri Pirenne, "Stages in the Social History of Capitalism," in Reinhard Bendix and Seymour Martin Lipset (eds.), *Class, Status, and Power: Social Stratification in Comparative Perspective* (New York: Free Press, 1966), 97–98. Pirenne makes clear precisely those forces and relationships Simmel ignores (97–107).

17. A substantial reference to Kroeber is included in Talcott Parsons, Edward Shils, Kaspar D. Naegele, and Jesse Pitts (eds.), *Theories of Society: Foundations of Modern Sociological Theory* (New York: Free Press, 1965), in Parsons's own essay "Culture and the Social System," 985; Alfred L. Kroeber, "On Culture," in ibid., 1032–36. Cf. Pitirim A. Sorokin, *Sociological Theories of Today* (New York: Harper, 1966), "Alfred L. Kroeber (1876–1960)," 263–78. Although Sorokin criticizes Kroeber for ignoring the "ideational" aspects of culture and the integralist theory of change, he nevertheless concludes that "the bulk of Kroeber's procedures and results appear to be sound and in essentials coincide with the results of my own studies of these problems" (278).

18. Alfred L. Kroeber, "On the Principle of Order as Exemplified by Changes of Fashion," *American Anthropologist* new series, 21 (1919): 235–63. Kroeber later used standard textbooks and encyclopedias as the main source of data in his better-known research on trends in art, literature, and science; his reasons for doing so are similar to the justifications he advanced for relying on fashion magazines in the study of changing styles in women's skirts. See Alfred L. Kroeber, *Configurations of Cultural Growth* (Berkeley: University of California Press, 1944), especially "Procedure," 21–27. In a later and more ambitious work, he used almost identical data to that assembled in his original study of fashions. See Alfred L. Kroeber, *Style and Civilization* (Ithaca: Cornell University Press, 1957), especially "Kinds and Properties of Styles," 1–29.

19. Kroeber, "Order as Exemplified by Changes of Fashion," 235, 236. Subsequent page numbers in text refer to this work.

20. "While however we are obviously hovering above a latent principle embodied in these phenomena, its expression in exact form, capable of successful application in the resolution of other events of human history, is difficult; chiefly because the variability of the phenomena is qualitative, whereas a workable law or deterministic principle must be quantitative in its nature" (ibid., 236). Serious methodological difficulties did in fact arise in Kroeber's own research precisely because of his attempt to represent qualitative changes in oversimplified quantitative terms; Kroeber overlooked these difficulties altogether. They are discussed later in this chapter.

21. "Order as Exemplified by Changes of Fashion," 242.

22. Ibid., 240–41.

23. That Kroeber should call such an extreme deficiency in his empirical portrait of fashions in women's skirts a consequence of "little circumstances" is a remarkable understatement in view of his own insistence on statistical thoroughness in the coverage of data. A means by which this deficiency could have been prevented, by examining fashion dolls rather than magazines and abandoning the artificial distinction between the "form" and "content" of social life, is considered below. Kroeber was primarily concerned with the measurement of the length of dress, waist width, width of the bottom of the dress. He ad-

mits that "there is no fixed limit of extremity" in these measurements; this leads to a number of problems in the interpretation of the statistical trends he attempts to portray.

24. Eleanor St. George, *The Dolls of Yesterday* (New York: Crown, 1948), especially "Milliners' Models," 69–75; "The Glass of Fashion," 80–87; and "American Doll Artists," 130–35. Since a substantial number of gifted doll artists were women rather than "workmen" or "craftsmen," part of the neglect of this crucial aspect of fashions in American history may be attributable to the ongoing resistance within the social sciences to the recognition of creative achievements by women in fields of aesthetic endeavor. To classify these artists merely as toy designers would be a gross distortion of the historical record in which they had a major role by reflecting as well as shaping the tastes of the time. The tragic life and brilliant work of such artists as Mabel Smith, for example, call into question Kroeber's narrow judgment of early American designers and "draftsmen." See 130–32.

25. "Order as Exemplified by Changes of Fashion," 256.

26. Ibid., 260.

27. Emile Durkheim, *Suicide: A Study in Sociology*, trans. John A. Spaulding and George Simpson (1897; reprint Glencoe: Free Press, 1951), "Relations of Suicide with Other Social Phenomena," 326–60; William Graham Sumner, *Folkways* (1906; reprint New York: New American Library, 1960), "Mores and Morals; Social Code," 203–4; Max Weber, *The Methodology of the Social Sciences*, trans. Edward Shils and Henry A. Finch (Glencoe: Free Press, 1949, originally published as separate essays between 1903 and 1917), "Critical Studies in the Logic of the Cultural Sciences," 113–88, wherein Weber searchingly criticizes the notion of free will as a mechanism of social change and control. All of these sources were available to Kroeber in 1919, and they clearly indicate the recognition of the need to study social regularities on an empirical basis.

28. See St. George, *Dolls of Yesterday*, especially "From the Cradle of Inventions," 6–13, "Association Dolls, I", 136–41.

29. "Order as Exemplified by Changes of Fashion," 261.

30. Ibid., 261.

31. Charles Horton Cooley, *Social Organization* (New York: Scribner's, 1909).

32. Albion Small, *General Sociology* (Chicago: University of Chicago Press, 1905, 1025), 74–75. Just as ethnocentrism is likely to lead a social scientist astray, the biased assumption that one's own culture and scientific community are inherently backward is equally misleading. Kroeber had harsh words for American craftsmen, and he further assumed that American social scientists were little more than pedestrian psychological reductionists in need of his corrective research. His portrait of American culture and scholarship was substantially misleading as a consequence of these assumptions

33. "Order as Exemplified by Changes of Fashion," 263.

34. The concern to establish sociology as a science was also a compelling theme in Weber's work and even more so in Durkheim's; many of the founding fathers of sociology were gravely concerned about the need for the discipline to become academically secure and respectable. Ernest Becker has indicated that Albion Small's once-radical approach to the study of society was increasingly watered down to the point of being virtually unrecognizable for the sake of this security; see Ernest Becker, *The Lost Science of Man* (New York: Braziller, 1970), "The Tragic Paradox of Small's Career," 19–29.

35. In the attempt to render social science objective and technically precise, Kroeber pursued a goal strikingly consonant with the new spirit of the times as industrialization gained momentum: the requirements of corporate power for standardization of the economic units of production and even of the social self were making themselves felt throughout American society. Kroeber's ahistorical intellectual lens of social statistics as the sure means to discover the underlying principles of order, change, and continuity in civilization

was itself an early symptom of the new orthodoxy of quantification everywhere and as though it were an end in itself. He went so far as to allow the presentation of seemingly hard data to substitute for relevant evidence in ascertaining the principles he wished to discover. The methodological tendencies generated by an expanding industrial system and crystallized in Kroeber's work eventually led such critics as Lynd to observe: "In the current social science world, but newly escaped from the era of over-easy theory-building into the world of patient empiricism and quantification, and overwhelmed by the number of things to describe and quantify in an era of rapid change, the prevailing tendency is heavily on the side of accepting institutional things and their associated values as given. The modern professor confines himself to professing facts, and radical criticism and generalization must wait until all the data are gathered." Robert S. Lynd, *Knowledge for What? The Place of Social Science in American Culture* (Princeton: Princeton University Press, 1939), 184.

2. The Embarrassment of Riches, the Nature of Scholarly Debate, and the Call for a Sociological Newton

1. Donald Horton, "Review of *Fads and Foibles in Modern Sociology and Related Sciences," American Journal of Sociology*, 62 (November 1956): 338–39; Pitirim Sorokin, "Letter to the Editor," *American Journal of Sociology*, 62 (March 1957): 515.

2. Horton, "Review of *Fads and Foibles*," 338. Subsequent citations of this article are indicated in text by page number.

3. Pitirim A. Sorokin, *Fads and Foibles in Modern Sociology and Related Sciences* (Chicago: Regnery, 1956), vii–viii.

4. George A. Lundberg, "Some Convergences in Sociological Theory," *American Journal of Sociology*, 62 (July 1956): 21–27. In view of the marked similarity between Dodd's and Parsons's work and the even more striking similarities between the work of Parsons and Sorokin as documented in detail by Sorokin himself, one can pose a number of questions about the extent to which Sorokin's work is as much of an alternative to the "fads and foibles of modern sociology" as he believes it is. I examine this matter later in the present study.

5. Sorokin, "Letter to the Editor," 515. (All subsequent quotations from this letter are from 515.)

6. Don Martindale, *The Nature and Types of Sociological Theory* (Boston: Houghton Mifflin, 1960), 541–42.

7. Alvin Boskoff, *The Mosaic of Sociological Theory* (New York: Crowell, 1972), 265.

8. Ibid., 264–65. Boskoff does not discuss Sorokin's analysis of the irrational elements in modern sociology or even include the title of *Fads and Foibles in Modern Sociology* in his own bibliography.

9. Ibid., 166–71.

10. See, for example, the exhortations in Alvin W. Gouldner, *The Coming Crisis in Western Sociology* (New York: Basic Books, 1970); Steven E. Deutsch and John Howard (eds.), *Where It's At: Radical Perspectives in Sociology* (New York: Harper, 1970); *Sociological Inquiry*, Winter 1970, an entire issue titled "Some Radical Perspectives in Sociology." Ibid., p. 265. One might also note that Boskoff equates Gouldner's work with "the sociological left," although there are many differences between the reflexive sociology advocated by Gouldner and the Marxist activism advocated by contributors to the radical works cited just above. Boskoff's portrait of Gouldner's position, however much one may disagree with it, is precisely the kind of caricature Boskoff exhorts his readers to avoid. See Boskoff's "Recent Currents in Sociological Orientation," in *Mosaic of Sociological Theory*, 25–26. If he

had been familiar with either Sorokin's *Fads and Foibles* or Sorokin's affiliation with leftist causes in the 1960s, Boskoff might have been inclined to place Sorokin in the same category of ideologues along with Gouldner, Deutsch, and Howard. Although some opinion leaders in sociology were calling for a "Newton" to rescue sociology from the horrors of chaos in the 1960s, at least one opinion leader had already anticipated the more tangible dangers of an eventual resurgence of radical scholarship even as early as the 1940s. Talcott Parsons himself was busily engaged in the clandestine recruitment of Nazi sympathizers and collaborators for appointments at elite American universities. His interest in such experts on Russian and ethnic studies went so far as to include providing them with assistance in circumventing U.S. immigration laws, ostensibly for the purpose of staffing centers for "Russian Studies" at Harvard and elsewhere. Although he was not successful in all instances of this international derring-do as the Cold War took shape, his efforts suggest that he anticipated the "need" for a hard core of anti-Communist intellectuals to contain any radical drift toward socialism or the Soviet Union in American universities. See John Wiener, "Talcott Parsons' Role: Bringing Nazi Sympathizers to the U.S.," *Nation* 248, 9 (March 6, 1989), 289, 306, 308–9.

3. Ambiguity and the Fashion Process in Kuhn's Study of Scientific Revolution

1. Thomas S. Kuhn, *The Structure of Scientific Revolutions* (Chicago: University of Chicago Press, 1966); originally published in the *International Encyclopedia of Unified Science*, vol. 2, no. 2 (1962). Page citations in text refer to the University of Chicago edition.

2. Ibid., viii–ix.

3. One could question the ideological assumptions implied in the use of such terms as "social" sciences and "natural" sciences; these terms connote that the social sciences are somehow peculiar or "unnatural" and obscure the real need for taking into account the special nature of the subject matter in every field of inquiry. Although Kuhn does occasionally drift into making this connotation, it is not unique to his work and will not be examined here in detail.

4. This emphatic approach to the study of anomalies does not imply that scientists individualistically or randomly impute any meaning they please to negative evidence in their discipline. The participation and communication in which such meaning is formed are themselves patterned largely by the social structure and language of the scientific community and of the larger society in which that community develops. This structure and language, in turn, can also be altered under various conditions by participants who make objects of even these seemingly immutable realities.

5. C. Wright Mills, "The Contribution of Sociology to Studies of Industrial Relations," *Berkeley Journal of Sociology*, 15 (1970); 11–32; Christopher Dominico, Anne Eisner, et al., "Violence Center: Technology for Repression," *Science for the People*, 6 (May 1974): 17–21; "Genocide of the Mind," in ibid., 8–15; for a critical analysis of sociological positivism as a legitimation of this manipulative research, see Alfred McClung Lee "Cultures and Personalities in Human Struggle," in his *Multivalent Man* (New York: Braziller, 1966), 342–61. For an analysis of new socialization techniques in the educational system that also reinforce the tendencies toward social adjustment, see Martin Carnoy, *Education as Cultural Imperialism* (New York: David McKay, 1974), especially "Education and the Ideology of Efficiency," 306–41. In assessing the proliferation of raw empiricist studies of social control, Mannheim stated that "limitation to practical problems of this kind tends to segregate single phenomena from the social fabric with which they are interwoven, thereby disintegrating

the whole of social life." Karl Mannheim, "American Sociology," in Maurice Stein and Arthur Vidich (eds.), *Sociology on Trial* (Englewood Cliffs, N.J.: Prentice-Hall, 1963), 4–5.

6. John David Ober and Juan Eugenio Corradi, "Pax Americana and Pax Sociologica: Remarks on the Politics of Sociology," *Catalyst*, 2 (Summer 1966): 41–54; John Horton, "Order and Conflict Theories of Social Problems as Competing Ideologies," *American Sociological Review*, 71 (May 1966): 701–13; Alan F. Westin, *Databanks in a Free Society: Computers, Record-Keeping and Privacy* (New York: Quadrangle Books, 1972), especially "The Federal Bureau of Investigation's National Crime Information Center," 47–64; an excellent analysis of new strategies used by social statisticians to manipulate the consciousness of workers through the dissemination of misleading data on unemployment is provided by John C. Leggett and Claudette Cervinka, "Countdown: How to Lie with Statistics," in James M. Henslin and Larry T. Reynolds (eds.), *Social Problems in American Society* (Boston: Holbrook Press, 1973), 234–57; General David M. Shoup, "The New American Militarism," in Arnold Birenbaum and Edward Sagarin (eds.), *Social Problems: Private Troubles and Public Issues* (New York: Scribner's, 1972), 217–27. Shoup's analysis was originally published in *Atlantic Monthly* April 1969, 51–56.

7. Thomas S. Szasz, *The Myth of Mental Illness: Foundations of a Theory of Personal Conduct* (New York: Dell, 1961), especially "The Logic of Classification and the Problem of Malingering," 37–51, and "Contemporary Views on Hysteria and Mental Illness," 85–96; Edwin M. Lemert, *Social Pathology* (New York: McGraw-Hill, 1951), "Psychological and Psychiatric Approaches to the Study of Sociopathic Behavior," 19–20, and "Sociopathic Individuation," 73–98. The most explicit and comprehensive rationale for the view that extremely disruptive behavior is evidence of pathology or mental illness is advanced by Talcott Parsons, *The Social System* (Glencoe: Free Press, 1951), "Deviant Behavior and the Mechanisms of Control," 249–325, and "The Processes of Change of Social Systems," 480–535, especially 485. Cf. Talcott Parsons et al., *Toward a General Theory of Action* (New York: Harper, 1962), 153, 106–7, 228; Parsons, *Essays in Sociological Theory* (Glencoe: Free Press, 1954), 125. For a cogent but unduly ignored analysis of the theory and practice of maintaining social order, see Alfred McClung Lee, "The Concept of System," *Social Research*, 31 (Winter 1964): 229–38. Cf. Sorokin, *Fads and Foibles*, 213–49. In addition to the endless search for new manipulative techniques aimed at the restoration of docile behavior, there is an endless search for new concepts to represent them. See Norman Bell and John Spiegal, "Social Psychiatry: Vagaries of a Term," *Archives of General Psychiatry*, 14 (1966): 337–45.

8. Kenneth Bock, "Evolution, Function and Change," *American Sociological Review*, 28 (April 1963): 229–37. Unlike most leading functionalists, Merton has admitted that this paradigm can be a conservative ideology; he subsequently argues that this is one logical possibility among many interpretations of this paradigm and continues uncritically to accept all of its biases. See Robert K. Merton, *Social Theory and Social Structure* (Glencoe: Free Press, 1957), "Functional Analysis as Conservative," 37–38, and "Functional Analysis as Ideology," 37–46. Cf. Dusky Lee Smith, "Robert King Merton: From Middle Range to Middle Road," *Catalyst*, 2 (Summer 1966): 11–40.

9. Even the saga of Watergate and the more recent "Iran-Contragate" scandal have been consistently defined as an accident or aberration in an otherwise well-ordered system. Nelson Rockefeller was regularly quoted by the news media as stating that "the tragedy of Watergate is the tragedy of men, not of our institutions"; he held fast to this view after Richard Nixon was forced to resign as president of the United States. The notion that every crisis is temporary or accidental leads to the policy of ad hoc reforms characteristic of modern liberalism and the impression of endless new improvements and innovations ranging from the New Deal and the Great Society to Dynamic Conservatism and the New

Frontier at various times after World War II. See James Weinstein, "Corporate Liberalism and the Modern State," in Richard C. Edwards, Michael Reich, and Thomas E. Weisskopf (eds.), *The Capitalist System: A Radical Analysis of American Society* (Englewood Cliffs, N.J.: Prentice-Hall, 1972), 188–92; James O'Connor, "The Expanding Role of the State," ibid., 193–99; James T. Bonnen, "The Effect of Taxes and Government Spending on Inequality," in ibid., 238–43; Michael Mann, "The Social Cohesion of Liberal Democracy," in Milton Mankoff (ed.), *The Poverty of Progress: The Political Economy of American Social Problems* (New York: Holt, 1972), 399–419. For a thorough analysis of the main features of modern liberalism and an appraisal of one of its chief opinion leaders, see Ralph Miliband, "Professor Galbraith and American Capitalism: The Managerial Revolution Revisited," in ibid., 46–58.

10. N. V. Novikov, "Modern American Capitalism and Parsons' Theory of Social Action," in Larry Reynolds and Janice Reynolds (eds.), *The Sociology of Sociology* (New York: David McKay, 1970), 256–73; Dusky Lee Smith, "The Sunshine Boys: Toward a Sociology of Happiness," in ibid., 371–87; Daniel Foss, "The World View of Talcott Parsons," in Stein and Vidich, *Sociology on Trial*, 96–126.

There is especially in sociology an ongoing search for new symbols to perpetuate the mystique of a scientifically certified restoration of order, minimization of change, and rationalization of crises to keep up with the rapidly changing times and to prevent the erosion of the credibility of the modern state: "On almost all levels of abstraction and on almost all levels of data-discovery or invention, many sociologists have fairly well integrated their sociologies with the ongoing market society. As the market society shifts because of national and international imperatives, as old symbols of legitimation lose their strength, new symbols are needed." Dusky Lee Smith, "The Scientific Institution: The Knowledge-Producing Appendage," in Larry T. Reynolds and James M. Henslin (eds.), *American Society: A Critical Analysis* (New York: David McKay, 1973), 145–70.

11. Alan Wolfe, *The Seamy Side of Democracy: Repression in America* (New York: David McKay, 1973), especially "Public Ideological Repression," 154–73; "Repression and the Liberal State," 207–32; and "Ideological Repression as Conscious Activity," 126–35. Cf. Robert Blauner, "Internal Colonialism and Ghetto Revolt," *Social Problems*, 16 (Spring 1969): 393–408; Douglas Davidson, "The Furious Passage of the Black Graduate Student," *Berkeley Journal of Sociology*, 15 (1970): 192–211, especially "The Colonial Model Applied to the Furious Passage of the Black Graduate Student," 192–85.

12. The classroom in which sociology itself is taught has now become an explicitly recognized arena in which these measures are implemented. The latest techniques in counseling, mate selection, behavior modification and the simulated society are attractively packaged in new "learn by doing" textbooks that professors assign to their students and that are openly represented as the most sensational means yet devised to teach undergraduates about important developments in social science. For some early examples of these trends, see the following manuals: Cathy S. Greenblatt, Peter J. Stein, and Norman F. Washburne, *The Marriage Game: Understanding Marital Decision Making* (New York: Random House, 1974), vi–53; William A. Gamson, *Simsoc: Simulated Society* (New York: Free Press, 1972), especially "Creating a Simforce," 26–31; Richard Mallot, *Contingency Management in Education* (Kalamazoo, Mich.: Behaviordelia, 1972), especially "The First Fly-By-Night Experimental College of Kalamazoo," 9–1 to 9–42. The manual on contingency management was adopted already for course use at over two hundred colleges and universities in the United States. According to the publisher's "Adoption List," the names of some of the most prominent institutions of higher learning are among those now using this device. It should also be noted that the manuals on marital decision making and "simsoc" were very well received in the 1970s. They were published by houses enjoying the highest

reputation in the social sciences, but their glamour, novelty, and some of their marketability have declined in favor of newer and even more sensational "audiovisual software" and "docudramas" in the 1980s.

13. These rationales were expressed to me by colleagues in sociology and psychology who have established reputations in the fields of behavior modification and various kinds of "applied psychology." In some instances, these colleagues have been engaged in consultation and research for prisons and mental hospitals. It should be emphasized that such consultation and research is not always unsound or inhuman; that behavior modification, for example, does often yield impressive results when applied to the treatment of acute mental retardation; and that the *prevailing* context, assumptions, and systematic uses of the aforementioned concepts and techniques in American social science and in the larger society as well as their representation in terms of unquestionable and sensational new discoveries are here at issue. Although these concepts and techniques are not the primary cause of the atomization, privatization, and alienation of the self, they do (a) represent means of encouraging fierce competition, individual therapy, and adjustment to institutions as given, and (b) imply that personal success is possible only when an impersonal expert has so decided. See Banesh Hoffman, *The Tyranny of Testing* (New York: Collier, 1962), especially "The Flight from Subjectivity," 43–58. For a profound study of the impact of these trends, see Richard Sennett and Jonathan Cobb, *The Hidden Injuries of Class* (New York: Random House, 1973), "Badges of Ability," 53–118, and especially the discussion of intelligence testing on 59–71.

14. Staughton Lynd, "The Responsibility of Radical Intellectuals," New University Conference Newsletter, May 24, 1968, 5–6, reprinted in Steven E. Deutsch and John Howard (eds.), *Where It's At: Radical Perspectives in Sociology* (New York: Harper, 1970), 61–70; David Horowitz, "Sociology and Society," in David Horowitz (ed.), *Radical Sociology* (San Francisco: Canfield Press, 1971), 1–12, especially 6–10. Significantly, research on the degree of political censorship exercised by the editors of prominent journals is very rarely discussed in the professional literature. One of the few studies of censorship ever to have appeared in any of these journals is concerned primarily with the customary forms of cronyism and elitism in editorial policy; its findings nevertheless could serve as a point of departure to investigate still further Horowitz's observations about the suppression of Marxist scholarship in American sociology. See Diana Crane, "The Gatekeepers of Science: Some Factors Affecting the Selection of Articles for Scientific Journals," *American Sociologist*, 2 (November 1967): 195–201. For examples of the systematic hostility directed against radical scholarship, see the series of articles by Philip M. Hauser, Richard H. Robbins, William A. Gamson, and Allen H. Barton reprinted in the section entitled "Critiques of Radicalism in Sociology," in J. David Colfax and Jack L. Roach (eds.), *Radical Sociology* (New York: Basic Books, 1971), 419–77.

15. J. David Colfax, "Varieties and Prospects of 'Radical Scholarship' in Sociology," in Colfax and Roach, *Radical Sociology*, 81–82. It might be added that Harold Garfinkel remarked after a guest lecture to the Graduate Sociology Club at Berkeley some years ago that anything of value in symbolic interactionism was already incorporated in ethnomethodology.

16. George Herbert Mead, "Scientific Method and Individual Thinker," in John Dewey et al., *Creative Intelligence: Essays in the Pragmatic Attitude* (New York: Holt, 1917), 178. The underlining is added. Cf. 176–227.

17. Kuhn, *op cit.*, p. 149.

18. The general conception of collective behavior according to which Kuhn's remarks are analyzed is found in Herbert Blumer, "Elementary Collective Groupings," in Alfred McClung Lee (ed.), *Principles of Sociology* (New York: Barnes & Noble, 1967), 178–98.

19. "The tension of individuals who are aroused by some stimulating event [e.g., disclosure of anomalies and intense competition among paradigms] leads them to move around and to talk to one another; in this milling, the incipient excitement becomes greater. The excitement of each is conveyed to others and . . . in being reflected back to each, intensifies his own condition. The most obvious effect of this milling is to disseminate a common mood, feeling or emotional impulse and to increase its intensity. This really leads to a state of marked rapport wherein individuals become very sensitive and responsive to one another and where, consequently, all are more disposed to act together as a collective unit." Ibid., 179.

20. Alvin W. Gouldner, "Anti-Minotaur: The Myth of a Value-Free Sociology," *Social Problems*, 9 (Winter 1962): 199–312; Irving M. Zeitlin, *Ideology and the Development of Sociological Theory* (Englewood Cliffs, N.J.: Prentice-Hall, 1968), "Max Weber," 111–58, and especially "Political Sociology and Political Values," 155–58.

21. Irving M. Zeitlin, "Karl Mannheim," in *Ideology*, 281–319, and especially "Diagnosis of Our Time," 315–19.

22. Joseph Ben-David, *The Scientist's Role in Society* (Englewood Cliffs, N.J.: Prentice-Hall, 1971), 152–60.

23. An excellent case study of this political socialization in the discipline of sociology is Irving Louis Horowitz, *Professing Sociology* (Chicago: Aldine, 1968), especially "Functionalist Sociology and Political Ideologies," 235–49.

24. Pio D. Uliassi, "Government Sponsored Research on International and Foreign Affairs," in Irving Louis Horowitz (ed.), *The Use and Abuse of Social Science* (New Brunswick, N.J.: Transaction Books, 1971), 309–42.

25. Jerome H. Skolnick, "The Violence Commission: Internal Politics and Public Policy," in Horowitz, *Use and Abuse of Social Science*, 234–48.

26. Gene M. Lyons, "The Social Science Study Groups," in Horowitz, *Use and Abuse of Social Science*, 133–52. There is, moreover, a growing body of evidence to support the view that the pressures operative upon social science are operative a fortiori upon the physical sciences. Cf. Walter Hirsch, *Scientists in American Society* (New York: Random House, 1968), especially "The Scientific Career," 85–115. An uncritical but factually detailed report on this trend is given by Carroll W. Pursell, Jr., "Science and Government Agencies," in David D. Van Tassell and Michael G. Hall (eds.), *Science and Society in the United States* (Homewood, Ill.: Dorsey Press, 1966), 223–49. For a more historically and theoretically adequate analysis of this trend, see Jerome R. Ravetz, *Scientific Knowledge and Its Social Problems* (New York: Oxford University Press, 1971), especially "Social Problems of Industrialized Science," 31–68.

27. Pitirim A. Sorokin, *Sociocultural Causality, Space, Time* (1943; reprint New York: Russell and Russell, 1964), especially 43–52.

28. Some of the crucial theoretical and substantive discoveries in social statistics, for example, took place in a context of practical or applied research in which various pressures were clearly operative. See Paul Lazarsfeld, "Notes on the History of Quantification in Sociology—Trends, Sources and Problems," in Harry Woolf (ed.), *Quantification: A History of the Meaning of Measurement in the Natural and Social Sciences* (New York: Bobs-Merrill, 1961), 147–203.

29. Kuhn ignores the importance of the scientist as an intellectual worker with real interests that are not necessarily identical to those of an allegedly value-free scientific community; he therefore fails to recognize the effects of alienated intellectual labor on scientists' willingness and capacity to solve arbitrarily imposed problems. But see Bertell Ollman, *Alienation: Marx's Conception of Man in Capitalist Society* (Cambridge: Cambridge University Press, 1971), 107–8, and "Activity, Work, Creativity," 99–105.

30. Waldemar A. Nielsen, *The Big Foundations* (New York: Columbia University Press, 1972), especially "Government and Foundation Programs: The Endless Ambiguous Interface," 379–98. Cf. Dusky Lee Smith, "The Sunshine Boys: Toward a Sociology of Happiness," in Reynolds and Reynolds, *The Sociology of Sociology*, 371–87.

31. M. King Hubbert, "Are We Retrogressing in Science?" *Science*, 139 (March 8, 1963): 884–90. Hubbert's crucial and unduly ignored appraisal of physical science was presented originally as his presidential address to the Geological Society of America in 1962. Kuhn shows no awareness at any point in the first or revised editions of *The Structure of Scientific Revolutions* of the matters astutely raised and documented by Hubbert.

32. Hubbert, 886.

33. In addition to the aforementioned evidence offered by Hubbert for the physical sciences, one should also recall that Sorokin shows in *Fads and Foibles in Modern Sociology* that the very opposite of these assumptions is true a fortiori for the social sciences. Although Sorokin does indicate the great degree to which modern textbooks are inundated with increasingly unreliable generalizations, his integralist explanation of this retrogression is inadequate and misleading. For a critical analysis of Sorokin's approach to the sociology of science, see Chapter 5 of the present study.

34. In his final chapter, "Progress through Revolutions," Kuhn does not acknowledge the bearing of collective tastes on the selection of a new paradigm despite his earlier emphasis on this very point. The extreme ambiguity in his definition of the paradigm is examined here in terms of the sociology of knowledge.

35. Kuhn does not explicitly recognize and defend some of the immediately preceding implications in his position. Had he been familiar with the writings of such evolutionists as Sumner and MacIver, however, he would have been able to spell out these conservative implications in terms of "the survival of the fittest" and the doctrine of immanent causation in a more sophisticated form than he was able to develop.

36. Kuhn is not alone in espousing this naive view of growth in the number of specializations that may appear in a given discipline. Studies of such proliferation in sociology, for example, ignore the substantive content of the problems and assumptions considered central to the new fields; they serve usefully to document the official *perception* of endless growth in new areas of inquiry as reported by academic departments of sociology and listed in university catalogs, although they do not indicate whether such perceptions correspond to any demonstrable evidence of intellectual growth or retrenchment in the discipline as a whole. See Nich Stehr and Lyle E. Larson, "The Rise and Decline of Areas of Specialization," *American Sociologist*, 7 (August 1972): 3, 5–6. Although Stehr and Larson offer evidence of the cyclical aspect of such apparent growth, they uncritically explain these phenomena in terms of a "generation gap" thesis and the strictly internal processes of change in the discipline per se. They explicitly agree with Kuhn on the validity of this analysis: "In Kuhn's terms, "the practitioners of a mature science are effectively insulated from the cultural milieu in which they live their extra-professional lives." The processes of change [in this case, proliferation] within sociology may also be internally induced. The rigidities of the process of professionalization may become a negative reference point and enhance the probability of generation-specific perspectives" (6). Although earlier in the same article the authors vaguely claim that such change is "responsive to the changing nature of social reality" (3), their main emphasis is on agreement with Kuhn's paradigm.

37. Robert Friedrichs, "The Potential Impact of B. F. Skinner upon American Sociology," *American Sociologist*, 9 (February 1974): pp. 3–8; Donald E. Tarter, "Heeding Skinner's Call: Toward the Development of a Social Technology," *American Sociologist*, 8 (November 1973): 153–58.

38. Friedrichs, "The Potential Impact of B. F. Skinner," 3–4.

39. Friedrichs ambiguously concludes his celebration of this new field of specialization by asserting that, in the long run, it "promises at the very least to nourish in its wake a less orthodox but competing paradigm that refuses to root itself in the radical subject-object dichotomization that is the presumptive soil of natural science" (8). Earlier in the same article, however, Friedrichs notes approvingly that operant conditioning is likely to receive greater acceptance in sociology than psychology and that it converges with existing assumptions in Parsons' and Homan's paradigms. See 4–5, 7.

40. Irving Louis Horowitz, *Professing Sociology: Studies in the Life Cycle of Social Science* (Chicago: Aldine, 1968), especially "Sociology for Sale," 167–73, and "Federally Sponsored Overseas Research: A Dilemma for Social Science," 305–13.

41. Horowitz, "Functionalist Sociology and Political Ideologies," in ibid., 235–49; Alvin W. Gouldner, *The Coming Crisis of Western Sociology* (New York: Basic Books, 1970), "From Plato to Parsons: The Infrastructure of Conservative Social Theory," 412–46.

42. Andre Gorz, "The Scientist as Worker: Speed-Up at the Think Tank," *Liberation*, 18 (May/June 1974): 12–18.

43. On those rare occasions when this possibility is aired in such journals, it is conveyed only as part of the chronology of events in radical sociology, as a moralistic and utopian commitment, or as a symptom of imperfect socialization into the profession. It is not seriously discussed therein as an alternative to the prevailing posture in the discipline. See Jack L. Roach, "The Radical Sociology Movement: A Short History and Commentary," *American Sociologist*, 5 (August 1970): 224–33; Thomas Ford Hoult, "Who Shall Prepare Himself to the Battle?" *American Sociologist*, 3 (February 1968): 3–7; William Gamson, "Sociology's Children of Affluence," *American Sociologist*, 3 (November 1968): 286–89.

44. Sociologists who see these phenomena as essential to the realization of a just society and as tendencies to be accelerated rather than as problems to be solved, contained, or eliminated are usually not recognized or even mentioned in passing in the major introductory textbooks of the discipline. See Mark Jay Oronmaner, "The Most Cited Sociologists: An Anaylsis of Introductory Text Citations," *American Sociologist*, 3 (May 1968): 124–26. The six most frequently cited sociologists are, in order, Merton, Weber, Parsons, Durkheim, Lipset, and Davis. All but Weber are avowed and influential spokesmen for the functionalist paradigm in sociological inquiry.

45. For a recent statement in defense of an elitist view of such research and a proposal for ongoing "projections of the future" through the use of databanks and computer simulation, see Henry Winthrop, "The Sociologist and the Study of the Future," *American Sociologist*, 3 (May 1968): 136–45. Winthrop endorses Moore's functionalist conception of a utopian future based upon consensus and order, and exhorts his fellow sociologists to take the leadership in promulgating this vision: "Various international organizations are now springing up that are specifically devoted to the study of the future. . . . But if sociologists remain overconservative professionally and ignore this new type of institution, then instead of leading the vanguard of the scientific procession in this emerging and important area, they may be forced later into something like a rearguard position. . . . Current conservatism with respect to forecasts of the future is the offspring of traditional methodologies of both undergraduate and graduate training." (143).

46. Thomas S. Kuhn, "Postscript – 1969," in *The Structure of Scientific Revolutions* (Chicago: University of Chicago Press, 1973), 208. One should recall that in the original edition of his study, Kuhn believed that little if any insight into paradigm shifts in the scientific community could be obtained from an investigation of art or philosophy because these and related fields (1) do not resemble a scientific community, and (2) fail to display signs of progress in any case. To appreciate the striking magnitude of Kuhn's own paradigm shift, which he does not acknowledge, one should recall the questions he posed at the be-

ginning of the crucial and final chapter, "Progress through Revolutions"; these questions clearly and fairly summarize his original position: "Why should the enterprise sketched above move steadily ahead in ways that, say, art, political theory or philosophy does not? Why is progress a perquisite reserved almost exclusively for the activities we call science?" In his 1969 postscript, however, Kuhn claims that historians of art and related fields actually gave him the insights into the nature of progress that he in turn merely applied to natural science.

47. Kuhn does correctly observe that modern textbooks can misrepresent the history of scientific discovery as though it were "linear or cumulative" with a culmination in the present and that such misrepresentation can lead to the appearance of an unheralded or "invisible" paradigm shift that is actually revolutionary in its scope. But he ignores the equally misleading and far more common tendency to misrepresent slight shifts and unoriginal revisions in a paradigm as if they were revolutionary: "Partly by selection and partly by distortion, the scientists of earlier ages are implicitly represented as having worked upon the same set of fixed problems and in accordance with the same set of fixed canons that the most recent revolution in scientific theory and method has made seem scientific. No wonder that textbooks and the historical tradition they imply have to be rewritten after each scientific revolution. . . . Whitehead caught the unhistorical spirit of the scientific community when he wrote, 'A science which hesitates to forget its founders is lost' " (137–38). Cf. "The Invisibility of Revolutions," 135–42.

48. Even this statement is somewhat ambiguous, for Kuhn appears far more antagonistic to authoritarianism from external sources than from within the discipline itself. Although this statement is at one level a disavowal of authoritarianism, it is at another level a further variation on the theme that laypersons must not meddle in the affairs of science and that this kind of interference is inherently authoritarian and corrosive to the scientific community. He ignores the possibility that each form of authoritarianism may well reflect and reinforce the other, and that both forms of authoritarianism may be produced directly or indirectly by the structure of domination in the larger society.

49. Still another striking instance of Kuhn's broad appeal is found in David Horowitz's outspoken Marxist critique of conventional sociology. Horowitz invokes Kuhn's paradigm to justify the radical demystification of repressive forces in the discipline: "Without an institutional funding source, it is virtually impossible for a radical perspective to establish itself as part of the "scientific" or "professional" academic canon. The work of Thomas Kuhn on the structure of scientific revolutions illustrates the obstacles nicely. As Kuhn points out, the acceptance (i.e., the social acceptance) of a paradigm marks a qualitative change in the development of any science. Until the paradigm is accepted and can be assumed, the individual scientist must in each work build his field anew, starting from first principles and justifying the use of each concept introduced. It is only when a textbook in his paradigm exists that he can abandon such elementary tasks, and begin his research where the textbook leaves off, and "thus concentrate exclusively upon the subtlest and most esoteric aspects of the phenomena that concern his group." Horowitz, "Social Science or Ideology," Berkeley Journal of Sociology, 15 (1970): 7; emphasis added. Horowitz disregards the possibility that Kuhn's paradigm at several other junctures serves even more strongly to support a conservative ideological defense of the scientific community and particularly of the sociological profession.

50. Robert W. Friedrichs, A Sociology of Sociology (New York: Free Press, 1972), 3.

51. The most explicit indications of a collectively felt need to defend the doctrine of value-neutrality are found in the previously cited articles in (i) the American Sociologist, and (ii) the criticisms of radical and activist scholarship reprinted in the anthology Radical Sociology, edited by Colfax and Roach. The extreme wrath expressed by Horton against

Sorokin and the muted scorn expressed by Merton against Mills's *Sociological Imagination* (which will be discussed below) are further instances of the defensive reactions exhibited by opinion leaders in the discipline when this doctrine is under assault. Kuhn's paradigm legitimizes this doctrine by conferring on it the appearance of scientific "progress" and even of "revolution."

52. The enthusiasm for "revolution" in society and in the social sciences should be further clarified. The crusade for racial integration was popular among Northern liberals during the 1950s and early 1960s, for example, until this issue was brought home in the form of demands for integrated neighborhoods and schools in the Northern states; "white backlash" and the decline of liberal support even for the abstract rhetoric of integration have most recently been manifested in the Boston school integration crisis in 1975 (more than twenty years after the Warren court issued its order for school desegregation "with all deliberate speed"). The abstract rhetoric of "revolution" must also be taken with a grain of salt. The term "revolution" enjoyed increasing currency in the book titles of even the most established publishers in the 1960s (e.g., the Free Press published Becker's *Revolution in Psychiatry* and the University of Chicago Press published Kuhn's *Structure of Scientific Revolution*); textbooks and articles on alleged "revolutions" in sociology, psychology, literature, cybernetics, demography, and other fields also appeared in rapid succession during this turbulent period. In the late 1960s and early 1970s, a growing number of courses with such titles as "Revolutionary Studies," "Revolution in Education," and "Sociology of Revolution" also appeared on many campuses in response to student interest and agitation. They were often part of a larger program of "experimental," "innovative," "interdisciplinary," or "Third World" studies. But the *substance* of revolutionary thought and action was only rarely and peripherally incorporated into the thrust of such publications and pedagogy. These courses, like the "experimental" programs in which they were usually offered, have in any case steadily declined in number and interest at campuses throughout the university and state college systems in California and New York (with which I am most familiar) as a result of political and budgetary retrenchment. The personal and political scenarios displayed by the late Abbie Hoffman, author of *Revolution for the Hell of It*, have culminated in his "letter of resignation" and in a drift toward privatization that call for a much more searching analysis of the original meaning of "The Revolution" than students and commentators on the New Left have advanced.

4. The Fashion Process and Historical Self-Awareness in Sociology: Continuities in Kuhn's Vision of the Scientific Community

1. Norman Birnbaum, "Foreword," in Robert W. Friedrichs, *A Sociology of Sociology* (New York: Free Press, 1972), ix–xviii. It will be shown below that Friedrichs regards his paradigm of dialectical pluralism as the only sound road to the advancement of sociology as a science, that he ignores the bearing of political and economic crises in American society upon the recent history of the discipline, and that his image of the sociological community is steeped in parochial self-celebration. Birnbaum, however, states in his enthusiastic foreword to Friedrichs's study that "Professor Friedrichs' conception of the development of thought is historical; he understands his work as an element in a situation which in itself inevitably will be transcended. . . . Professor Friedrichs has not shown a limited and provincial viewpoint. Rather, by bringing to bear on that scene an array of arguments rooted in other traditions, *he has contributed to the future attainment of a goal much to be desired: the reduction of our provincialism and the internationalization of scholarly debate in sociology*" (ix–x, xvii–xviii; emphasis added). The reasons for widespread praise of

Friedrichs's study and the imputation to it of features it does not in fact have are examined below in terms of the sociology of knowledge.

2. Friedrichs, A *Sociology of Sociology*, 290.

3. "Sociology: The Prophetic Mode," 55–75, especially "The Hebraic Analogue," 64–68; "Sociology: The Priestly Mode," 93–109, especially "Faith in Order," 106–9. " 'Normal' and 'Revolutionary' Sociology," 11–56; "Dialogical Possibilities," 314–23; "Prophecy or Priest-craft?", 292–93.

4. "Legacy of Talcott Parsons," 293–95; "Conflict or System?", 295–96; "Conflict Theory," 45–51.

5. After an impressionistic sketch of Marcuse's alleged influence on the thinking of graduate students, Friedrichs conjectures that "if the political activism that began to evidence itself with the American Sociological Association's 1967 meetings and the emergence of both 'black' and 'radical' caucuses at the 1968 convention, together with the appearance of a spate of 'underground' sociological periodicals, are more than momentary manifestations of the larger temper of the times, the conflict image has yet to reach its apogee" (50–51). Friedrichs makes no attempt to investigate or to suggest how others might investigate the "temper of the times."

6. He repeatedly touches upon these issues at a distance and as though they have been rendered obsolete by virtue of what he deems to be a conciliatory proposal. See "Division in the Ranks," 23–29. Friedrichs allows those who were most challenged at the time to characterize this period of confrontation in highly subdued terms and then proceeds to treat their characterization of it as self-evident: "Among the many who offered more modest routes to the articulation of function and change were Barber, Bredemier, Buckley, Cancian, Dore, Fallding, Hempel, Simpson and Smelser. . . . Wilbert Moore, however, may have captured the nature of the challenge most succinctly when he titled a series of essays *Order and Change. Clearly, both the ad hoc adjustments and the stubborn resistance that Kuhn sets forth as characteristic of the early stages of a scientific revolution were abundantly evident as sociology moved from the consensus of the fifties to the division of the sixties*" (29; emphasis added). The logic by which Friedrichs reaches the conclusion that sociology has attained a new and permanent stage of scientific revolution is examined below.

7. "The Calling of Sociology," 289–328, especially "The Dialectical Image," 296–97, and "Epistemological Pluralism," 297–300. Although he expresses opposition in principle to "a well-intentioned but wooly-headed confusion of tongues" (298), we will examine below the degree to which his paradigm is symptomatic of just this kind of poorly digested eclecticism and pluralism.

8. Although Friedrichs is often considered to be a completely original theorist, he does at one point emulate Kuhn's practice of realistic self-appraisal: "My indebtedness to Kuhn's insight into the life cycle of paradigms will become so apparent in the pages ahead that I need do little more here than express my profound admiration for him. From that point on the jigsaw puzzle fell into place. All that remained was the burden of rhetoric and style" (xxi). The reasons for the widespread imputation of an original, long overdue, sensational, and revolutionary character to Friedrichs' work are examined below.

9. Friedrichs claims that he is critical of Kuhn's purist view of value-neutral paradigms in the scientific community and that the social sciences do play host to paradigms on two levels because "such sciences are forced to encompass the scientist, his activity and his subject matter" (290). Had he applied this flash of insight to his own dialectical and pluralistic worldview, he might have been able to correct for some of the biases that led him astray.

10. Whether or not one agrees with Sorokin's earlier writings in this domain, for exam-

ple, one could not possibly regard them as altogethr relativistic. Mannheim's analysis of the situational determinants of thought, moreover, can hardly be dismissed as an idle exercise in relativism, much less solipsism. Pitirim A. Sorokin, *Sociocultural Causality, Space, Time* (New York: Russell & Russell, 1964), especially "Referential Principles of Integralist Sociology," 226–37; Karl Mannheim, *Ideology and Utopia*, trans. Louis Wirth (New York: Harcourt, 1936), especially "Utopia, Ideology and the Problem of Reality," 192–204. Mills studied *empirically* the relationship between ideology and modes of cognition; see C. Wright Mills, "The Methodological Consequences of the Sociology of Knowledge," in Horowitz (ed.), *Power, Politics and People*, 453–68. Cf. Leon Shaskolsky, "The Development of Sociological Theory in America – A Sociology of Knowledge Interpretation," in Reynolds and Reynolds, *The Sociology of Sociology*, 6–30.

11. The rank and file of the sociological profession made no secret of the identity crisis facing the bastions of "normal science" in the early 1970s. The symptoms of organized insecurity were everywhere. Nearly every issue of *American Sociologist* includes a major article (or sometimes several) on the topics of (1) the respectability of the profession in the eyes of the public or academic administrators, (2) the prospects for vertical mobility through publications, (3) problems of licensing or certification of one or another kind, and (4) the maintenance of government and corporate funding levels for "sociologists on the move" and closely related concerns. See, for example, Philip E. Hammond and Charles E. Higbie, "This Time a More Personal View of the Press Coverage of a Sociological Convention," *American Sociologist*, 3 (February 1968): 51–53; Albert D. Biderman, "On the Influence, Affluence and Congruence of Phenomena in the Social Sciences," *American Sociologist*, 4 (May 1969): 128–30; David Schichor, "Prestige of Sociology Departments and the Placing of New Ph.D.'s," *American Sociologist*, 5 (May 1970): 157–60; Jay Demerath, "From the Executive Office," *American Sociologist*, 6 (February 1971): 55–56; Clyde W. Franklin, "Sociologists on the Move," *American Sociologist*, 7 (November 1972): 15–16; Richard Doering, "Publish or Perish: Book Productivity and Academic Rank at Twenty-Six Elite Universities," ibid., 11–13; Walter F. Abbott, "Prestige Mobility of University Sociology Departments in the United States: 1964–1969," *American Sociologist*, 8 (February 1973): 38–41; Robert McGinness and Louise Solomon, "Employment Prospects for Ph.D. Sociologists During the Seventies," *American Sociologist*, 8 (May 1973): 57–63; Dennis Wrong, "On Thinking about the Future," *American Sociologist*, 9 (February 1974): 26–31. Wrong's condemnation of an activist conception of social science and his sympathy for Weber's and Hannah Arendt's views on the politics of scholarship are illustrative of the conservative bias in the aforementioned studies; he espouses a narrow conception of professionalism and concludes: "I choose therefore to be a truthteller rather than a political actor; to quote Arendt again, 'to look upon politics from the perspective of truth means to take one's stand out of the political realm. This standpoint is the standpoint of the truthteller who forfeits his position – and, with it, the validity of what he has to say – if he tries to interfere directly in human affairs and to speak the language of persuasion or violence' " (30). By the term "truthteller," Wrong is by implication referring to the kind of sociologist who is preoccupied with the public image of the profession and with his own mobility from a careerist standpoint. A more direct admission of the same fear of a radicalization of the discipline and a loss of professional stature is made by Gove: "If the public confuses moral position with sociological knowledge, it will tend to see sociology as an ideology, not a science. It may then come to pass that sociologists will not be sought for situations where they could help, and sociological knowledge will not be used even when it is valid, for sociologists and sociology will not be trusted." Walter R. Gove, "Should the Sociology Profession Take Moral Stands on Political Issues?", *American Sociologist*, 5 (August 1970): 222.

12. Friedrichs does not actually specify the nature of this "highest tradition" in the so-

ciology of knowledge. He frequently treats this field of study as though it were excess baggage to be discarded rather than taken seriously in the study of the scientific community. He is plainly unaware of the extent to which his ahistorical view of evolutionism might itself reflect a series of highly misleading ideological presuppositions about science and society. In this light, Friedrichs is hardly doing justice to any traditions, the highest or otherwise, in the sociology of knowledge.

13. One might ask whether Friedrichs is proposing a psychological, cultural, or structural model to explain and defend the present state of sociology. In attempting to answer this question, however, one could cite examples of psychological, cultural, and structural overdeterminism in various sections of Friedrichs's work. One could also cite examples of his judicious words of caution that are then quickly put aside. One could cite still other examples of a voluntaristic conception of alternative modes of inquiry in his dialectical and pluralistic paradigm. Friedrichs criticizes functionalism and relativism at one point, for example, only to espouse the basic assumptions in both doctrines in his substantive exposition. See A Sociology of Sociology, "The Retreat to Relativism," 242–53; "The Presumptive Faith of Science," 197–222; and "The Derivation of Value from Cognition," 94–98.

14. Ibid., "Division in the Ranks," 25; " 'Normal' and 'Revolutionary' Sociology," 27; "Introspection," 29. Although Friedrichs's haste in attributing the crisis to the natural or immanent development of the scientific community is interspersed with occasional observations about the impact of the antiwar movement and the Black Power movement, these observations are not logically related to his model of an insulated scientific community constituted by free-floating intellectuals with vaguely humanistic outlooks. Cf. "Recovery of the Prophetic Mode," 111–34, especially Professional Uneasiness," 114–17.

15. Friedrichs at times sees himself as mediator between the radical and conservative forces in the discipline, at other times as a passive witness to the unfolding of the human drama, and at yet other times as the savior of the discipline by virtue of his discovery of a new dialectical model that allows all contending factions an allegedly honorable basis for a truce. There are even times when Friedrichs insists that he has repudiated Kuhn's major assumptions about the scientific community: "Sociology did tend to move out of an eclectic adolescence and toward coalescence about an orthodoxy spelled out in terms of system and the derivative notion of function. . . . The late 'fifties and early 'sixties found the field wrestling with the issue of fundamental social 'change'—a stubborn anomaly when addressed by a conceptual model which saw in stability its final point of reference. . . . The 'sixties brought with them a major movement, particularly among younger sociologists, toward replacing system with conflict in the position of prime paradigmatic honor. At the edge of the battle stood a small band of mediators proferring a 'dialectical' flag as a means to an honorable peace without victory or defeat. . . . The prophetic and the priestly modes will continue in dialogue—as they do in the larger religious-philosophical life of our kind. If one would seek a term that would envelop both the active and the passive, the liberating and the ordering, nature of our calling as sociologists, perhaps witness may do. The sociologist would be witness to the profoundly social dialogue that is man" (324, 328; emphasis added). Vague and ambiguous mandates of this kind are so frequently found in Friedrichs's work as to render extremely difficult any effort to ascertain just what he might have in mind that would differ from the traditional defense of academic fence-straddling and the posture of noncommittal reasonableness. Cf. Max Weber, "Science as a Vocation," in Hans Gerth and C. Wright Mills (eds.), From Max Weber: Essays in Sociology (New York: Oxford University Press, 1958), 129–56. As discussed above, Friedrichs has succeeded in making this traditional doctrine seem plausible, modern, and progressive to those who otherwise might have misgivings about its viability.

5. Sorokin, Merton, and the Many Faces of the Fashion Process

1. *Fads and Foibles in Modern Sociology* has been out of print and unavailable from the publisher, Henry Regnery, for several years. Of the fourteen members in the Department of Sociology in which I teach, only two have ever read it. Graduate students in large as well as small departments in which the doctorate in sociology is offered and with which I am familiar are today generally unaware of the importance or even the existence of this book.

2. This is not to say that Sorokin ever deliberately compromised his intellectual or personal integrity or that he merely wished to echo the prevailing trends in American culture. Although it is true that he opposed the Russian Revolution and that he originally believed that American capitalism presented "freedom for the individual," it is also true that Sorokin's views changed slowly—especially after his formal academic career had ended. He was familiar with the Marxist orientation in the Sociology Liberation movement, for example, and he enthusiastically approved of its activities in the 1960s. I received a forthright statement from him to this effect that was read at the 1968 counterconvention in San Francisco. Most radicals in sociology now dismiss Sorokin's work categorically without ever having read it, thus having a grossly misinformed posture in common with the conservatives (albeit for different reasons). The caricatures to which he has been subjected would be an instructive area of study in their own right. Sorokin's Center for the Study of Altruism and Creative Integration, for example, was originally sponsored by the Eli Lilly Foundation—an organization noted for its very conservative sympathies. The publisher of *Fads and Foibles in Modern Sociology*, Henry Regnery, is also known for its sponsorship and publication of conservative works in various fields of endeavor. That Sorokin's charismatic efforts eventually attracted the attention of some pacifist groups involved in draft resistance and the antiwar movement and that his writings became increasingly sympathetic to the left (and he himself became a generous sponsor of a radical journal, *The Minority of One*) serve to illustrate the complexity of his views and his own political reeducation after his separation from Harvard University.

3. Herbert Blumer, "Fashion: From Class Differentiation to Collective Selection," *Sociological Quarterly*, 10 (Summer 1969): 289.

4. Ibid., 275–91, especially pp. 280–81 and 287.

5. Sorokin's influence, particularly through his role at Harvard as chairman and mentor to a larger number of graduate students destined to attain prominence in their own right, is often underestimated or ignored by commentators on the state of the profession. His *Contemporary Sociological Theories* and *Social and Cultural Dynamics* continue to be well-regarded by many opinion leaders in the discipline; these works (or at least parts of them) are still often designated as assigned reading in graduate courses at leading universities. But few sociologists are familiar with the more explosive side of his work (e.g., his views in *Fads and Foibles in Modern Sociology*) and his leftist ideologist drift (e.g., his sponsorship and writing for *The Minority of One*) after his separation from Harvard University.

6. Sorokin's sketchy and fleeting treatment of Mannheim's work is noted by Robert K. Merton, "Sorokin's Formulations in the Sociology of Science," in *The Sociology of Science: Theoretical and Empirical Investigations* (Chicago: University of Chicago Press, 1973), 155. Merton also neglects the instructive parallels in the writings of Sorokin and Mannheim.

7. Although Mannheim is often portrayed as a neo-Marxist in his studies in the sociology of knowledge, his position is far closer to Weber's than is generally believed. Mannheim is even more careful than Weber to avoid using the term "social class," whereas We-

ber already surgically removed the materialist emphasis on ownership or nonownership of the means of production from it. Mannheim consistently refers to the abstraction of "interests" or "total situation" as the alleged determinant of ideology, for example, without acknowledging the impact of class domination on these "interests." It is true that he sometimes loosely uses such terms as "attitude" and "worldview" as though they were equivalent to "ideology," thereby leaving his position open to a number of psychologically reductionist and relativistic interpretations. But he clearly does assume (1) that ideology determines or conditions the perceptions and actions of the individual, and (2) that it is virtually unamenable to reconstruction except through the global synthesis of values and cultural transcendence he himself proposed but never accomplished. To claim that "the situation" determines ideology and that ideology determines consciousness with only the remotest hope of critical response through a form of transcendence no one has yet achieved is to relegate the self to an acquiescent role in the making of history.

8. *Fads and Foibles in Modern Sociology*, 316.

9. Ibid., 158–59.

10. Ibid., "The Nemesis," 304–15.

11. Ibid., "The Grand Cult of Social Physics and Mental Mechanics," 174–212.

12. Ibid., "Predictability and Scientific Theory," 250–72.

13. Ibid., "Amnesia and the Discoverer's Complex," 3–16.

14. Sorokin vaguely admits to his own culpability: "As to the irritation and distress which this . . . cleansing operation . . . is bound to provoke, especially among the devotees of the exposed half-truths and sham-verities, the author must humbly confess that he himself is also one of these 'sinners' " (v). But Sorokin never examines the magnitude of his "sins," the possible reasons behind their commission, or the extent to which they may have *helped* to ensure a favorable reception for some of his writings.

15. Robert K. Merton, *The Sociology of Science: Theoretical and Empirical Investigations* (Chicago: University of Chicago Press, 1973). This substantial volume (over 600 pages in length) includes all of Merton's major studies and several minor ones dealing with the nature of contemporary science and the sociology of knowledge. An adulatory orientation to the volume is provided by Norman W. Storer's introduction (xi–xxxi); all of Merton's articles therein are selected and edited for republication by Storer and with Merton's complete approval. One may conclude that this volume represents Merton's most considered judgment regarding those of his contributions that are most pertinent to the sociological study of contemporary science.

16. Robert K. Merton, *Social Theory and Social Structure*, rev. ed. (Glencoe: Free Press, 1957), "Continuities in the Theory of Reference Groups and Social Structure," 281–386.

17. Merton, *The Sociology of Science*, "Znaniecki's *The Social Role of the Man of Knowledge*," 41–46, especially 44; "Singletons and Multiples in Science," 343–70; "Social Conflicts over Styles of Sociological Work," 47–49.

18. Merton, *Sociology of Science*, "Changing Foci of Interests in the Sciences and Technology," 191–203; " 'Recognition' and 'Excellence': Instructive Ambiguities," 419–38; "The Ambivalence of Scientists," 383–418; "Institutionalized Patterns of Evaluation in Science," 460–96; "The Neglect of the Sociology of Science," 210–20. One might note that Merton originally published his essay on the neglect of the sociology of science as an adulatory foreword to Bernard Barber's *Science and the Social Order* in 1952, that he correctly anticipated therein a forthcoming revival of interest in this domain, and that he nevertheless ignored the concrete structural and ideological factors which are responsible for suppressing or nurturing its development. See ibid., 211–13.

19. It should be recalled that Sorokin singled out for special denunciation in *Fads and Foibles* the highly influential essay by Davis and Moore on the functional analysis of social

stratification, not because Davis and Moore advanced unsound principles in Sorokin's judgment, but rather because (1) Davis (and many other leading functionalists) first learned about this mode of analysis in Sorokin's graduate seminars and (2) these and other authors failed to cite Sorokin's own previous studies that had already documented these principles in great detail and that were assigned readings during their days at Harvard under Sorokin's direction. Sorokin held with considerable justification that these authors failed to give credit where it was in fact due. See Sorokin, 16 and 323–25 (notes 47 and 48).

20. "Institutionalized Patterns of Evaluation in Science," in *The Sociology of Science*, 460–96. This essay was originally published in 1971, although Merton does not attempt to investigate therein the ways in which the selection process might affect what Kuhn meant by the resolution of conflicting paradigms and the response of the scientific community to the uncovering of anomalies.

21. Ibid., 460.

22. Many professional societies, particularly including the American Sociological Association, for example, display a high degree of institutionalized racism and sexism; some of them, such as the American Medical Association, are not only inaccessible to women and ethnic minorities but also hostile even to such moderate reforms as the graduated income tax and social security benefits for the aged. For an analysis of the AMA's opposition to federally funded health services for the poor, see James Howard Means, "Homo Medicus Americanus," in Kenneth S. Lynn (ed.), *The Professions in America* (Boston: Houghton Mifflin, 1965), 47–69.

23. David Horowitz, "Social Science or Ideology," *Berkeley Journal of Sociology*, 15 (1970): 1–11; Marcel Rioux, "Critical versus Aseptic Sociology," ibid., 33–47. Rioux's article originally appeared in *Sociologie et Sociétés*, 1 (May 1969): 53–67, and was translated by Jean-Guy Vaillancourt and Robert Dubois. See especially Rioux's cogent discussion "American Sociologists and Their Society," 42–45.

24. Diana Crane, "The Gatekeepers of Science," 195–201; Gouldner, "Anti-Minotaur: The Myth of a Value-Free Sociology," 199–213; David Horowitz, "Social Science or Ideology," 1–11. For a criticism of the view that the decision-making processes and the decision makers themselves are or could be value-neutral regarding the maintenance of vested interests in the profession or the larger society, see Irwin Sperber, "The Road to Objective Serfdom," *Berkeley Journal of Sociology*, 14 (1969): 111–21. The rise of the sociological profession largely in the service of legitimizing the structure of privilege in American society is extensively documented by the Schwendingers in *The Sociologists of the Chair*. Albion Small's goal of a progressive social science was undermined as much by the vested interests of decision makers in the profession itself as by the conservative forces in the larger society. Cf. Becker, *The Lost Science of Man*.

25. Robert K. Merton, "Paradigm for the Sociology of Knowledge," in *The Sociology of Science*, 7–40, especially "The Existential Basis," 13–18. It should be noted that Merton even follows some of Marx's and Mannheim's arguments in favor of studying the existential bases for intellectual life; in this connection, he goes so far as to criticize Sorokin's worldview on the ground that integralism is "not [suitable] for analysing connections between varied existential conditions and thought within a society" (18).

26. Ibid., 494.

27. Ibid., "Relativism and the Criteria of Scientific Truth," 163–66.

28. In one brief passage, Merton appears almost sympathetic to the kind of radical sociology that insists on getting at the root of things, raising social consciousness even if the wrath of the state is incurred, and assaulting the bastions of conservative scholarship: "Science which asks questions of fact, including potentialities, concerning every aspect of nature and society may come into conflict with other attitudes toward these same data

which have been crystallized and often ritualized by other institutions" ("The Normative Structure of Science," 277).

29. Ibid., "Social Conflict over Styles of Sociological Work," 47–69.

30. Ibid., 55.

31. Robert K. Merton and Bernard Barber, "Sorokin's Formulations in the Sociology of Science," in Philip J. Allen (ed.), *Pitirim A. Sorokin in Review* (Durham, N.C.: Duke University Press, 1963), 332–68; reprinted in Merton, *The Sociology of Science*, 142–72. One could note that the first article Merton ever published was written in collaboration with Sorokin: "The Course of Arabian Intellectual Development, 700–1300 A.D.," *Isis*, 22 (February 1935): 516–24. Although such descriptive historical research is of interest in its own right it does not immediately bear upon the issues raised by the present view of his conception of the scientific community in modern society.

32. Merton, *The Sociology of Science*, 143. One should note that Merton has in mind primarily the prewar era during which there were sharp upswings and downswings in the American economy and the chronic and severe depression lingering until the onset of World War II. American universities in that era were far more rigid as bastions of conservative ideology and traditional pedagogy than they are today, and the surplus of available candidates for the very limited number of teaching positions allowed them to be highly selective in the recruitment and retention of personnel with the desired background. European universities at the same time only to a limited degree approximated the mentor-disciple relationship, with its absolute requirements of personal and ideological loyalty, which Merton has postulated. See Martin Carnoy, *Education as Cultural Imperialism* (New York: David McKay, 1974), especially "Education as Internal Colonialism: Educational Reform and Social Control in the United States, 1830–1970," 233–69. Veblen was himself a victim of this state of affairs at the University of Chicago and Stanford University, and he drew upon his unhappy experiences in his study of American universities. See Thorstein Veblen, *The Higher Learning* (New York: Hill & Wang, 1957), 62–97, 124–39.

33. Pradeep Bandyopadhyay, "The Many Faces of French Marxism," *Science and Society*, 36 (Summer 1972): 129–57. This survey of French Marxism tends to be sympathetic to the writings of Althusser and to ignore the problem of specifying criteria by which to ascertain whether one or another of the academic varieties of Marxist social science in France might be (a) objectively valid and (b) relevant to the goals of socialist revolution. Neither the twin possibilities of dilettantism and opportunism nor the even greater likelihood of the fashion process operating in radical research institutes and intellectual collectives are recognized in this extensive survey. Symptomatic of many idle appeals for future research and scholarly debate is Bandyopadhyay's conclusion that "the aim in this survey has been to draw attention to recent Marxist researches in France, stressing the academic and scientific concerns and the still powerful role of the Communist Party. It is to be hoped that this enormous effort will not remain unknown to Anglo-Saxon researchers, and that a serious debate with the brilliant new Marxists of France can begin" (157). But in the absence of any explicit and rational criteria by which to select the French, American, and British models to be compared and without the specification of any political purpose behind the ensuing debates, the call for "serious debate" is not convincing. In view of the conservative role of the Communist Party and many of its foremost intellectuals in the 1968 uprising in France, the possible grounds for debating the allegedly "brilliant Marxists" in French universities might well be far more politically focused and historically urgent than this survey implies. Exactly why brilliant *new* Marxists should be considered intrinsically more worthy of attention than classical Marxists, moreover, is not explained. The possibility that collective tastes rather than revolutionary objectives may have lead to the identification of certain scholars rather than others as allegedly "brilliant" is also ignored in that study.

34. Paul Breines, "Recent Studies in Critical Social Theory," *Continuum*, 8 (Spring–Summer 1970): 96–101; Gunnar Anderson, "Anglo-Saxon and Continental Schools of Metascience," ibid., 102–10.

35. I am indebted to Professor Alfredo Fasola-Bologna for details about the varieties of radical and Marxist scholarship in Italian universities; for discussions of theoretical and political ferment in American sociology and the ideological pressures toward monolithic control of its academic development in the 1970s, see Alfredo Fasola-Bologna, "The Inevitable Radicalization of Liberal Sociologists," *Human Factor*, 8 (Spring 1969): 19–30; Alfredo Fasola-Bologna, "The Sociological Profession and Revolution," *Sociological Inquiry*, 40 (Winter 1970): 35–43.

36. A candidate for a faculty position in the Department of Sociology at Columbia University once expressed his dismay to me because a senior member of that department had straightforwardly asked him if he was committed "to the profession" or "to the revolution"; according to this candidate, that same senior faculty member also suggested that the answer to such a question would be taken into account when the decision about whether to appoint him would be made. Mills's banishment from Columbia's Department of Sociology and his inaccessibility to doctoral candidates in that department – a process of ostracism that intensified as Mills identified with revolutionary movements in the Third World and openly attacked the "bureaucratic ethos" in the discipline – is another indication that the very opposite of Merton's notion of academic pluralism in American universities might well be closer to the truth. Mills's own doctoral dissertation, now published as *Sociology and Pragmatism* and edited by Irving Louis Horowitz, was in grave danger of never being certified by the University of Wisconsin because none of his professors were sympathetic to or even familiar with the work of Peirce and Dewey. Such a state of affairs hardly testifies to the alleged pluralism of American universities. See in this connection Horowitz's cogent introduction to Mills's most important study in the sociology of knowledge; Irving Louis Horowitz, "The Intellectual Genesis of C. Wright Mills," in C. Wright Mills, *Sociology and Pragmatism: The Higher Learning in America* (New York: Oxford University Press, 1966), 11–31, especially 30.

37. Albion Small's abortive effort to establish a center for progressive sociological research at Chicago and the negative reception given to critical theory in the United States are two among many cases in point that could be cited. See Ernest Becker, *The Lost Science of Man*, especially "The Dénouement, 1883–1929," 27–33, and "The Break-up of the American Social Science Association," 33–35; Martin Jay, "The Institut für Sozialforschung and the Origins of Critical Sociology," *The Human Factor*, 6–18, especially 18. A detailed and historically oriented study of the difference between the appearance of pluralism and academic freedom on the one hand and the reality of ideological constraint on the other hand in the development of American sociology is provided by Herman Schwendinger and Julia Schwendinger, *The Sociologists of the Chair: A Radical Analysis of the Formative Years of American Sociology*, "Political Repression and the Academic Social Sciences," 539–48.

38. Merton, The Sociology of Science, 144.

39. Ibid., 145–46.

40. See Merton, *Social Theory and Social Structure*, "A Typology of Modes of Individual Adaptation," 140–57. His discussion of "rebellion," the rejection of prescribed means and ends, and the effort to replace them with new ones in his model, is particularly vague and mechanistic. Cf. 155–57.

41. "Empirical Research: Quantitative Indicators in the Sociology of Science," 156–63. For a still more striking example of Sorokin's meandering in the direction of raw empiricism and a more disconcerting sign of his occasional capitulation to the sensate culture

than that cited by Merton, see Pitirim A. Sorokin and Clarence Q. Berger, *Time-Budgets of Human Behavior* (Cambridge, Mass.: Harvard University Press, 1939).

42. Merton, "Relativism and the Criteria of Scientific Truth," 163–66.

43. "The Selective Cumulation of Scientific Knowledge," 167.

44. Ibid., 169.

45. "In 1961, approximately 75 percent of faculty in Canadian universities were Canadian. In 1968, this proportion had dropped to 49 percent and has almost certainly dropped further since then. [In 1969,] Canadian universities made about 2,642 new appointments. Of these appointments, 1013 were Americans, 545 British, 722 others. The truly devastating statistic is the one which indicates that only 362 were Canadians—*the smallest single group*. [In 1968,] Canadian universities engaged only 9.5 percent of the total Canadians available to fill academic positions." Hugh MacLennon, "On De-Canadianization," in Robin Mathews and James Steele (eds.), *The Struggle for Canadian Universities* (New Press, 1970), 141–51; cf. James MacKinnon and David Brown, "Political Science in the Canadian University, 1969," in ibid., 151–62. Louis Parai, *Immigration and Emigration of Professional and Skilled Manpower During the Post-War Period*, Special Study No. 1 (Ottawa: Economic Council of Canada, 1965), 224. Although the specific period to which C. P. Snow refers does to some degree fit Merton's generalization about modern physics, Merton intends fully to use these reminiscences as a justification for unqualified praise of modern science in general and is accordingly open to criticism on empirical grounds. Although commitment to the "personal development" of university students remains vigorous in the United Kingdom, actual plans for the funding of universities are conceived largely in terms of prospects for the future employment of graduates: "The fastest expansion should continue to be in the polytechnics and the non-university colleges." Margaret Thatcher, Secretary of State for Education and Science, "White Paper on Educational Expansion in England and Wales," *Keesing's Contemporary Archives*, 19 (1973): 25692–6. The combined effects of inflation and recession *before* 1973 had already begun to make themselves felt in British universities; they help to explain why this extensive White Paper indicates virtually no commitment to the maintenance of programs in "pure science" or long-term research in those universities. They have been greatly intensified by inflationary spirals, soaring unemployment, business failures, and nationwide strikes associated with economic setbacks in that country; they continue to produce ominous developments for British universities in the near future.

46. Norman W. Storer, Introduction, xxx; xvii–xviii.

47. "Age, Aging and Age Structure in Science," ibid., 554.

48. Ibid. Merton here is citing Kuhn's remarks delivered in response to various critics and supporters in the anthology assembled by Imre Lakatos and Alan Musgrave (eds.), *Criticism and the Growth of Knowledge* (Cambridge: Cambridge University Press, 1970). In view of the discussion of Kuhn's paradigm about scientific revolutions presented earlier in this study, however, it should be emphasized that there is little correspondence between Kuhn's abstract statements about the sociology of science to which Merton misleadingly refers and his actual analysis of scientific revolutions in his famous monograph.

49. Although a detailed analysis of the flood of research on citation behavior is beyond the scope of the present study, Merton's alarm over the mediocre scholarship usually represented by such research is well taken and instructive: "Ever since the invention of the Science Citation Index, citation studies have been increasing at such a rapid rate that they threaten to get out of hand. Many methodological problems are being neglected in their frequently uncritical use" (556). Despite his alarm and words of caution about their indiscriminate use, Merton proceeds to invoke them in support of his sweeping assumptions about citation behavior. See 549–50, 558. He ignores the considerable extent to which

he, his students, his colleagues and followers have been in the vanguard of teaching and research on behalf of citation studies. Although such studies might be helpful in testing hypotheses about the priorities and shifting tastes in the scientific community, they have tended to proliferate rapidly in the direction of raw empiricism; and they are all but useless in the absence of a rigorously defined and historically informed perspective through which their results could be interpreted. Merton does not come to grips with the need for developing such a perspective or examining the degree to which citation studies themselves are caught up in the fashion process.

50. Robert K. Merton, "Social Conflict over Styles of Sociological Work," *Transactions* (Louvain: International Sociological Association, 1961), 3, 21–46; reprinted in Merton, *The Sociology of Science*, 47–69 (further citations from the latter text are indicated in the text by page number).

51. Although Merton's *Sociology of Science* is over 600 pages in length and ostensibly devoted to the sociology of science and the sociology of knowledge, he never refers to Mills's *Sociological Imagination* by its title or in any serious sense at all. He does mention briefly some of Mills's earlier and much less germane studies on language, ideologies of social pathology, and character and social structure, but he neither cites nor comes to grips with Mills's more far-reaching and influential contributions to these scholarly domains in *Sociological Imagination* and *Sociology and Pragmatism*. This and similar modes of responding to serious criticism of the discipline take on special relevance below in the analysis of Merton's image of intellectual debate and heterodoxy during the present period of alleged maturation in the growth of modern sociology.

52. A feature of Merton's expositions on contemporary issues in sociological theory is his insistence on his own statesmanship in transcending the bitter controversies of the day and his skill in caricaturing those with whom he disagrees as so misguided (partisan, petty, fanatic, vulgar, and so forth) as to be unworthy of attention in any case. Hence, he presumes to settle the probable outcome of a controversy without airing the explosive issues at hand. Cf. his wry contempt for Feuer (187–89), and his impatience with Marxists who, he declares, are responsible for "merely a pseudo-theory" (31).

53. Merton gives an even sketchier and more dubious account of "The Lone Scholar and the Research Team," ibid., 64. He ignores the extent to which Sorokin's work has been attacked by Horton and others as unworthy of serious attention on the grounds that it was not produced in the congenial and collaborative spirit of mainstream sociology.

54. C. Wright Mills, "The Contribution of Sociology to Studies of Industrial Relations," 18–23.

55. The two most influential works in this tradition are George Homans's *The Human Group* and Talcott Parsons's *The Social System*, especially Chapters 7 and 11 (on deviance and social change).

56. The social and ideological forces behind these ostensibly benign research interests are most clearly identified by Herbert Marcuse, "The New Forms of Control," in Maurice Zeitlin (ed.), *American Society, Inc.* (Chicago: Rand McNally, 1973), 373–87.

57. Susanne J. Bodenheimer, "The Ideology of Developmentalism: American Political Science's Paradigm-Surrogate for Latin American Studies," *Berkeley Journal of Sociology*, 15 (1970): 95–137.

58. Merton does not specify the criteria by which the presumably ensuing synthesis of "combinations of position" or the flowering heterodoxies "on the worldwide scale of sociology" might be differentiated from a potpourri of half-digested ideologies. But even if the many heterodoxies that are now allegedly developing in "world sociology" were eventually to converge or to complement one another, their substantive validity or truth-content would still be problematic. The fact that many ideologies or theoretical assump-

tions happen to converge has no bearing on their empirical and logical verifiability. The fact that a given doctrine or a set of doctrines is in fashion at a given time, whether on a local, national, or "worldwide" scale, must not be equated with a demonstration of their validity. Merton's eagerness to accept this very equation indicates the operation of the fashion process in his judgment of what is true or false in sociological inquiry.

59. Dusky Lee Smith, "Robert King Merton: From Middle Range to Middle Road," *Catalyst*, 2 (Summer 1966): 11–40. See especially "Social Change and Social Problems," 24–32. Smith observes that "despite his hypersensitive pronouncements concerning the . . . non-ideological nature of Middle Range functionalism, [Merton's] adroit and dexterous employment of it only contributes further substantiation to the argument that functionalism primarily adheres to the world of the *given*, that its criticism is non-transcendent, that 'functions in both theory and especially practice become mere adaptations to the basic structure of the 'Is' '" (11). Merton's apparent willingness to tolerate an indefinite range of controversial or even radical positions in the discipline and his occasional nod to such mavericks in the sociology of knowledge as Mannheim and Sorokin may help to explain why his writings are accepted, often uncritically, even by those associated with radical perspectives in the sociology of knowledge. The anthology on the sociology of knowledge and its application to the sociological profession edited by Reynolds and Reynolds, *The Sociology of Sociology*, is illustrative of this tendency. This particular anthology, representing largely radical and neo-Marxist analyses of contemporary sociology, also includes Merton's essay "Social Conflict over Styles of Sociological Work." That Merton's toleration of unorthodox perspectives might be more apparent than real is a possibility generally ignored by those who are grateful even for the facade of approval that his declarations about "heterodoxy" bestow upon radicalism and cleavage in the discipline.

6. The Functional Theory of Inequality: The Problem of Rewarding Merit or Mediocrity

1. Jeffrey Alexander, "General Theory in the Postpositivist Mode: The 'Epistemological Dilemma' and the Search for Present Reason," in *General Theory and Its Critics: Contemporary Debates* (Albany: Department of Sociology at SUNY Albany, April 15–16, 1988), pp. 1–71.

2. Cf. 1–17 and passim.

3. Ibid., 62.

4. The guidelines themselves can be seen as a set of boundaries for acceptable academic conduct, as a statement of collective tastes, with implied sanctions for doing research in bad taste and mandates for keeping in step with the latest developments. The tendency toward futurism and utopianism is especially discernible in the presumed leap into the next generation of *post*modernism, *post*structuralism, *post*positivism and *neo*-functionalism as though all vestiges of supposedly obsolescent paradigms can be left behind through instant acts of will power. The epistemological and historical linkages among the decline of the capitalist state at the hands of omnipotent multinational corporations, the proliferation of ahistorical visions of a postindustrial, postmodern, and postrational world, and pervasive cynicism in the language and logic of social theory deserve separate investigation. An excellent first step toward an analysis of these linkages is taken by Elizabeth Bowman, "Sartre and Foucault: Postmodern Consciousness and the Carceral State," unpublished paper presented at a lecture series on "Modernism and Postmodernism," Memphis State University Center for the Humanities, November 13, 1987, 1–19.

7. Conclusion: The Fashion Process, Science, and Society

1. Although neither Friedrichs nor Merton is successful in resolving these issues, both deserve credit for acknowledging their gravity. Merton is the first opinion leader in the mainstream of American sociology to go so far as to enumerate the forms of confrontation that were already emerging in the 1950s and to identify the political impetus behind many of them. See Merton, *The Sociology of Science*, "Social Conflict over Styles of Sociological Work," 47–69. His clear and candid admission that the polarization was taking place, it should be reemphasized, is not in question; his effort to explain away the nature of this underlying political conflict as "pervasive polemics" (ibid., 59) is, as previously noted, on extremely shaky ground and is particularly questionable even in terms of his own paradigm for the sociology of knowledge.

2. Robert K. Merton, *On the Shoulders of Giants: A Shandean Postscript* (New York: Free Press, 1965). Unfortunately, Merton uses this work as an occasion merely to satirize the kind of academic dogmatism and cynicism found in the mainstream of American sociology. Typical of the aphoristic comments he tenders is this disclosure so reminiscent of Parsons's view of "striking convergences" in the history of social theory: "What we have before us, then, is virtually a self-exemplifying theory: in the very letter in which Newton is about to set down his immortal version of the Shoulders-of-Giants Aphorism, he first exemplifies the Aphorism itself by building on Hooke's rationale for a private correspondence to arrive at what must hereafter be known as the Hooke-Newton-Merton principle of interaction among scientists" (29, ad infinitum, ad nauseam).

3. Even in seemingly exhaustive empirical studies of the production and consumption of knowledge, the effects of this doctrine are usually ignored. Symptomatic of such studies is Fritz Machlup, *The Production and Distribution of Knowledge in the United States* (Princeton: Princeton University Press, 1962). Machlup declares, for instance: "My concepts of knowledge and knowledge-production are unusually wide, particularly because I recognize and work with both meanings of knowledge: *as that which is known*, and as *the state of knowing*. Hence to 'produce knowledge' is not only to add to the stock of what is known but also to create a state of knowing in anybody's mind" (vi). But how can one be sure that the material represented as "knowledge" is in fact valid in any significant sense? Is orthodoxy to be equated with validity? How can one differentiate the body of allegedly reliable knowledge from those models that are in fashion at a given time in the development of a scientific discipline? Questions of this kind are consistently ignored in Machlup's innocent acceptance of officially certified and culture-bound products of the knowledge industries.

4. The doctrine of "knowledge for its own sake" opens the door to cultural experimentation and intellectual novelties. We have seen earlier in the present study that the tendency to reject traditional ideas in favor of new ones regardless of the latter's shortcomings can lead to the proliferation of increasingly dubious paradigms and the erosion of intellectual integrity in the scientific community. The popularity and sanctity of this doctrine, especially in the social sciences, deserve careful analysis. If we were examining it from the standpoint of nineteenth-century rationalism, the questions posed above could be more pointedly formulated: *How can a doctrine promoting intellectual self-indulgence and the play of fashion be upheld in the very community most dedicated to the primacy of reason in the selection, construction and evaluation of new paradigms?*

5. Cf. Erving Goffman, *The Presentation of Self in Everyday Life* (Garden City, N.Y.: Doubleday, 1960). Goffman's thesis is that social participants and even whole communities may respond to the *impressions* and *appearances* of reality and not to the objective reality itself, that such responses are all the more likely when there are embarrassing or painful

problems in the "backstage" area no one wishes to acknowledge. We might add that the most painful fact of life to which scientists are driven to respond is the alienation of intellectual labor in their own community. Goffman applied his dramaturgical model to the study of mental patients, gamblers, the handicapped, psychiatrists, transients, and urban dwellers in general; a direction for future research would be a more systematic application of his model to the study of collective behavior among scientists than has been suggested here.

6. George Becker, "Pietism and Science: A Critique of Robert K. Merton's Hypothesis," *American Journal of Sociology*, 89 (March 1984): 1065–90.

7. Robert K. Merton, "The Fallacy of the Latest Word: The Case of 'Pietism and Science,' " ibid., 1091–1121.

8. George Becker, "The Fallacy of the Received Word: A Reexamination of Merton's Pietism-Science Thesis," *American Journal of Sociology*, 91 (March 1986): 1203–18.

9. If the present study were to focus on the distinctions between false and heightened political consciousness among scientists per se, these observations could be posed as follows. Whatever the material and symbolic rewards conferred upon scientists, however much they subjectively perceive themselves as superior to those engaging in manual labor, the fact remains that they can be hired and fired; that they do not own or control the uses or enjoy the benefits of the paradigms they produce for their employer; that they are just as dependent on wages obtained by selling their labor time and energy to their employer as are the clerks and hard hats who seem at first glance to be in an inferior social class, in a totally different world of toil and servitude.

10. The capitalist system creates a long, complex, even endless series of discontents experienced by the working class as a whole; it conveys the message that the real wealth and progress of society are attributable to individual capitalists whose great vision, energy, and courage were the driving force behind the growth of modern civilization. The working class, by contrast, is conditioned by the belief that it contributes little or nothing of value to social progress; that it has neither the right nor the ability to shape its own destiny or to participate in the decision-making process in the larger society. The advertising industry obscures the ways in which the working class can shape its own destiny and participate in the decision-making process in the larger society. Madison Avenue also does much to play upon the resulting perceptions of self-doubt felt throughout the working class.

11. The capitalist class does not rely on the usually unrecognized fashion process alone to generate new paradigms. It has other and more controllable techniques at its disposal to accomplish this end. It has been generally successful in passing off the costs and risks of doing business, in transferring the burdens of research and development programs, to the public sector of the economy. The immense costs, risks, and burdens of research and development are passed on to such agencies of state power as the National Science Foundation, NASA, and fuel and energy "commissions" and "task forces." The costs are then borne primarily by the working class, which pays for these programs through income taxes, fuel bills, and tax surcharges. The upper echelons of these agencies are staffed by executive appointees temporarily "on loan" from those corporations having vested interests in the research to be carried out.

12. I conducted this "survey," admittedly at most an illustrative and anecdotal one, during the years 1960–63, while a graduate student at the City University of New York and then at the University of California at Berkeley.

13. Stephen F. Mason, *A History of the Sciences* (New York: Collier, 1962), 606.

14. Reference is made here to the objective level of access to the decision-making process, and not to the subjective belief that "we control our own destinies." In the early 1970s, for example, a coalition of mavericks, antiestablishment liberals, and remnants of what

had been the "Union of Radical Sociologists" finally succeeded in having their candidate for the presidency of the American Sociological Association elected to office. Because of the continuing grip on key administrative positions and committee assignments (not to mention control over the referral of mail, disbursement of funds, and forwarding of messages) by the Old Guard, the real forces in charge of this organization and its influential journals remained the same even though there was a nominal change in executive leadership for a year. Few sociologists today recall the sense of alarm within the ranks of the ASA's opinion leaders when Alfred McClung Lee waged a successful grass-roots campaign for the organization's highest office. The panic turned out to be unnecessary and short-lived, for there were a good many administrative personnel and procedures already in place to undermine Lee's ability to wield any substantial influence at all. Thus, the conservative ideology and politics of structural-functionalism remained viable despite the temporary state of siege by a strange and fragile potpourri of disaffected liberals, radicals, restless graduate students, and "outside agitators."

15. Leon Kamin, *The Science and Politics of I.Q.* (New York: Halstead Press, 1974).

16. Quoted in Collins, *History of the Sciences*, 176; emphasis added.

17. Cf. Mason, *A History of the Sciences*, 424.

18. Irwin Sperber, "AIDS Research and Social Policy: Historical and Iatrogenic Aspects of the AIDS-Syphilis Connection," *Whetstone* I (Spring, 1989), 9–11, 58–81, especially "Applying Kuhn's Model of the Scientific Community to AIDS Research," 68–70, and "Structural Forces Shaping the Viral Hypothesis," 81–83, and note 18.

BIBLIOGRAPHY

BIBLIOGRAPHY

Abbott, Walter F. "Prestige Mobility of University Sociology Departments in the United States: 1964–1969." *American Sociologist*, 8 (February 1973): 38–41.

Allen, Philip J., editor. *Pitirim A. Sorokin in Review*. Durham, N.C.: Duke University Press, 1963.

Anderson, Charles H., and Murray, John D., editors. *The Professors: Work and Life Styles among Academicians*. Cambridge, Mass.: Schenkman, 19971.

Anderson, Gunnar. "Anglo-Saxon and Continental Schools of Meta-Science." *Continuum*, 8 (Spring–Summer 1970): 102–10.

Bandyopadhyay, Pradeep. "The Many Faces of French Marxism." *Science and Society*, 36 (Summer 1972): 129–57.

Becker, Ernest. *The Lost Science of Man*. New York: Braziller, 1970.

——. *The Structure of Evil: An Essay on the Unification of the Science of Man*. New York: Braziller, 1968.

——. *The Revolution in Psychiatry: The New Understanding of Man*. New York: Free Press, 1964.

Bell, Norman, and Spiegal, John. "Social Psychiatry: Vagaries of a Term." *Archives of General Psychiatry*, 14 (1966): 337–45.

Ben-David, Joseph. *The Scientist's Role in Society*. Englewood Cliffs, N.J.: Prentice-Hall, 1971.

Bendix, Reinhard. *Max Weber: An Intellectual Portrait*. Garden City, N.Y.: Doubleday, 1962.

Bendix, Reinhard, and Lipset, Seymour Martin, editors. *Class, Status and Power: Social Stratification in Comparative Perspective*. New York: Free Press, 1966.

Biderman, Albert D. "On the Influence, Affluence and Congruence of Phenomena in the Social Sciences." *American Sociologist*, 4 (May 1969): 128–30.

Birenbaum, Arnold, and Sagarin, Edward, editors. *Social Problems: Private Troubles and Public Issues*. New York: Scribner's, 1972.

Birnbaum, Norman. Foreword. In Robert W. Friedrichs, *A Sociology of Sociology*. New York: Free Press, 1972, ix–xviii.

Blackburn, John A. "Clothing Trade." *Chambers' Encyclopedia*, 3 (1967): 655–59.

Blauner, Robert. "Internal Colonialism and Ghetto Revolt." *Social Problems*, 16 (Spring 1969): 393–408.

Block, Fred. "Expanding Capitalism: The British and American Cases." *Berkeley Journal of Sociology*, 15 (1970): 138–65.

Blumer, Herbert. "Social Movements." In Alfred McClung Lee, editor, *Principles of Sociology*. New York: Barnes & Noble, 1967, 119–220.

———. "Fashion." *International Encyclopedia of the Social Sciences*, 5 (1968): 341–45.

———. *Symbolic Interactionism: Perspective and Method*. Englewood Cliffs: Prentice-Hall, 1969.

———. "Fashion: From Class Differentiation to Collective Selection." *Sociological Quarterly*, 10 (Summer 1969): 275–91.

Bock, Kenneth. "Evolution, Function and Change." *American Sociological Review*, 28 (April 1963): 229–37.

Bodenheimer, Susanne J. "The Ideology of Developmentalism: American Political Science's Paradigm-Surrogate for Latin American Studies." *Berkeley Journal of Sociology*, 15 (1970): 95–137.

Bonnen, James T. "The Effect of Taxes and Government Spending on Inequality." In Michael Reich and Thomas E. Weisskopf, editors, *The Capitalist System: A Radical Analysis of American Society*. Englewood Cliffs: Prentice-Hall, 1972, 238–43.

Boskoff, Alvin. *The Mosaic of Sociological Theory*. New York: Crowell, 1972.

Breines, Paul. "Recent Studies in Critical Social Theory." *Continuum*, 8 (Spring–Summer 1970): 96–101.

Carnoy, Martin. *Education as Cultural Imperialism*. New York: David McKay, 1974.

Chambers, Bernice Gertrude. "Fashion and Clothing." *Collier's Encyclopedia*, 9 (1966): 577–86.

Cirino, Robert. *Don't Blame the People*. New York: Random House, 1971.

Colfax, J. David. "Varieties and Prospects of 'Radical Scholarship' in Sociology." In J. David Colfax and Jack L. Roach, editors, *Radical Sociology*. New York: Basic Books, 1971, 81–92.

Cooley, Charles Horton. *Social Organization*. New York: Scribner's, 1909.

Crane, Diana. "The Gatekeepers of Science: Some Factors Affecting the Selection of Articles for Scientific Journals." *American Sociologist*, 2 (November 1967): 195–201.

Davidson, Douglas. "The Furious Passage of the Black Graduate Student." *Berkeley Journal of Sociology*, 15 (1970): 192–211.

Demerath, Jay. "From the Executive Office." *American Sociologist*, 6 (February 1971): 55–56.

Deutsch, Steven E., and Howard, John, editors. *Where It's At: Radical Perspectives in Sociology*. New York: Harper, 1970.

Doering, Richard. "Publish or Perish: Book Productivity and Academic Rank at Twenty-Six Elite Universities." *American Sociologist*, 7 (November 1972): 11–13.

Dominico, Christopher, and Eisner, Anne. "Violence Center: Technology for Repression." *Science for the People*, 6 (May 1974), 17–21.

Durkheim, Emile. *Suicide: A Study in Sociology*, trans. George Simpson and John A. Spaulding. Glencoe: Free Press, 1951.

Edwards, Richard C. "The Logic of Capitalist Expansion." In Richard C. Edwards and Thomas E. Weisskopf, editors, *The Capitalist System*. Englewood Cliffs: Prentice-Hall, 1972, 98–106.

Fasola-Bologna, Alfredo. "The Inevitable Radicalization of Liberal Sociologists." *Human Factor*, 8 (Spring 1969): 19–30.

——. "The Sociological Profession and Revolution." *Sociological Inquiry*, 40 (Winter 1970): 35–43.

Flacks, Richard. *Youth and Social Change*. Englewood Cliffs: Prentice-Hall, 1970.

Foss, Daniel. "The World-View of Talcott Parsons." In Maurice Stein and Arthur Vidich, editors, *Sociology on Trial*. Englewood Cliffs, N.J.: Prentice-Hall, 1963, 96–126.

Franklin, Clyde W. "Sociologists on the Move." *American Sociologist*, 7 (November 1972): 15–16.

Freeman, Jack. "Fashion and Clothing in the Nineteenth and Twentieth Centuries." *Collier's Encyclopedia*, 9 (1966): 586–89.

Friedrichs, Robert W. *A Sociology of Sociology*. New York: Free Press, 1972.

——. "The Potential Impact of B. F. Skinner upon American Sociology." *American Sociologist*, 9 (February 1974): 3–8.

Fromm, Erich. *Escape From Freedom*. New York: Avon, 1965.

Gamson, William. "Sociology's Children of Affluence." *American Sociologist*, 3 (November 1968): 286–89.

——. *Simsoc: Simulated Society*. New York: Free Press, 1972.

Glaberman, Martin, and Rawick, George P. "The Economic Institution." In Larry T. Reynolds and James M. Henslin, editors, *American Society: A Critical Analysis*. New York: David McKay, 1973, 25–65.

Gorz, Andre. "The Scientist as Worker: Speed-Up at the Think Tank." *Liberation*, 18 (May–June 1974): 12–18.

Gouldner, Alvin W. *The Coming Crisis of Western Sociology*. New York: Basic Books, 1970.

——. "Anti-Minotaur: The Myth of a Value-Free Sociology." *Social Problems*, 9 (Winter 1962): 199–213.

Gove, Walter R. "Should the Sociology Profession Take Moral Stands on Political Issues?" *American Sociologist*, 5 (August 1970): 222.

Greenblatt, Cathy S., Stein, Peter J., and Washburne, Norman F. *The Marriage Game: Understanding Marital Decision Making*. New York: Random House, 1974.

Hammond, Philip E., and Higbie, Charles E. "This Time a More Personal View of the Press Coverage of a Sociological Convention." *American Sociologist*, 3 (February 1968): 51–53.

Hauser, Philip M., Robbins, Richard H., Gamson, William A., and Barton, Allen H. "Critiques of Radicalism in Sociology." In J. David Colfax and Jack L. Roach, editors, *Radical Sociology*. New York: Basic Books, 1971, 419–77.

Henslin, James M., and Reynolds, Larry T., editors. *Social Problems in American Society*. Boston: Holbrook Press, 1973.

Hirsch, Walter. *Scientists in American Society*. New York: Random House, 1968.

Hoffman, Banesh. *The Tyranny of Testing*. New York: Collier, 1962.

Horowitz, David. "Sociology and Society." In David Horowitz, editor, *Radical Sociology*. San Francisco: Canfield Press, 1971, 1–12.

——. "Social Science or Ideology." *Berkeley Journal of Sociology*, 15 (1970): 1–11.

Horowitz, Irving Louis. "The Intellectual Genesis of C. Wright Mills." In C. Wright Mills, *Sociology and Pragmatism: The Higher Learning in America*. New York: Oxford University Press, 1966, 11–31.

——. *Professing Sociology: Studies in the Life Cycle of Social Science*. Chicago: Aldine, 1968.

Horowitz, Irving Louis, editor. *The Use and Abuse of Social Science*. New Brunswick, N.J.: Transaction Books, 1971.

Horton, Donald. "Review of *Fads and Foibles in Modern Sociology and Related Sciences*." *American Journal of Sociology*. 62 3 (November 1956): 338–39.

Horton, John. "Order and Conflict Theories of Social Problems as Competing Ideologies." *American Sociological Review*, 71 (May 1966): 701–13.

Hoult, Thomas Ford. "Who Shall Prepare Himself to the Battle?" *American Sociologist*, 3 (February 1968): 3–7.

Hubbert, M. King. "Are We Retrogressing in Science?" *Science*, 139 (March 8, 1963): 884–90.

Jay, Martin. "The *Institut für Sozialforschung* and the Origins of Critical Sociology." *Human Factor*, 8 (Spring 1969): 6–18.

Kamin, Leon. *The Science and Politics of I.Q.* New York: Halstead Press, 1974.

Keast, William R., editor. *Faculty Tenure: A Report and Recommendations by the Commission on Academic Tenure in Higher Education.* San Francisco: Jossey-Bass, 1973.

Kroeber, Alfred L. "On the Principle of Order as Exemplified by Changes of Fashion." *American Anthropologist*, n.s., 21 (1919): 235–63.

——. *Configurations of Cultural Growth.* Berkeley: University of California Press, 1944.

——. *Style and Civilization.* Ithaca, N.Y.: Cornell University Press, 1957.

——. "On Culture." In Talcott Parsons, Edward Shils, et al., editors, *Theories of Society: Foundations of Modern Sociological Theory.* New York: Free Press, 1965, 1032–36.

Kuhn, Thomas S. *The Structure of Scientific Revolutions.* Chicago: University of Chicago Press, 1966. Originally published in *International Encyclopedia of Unified Science*, 2 (1962).

——. *The Structure of Scientific Revolutions.* rev. ed. Chicago: University of Chicago Press, 1973.

Lakatos, Imre, and Musgrave, Alan, editors. *Criticism and the Growth of Knowledge.* Cambridge: Cambridge University Press, 1970.

Lazarsfeld, Paul. "Notes on the History of Quantification in Sociology—Trends, Sources and Problems." In Harry Woolf, editor, *Quantification: A History of the Meaning of Measurement in the Natural and Social Sciences.* New York: Bobbs-Merrill, 1961, 147–203.

Lee, Alfred McClung. "The Concept of System." *Social Research*, 31 (Winter 1964): 229–38.

——. *Multivalent Man.* New York: Braziller, 1966.

Lee, Alfred McClung, editor. *Principles of Sociology.* New York: Barnes & Noble, 1967.

Leggett, John C., and Cervinka, Claudette. "Countdown: How to Lie with Statistics." In James M. Henslin and Larry T. Reynolds, editors, *Social Problems in American Society.* Boston: Holbrook Press, 1973, 234–37.

Lemert, Edwin M. *Social Pathology.* New York: McGraw-Hill, 1951.

Lewis, George H. "Pop Society and the *Nouveau Riche*." In George H. Lewis, editor, *Side-Saddle on the Golden Calf: Social Structure and Popular Culture in America.* Pacific Palisades, Calif.: Goodyear, 1972, 173–81.

Lundberg, George A. "Some Convergences in Sociological Theory." *American Journal of Sociology*, 62 (July 1956): 21–27.

Lynd, Robert S. *Knowledge for What? The Place of Social Science in American Culture.* Princeton: Princeton University Press, 1939.

Lynd, Staughton. "The Responsibility of Radical Intellectuals." *New University Conference Newsletter*, May 24, 1968, 5–6. Reprinted in Steven E. Deutsch and John Howard, editors, *Where It's At: Radical Perspectives in Sociology.* New York: Harper, 1970, 61–70.

Lynn, Kenneth S., editor. *The Professions in America.* Boston: Houghton Mifflin, 1965.

Lyons, Gene M. "The Social Science Study Group." In Irving Louis Horowitz, editor, *The*

Use and Abuse of Social Science. New Brunswick, N.J.: Transaction Books, 1971, 133–52.

Machlup, Fritz. *The Production and Distribution of Knowledge in the United States.* Princeton: Princeton University Press, 1962.

MacIntyre, Alasdair. *Against the Self-Images of the Age: Essays on Ideology and Philosophy.* New York: Schocken, 1971.

Mallot, Richard. *Contingency Management in Education.* Kalamazoo, Mich.: Behaviordelia, 1972.

Mankoff, Milton, editor. *The Poverty of Progress: The Political Economy of Social Problems.* New York: Holt, 1972.

Mann, Michael. "The Social Cohesion of Liberal Democracy." In Milton Mankoff, editor, *The Poverty of Progress: The Political Economy of American Social Problems.* New York: Holt, 1972, 399–419.

Mannheim, Karl. *Ideology and Utopia,* trans. Louis Wirth. New York: Harcourt, 1936.

——. "American Sociology." In Maurice Stein and Arthur Vidich, editors, *Sociology on Trial.* Englewood Cliffs: Prentice-Hall, 1963, 3–11.

Marcuse, Herbert. "The New Forms of Social Control." In Maurice Zeitlin, editor, *American Society, Inc.* Chicago: Rand-McNally, 1973, 373–87.

——. *An Essay on Liberation.* Boston: Beacon Press, 1969.

Martindale, Don. *The Nature and Types of Sociological Theory.* Boston: Houghton Mifflin, 1960.

McGinness, Robert, and Solomon, Louis. "Employment Prospects for Ph.D. Sociologists During the Seventies." *American Sociologist,* 8 (May 1973): 57–63.

Means, James Howard. "Homo Medicus Americanus." In Kenneth S. Lynn, editor, *The Professions of America.* Boston: Houghton Mifflin, 1965, 47–69.

Merton, Robert K. *On the Shoulders of Giants: A Shandean Postscript.* New York: Free Press, 1965.

——. *Social Theory and Social Structure,* rev. ed. Glencoe: Free Press, 1957.

——. *The Sociology of Science: Theoretical and Empirical Investigations,* edited and with an introduction by Norman W. Storer. Chicago: University of Chicago Press, 1973.

Merton, Robert K., and Barber, Bernard. "Sorokin's Formulations in the Sociology of Science." In Philip J. Allen, editor, *Pitirim A. Sorokin in Review.* Durham, N.C.: Duke University Press, 1963, 332–68.

Miliband, Ralph. "Professor Galbraith and American Capitalism: The Managerial Revolution Revisited." In Milton Mankoff, editor, *The Poverty of Progress: The Political Economy of American Social Problems.* New York: Holt, 1972, 46–58.

Mills, C. Wright. "The Methodological Consequences of the Sociology of Knowledge." In Irving Louis Horowitz, editor, *Power, Politics and People.* New York: Oxford University Press, 1963, 453–68.

——. *Sociology and Pragmatism: The Higher Learning in America.* New York: Oxford University Press, 1966.

——. *The Sociological Imagination.* New York: Oxford University Press, 1967.

——. "The Contribution of Sociology to Studies of Industrial Relations." *Berkeley Journal of Sociology,* 15 (1970): 11–32.

Nielsen, Waldemar A. *The Big Foundations.* New York: Columbia University Press, 1971.

Nisbet, Robert A. "The Permanent Professors." In Charles H. Anderson and John D. Murray, editors, *The Professors: Work and Life Styles among Academicians.* Cambridge, Mass.: Schenkman, 1971, 105–21.

Novikov, N.V. "Modern Capitalism and Parsons' Theory of Social Action." In Larry Reynolds and Janice Reynolds, editors, *The Sociology of Sociology.* New York: David McKay, 1970, 256–73.

Ober, John David, and Corradi, Juan Eugenio. "Pax Americana and Pax Sociologica: Remarks on the Politics of Sociology." *Catalyst,* 2 (Summer 1966): 41–54.

O'Connor, James. "The Expanding Role of the State." In Richard Edwards, Michael Reich, and Thomas E. Weisskopf, editors, *The Capitalist System: A Radical Analysis of American Society.* Englewood Cliffs: Prentice-Hall, 1972, 193–99.

Ollman, Bertell. *Alienation: Marx's Conception of Man in Capitalist Society.* New York: Cambridge University Press, 1971.

Oromaner, Mark Jay. "The Most Cited Sociologists: An Analysis of Introductory Text Citations." *American Sociologist,* 3 (May 1968): 124–26.

Parsons, Talcott. *The Social System.* Glencoe: Free Press, 1951.

———. *Essays in Sociological Theory.* Glencoe: Free Press, 1954.

———. "Culture and the Social System." In Talcott Parsons, Edward Shils, et al., editors. *Theories of Society: Foundations of Modern Sociological Theory,* New York: Free Press, 1965, 985.

Parsons, Talcott, et al., editors. *Toward a General Theory of Action.* New York: Harper, 1962.

Parsons, Talcott, Edward Shils, et al., editors. *Theories of Society: Foundations of Modern Sociological Theory.* New York: Free Press, 1965.

Pirenne, Henri. "Stages in the Social History of Capitalism." In Reinhard Bendix and Seymour Martin Lipset, editors, *Class, Status and Power: Social Stratification in Comparative Perspective.* New York: Free Press, 1966, 97–107.

Pursell, Caroll W., Jr. "Science and Government Agencies." In David D. Van Tassel and Michael G. Hall, editors, *Science and Society in the United States.* Homewood, Ill.: Dorsey Press, 1966, 223–49.

Raab, Earl, and Selznick, Gertrude Jaeger. *Major Social Problems.* New York: Harper, 1964.

Ravetz, Jerome R. *Scientific Knowledge and Its Social Problems.* New York: Oxford University Press, 1971.

Reynolds, Larry T., and Henslin, James, editors. *American Society: A Critical Analysis.* New York: David McKay, 1973.

Reynolds, Larry T., and Reynolds, Janice M., editors. *The Sociology of Sociology.* New York: David McKay, 1970.

Rioux, Marcel. "Critical versus Aseptic Sociology," trans. Jean-Guy Vaillancourt and Robert Dubois. *Berkeley Journal of Sociology,* 15 (1970): 33–47.

Roach, Jack L. "The Radical Sociology Movement: A Short History and Commentary." *American Sociologist,* 5 (August 1970): 224–33.

Rogers, Everett M., and Shoemaker, F. Floyd. *Communication of Innovations: A Cross-Cultural Approach.* New York: Free Press, 1971.

Sapir, Edward. "Fashion." *Encyclopedia of the Social Sciences,* 6 (1931): 139–44.

St. George, Eleanor. *The Dolls of Yesterday.* New York: Crown, 1948.

Schichor, David. "Prestige of Sociology Departments and the Placing of New Ph.D.'s." *American Sociologist,* 5 (May 1970): 157–60.

Schwendinger, Herman, and Schwendinger, Julia. *The Sociologists of the Chair: A Radical Analysis of the Formative Years of American Sociology (1883–1922).* New York: Basic Books, 1974.

Sennett, Richard, and Cobb, Jonathan. *The Hidden Injuries of Class.* New York: Random House, 1973.

Shoup, General David M. "The New American Militarism." In Arnold Birenbaum and Edward Sagarin, editors, *Social Problems: Private Troubles and Public Issues.* New York: Scribner's, 1972, 217–27.

Simmel, Georg. "Fashion." *International Quarterly,* 10 (October 1904): 130–55. Reprinted in *American Journal of Sociology,* 62 (May 1957): 541–58.

——. *The Sociology of Georg Simmel,* ed. and trans. Kurt H. Wolff. Glencoe: Free Press, 1950.

Skolnick, Jerome H. "The Violence Commission: Internal Politics and Public Policy." In Irving Louis Horowitz, editor, *The Use and Abuse of Social Science.* New Brunswick, N.J.: Transaction Books, 1971, 234–48.

Small, Albion. *General Sociology.* Chicago: University of Chicago Press, 1905 and 1925.

Smith, Dusky Lee. "Robert King Merton: From Middle Range to Middle Road." *Catalyst,* 2 (Summer 1966): 11–40.

——. "The Sunshine Boys: Toward a Sociology of Happiness." In Larry T. Reynolds and Janice M. Reynolds, editors, *The Sociology of Sociology.* New York: David McKay, 1970, 371–87.

——. "The Scientific Institution: The Knowledge-Producing Appendage." In Larry T. Reynolds and James M. Henslin, editors, *American Society: A Critical Analysis.* New York: David McKay, 1973, 145–70.

Sorokin, Pitirim A. *Sociocultural Causality, Space, Time.* 1943. Reprint. New York: Russell and Russell, 1964.

——. *Fads and Foibles in Modern Sociology and Related Sciences.* Chicago: Henry Regnery, 1956.

——. "Letter to the Editor." *American Journal of Sociology,* 62 (March 1957): 515.

——. *Sociological Theories of Today.* New York: Harper, 1966.

Sorokin, Pitirim A., and Berger, Clarence Q. *Time-Budgets of Human Behavior.* Cambridge, Mass.: Harvard University Press, 1939.

Sperber, Irwin. "The Road To Objective Serfdom." *Berkeley Journal of Sociology,* 14 (1969): 111–21.

——. "The Marketplace Personality." In James M. Henslin and Larry T. Reynolds, editors, *Social Problems in American Society.* Boston: Holbrook Press, 1974, 131–39.

——. "Methodology as a Changing Field of Specialization." In George H. Lewis, editor, *Fistfights in the Kitchen: Major Issues Facing Social Research.* Pacific Palisades, Calif.: Goodyear, 1975.

——. "AIDS Research and Social Policy: Historical and Iatrogenic Aspects of the AIDS-Syphilis Connection." *Whetston I* (Spring, 1989): 9-11, 58-81. Available through FIFE Publishers, P.O. Box 98145, Seattle, Wash. 98145-0792.

Stehr, Nich, and Larson, Lyle E. "The Rise and Decline of Areas of Specialization." *American Sociologist,* 7 (August 1972): 3, 5–6.

Storer, Norman W. Introduction. In Robert K. Merton, *The Sociology of Science: Theoretical and Empirical Investigations.* Chicago: University of Chicago Press, 1973, xi–xxxi.

Sumner, William Graham. *Folkways.* 1906. Reprint. New York: New American Library, 1960.

Szasz, Thomas S. *The Myth of Mental Illness: Foundations of a Theory of Personal Conduct.* New York: Dell, 1961.

Tartar, Donald Thomas. "Heeding Skinner's Call: Toward the Development of a Social Technology." *The American Sociologist,* 8 (November 1973): 153–58.

Teggart, Frederick J. *Theory and Processes in History.* Berkeley: University of California Press, 1960.

Uliassi, Pio D. "Government Sponsored Research on International and Foreign Affairs." In Irving Louis Horowitz, editor, *The Use and Abuse of Social Science.* New Brunswick, N.J.: Transaction Books, 1971, 309–42.

Valency, Maurice. "Fashion." *Encyclopedia Americana*, 11 (1973): 40–41.

Van Tassel, David D., and Hall, Michael G., editors. *Science and Society in the United States*. Homewood, Ill.: Dorsey Press, 1966.

Veblen, Thorstein. *The Higher Learning in America: A Memorandum on the Conduct of Universities by Businessmen*. 1918. Reprint. New York: Hill & Wang, 1957.

——. *The Theory of the Leisure Class*. New York, Vanguard Press, 1928.

Weber, Max. *The Methodology of the Social Sciences*. Glencoe, Ill.: Free Press, 1949.

Weinstein, James. "Corporate Liberalism and the Modern State." In Richard C. Edwards, Michael Reich, and Thomas E. Weisskopf, editors, *The Capitalist System: A Radical Analysis of American Society*. Englewood Cliffs: Prentice-Hall, 1972, 188–92.

Westin, Alan F. *Databanks in a Free Society: Computers, Record-Keeping and Privacy*. New York: Quadrangle Books, 1972.

Winthrop, Henry. "The Sociologist and the Study of the Future." *American Sociologist*, 3 (May 1968): 136–45.

Wolfe, Alan. *The Seamy Side of Democracy: Repression in America*. New York: David McKay, 1973.

Wrong, Dennis. "On Thinking About the Future." *American Sociologist*, 9 (February 1974): 26–31.

Zeitlin, Irving M. *Ideology and the Development of Sociological Theory*. Englewood Cliffs: Prentice-Hall, 1968.

INDEX

INDEX

Irwin Sperber earned a master's degree in sociology from the City University of New York and a doctorate in sociology from the University of California at Berkeley. He was a founder and editor of the *Insurgent Sociologist* and an editor of the *Berkeley Journal of Sociology*. He is on the faculty at SUNY, New Paltz, and teaches primarily in the areas of medical sociology and social theory.